RED  *ION*

Gregg R. Jones

RED REVOLUTION

INSIDE THE PHILIPPINE GUERRILLA MOVEMENT

Westview Press

BOULDER • SAN FRANCISCO • LONDON

Photographs were taken by the author, unless otherwise noted.

Published in 1989 in the United States of America by Westview Press, Inc., 5500 Central Avenue, Boulder, Colorado 80301, and in the United Kingdom by Westview Press, Inc., 13 Brunswick Centre, London WC1N 1AF, England

Library of Congress Cataloging-in-Publication Data
Jones, Gregg R.
  Red revolution: inside the Philippine guerrilla movement / Gregg R. Jones.
     p.   cm.
  Bibliography: p.
  Includes index.
  ISBN 0-8133-0644-2—ISBN 0-8133-0877-1 (pbk.)
  1. Philippines—Politics and government—1946–   . 2. Insurgency—
Philippines—History—20th century.   3. Communism—Philippines—
History.   4. Guerrillas—Philippines—History—20th century.
I. Title.
DS686.5.J64 1989
959.904—dc20   89-32833
                                                                                                        CIP

Printed and bound in the United States of America

The paper used in this publication meets the requirements of the American National Standard for Permanence of Paper for Printed Library Materials Z39.48-1984.

10   9   8   7   6   5   4   3   2   1

To my parents,
Bob and Pauline Jones,

and to my wife,
Aleli Nucum-Jones

Contents

List of Illustrations		ix
Preface		xi
Acknowledgments		xvii
List of Acronyms		xxi

	Introduction	1
1	A Resilient Revolution	5
2	Launching the Struggle	17
3	A People's Army Takes Shape	31
4	Collapse and Retreat	45
5	The Ghosts of Plaza Miranda	59
6	Prisoners in a Gilded Cage	71
7	Shaping the Revolution	85
8	Indigenizing "People's War"	95
9	Martial Law and the Urban Underground	103
10	The Manila Rebellion	113
11	The New People's Army Tastes Success	123
12	The Battle for Davao	133
13	The Elusive United Front	145
14	The Election Boycott and Strategic Debates: 1985–1987	155
15	Talking Peace While Preparing for War	165

16   "Land to the Tillers"   175

17   Barangay Rose: Life in a Communist Village   185

18   Revolution in the Church   201

19   Inside the Labor Front   215

20   Inside the New People's Army   223

21   People's War: The Third Decade   239

22   The Faces Behind the Revolution   251

23   "A Terrible Time"   265

24   "People's Republic of the Philippines"   277

25   Red Christmas   285

26   Facing the Future   295

Notes   315
Glossary   337
Bibliography   339
Index   347

Illustrations

MAPS

The Philippines, xxiii

PLATES (*at center of book*)

1 The author on the trail with his bodyguard, "Ka" (Comrade) Baldo

2 Surrendered communist guerrillas construct a hut at Mindanao's Gambalay rehabilitation center

3 Communist Party officials and organizers sing the communist anthem, the "Internationale"

4 NPA guerrillas on patrol in southern Quezon province take a break in the yard of a sympathetic farmer

5 Peasants and guerrillas celebrate the CPP anniversary on December 26, 1987

6 CPP Central Committee member Sotero Llamas in his jungle "office" in a forward base camp, Albay province

7 The communist military commander for the Southern Tagalog region punches a coded radio message into a hand-held Casio computer

8 NPA guerrillas share a communist newspaper as they rest on Christmas Day, 1987

9 NPA regulars, communist militiamen, and peasant supporters gather to celebrate the Party anniversary, December 26, 1987

10 A communist peasant and his daughter prepare a chicken for lunch at their home, Christmas Day, 1987

11   A Communist Party cadre enjoys a meal with the peasant Dante and his family in Barangay Rose

12   Office work in a jungle camp, Bondoc peninsula

13   Guerrillas take a break in a Quezon province camp

14   A guerrilla hangs laundry to dry in a Quezon province jungle camp

15   A jungle kitchen

16   Guerrillas on patrol chat with a peasant farmer taking a load of coconuts to market

17   Manila's Plaza Miranda minutes after communist operatives hurled fragmentation grenades onto the stage where a Liberal party political rally was underway

18   A young boy wounded in the stomach by grenade shrapnel, Plaza Miranda

19   Workers on a Negros sugar hacienda, March 1985

20   Faces of poverty in northern Luzon

21   A military escort removes José María Sison's handcuffs before his court hearing, June 23, 1978

22   Rodolfo Salas, Sison's successor as chairman of the CPP

23   "Wanted" poster for Bernabe Buscayno, the founding NPA commander, better known as Commander Dante

24   Government soldiers inspect Chinese-made rifles and ammunition captured from NPA units at Digoyo Point

25   The M/V Karagatan, aground on a sandbar off Digoyo Point, after Chinese weapons were unloaded for Philippine communist forces

26   Filipino communists wash clothes at their Hunan province compound, April 1976

Preface

My fascination with an Asian archipelago beset by a burgeoning communist revolution began in 1983, when I was a 24-year-old reporter in Atlanta. I was drawn to Asia almost by accident, by reading *In Search of History*, Theodore White's account of his youthful reportorial travels through China as the revolution led by Mao Zedong edged toward victory. I started clipping brief wire service articles on the worsening conflict in the Philippines—10 soldiers dead in an ambush along some isolated provincial road, 8 New People's Army (NPA) guerrillas killed in a remote jungle encounter elsewhere, and so on. By late 1983, as the Philippines seemed to totter on the brink of cataclysm in the aftermath of Benigno Aquino's assassination, I had decided to witness firsthand a revolution in the making. Late in the sweltering evening of May 3, 1984, I arrived in Manila to begin a career as a free-lance correspondent. For the next five years, I traveled throughout the Philippines, observing and reporting on the various political and social forces shaping and tearing the nation. I witnessed the decline and fall of the Marcos regime and the first three years of Corazón Aquino's rule. In 1987, my interest in the forces of revolution in the Philippines brought me together with a publisher interested in a book on the Communist Party of the Philippines (CPP) and its guerrilla army.

When I began this project, I was unsure how much access I would have to the Communist Party and its political and armed forces in the countryside and the cities. The Party is, after all, an outlawed organization, and the affairs of the revolution have by necessity been shrouded in secrecy. I was told by Party cadres at one point during my research that a lower CPP organ had recommended against cooperating for a book about the revolution written by a foreigner. But high-level Party officials overruled, and I was allowed to proceed. As it turned out, I was surprised and pleased by the extent of the cooperation I received from Party and guerrilla units. By late 1988, I had been given a rare look inside a clandestine revolutionary movement in the midst of, rather than after, its struggle for power.

I have focused this book as narrowly as possible on the revolutionary underground—that is, on the activities of the CPP and its guerrilla army. A meaningful examination of the Armed Forces of the Philippines and government responses to the communist-led revolution would require another volume. In order to devote more attention to those aspects of the revolution about which little is known, I have treated more briefly some of those recent historical events in the Philippines (the 1986–1987 cease-fire between Corazón Aquino's government and the guerrillas, for example) that have been exhaustively covered by the international media and by scholars.

The material for this book derives from three principal sources: my interviews and conversations with CPP and NPA leaders, rank-and-file guerrillas and Party members, legal left-wing activists, rebel defectors, and Filipinos living in communist-controlled rural barrios and urban slums; CPP and government documents, both published and unpublished; and my experiences and observations as a reporter covering the Philippines for U.S. and British newspapers between 1984 and 1989, during which time I visited 40 of the country's 73 provinces. I discovered that many early "official" Party documents written for public consumption were embellished, and so I have treated such sources with caution.

I have relied primarily on the interviews I conducted with men and women who had joined the revolution. The overriding value of basing this book to a large extent on hundreds of interviews with the leaders and members of the CPP and communist army, as well as sympathetic peasants and slum dwellers, lies in the vivid personal accounts that have brought the revolution to life in human terms. I have sought to depict the history and development of this revolutionary movement as seen through the eyes of actual participants. This methodology, of course, has inherent strengths and weaknesses. Memories can be selective and self-serving, and therefore I attempted to corroborate information as much as possible with one or more sources. Sometimes, documents or the historical record helped resolve conflicts. In a few instances, I was unable to resolve discrepancies, and so I have offered the conflicting versions of events.

At the outset of every interview, I took pains to explain the nature of my project, so that it would be clear to my sources that they were speaking for publication. In general, I found lower-ranking Party cadres, guerrillas, and peasants to be the most candid sources, sometimes remarkably so, although some ranking CPP officials with whom I developed relationships during the course of months became more forthcoming in our discussions. Scores of interviews were impromptu. Whenever I arrived in a guerrilla camp or in a peasant's house in a communist-controlled barrio, I tried to interview as many people as I could. Since I was always escorted by a Party cadre, I was viewed as an "official," and therefore welcome, guest by most of the combatants, political cadres, and peasants I met in the countryside. I was always on the alert for the possibility that interviewees might be telling me what they thought I wanted to hear or what Party cadres expected them to say. Armed with a reporter's skepticism, I had to judge the credibility and candor of a source. The reader must decide how successful I have been in this endeavor.

I conducted a majority of the interviews during eight forays with NPA and Party units in the countryside during 1987 and 1988; on other reporting trips I spoke with Party cadres and relevant military, political, and private figures in different areas of the country. My trips and interviews inside guerrilla zones were geographically dispersed enough, I believe, to have given me an overview and a sense for the revolution as a national movement. I selected a CPP-controlled barrio in southern Quezon for a case study of life under revolutionary rule, and I was allowed to travel freely through the area, although always escorted by a Party cadre.

Some of my most valuable sources were ranking Party and NPA officials who had been imprisoned for years and who had not returned underground upon their release. It took months to locate and arrange interviews with most of the former top Party leaders. Most were quietly going about their lives and never before had spoken to an "outsider" about their experiences in the revolutionary movement. Their candor, however, usually far exceeded that of active CPP officials. No longer bound by strict Party discipline, some of these sources provided invaluable details on the early history and inner workings of the movement. I repeatedly interviewed several sources during the course of many months.

I interviewed five of the eleven founding CPP Central Committee members who are still alive. The founding NPA commander, Bernabe Buscayno, declined to be interviewed, but I was able to speak with several of his closest colleagues who were with him in the countryside from 1969 until his arrest in 1976. In April 1988, I traveled to Europe to conduct extensive interviews with past and present leaders of the revolution, including founding CPP chairman José María Sison and Central Committee member Luís Jalandoni, who is the chief international representative of the revolution's political front, the National Democratic Front (NDF). I spent nine hours in two sessions interviewing former CPP chairman Rodolfo Salas in his cell in the Philippine Constabulary stockade in Camp Crame, Quezon City. During those visits, I met and talked briefly with several other top leaders of the revolution, including NPA commander in chief Romulo Kintanar.

Whenever possible, I have tried to cite sources by name in the text. Unfortunately, often this was not possible. First, in many cases, I knew my sources only by their underground names. Second, former Party officials and guerrillas who spoke with me, sometimes with astonishing candor, did so at considerable personal risk; it was only because of my guarantee of anonymity that they could talk so freely without fear of retribution from either the military and violent right-wing elements or former colleagues still in the underground. Almost all of the former Party officials with whom I spoke had been captured and imprisoned and were trying to get on with their lives. Several still maintained close contacts with their former colleagues in the revolution. Although in some cases former Party officials spoke without asking for anonymity, in all but a few instances I judged their information to be of such a sensitive or controversial nature that I have not named them in order to spare the sources and their families from possible harassment and even violence from elements on the Right or the Left.

The chapters on Plaza Miranda and the CPP's secret China delegation presented particular difficulties because of their extremely controversial nature. When I began this project, I assumed that the commonly accepted version of history—that Marcos was responsible for the Plaza Miranda bombing—was true. I was astonished when a few former Party officials disclosed that the bombing was planned and carried out by CPP forces. During the course of several months of interviews with former senior Party officials, I was able to piece together details that shed light on the CPP leadership's motivations for carrying out the Plaza Miranda attack, as well as details concerning the plan itself. In separate interviews, my principal sources provided information that dovetailed. Only after having conducted lengthy interviews on the subject, and having become absolutely convinced of the credibility of my sources, did I decide to write the chapter.

That these former CPP officials revealed to an outsider their knowledge of the Plaza Miranda plan could warrant severe punishment—even assassination—at the hands of former colleagues who will undoubtedly view the disclosures of such sensitive Party secrets as an unforgivable betrayal. I have agonized over this knowledge, and as a result I have tried to protect my sources as best I could while trying to clearly establish the historical record on the Plaza Miranda bombing. Similarly, as no details of the CPP's secret mission to China in the 1970s have ever been publicly disclosed, I have tried to protect my sources as much as possible. On this subject, I have relied heavily on one source, a member of the CPP's China delegation known personally to me, whom

I interviewed for more than 15 hours during the course of three sessions. Much of this person's information was corroborated in other interviews with past and present CPP officials and with three other members of the China delegation.

Although CPP officials at the highest levels approved this project, presumably attracted by the international exposure such a book would give the movement, the Party cadres with whom I worked in arranging interviews and visits to guerrilla zones in various regions of the countryside made no attempt to shape the manuscript once I began writing. From the beginning, it was understood that I was undertaking this project not to advocate one side or the other but to record the history and development of the Philippine revolutionary movement and to depict accurately the radical changes the movement has effected in many areas of the country. To the CPP's credit, I was allowed to conduct my research and interviews with few restrictions.

Finally, my objective is not to offer solutions to those in the Philippines and the United States who seek to undermine or defeat the revolutionary movement. I approached this book as a neutral observer, and I have tried to offer the reader a close-up look and analysis of the revolution based on the rare access I gained inside the movement. As far as generalizations are valid, this book may serve as a case study of the inner workings of one of the most successful communist revolutionary movements existing in the world today.

Gregg R. Jones
Manila, Philippines

Acknowledgments

This book would not have been written without the extraordinary cooperation and assistance of scores of men and women in the Communist Party of the Philippines and the New People's Army and their supporters. Most of my interviews within the underground and trips to the countryside with NPA units were the result of the diligent efforts of a veteran Party cadre whom I will identify only as George. When some CPP members sought to restrict the access that was being granted to a foreign writer, George argued on behalf of the project. For this and many other reasons, George has my deepest appreciation and respect.

The leaders, staff, and the Party and NPA rank and file of the CPP's Southern Tagalog region deserve special mention for their unfailing assistance in arranging interviews and visits to guerrilla zones. I offer heartfelt thanks to Tibbs, Francisco, Roger, Mike, Mila, Leny, Lisa, and Joy (my helpful Party guide who looked after me on several trips to guerrilla zones). I thank the peasants of Barangay Rose, who shared their simple homes and meager food and revealed themselves to a stranger. I am especially grateful for the hospitality and kindnesses shown by the peasant couple known as Kulas and Guring and by the late Dante and his widow. Other Party officials, guerrillas, and peasants—too many to name—also deserve my gratitude. I hope I have lived up to the trust and confidence they placed in me by accurately reporting their views and aspirations.

I owe an enormous debt to my wife, Aleli Nucum-Jones, who in so many ways was responsible for bringing this book to fruition. I dragged her along with me to spend a Christmas in a communist barrio, and she rose magnificently to the occasion. Her instant rapport with the peasants and guerrillas and her superb translating skills provided the book with its richest and most colorful material from Barangay Rose. She accompanied me to Europe for several important—and sometimes excruciatingly long—interviews with past and present leaders of the revolution, then spent days performing the tedious task of transcribing hours of tapes. She also performed the even more mundane chores of bringing me meals while I worked at the word processor and managing the affairs of a household. With strength and silence, she suffered my many weeks of absence as I traveled with the guerrillas. I can only offer my deepest love and gratitude.

Some of this book's most gratifying by-products were the friendships it produced or strengthened. Marites Vitug, a remarkably energetic and talented journalist, provided me with invaluable names, introductions, and suggestions at the outset of this project. Alex and Susan Magno generously helped me in ways too numerous to mention, and I will be eternally grateful for their many kindnesses. Jojo Abinales was similarly gracious in his advice and assistance, and I hope the political atmosphere in the Philippines will enable him to write his own book in the near future. I owe much to David Timberman, a dear friend, worthy tennis opponent, and rigorous scholar who cares deeply about the Philippines. After arranging my initial contacts with Westview Press, David then offered much encouragement, advice, and constructive criticism through-out the course of this project. At Westview, I am indebted to many cheerful and supportive people. I offer deep gratitude to senior acquisitions editor Susan McEachern for her patience, enthusiasm, and support throughout the project. A writer often is only as good as his (or her) copy editor, and I was fortunate enough to have Janice Murray, one of the most talented and rigorous editors with whom I have ever worked. My thanks to Beverly LeSuer, my project editor at Westview, who steered the manuscript through the final stages of production in record time.

Julius Fortuna, Leoncio Co, and Romeo Candazo were generous with their time and exceptionally helpful as they patiently explained the history of the Philippine revolutionary movement to an outsider. This book benefited immensely from the cooperation and recollections of Fidel Agcaoili, Monico Atienza, Ibarra Tubianosa, Reuben Guevarra, Victor Corpus, Mila Aguilar, and Mario and Alma Miclat. Romeo Capulong provided valuable insights into the cease-fire period and facilitated interviews with jailed communist leaders. My thanks to Rudy Salas, for his hours of anecdotes and analysis, and to his wife, Josie, who made my visits possible.

Seth Mydans' keen intellect, superior journalistic instincts, and prowess as a writer are reflected throughout this book. His excitement and encouragement helped me through the difficult latter stages of the project. He devoted many days to reading the unfinished manuscript, raised questions that needed to be answered, and offered invaluable advice.

This book would have been much the poorer without Seth's friendship and counsel.

I am deeply appreciative of the friendship and support offered by Armando and Paula Malay, their son, Buddy, and his wife, Odile. Dick Malay provided my wife and me with a warm home during several days of interviews in the Netherlands, and he regaled us with hours of priceless remembrances and insights into the revolutionary movement. I hope before too long Dick will write a book about his experiences representing the CPP in China during the 1970s. Charito Ramirez was a gracious hostess during our stay in Amsterdam.

Luís and Consuelo Jalandoni arranged crucial interviews and facilitated my stay in Europe. My personal secretary, Claire Ferrer, assisted in many ways throughout the project. Robert Dietz introduced me to valuable sources, an all-too-rare occurrence among journalists. Steve Le Vine not only generously shared sources but offered unfailing friendship and support. William Branigin taught me much about being a journalist and also shared sources, information, and friendship before leaving Asia in 1986. My brother, Steve, read portions of the manuscript and offered helpful suggestions as well as his prayers. Jim and Becky Rupert provided a place to stay and warm hospitality during several days of research in Washington, D.C. George Gascon, a superb photographer, reshot the historical photographs that appear in the book. Others whom I thank for their encouragement or assistance are Louise Williams, Joan Orendain, Joey and Lynn Reaves, Melinda Liu, James Clad, Keith Richburg, Lin Neumann, Mark Fineman, Lawrence Walsh, Humphrey Hawksley, Juan Gatbonton, José Feliciano, Ariel Almendral, and Dr. Ervin Nucum.

I am deeply grateful to several people who have kept me employed as a journalist in the Philippines during the past five years: Randal Ashley of the *Atlanta Constitution,* Michael Getler of the *Washington Post,* Kathy Tolbert of the *Boston Globe,* Martin Woolacott of *The Guardian,* Jack Payton of the *St. Petersburg* (Fla.) *Times,* Janie Paleschic, formerly of the *Dallas Morning News,* Fran Maier of the *National Catholic Register,* Karen Johnson and Jon Funabiki of the *San Diego Union,* and Carey English of *U.S. News & World Report.*

I owe a special debt to Monte Plott, my friend and editor at the *Atlanta Constitution.* Throughout late 1983 and early 1984, Monte encouraged a young, restless reporter to follow his dream to Asia. It was all I needed to hear.

Most importantly, I offer thanks to God. Without His inner strength and guidance, I could not have completed this journey.

G.R.J.

Acronyms

AFP	Armed Forces of the Philippines
BAR	Browning automatic rifle
Bayan	Bagong Alyansang Makabayan (New Nationalist Alliance)
BCC	Basic Christian Community
CAFGU	Civilian Armed Forces Geographical Unit
CHDF	Civilian Home Defense Force
CNL	Christians for National Liberation
CPP	Communist Party of the Philippines
DPA	deep penetration agent
FFF	Federation of Free Farmers
GTU	general trade unionism course
Hukbalahap	Hukbong Bayan Laban sa Hapon (People's Anti-Japanese Army)
JAJA	Justice for Aquino, Justice for All
KADENA	Kabataan para sa Demokrasya at Nasyonalismo (Youth for Democracy and Nationalism)
KM	Kabataang Makabayan (Patriotic Youth)
KMU	Kilusang Mayo Uno (May First Movement)
KOMPIL	Kongreso ng Mamamayang Pilipino (Congress of the Filipino People)
MAN	Movement for the Advancement of Nationalism

MASAKA   Malayang Samahan ng Magsasaka (Democratic Union of Peasants)

MDP   Movement for a Democratic Philippines

NATU   National Association of Trade Unions

NDF   National Democratic Front

NPA   New People's Army

PKM   Pambansang Katipunan ng Magsasaka (National Farmers Movement)

PKP   Partido Komunista ng Pilipinas

PMA   Philippine Military Academy

PnB   Partido ng Bayan (People's Party)

PSR   *Philippine Society and Revolution*

SCAUP   Student Cultural Association of the University of the Philippines

SDK   Samahang Demokratiko ng Kabataan (Democratic Youth Organization)

SOT   special operations team

TO   tactical offensive

UP   University of the Philippines

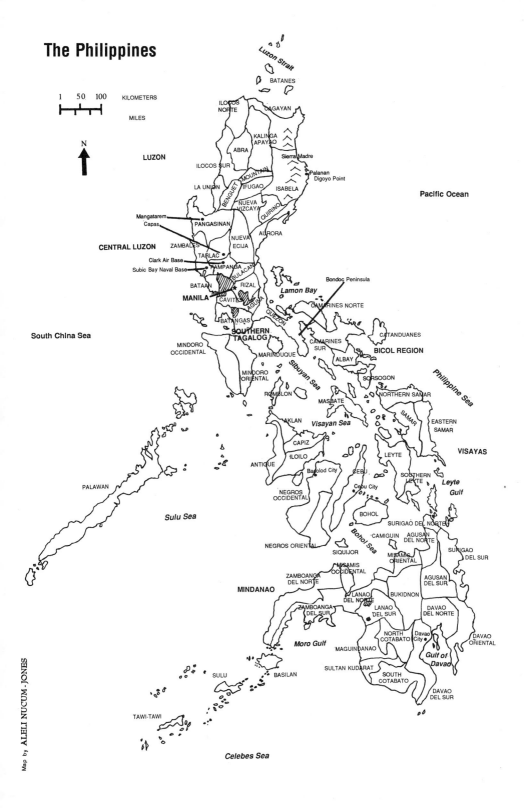

The Philippines

KILOMETERS
1   50   100

MILES

N

Map by ALELI NUCUM-JONES

Luzon Strait

BATANES

LUZON

ILOCOS NORTE
CAGAYAN
KALINGA APAYAO
ABRA
ILOCOS SUR
Sierra Madre
LA UNION
MOUNTAIN
IFUGAO
BENGUET
NUEVA VIZCAYA
ISABELA
Palanan
Digoyo Point
QUIRINO

Pacific Ocean

Mangatarem
Capas
PANGASINAN

CENTRAL LUZON
ZAMBALES
NUEVA ECIJA
AURORA

Clark Air Base
TARLAC
Subic Bay Naval Base
PAMPANGA
BULACAN
BATAAN
RIZAL
MANILA
CAVITE
LAGUNA
BATANGAS
QUEZON
SOUTHERN TAGALOG

Bondoc Peninsula
Lamon Bay
CAMARINES NORTE
CATANDUANES

South China Sea

MINDORO OCCIDENTAL
MARINDUQUE
CAMARINES SUR
ALBAY
BICOL REGION

MINDORO ORIENTAL
Sibuyan Sea
SORSOGON

Philippine Sea

ROMBLON
MASBATE
NORTHERN SAMAR

AKLAN
Visayan Sea
SAMAR
EASTERN SAMAR

CAPIZ
ILOILO
LEYTE
VISAYAS

ANTIQUE
Bacolod City
CEBU
SOUTHERN LEYTE
Leyte Gulf

PALAWAN
Cebu City
NEGROS OCCIDENTAL

Sulu Sea
BOHOL
SURIGAO DEL NORTE

NEGROS ORIENTAL
Bohol Sea
CAMIGUIN
AGUSAN DEL NORTE
SURIGAO DEL SUR

SIQUIJOR
MISAMIS ORIENTAL

ZAMBOANGA DEL NORTE
MISAMIS OCCIDENTAL
AGUSAN DEL SUR

MINDANAO
LANAO DEL NORTE
BUKIDNON

ZAMBOANGA DEL SUR
LANAO DEL SUR
DAVAO DEL NORTE

Moro Gulf
NORTH COTABATO
Davao City
DAVAO ORIENTAL

MAGUINDANAO
Gulf of Davao

SULTAN KUDARAT
SOUTH COTABATO

SULU
BASILAN
DAVAO DEL SUR

TAWI-TAWI

Celebes Sea

Introduction

"Please, God, let them be NPA."

That was my silent prayer when our aging Volkswagen sedan rounded a sharp curve deep in the rugged countryside of the Philippines' southern Quezon province and I saw that the way was blocked by fatigue-clad men cradling automatic rifles. I prayed that the armed men were New People's Army (NPA) guerrillas because a military roadblock could mean arrest or death for the men in the car with me. At my side was a former university physics professor, now Comrade Mike, the Communist Party secretary running the war in the southern Quezon sector against Corazón Aquino's government. In the front passenger seat was a sinewy, 19-year-old peasant guerrilla named Bel who was to guide us to an NPA camp deep in the interior of the Bondoc peninsula.

Panicking at the sight of the armed men, our driver slammed his fist against the horn—as though that would make the terrifying sight disappear. The armed men, soldiers of the Philippine Army's Thirty-first Infantry Battalion, merely scowled and waved us to a stop. My hands were shaking as I fumbled for my wallet and the government press pass inside. "I'm a journalist," I explained to a soldier who was standing outside my window.

The soldiers crowded around our car, peering inside at me, a foreigner venturing so far into a countryside that was for them so dangerous. One of the soldiers, as young and fresh-faced as the peasant guerrilla in the front seat, spotted my military-issue knapsack on the floor. The communist commander and I stepped out of the car and as we watched anxiously, the soldiers emptied my pack, item by item, onto the car hood. They pointed suspiciously at my camouflage poncho and mosquito net. I hurriedly explained that I had bought the gear at Manila's Quiapo flea market, and the soldiers laughed, breaking the tension. They crammed my gear haphazardly back into the canvas pack, and it seemed that we were free to go. Our driver had begun easing the car through the roadblock when a stern-looking sergeant suddenly shouted at us to stop. The battalion commander would like to see me.

Mike and other communist rebels I had met in Manila had spoken fearfully of Captain Juanito Laudiangco, an unusually aggressive opponent of the NPA. A few days earlier, two guerrillas had been arrested at the checkpoint. They had been forced to lead an army patrol into the jungle, and afterward, Mike said, the two had been found with bullets in their heads. I wondered what the captain would do to my companions, and to me, if he discovered that his chief adversary, the communist front commander, was sitting in the car stopped at his checkpoint.

The short, dark-complexioned captain looked rather comical as he swaggered down the hillside wearing shorts, an olive-green T-shirt, and knee-high black rubber boots. He brushed aside my greeting. "What are you doing here? This is a critical area. You should not be here. You might be kidnapped by the rebels," he scolded. "You must get permission from brigade headquarters before you can go any further."

Two soldiers ordered my companions—the rebels Mike and Bel, our driver, and his nephew—out of the car and led them before the glowering captain. My heart was pounding as I introduced Mike as my translator, which was true, and Bel, the peasant guerrilla, as our guide. The captain's eyes darted from one man to the next, sizing up each of them.

"What's your name? Where do you live?" he demanded of Mike, who cooly offered Laudiangco an alias and false address. One by one, the captain interrogated the others. In a stroke of luck, he focused his attention on the driver's nephew—a fellow who knew nothing of Mike's identity or of our destination. After several minutes, Laudiangco seemed to lose interest. "You may proceed," he said with a touch of self-importance. Then as an afterthought, the captain leveled a menacing glare at the men standing before him. "I hope you're not NPAs," he muttered and then turned away.

Once safely beyond the checkpoint, we giddily celebrated our escape. Bel giggled and slapped himself in the face. "That was Captain Laudiangco!" he shouted, amazed that he had come eye to eye with the dreaded enemy and was still alive to talk about it. Mike was reserved, although he allowed himself a wan smile and a sigh of relief. "I was trying to hold myself together," he said quietly. "I thought it was all over."

From the outside, the bamboo hut was indistinguishable from the others that lined the rough gravel road that wound for miles through the forest. Mike, Bel, and I slipped out of the car and hurried inside. The old man and woman who greeted us were staunch supporters of the revolution, and their house was the final way station on the route from Manila to this communist "consolidated zone." After hurriedly exchanging whispered farewells with the old peasant couple, we plunged into the damp, black forest.

Bel led the way along the muddy track, walking quickly despite the weight of my bulging pack, which he had insisted on carrying. The trail had been churned into a yellowish glue by the hooves of *carabaos* (water buffalos) and by the steady passage of peasants and NPA guerrillas. We moved silently past darkened bamboo huts, arousing sleeping dogs whose furious barking quickened our pace. Sometimes, through the frail bamboo walls of a peasant's house, we could see the glow of an oil lamp or hear the murmur of quiet conversation. Bel knew these hills intimately, and he paused only momentarily before plunging right or left along the many forks that led deeper into the forest.

After an hour, we struggled up an especially difficult hill and emerged onto the crest of a ridge. To the west, perhaps 10 miles away, we could see the lights of fishing boats flickering like fireflies on the Ragay Gulf. Bel pointed south toward a jumble of hills that rose ominously in the darkness. Our destination, he declared, was one hour in that direction.

We cut across a field of sickly corn that sprawled down the steep hillside, and then we were engulfed again by the palm forest. As the terrain became more rugged, the forest gave way to a dripping, tangled jungle. Our shoes became encased in thick mud, which made each step a laborious effort. I was already drenched in sweat, and my breathing became more and more ragged. Mike was a few pounds overweight, and I could hear him panting heavily behind me. I took heart when even Bel began to labor.

The trail led up steep hills and then plunged quickly into deep ravines, only to cut up another hill and down, on and on. Our supposed two-hour journey had become nearly three when we arrived at a wood-frame, palm-roofed farmhouse set into a steep hillside. Fifteen guerrillas, their U.S.-designed M-16 rifles beside them, were sleeping inside, stretched out on wooden benches downstairs or lying in rows on the bamboo-slat floor upstairs, which they shared with the peasant family. They slept soundly without fear, for it was rare that soldiers ventured this far into the interior of the Bondoc peninsula, and never at night.

Although we were not even 20 miles from Captain Laudiangco's army battalion, we might as well have been 2,000 miles away. The distance we had traveled was not physical as much as it was spiritual, metaphorical. We had crossed the invisible boundary that sometimes cleaved urban communities and adjacent barrios, the boundary that separated the communist revolution from the old Philippine society it sought to transform.

1

A Resilient Revolution

The revolution began in the fertile mind of a college English literature teacher fond of poetry and philosophy, but ultimately drawn to the writings of Karl Marx, V. I. Lenin, and Mao Zedong. Indeed, the latter's works provided José María Sison with the framework for an armed revolution, a "protracted people's war" in which, he envisioned, historically oppressed Philippine peasants would form the nucleus of a communist army. From the countryside, the rebel army would gradually "encircle the cities" and advance "wave upon wave," as he put it, at the vanguard of a social and political revolution that would sweep to power.

The Philippine revolution was a product of the classical Third World fusion of peasant unrest and nationalism, and it was shaped by a convergence of forces at work in the 1960s: the war in Vietnam, humiliating inequities in the relationship between the Philippines and the United States, the political radicalism that was sweeping college campuses from Michigan to Manila, and the Cultural Revolution in the People's Republic of China.

Sison began in Manila in the early 1960s by organizing small groups of students and workers around nationalist political and economic issues. While most leading Filipino intellectuals of the day dismissed him as a harmless crackpot, Sison was training a fanatically loyal and dedicated cadre of followers. By coopting a succession of nationalist issues, Sison and his protégés gradually built a radical student movement that gained thousands of adherents amid the social and political decay of the Philippines in the late 1960s. The exhortations of Mao and the Cultural Revolution attracted and inspired the newly converted Filipino radicals, thereby providing the fledgling movement with its ideological cement.

By early 1969, Sison had secretly formed a tiny revolutionary party from among his most trusted followers. Within a few weeks, the students forged an alliance with a few dozen peasant rebels who were remnants of previously failed communist-led rebellions in Central Luzon (the country's rice bowl), and a guerrilla war was launched.

Hundreds, perhaps thousands, of radical students by then had come to accept Sison's argument that an armed revolution was necessary to "liberate" the Philippines from the forces of imperialism and feudalism. By the time Ferdinand Marcos declared martial law and moved to crush dissent in September 1972, Sison's Communist Party of the Philippines (CPP) had grown to nearly 2,000 members, and poorly armed New People's Army (NPA) squads were launching hit-and-run ambushes in Central Luzon, the Sierra Madre of northeast Luzon, and a few other pockets of the 1,000-mile-long archipelago.

In their zeal to emulate Mao's Red Guards, the student revolutionaries were given to excesses. They forbade the use of English, banned all music except for revolutionary songs, and even executed members who violated the movement's strict code of discipline. "When we joined, our strength and inspiration were what Mao told us," one veteran Party leader recalled years later, able now to laugh at the early movement's rigidity. "We were like kids, but we were able to survive."

Martial law marked the first critical test of survival for the struggling revolutionary movement. Hundreds of activists and Party members were arrested in Manila and other cities. In the countryside, coordinated assaults by government troops nearly wiped out the rebel armed forces. A misguided attempt in the northern Luzon province of Isabela to replicate Mao's self-contained Shensi province stronghold resulted in heavy losses and the dispersal of the few hundred guerrillas and supporters who survived. Similarly amateurish attempts to adopt Chinese and Vietnamese communist tactics ended in demoralizing failures. The key to survival, however, was the scattering of remaining Party cadres and guerrillas across several islands. By the late 1970s, military abuses against peasants in the countryside, worsening poverty, and unprecedented levels of official corruption had resulted in the steady growth of the CPP and its army.

For years, Marcos as well as the U.S. State Department and Pentagon had dismissed the NPA as little more than a nuisance. But by 1984 U.S. officials had been jolted from their lethargy by the spectacular expansion of guerrilla operations in the countryside and communist political activities in the cities. Dire assessments from Washington raised the specter of the CPP seizing power or forging a coalition government with moderate opposition forces. At the same time, government forces were spread dangerously thin by small, mobile rebel units scattered throughout 60 of the country's 73 provinces. Marcos and his political allies were discredited; the nonviolent political opposition was fragmented and lacked an alternative vision for governing.

In contrast, the revolutionary forces were well organized and well disciplined. The rebel movement offered a clear vision of the future, and its leaders were some of the brightest and most dedicated Filipinos who had come of age since the 1960s. By the eve of the February 1986 presidential election pitting Marcos against a political neophyte named Corazón Aquino—who offered herself as "the complete opposite of Marcos"—the forces of the Party-led National Democratic Front (NDF) seemed to be close to victory.

The communists had always smugly described Marcos as their best recruiter, and his sudden exit in 1986—and the rise of the popular Aquino—threw the movement into disarray. Recriminations about the Party's decision to boycott the 1986 presidential election resounded through the ranks of the CPP and the rebel army. A significant number of Party leaders and cadres argued that the revolutionary movement should cooperate with the new government and try its hand at legal politics. Yielding to pressure from the public and within the movement, the CPP leadership entered into cease-fire negotiations with the Aquino government. Four months of contentious talks led to a 60-day cease-fire, and when that lapsed in February 1987, the war resumed. By that time, the CPP leadership had dropped its conciliatory stance and had adopted a new, critical posture toward the Aquino government. Aquino's movement to the Right, brought about by her attempt to placate a restive military, made it easier for Party leaders to convince their forces of the correctness of the tougher line.

By 1989, as the guerrilla war entered its twentieth year, the revolution had reached a crossroads. CPP officials conceded that victory, either military or political, was at best years distant. Aquino's popularity and the CPP's unresolved internal debates about ideology and strategy stood as formidable challenges to the movement. Military-backed anticommunist vigilantes posed new problems for communist forces attempting to expand in the countryside, and in some areas the NPA had even been rolled back from former strongholds. Buoyed by the arrests of several top communist leaders and persistent rumors of wrangling over revolutionary strategy and tactics, Aquino boasted that 1988 would be remembered as the year the insurgency was broken. Armed forces strategists suddenly began talking of defeating the rebels by 1992, the end of Aquino's term.

For all the optimistic talk emanating from the government, the CPP and its armed and political forces were far from beaten and in fact remained a formidable long-term challenge to the government. By the military's estimates, in early 1989 the NPA had about 24,000 guerrillas, with an arsenal of more than 10,000 high-powered rifles, grenade launchers, and a few mortars—virtually all captured from government forces. The rebels controlled or influenced more than 8,000 of the country's 41,000 *barangays*, according to the military.[1] In Manila and other cities the communists had succeeded in gaining varying degrees of control over hundreds of labor unions and in establishing slum bases for urban guerrillas. The movement had succeeded in integrating a significant number of Catholic Church elements—priests, nuns, lay-workers, and even one or two bishops—into the National Democratic Front, a crucial development in a nation that is 85 percent Catholic. The participation of Church elements in the revolution had helped the movement overcome to some extent strong anticommunist sentiments imbedded in the psyche of most Filipinos. More practically, radical Church elements were providing support services to the guerrilla army in the countryside, while building links with middle-class, business, and professional elements in the cities.

From the beginning, the CPP had stressed political organizing over military action, and that still held true in early 1989. Lacking heavy weapons, the NPA remained incapable of challenging the Armed Forces of the Philippines (AFP) in a conventional sense. After 20 years of war, the movement had to be content with ambushing army convoys and patrols and overrunning isolated town halls, police stations, and small military detachments. The total number of deaths attributed to the guerrilla war in 1988 was approximately 5,000 soldiers, civilians, and rebels, which was modest when compared to other modern conflicts.

For years, the Philippine communists had proudly waged an indigenous revolution and had relied primarily on arms and materiel captured or bought from the AFP. In the early days of slavish Maoism, the revolution received token aid from China. But the aid pipeline was cut in 1975–1976 with the opening of diplomatic relations between Manila and Beijing and the death of Mao, leaving the NPA to survive by its own devices. The rebels pioneered a campaign called *agaw armas* (literally, grab guns), which relied on small unit attacks and assassinations to painstakingly build the communist arsenal gun by gun.

Building the revolution without foreign aid became a point of pride with the rebels, and it also gave the movement the flexibility to make its own decisions without having to worry about how a foreign benefactor would react. The indigenous nature of the revolution also had a soothing effect on many middle- and upper-class Filipinos, who argued that the absence of foreign involvement was proof that the movement was "uniquely Filipino" and not really a classic Marxist-Leninist revolution.

But communist leaders had mapped out a strategy that called for an escalation of the war in 1989–1990, with the hope of forcing a military stalemate by 1992. Virtually every Communist Party official and guerrilla commander with whom I spoke emphasized that the NPA would have difficulty attacking larger military camps and advancing the war to a stalemate without mortars, bazookas, and even surface-to-air missiles. But without heavier weapons, the guerrilla war could stagnate, and as a result the NPA would find it difficult to convince more peasants to support a movement that did not seem to have a chance of winning. So for the first time in the movement's history, CPP leaders were appealing openly to communist countries and radical movements to aid the Philippine revolution. There were hints by some rebel officials that a source of heavy weapons had already been arranged and that NPA officers were abroad being trained to use the weapons.

North Korea, rather than China or the Soviet Union, loomed as the most likely source of aid for the rebels. The CPP had developed cordial ties with the communist regime in Pyongyang. (The Soviet Union and China, on the other hand, had worked hard to improve relations with the Philippines and appeared as of early 1989 to have little to gain by aiding the NPA.) The rebel movement had also developed close relations with Nicaragua and to a lesser extent with Cuba, Libya, and elements of the Palestine Liberation Organization.

The acquisition of heavy weapons by the NPA would dramatically change the complexion of the war and rapidly bring the guerrillas close to parity with government forces. As of early 1989, the AFP had only an estimated 70,000 combat-effective troops with which to oppose the NPA and the Muslim insurgents in the south—far less than the 10 to 1 ratio deemed necessary to wage a successful campaign against a guerrilla army. The infusion of heavier military hardware into the conflict would also raise the stakes for the United States, and with two prized military bases on the line, the Pentagon would likely respond by supplying the Philippines with even more sophisticated U.S. weaponry and other forms of support.

The talk of heavy weapons drew attention away from the realm in which the rebels were most dangerous and had advanced the farthest in 20 years of struggle—the political front. The broad extent of the communist political network became apparent to me as I journeyed inside the revolution, in urban areas and the countryside. The CPP cadres I met represented a cross-section of Philippine society: government bureaucrats, parish priests, labor organizers, human rights workers, journalists, teachers, lawyers, farmers, fishermen, and students. Even more astonishing in its breadth was the revolution's support network of allies—some of them reluctant—and sympathizers, which included members of congress, provincial governors, Catholic bishops, mayors, wealthy businesspeople, and powerful landowners.

Aquino had frustrated the rebel movement's inroads with the urban middle-class, students, labor, and other key groups in Manila and other major urban centers. But in one of the most striking and little-noticed developments I observed, in the smaller cities and towns of the countryside—where NPA influence was far more pronounced, yet hardly noted by the Manila press—communist forces were enjoying remarkable success in weaving a web of alliances with the middle and upper echelons of power. That point was driven home to me during a bizarre encounter in March 1987.

Escorted by four or five Party cadres and peasant guerrillas, I arrived one day at noon in a small town only 60 miles from Manila. At a busy restaurant within sight of the town hall and police station, we were joined by an elderly woman with fair Spanish features who was clearly a member of the local aristocracy. Waving a silk fan to ward off flies and the sultry noonday heat, the old woman chatted gaily with my guerrilla guide, a woman named Damit, and the young communist in turn affectionately addressed the matron as "grandmother." Later, Damit explained that the woman was matriarch of the town's wealthiest and most politically powerful family. The family owned all the prime agricultural land for miles around, the town's only pharmacy, and the only bus company traveling the only road linking the town to the outside world. Indeed, this family represented everything the NPA guerrillas had been fighting to destroy, and yet, Damit told me, the family was providing food, money, medicine, and other assistance to the rebels. As the encounter in the restaurant illustrated, neither side was making any effort to hide the fact. "How had this 'feudal ruler' been persuaded to support her sworn enemies?" I asked Damit.

"We talked to her," the young guerrilla replied with a knowing smile. "We explained the movement to her."

Damit and her companions never had to threaten the family. By then, everyone in the Philippines knew that the rebels were capable of killing their enemies. Everyone also knew it was far easier, far safer, and certainly far more profitable—at least in the short term—to make peace with the rebels and give them what they wanted, up to a point.

By the late 1980s, such arrangements were hardly isolated, as I was reminded repeatedly. Politicians, landlords, businesspeople, even Catholic bishops, were reaching accommodations with the rebels and supplying them with money, shelter, and weapons in exchange for protection from criminals, guarantees against assassination, support on election day, the right to travel through communist-dominated areas, and unhampered business activities. In much of the countryside and even in some major cities, those Filipinos who would have the most to lose after a triumphant revolution had come to view support of the rebels as a price of doing business.

Through a skillful blend of coercion and persuasion, the rebels are weaving themselves into the fabric of Philippine society, stitching together thousands of relationships and arrangements that are slowly neutralizing members of the traditional economic and political elite. The scenes of cooperation between the communist underground and the nation's elite, as represented most vividly to me in the person of the fastidious provincial matriarch with her silk fan, raise the possibility of a time, perhaps years in the future, when the revolutionary movement will have consolidated a position of influence over large portions of the establishment in areas of the countryside. Spanish, U.S., and Japanese conquerors all used the cooptation of the Philippine elite to maintain power, and the NPA in its drive to seize power appears to be applying with some success the same strategy from below. The extent to which such cooptations could be a factor in the revolution's success or failure was not clear by the late 1980s, but the phenomenon seemed potentially disturbing for those who viewed the revolution as an isolated rural movement estranged from the establishment. How have the Communist Party of the Philippines and its NPA guerrillas reached the point where some of the Philippines' richest and most powerful figures are paying homage? The answer lies in the history and inner workings of this independent and innovative revolutionary movement.

Having demonstrated considerable resiliency and prowess throughout two decades of guerrilla warfare and political struggle, the CPP and New People's Army have established a position as long-term players for political power in the Philippines. The movement has weathered many crises since 1969—periods of intense doctrinal debates and internal disputes among the leadership, arrests, political blunders, and military failures—and has emerged each time to flourish. Although the 1988 arrests of several rebel leaders hurt morale within the ranks of the revolutionary movement to some extent, the loss of national Party leaders had little or no effect on the ability of the regional communist commands to continue the revolution. The period of rapid expansion that the CPP and its army had enjoyed from the late 1970s until the mid-1980s had been stalled, but there was little evidence the movement was in strategic decline. Rebel losses—in personnel, weapons, and territory—in many cases were offset by corresponding gains in other areas. The stunning rollback of the communists on the island of Mindanao in 1986 and 1987, for example, was answered by dramatic NPA expansion on the main island of Luzon.

From what I witnessed in the countryside, the NPA has become a significant national movement not so much by terror and killing— although these tactics are selectively employed—but by the painstaking forging of bonds with an impoverished, landless peasantry that has been ignored by a succession of governments. The rebel movement has expanded its base by addressing a number of key issues that the government has either been unwilling or unable to resolve. Agrarian reform, social services, rudimentary health care, law enforcement, justice, and other local services are being provided in an effective, if sometimes brutal, fashion by the rebels. To the average peasant who has never known a government to do much more than collect taxes, these are all dramatic developments. By early 1989, the revolutionary movement had succeeded in sinking deep roots throughout the archipelago, and it had altered, perhaps irreversibly, Philippine politics and society.

The revolution was in its tenth year when it reached the rugged hills of southern Quezon province in 1979, and like most of his neighbors, Dante vividly remembered the day. It was nearing nightfall when eight weary looking young men and women armed with pistols and one-shot derringers walked into the hilltop clearing Dante had carved from the coconut palm forest and approached the peasant's bamboo-and-palm hut.

"I'm Comrade Boy," one of the men announced, holding out his hand in greeting. "We are from the New People's Army."

Since the early 1970s, Dante had heard occasional rumors about the rebel army and its activities in other provinces. The guerrillas were said to be helping poor farmers in Central Luzon and Bicol by punishing robbers and thieves. Dante invited the NPA squad into his hut to share a dinner of rice and dried fish, and by the light of a small homemade lamp, he and his wife listened as the young rebels explained their reasons for taking up arms against the government. They were fighting to improve the lives of poor farmers like Dante, Boy said. The revolution was against the big landlords, the "oppressors" and "exploiters" who, he said, got rich from the labor of peasants such as Dante. Later, the rebels encouraged Dante to tell them about his problems and the difficulties of other local farmers. Dante mentioned that the barrio was plagued by a gang of *carabao* rustlers, who operated with the knowledge, if not collusion, of the military.

The rebels returned, occasionally at first, then more and more frequently as time passed. Within a few months, they won the gratitude of the peasants by catching and executing the leaders of the *carabao* rustling gang. If some in the village were uncertain about supporting the guerrillas, the killings served as a reminder that it was prudent to stay in their good graces.

Soon, the regular political sessions conducted by the visiting Communist Party cadres moved beyond discussion of local grievances. They began to teach Dante and his neighbors that "U.S. imperialism, feudalism, and bureaucrat capitalism" were the three great evils responsible for their poverty. Gradually, to deepen the process of politicization, the cadres organized entire families into separate clandestine organizations for farmers, women, and youths.

In three years, Barangay Rose—as the rebels had code-named Dante's barrio—had become one of the most organized villages in southern Quezon's Bondoc peninsula. Virtually all of the farmers and their families were members of Party organizations and attended regular political classes as well as fed and sheltered guerrillas and CPP cadres. That same year, the rebels helped the peasants establish a barrio revolutionary council, a Party shadow government, that provided everything from health services to political education to marriage counseling. With armed guerrillas frequenting the barrio, the legal *barangay* council was persuaded to defer its most important functions to the communist government.

To continue the process of political indoctrination among the peasants, an armed propaganda unit of a half dozen men and women with rifles and pistols was assigned full-time to Barangay Rose. Increasingly, the peasants were mobilized to aid the communist war effort. They contributed portions of their rice and banana harvests to local rebel units, acted as couriers, and reported military movements to the closest NPA camp.

By 1985, the barrio revolutionary council—which by now included some members of the legal *barangay* council—was openly governing Barangay Rose. The communists organized Dante and a few other trusted farmers into a village militia. Armed with shotguns and a few antiquated Springfield and Garand rifles, the peasants patrolled the barrio, arresting and sometimes executing lawbreakers and adjudicating minor disputes, including domestic quarrels. Occasionally, the militia would even join guerrilla units in ambushing army patrols and raiding government outposts. In guerrilla parlance, Barangay Rose was now a consolidated zone, a secure base from which the revolution was spreading to neighboring towns and villages. The communists counted the barrio as a measure of the revolution's success, a place where 80 out of 85 families had at least one member working in the rebel movement. That success was anchored on people such as Dante.

A humid tropical dusk was settling on the jungled hills of southern Quezon one day in October 1987 as a 20-year-old Party cadre named Joy led me for the first time along a twisting, muddy trail to the clearing where Dante lived with his wife and four children. Dante was standing outside his hut, burning brush in the twilight as filthy pigs and scrawny chickens shuffled about his feet. He greeted Joy with a smile, shook my hand, then studied me carefully. For years, the Party had taught him that U.S. imperialism was one of the root causes of his poverty and the number one enemy of the revolution. Now, face to face with a visitor from the United States, he seemed uncertain whether to be curious or suspicious.

At 38, Dante stood barely five feet but looked as stout and strong as a *carabao*. His chest was broad, and his arms and legs rippled with well-developed muscles. His bearded face, darkened by years in the sun, was remarkable for its gentleness and after a few minutes of sizing me up, he began to smile easily.

Dante was by now deeply involved in the communist revolution that had swept Barangay Rose, and his dedication had not gone unrewarded by Party officials. In 1980, he had been selected to head the communist barrio peasants' association. Five years later, when the village militia was formed, Dante was named deputy commander. He was one of 20 peasants in Barangay Rose to be given membership in the exclusive Communist Party, even though he had never attended school beyond the elementary level.

Cursed by poor soil, primitive farming techniques, and lack of education, most Philippine peasants are reduced to a life of subsistence and struggle. Like his father before him, Dante toiled to support his family by slash-and-burn farming on plots cleared from the steep hillsides and by gathering coconuts to sell for a few centavos in the nearest town.

By all indications, the war between Aquino's government and the guerrillas had reached a stalemate here as in other areas of the Philippines. After army units abandoned small, vulnerable outposts in villages such as Barangay Rose, they concentrated in fortified camps along the National Highway on the peninsula's northern fringe or along secondary roads that hugged the coast. Even along these roads, the soldiers traveled at great peril. Every few months, in an increasingly familiar pattern, NPA units would ambush an army convoy or patrol, usually destroying an armored car or troop truck with a homemade land mine and capturing 10 or 15 rifles. The army would announce it was in hot pursuit of the guerrillas, step up patrols, and increase its checkpoints; then after a few days of fruitless activity the army would settle back into its fortified camps to await the next NPA ambush or raid. Meanwhile, Communist Party cadres continued their organizing work among the peasants.

After nearly a decade of political organizing and guerrilla warfare in southern Quezon, the communists claimed to have developed a support network of 30,000 men, women, and children in an underground network of Party organizations. From a single propaganda unit armed with pistols and derringers in 1979, the NPA's Southern Quezon Front had built 2 combat-savvy guerrilla companies numbering more than 120 local peasant fighters armed with captured U.S.-designed M-16 automatic rifles and M-79 grenade launchers. Each of the 3 district CPP committees of the front had established 15-member guerrilla units, which conducted small local attacks on militia squads or anticommunist vigilantes and joined the companies for major operations. Another 100 farmers were organized into a front militia, which performed police functions in communist-dominated barrios and supplemented the companies and district units in larger operations.

In sufficient force, the Philippine armed forces could travel to any barrio in southern Quezon, including Barangay Rose. Sometimes the military succeeded in disrupting NPA activities and forced the guerrillas to move to other villages. But, surrounded by an often hostile populace, the troops would rarely remain for more than a few tense days. Even if some peasants preferred to support the government, the military could not guarantee their safety. As soon as the army left an area, the Party cadres and guerrillas returned, and anyone who had shared with the military information about communist activities was summarily executed.

After years of relative peace and prosperity under communist rule, the war unexpectedly brushed Barangay Rose one day in mid-February 1988. Early that morning, the army airlifted 58 soldiers to a village a few miles away. Throughout the day, the NPA peasant network tracked the soldiers and warned the guerrillas and their supporters of the approaching danger. In the past, the occasional patrols had turned back toward the coastal road before reaching Barangay Rose, but this time they pushed onward. Dusk was settling when the soldiers arrived in the "barrio center," a collection of several shopping stalls, bamboo houses, and a wooden schoolhouse. Brusquely, the soldiers ordered the frightened villagers to remain in their houses, and they obliged.

At about the same time, a Party cadre arrived at Dante's house and asked the peasant to guide him to an NPA camp hidden in the jungle a few miles away. Unaware of the presence of soldiers nearby, they set out after dinner for the barrio center, a 15-minute walk, Dante in the lead with his old Springfield rifle in one hand and a palm-frond torch in the other.

Dante may not have seen the army sentry outside the schoolhouse before he opened fire with his M-16 automatic rifle at a distance of 20 feet. One slug ripped through Dante's jaw, but he managed to run a few hundred yards to a nearby creek before collapsing. Finding him there, the soldiers sprayed him with automatic rifle fire. The next day, the troops displayed Dante's bullet-riddled corpse on the lawn outside the school as a warning to the residents of Barangay Rose. Summoning villagers to the school, the soldiers forced them to sign an affidavit attesting that Dante was an NPA guerrilla.

The NPA immediately sought to avenge Dante's death, and they took up ambush positions along the road that the army patrol would have to take upon exiting Barangay Rose. But the troops were wary, and they waited in a schoolhouse in the next barrio, shielded by villagers. After two days, the guerrillas withdrew. On the third day, the soldiers passed without incident along the road where the rebels had lain in ambush.

One of the first to greet the communist organizers when they arrived in the coconut palm forest of southern Quezon a decade earlier, Dante was the first of their supporters to be killed. After 10 years of quiet rebellion, war had come to Barangay Rose.

2

Launching the Struggle

The Philippine communist guerrillas and their supporters celebrate December 26, 1968, as the day the revolution began. Officially, the date marks the "reestablishment" of a dying communist party and its emergence as the Communist Party of the Philippines–Marxist-Leninist (Mao Zedong Thought). Not coincidentally, the date was the seventy-fifth anniversary of Mao's birthday.

In fact, the date is myth. The founding congress, as José María Sison grandiosely billed the gathering with 11 of his followers under a grove of trees in Pangasinan province, was canceled when the would-be revolutionaries discovered their plans had been leaked to outsiders. Fearing a military raid or possible attack by political rivals, Sison delayed the gathering for a week, and it began without incident on January 3, 1969. The 12 founding Party members agreed that the official date would be recorded as December 26, 1968.[1]

The recreation of the communist party and the rebirth of armed revolutionary struggle were dreams Sison had nurtured throughout much of the 1960s. When in 1967 he broke with the existing, moribund Philippine communist party, the Partido Komunista ng Pilipinas, or PKP, Sison was finally free to gather his loyal following of radical students and workers and pursue his vision. In September 1968, after months of planning and more than a few setbacks, Sison sat down at a typewriter in his apartment in a working-class neighborhood of suburban Manila and began drafting the blueprint for an armed revolution. He sketched out a plan to reestablish the communist party, which he argued had effectively died under the hapless leadership of brothers Jesús, José, and Francisco Lava. By early December, a party constitution, bylaws, and a revolutionary program were ready, and Sison and 12 of his handpicked followers began approaching members of the PKP who were disgruntled with the Lavas' leadership to convince them to join the venture. One of the old party members to whom Sison had entrusted a copy of the documents passed them on to a newspaper publisher. Horrified at the breach of security, Sison demanded the documents back from the indiscreet PKP cadre and immediately ceased all attempts to recruit members of the old party. With their plans compromised, the founding congress planned for the day after Christmas was scrapped, then reset for the following week. Sison and his tiny band of Maoist protégés were on their own.

If Sison ever had doubts about the wisdom of his plan, he was careful to conceal them when he asked 13 of his most trusted disciples to meet him in Quezon City at. the suburban Pantranco bus terminal on the evening of January 2, 1969. Of the group, all men in their twenties, Sison alone brimmed with confidence. Arthur García, a labor organizer who was Sison's most trusted aide, tried to mirror his mentor's buoyancy, but the rest, although loyal to Sison, secretly harbored serious misgivings. "We were hopeful, but there was a certain amount of cynicism," one recalled years later. "If there was optimism, it was 90 percent Joema's [Sison's]."[2]

Sison's brother-in-law, Carlos del Rosario, who was one of the young Marxists invited to join the founding congress, was so skeptical of the endeavor that he simply did not show up at the bus station. When it came time to board the bus, another of Sison's inner circle, a radical student and labor organizer named Rodolfo Salas, walked away in silent protest of Sison's attempts to forge an alliance with Commander Sumulong, Faustino del Mundo, the corrupt Central Luzon Huk warlord.[3] Careful to keep up an air of insouciance lest he weaken the resolve of his followers, Sison never mentioned Salas' name again during the trip.

Their destination was a secluded farm owned by Arthur García's brother-in-law outside the Pangasinan town of Mangatarem, about 100 miles north of Manila. Sison had purposely selected Pangasinan as the site for the founding congress because the area marked the boundary between the Central Luzon rice plains—the focal point of agrarian unrest—and Luzon's rugged Cordillera Mountains, which Sison envisioned as a potential stronghold for the Maoist army of his dreams.

The 12 men who were to form the new party's central committee and two security escorts had broken into three groups in the Quezon City bus station, and the first rebels arrived at Mangatarem at dawn. The group led by Sison arrived later, and the men set off walking down an isolated dirt road. Nervous, and at the same time excited, they bantered and joked among themselves. García swaggered ahead of the column, a big straw sombrero on his head and a .38-caliber revolver tucked into his waist. If they were stopped by soldiers, García joked, he would direct the troops to "the thin guy with the mustache [Sison] and the little guy with the limp," Ibarra Tubianosa, one of Sison's first recruits from the Lyceum University, and a victim of polio as a child.

After walking more than an hour in the blazing tropical sun, they arrived at the house of García's sister. A child's baptismal party was under way, and so the rebels waited outside until the festivities were over. When the last guests had finally left, the men walked to a grove of cayumito trees in a nearby field. García's brother-in-law patrolled the area with an old Springfield rifle and a shotgun, and the two security escorts who had accompanied the group—both members of a radical union organized by Sison's men at U.S. Tobacco Company in Manila—took up positions with pistols.

As Sison began reading the voluminous documents he had crafted, a loud noise brought the proceedings to an abrupt halt. Some of the startled men thought it was a military raid, but they were relieved to discover that it was only one of their security guards who had fallen asleep and tumbled from a tree. The guard sheepishly dusted himself off as the others broke into relieved laughter, and Sison resumed.

If the others were still trying to convince themselves of the importance of the occasion, Sison carried on with a flair that suggested a heightened sense of history. He read each of the carefully prepared documents, including a scathing, meticulously detailed denunciation of the Lava brothers entitled, "Rectify Errors and Rebuild the Party," and a new communist party constitution. The session dragged on until nearly 11 P.M., when Sison finally called a recess.

The following morning, the jittery group moved to a nearby house to continue their deliberations, which included the election of party officers. Sison was unanimously elected chairman, and Nilo Tayag, an amiable student leader, was chosen secretary-general. Late in the morning, Sison adjourned the congress, and the Communist Party of the Philippines was officially reestablished. The uncertain revolutionaries, relieved that it was all over, boarded a bus for the long ride back to Manila.

The 1960s had begun calmly enough in the Philippines, with the agrarian rebellion that had simmered in the Central Luzon provinces for the past 20 years finally on the wane and radical politics discredited. The PKP was a political pariah, a victim of its own errors and of virulent anticommunist crusades spawned by cold war fears during the 1950s. Even among intellectuals, interest in Marxism was scant. Although the old social and economic problems had not been resolved, there was no viable movement to champion the cause of reforms.

Sison's entree to a small but vocal nationalist movement had been through an organization he had founded at the University of the Philippines in 1959, the Student Cultural Association of the University of the Philippines (SCAUP). When a congressional committee began conducting a McCarthy-style witchhunt at the university in 1961, Sison saw an opportunity for his obscure group. SCAUP organized student demonstrations outside Congress that forced the Committee on Anti-Filipino Activities to abandon its investigation into "communist infiltration" on university campuses. Overnight, the successful demonstrations thrust SCAUP and its young founder into prominence in nationalist circles.

To his peers, Sison seemed an unlikely personage around which to build a radical political movement. Francisco Nemenzo, a University of the Philippines (UP) political science professor who was a young radical at the time, recalled his impressions of the frail English literature teaching assistant: "The first time I met Joe [in the 1950s], he was more of a poet. I didn't think of him as a political man. I was already leaning toward Marxism. Joe was flirting with existentialism. I simply underestimated Joe's capability for building something serious."[4]

Sison had grown up in northwestern Luzon's Ilocos Sur province, the son of affluent landowners who thrived on the country's feudal agricultural system. After each harvest, the family's tenants would settle their rent by carrying great bales of tobacco leaves to the Sisons' big house, which was prominently located on the town square.[5] The area had gained notoriety for its stiff resistance to Spanish, and later to U.S., colonizers, and Sison's forebears personified that spirit. A great grandfather had supported Andrés Bonifacio's Katipunan, the secret society plotting a revolution against Spain in the 1890s, and was hauled before Spanish authorities to explain his "treasonous" actions. A few years later, a great uncle was killed by U.S. soldiers for aiding Emilio Aguinaldo's revolutionary army in its fight for Philippine independence from the United States.

Sison deepened his appreciation of nationalism while compiling a strong academic record in high school and college in Manila. He devoured the works of such contemporary nationalist writers as Teodoro Agoncillo, Hernando Abaya, Cesar Adib Majul, and Claro Recto. Sison later began reading Marx but displayed a stronger interest in poetry and English literature.[6] In the 1950s, the common theme of Filipino nationalist writers was the unjust nature of the country's relationship with the United

States. They dissected postwar economic and military treaties, which were heavily weighted in favor of the United States, and articulated nationalist positions on U.S. bases and the U.S.-imposed free-trade arrangement. But like Central Luzon peasants who sought only a more just arrangement with landlords, the old nationalists were merely in quest of a partnership of equals with the United States, not a severing of ties.

The postwar generation of Filipinos was far less accommodating, and by the early 1960s, antagonism toward the United States was rising. "You had a new generation of Filipinos who had no recollection of MacArthur and the war experience," recalled Nemenzo, who had been in the midst of the nationalist movement. "Their recollection of America was a country that was shooting Filipinos inside Clark Air Base, throwing its weight around, bullying little Cuba."[7]

Two incidents at the U.S. military bases breathed life into the crusade and galvanized public opinion behind the nationalists. On November 25, 1964, an off-duty U.S. soldier shot and killed a Filipino boy collecting scrap items inside Clark Air Force Base. Barely two weeks later, two U.S. naval sentries at Subic Bay Naval Base shot and killed a Filipino fisherman paddling his small boat inside the territorial waters of the base.[8] The killings, and the callous official U.S. reactions, touched off angry protests against the U.S. presence in the Philippines. Overnight, paltry demonstrations outside the U.S. Embassy mushroomed into huge affairs attended by tens of thousands of students, workers, and intellectuals. Spearheading the peaceful demonstrations was another organization created by Sison, the Kabataang Makabayan (Patriotic Youth, or KM).

Following his success with the student protests in 1961, Sison had organized a secret Marxist study group within SCAUP and in 1963 had accepted an invitation to join the withering PKP. Sison became head of the party's youth department and sketched out plans for the creation of an organization that would link urban students and the children of former peasant guerrillas in a nationalist crusade—with a hidden revolutionary agenda. Sison contacted radical student leaders at the major Manila universities. At the same time, he pursued connections with peasant groups and cultivated members of the militant National Association of Trade Unions (NATU). Working from the NATU offices, Sison gradually tied all the threads together, and on November 30, 1964, the KM was formally launched. The organization brought together not only NATU workers and the brightest and most militant students of UP and the Lyceum; it also fused the urban protest movement with the decades-old agrarian reform struggle by incorporating the children of the PKP's Luzon farmers' league—Malayang Samahan ng Magsasaka (the Democratic Union of Peasants, or MASAKA).

From the outset, Sison and KM leaders sought to give members in the organization a sense of belonging to a broader, class-oriented movement. Field trips were organized to MASAKA-controlled villages in the countryside, so KM students could be exposed to the living conditions of the peasants and to their legacy of militant struggles for agrarian reforms. Leoncio Co, a founding CPP member, recalled making such a trip to Nueva Ecija province as a young student in 1966, accompanied by future Party leaders Rodolfo Salas and Fernando Tayag:

> We went to this barrio of old [communist-led Hukbalahap guerrilla] veterans, and we saw them attending political schooling. They were discussing land reform, even dialectical materialism. We viewed them romantically. When it started to rain, one of the old men complained that an old war wound was starting to ache. To a 19-year-old kid fresh from reading Marx, this was something romantic.[9]

Although KM was conceived and organized by Sison in his clandestine capacity as chief of the PKP youth section, the organization began by coopting the issue of nationalism. KM discussion groups were formed in which students read and analyzed the writings of Recto and other nationalists and discussed imperialism and its relevance to the problems of Philippine society. When the groups exhausted the works of Recto, they turned to Marx and Lenin. That leap from nationalism to Marxism came so gradually with most student activists that today they recall the transition as a natural progression. One student who later became a top CPP official told me that students simply lost confidence in the non-Marxist nationalists. "We felt they couldn't lead a revolution, so we looked for a new direction to achieve meaningful social change."

By 1966, the Vietnam War had become the galvanizing issue of the day and had pushed the growing radical movement beyond what one activist called the "bourgeois nationalism" of Recto. The United States was seeking to make the war more of a joint effort by Asian allies— "More flags," as Lyndon Johnson styled it—and in September 1966, President Ferdinand Marcos acceded to LBJ's pressure and dispatched 2,000 Filipino troops for "civic action" duty in South Vietnam. That coupled with the growing role of the Clark and Subic bases in supporting the U.S. war machine fueled opposition to the war in the Philippines.

Just as it had coopted the nationalist crusade, the KM had already zeroed in on the Vietnam War as an issue around which it could rally students, workers, and intellectuals. From the perspective of the demonstrators, the United States was the imperialist bully oppressing the liberation-minded Vietnamese nationalists. Julius Fortuna, a radical student leader of the late 1960s who subsequently headed the CPP's Manila region, entered UP in 1965 as the war protests were beginning to grow, and he cut his activist teeth on the antiwar movement. "The Vietnam War helped change many Filipinos' perception toward communism," Fortuna recalled. "To us, the [communist-led] National Liberation Front was the hero in Vietnam."[10]

The antiwar protests began to attract many students who knew little about ideology but were opposed to what they considered another flagrant case of "U.S. intervention." KM propagandists likened the U.S. involvement in Vietnam to the U.S. suppression of Filipinos' turn-of-the-century war for independence. Opposition to the Vietnam War continued to build as President Johnson and other Asian leaders arrived in Manila in October 1966 for a U.S.-arranged summit to drum up broader regional support for the war effort.

The KM united with other student and labor organizations for a massive rally on the opening day of the Manila summit, October 24, 1966. Tens of thousands of demonstrators chanting "Johnson go home!" and "Hey, hey, LBJ, how many kids did you kill today?" marched to the seaside U.S. Embassy and then turned down the street to the Manila Hotel, the summit site. At one point, Saturnino Ocampo, a founding KM member who was also a reporter covering the summit for the *Manila Times*, walked out of the hotel and joined the throng of screaming demonstrators. Within a decade, Ocampo would be a CPP Central Committee member. Later that day, in the first bloody confrontation of the movement, nervous police roughly dispersed the demonstrators with truncheons and firehoses. Sison and others were arrested, several protesters were wounded by gunfire, and many others were bruised and beaten, although nobody was killed.

The final significant influence that shaped the Philippine communist movement in its formative years was the Chinese Cultural Revolution. By the 1960s, China had taken an active interest in Third World radical movements, particularly those in Asia. The Partai Kommunist Indonesia had become the world's fastest growing communist party thanks to generous aid and encouragement from China, and the potential for Chinese support was not lost on Filipino radicals. Small groups of Filipino students were already visiting China in 1965, lured by utopian accounts of that country's "socialist experiment."

By late 1966, news of the Cultural Revolution being waged by the Red Guards was filtering back to the Philippines, thereby deepening interest in China and Mao. In attempts to emulate the Cultural Revolution and embrace Mao's directive to "learn from the people," hordes of Filipino students wearing Mao caps, jackets, and badges and clutching copies of Mao's *Little Red Book* began flocking to the countryside on KM-sponsored outings. In time, the China craze reached comical proportions; even conservative, middle-class students donned Mao caps and buttons and learned the songs of the Cultural Revolution. The UP student newspaper, *The Philippine Collegian*, began serializing Mao's writings, and scarce copies of the *Peking Review*, painstakingly retyped and mimeographed, became must reading in student and intellectual circles.

The most important effect of the China mania was the increased interaction between the student activists and peasants in the countryside. KM members formed Serve the People Brigades (coined from another directive of Chairman Mao) and the Nationalist Corps to foster contact with "the masses" in the countryside. Every weekend, Serve the People Brigades of 10 to 20 students fanned out to the provinces surrounding Manila to share quotations from Mao and learn about the lives of peasants. For idealistic students, the experience was one more step in the transition from "bourgeois nationalists" to Marxist revolutionaries. Fortuna concluded years later that the forays to the countryside were "more for our self-transformation than for organizing the peasants in the countryside."

Returning from China in early 1967 with four volumes of Mao's collected works, Sison commissioned his most advanced cadres to translate the works into Tagalog. Later, Sison's disciples discussed what they had read in secret Marxist study cells formed within KM and SCAUP. Aside from offering a concrete plan for organizing an armed revolution, Mao's writings convinced the activists that "there is a possibility of victory for a weak group against a more powerful group," as Monico Atienza, a student leader who later became a founding CPP member, told me. For years, Filipino nationalists had been paralyzed by their belief that nothing they could do would shake the grasp of U.S. imperialism. Now, Mao was telling the students that they could shape their own destiny, that with enough patience, discipline, and sacrifice, they could make a revolution. "We were convinced by Mao's writings," Atienza said, "that if we followed his guidelines, eventually victory would come forth."

Sison's growing power as the guiding hand behind the student movement and his confrontational tactics began to make the cautious PKP leaders nervous. Although the elder PKP stalwarts professed to be loyal Stalinists, the party's theoretical moorings had never been particularly strong. During the Hukbalahap insurgencies of the 1940s and 1950s in Central Luzon, the party's ideological basis was diluted further by the infusion of poorly educated peasant members. The old PKP hands were increasingly uncomfortable with the highly ideological Sison and his well-read radicals who could quote the Marxist classics and the latest treatises on Maoist revolution.

The PKP's elder generation and Sison's youth brigade differed further on the question of tactics. The Lava faction was content to slowly build front organizations among students, workers, and peasants, not for the purpose of forcing a confrontation with the government, but for use as a springboard in a parliamentary struggle. Still haunted by an ill-conceived grab for power through armed revolution in 1950, the old men wanted nothing to do with what they viewed as Sison's "adventurist" talk of revolution.

The youth movement's plunge into Maoism pushed the widening generation gap to the verge of a schism. The hordes of students waving the *Little Red Book* who descended on PKP-controlled villages horrified some of the old peasants and party faithful, who were trying to convince the government of their legal, nonviolent intentions. The peasants had borne the brunt of the military repression and bloodshed of the 1950s, and they, too, were not eager to repeat the experience.

As early as 1965, Sison had been trying to convince PKP members that the dying party needed to undertake a "rectification" campaign that would criticize the Lavas' past errors and explain to party members the reasons for the failure of the Huk movement. Only by cleansing itself through rectification could the party hope to redeem itself with younger radicals, Sison argued. The old guard finally acceded, and Sison set to work preparing a draft in early 1967. What emerged was a blistering, detailed denunciation of the Lavas' failings in party leadership dating back to 1942. Infuriated, the Lava faction removed Sison as head of the PKP youth section, accusing him of adventurism and of encouraging a Maoist cult within KM. In April 1967, the Lava faction convened a special session of the PKP executive committee and formally expelled Sison and his followers from the party.[11]

Sison immediately went on the offensive. He attempted to seize control of key front organizations such as the Bertrand Russell Peace Foundation and a broad nationalist coalition called the Movement for the Advancement of Nationalism (MAN). The bitter polemics between the Lava and the Sison factions were aired in the UP student newspaper and in the meetings of MAN and other organizations. The PKP pulled peasant children of old Hukbalahap guerrillas out of KM in order to establish a rival youth organization. By the end of the year, Sison had been ousted as chairman of MAN and in retaliation had pulled KM from the coalition. Even KM was affected by the bitter polemics, and Sison barely maintained control of the organization that formed his power base. Believing Sison's confrontational leadership had caused the chaos within the radical movement, an embittered faction within KM broke away and established a rival Maoist student organization, the Samahang Demo-kratiko ng Kabataan (Democratic Youth Association, or SDK).

Shortly after his expulsion from the PKP, Sison issued a May Day Statement, published in a pro-Chinese communist newspaper in New Zealand, scorning the "Lavaists" as "modern revisionists" in the traitorous mold of China's fallen Liu Shaoqi and the Soviet Union, the latter having broken with China over ideology. Sison signed the statement on behalf of the "provisional Politburo" of the Communist Party of the Philippines, which in reality was a loose collection of his student protégés and PKP allies.

The loss of the rural KM base caused by the split with the PKP for the moment hurt Sison's plans for a rural-based revolution, so he set to work feverishly strengthening his student base. SCAUP and KM intensified recruiting efforts and stepped up the political education of members. Sison also ordered his Central Luzon KM leader, Rodolfo Salas, to contact Huk commanders about a possible alliance. On their own, the young communists began stockpiling handguns and single-shot hunting rifles in Batangas province, south of Manila. "There was already the conclusion that only armed revolution could promote social change," Fortuna recalled. "The conclusion was that the national situation was favorable for revolution."[12] In the end, the decision to form a new communist party and build an army was in part dictated by self-preservation. The Lava faction had earned a reputation for eliminating its political rivals, and Sison and his lieutenants were convinced they were targeted for assassination.

By 1968, Sison had gained a sizable following among activist ranks for his rectification campaign. Many students had come to believe in the practical need for a party reassessment, if for no other reason than to explain to the growing ranks of activists the reasons behind the chaos of the preceding year. In September, Sison set to work drafting a new communist party constitution and a plan for launching an armed rev-olution, while revising the rectification document. By early December, all that remained to be done was for Sison and a handpicked Central Committee to formally launch the new party and the armed revolution.

In the weeks immediately following the Pangasinan congress, the young CPP leaders were at a loss about how to advance the revolution they had declared. "The question after a few days was, 'Now what?' " Leoncio Co, one of the founding CPP members, told me 20 years later. The immediate task was to build the fledgling Party. Sison assigned his Central Committee members, all of whom remained above ground until spring 1969, to press the expansion of KM. Sison was more preoccupied with finding an army to protect his party and to launch the "people's war" he had detailed on paper. Years later, ranking CPP associates of Sison recalled that the Party leader had on two occasions traveled to Central Luzon to meet Commander Sumulong to discuss a possible alliance, but the Huk warlord had not appeared.[13]

In late 1968, Salas told Sison about another possible ally, a young Tarlac province Huk commander named Dante. A few weeks after the Pangasinan congress, in late January 1969, Sison was summoned to the Manila office of Congressman José Yap, the protégé of a nationally prominent Tarlac senator, Benigno Aquino, Jr. Yap told Sison that a Tarlac Huk leader wanted to meet him. Would he be interested in a rendezvous with Commander Dante?[14]

Sison knew little about the Huk commander, but the wiry rebel was well known to the peasants as well as to the powerful landowners of Tarlac. Born Bernabe Buscayno, Dante had for years been leading a ragged Huk band that controlled the barrios of southern Tarlac and collected tribute from peasant rice farmers and wealthy sugar plantation owners. Dante's superior, Commander Sumulong, the supreme Huk commander, acted as a power broker, deciding who would run for what office in Central Luzon.[15]

The region's politicians knew the rules, and many prominent officials developed close relationships with local Huk commanders. Aquino, the scion of one of Tarlac's wealthiest and most powerful families, had learned to play the game well. In the 1950s, Aquino had added to his power and fortune by marrying the daughter of another wealthy Tarlac family, Corazón Cojuangco. In 1957, Cojuangco's family bought a 15,000-acre sugar plantation in central Tarlac. The estate, Hacienda Luisita, was one of the country's major sugar producers, and thousands of Central Luzon agricultural workers earned a living planting and cutting cane on the vast plantation.

Buscayno grew up in the shadow of Hacienda Luisita, one of eight children born to a poor tenant farmer in a primitive barrio of Capas, Tarlac. His father had joined the communist-led Hukbalahap guerrilla army during World War II and later took up arms against the government in the postwar peasant rebellions. By the 1950s, the elder Buscayno had given up the rebel life. He settled his growing family in a small thatch shack built in a mango orchard owned by a prominent local doctor and tried to scrape out a living. But like many of the region's peasants, the elder Buscayno found it impossible to make ends meet, so Bernabe and his younger brother José were sent to a Manila suburb to live with their landlord and attend school while working as houseboys. Buscayno reached the second year of high school before he and his brother left the city to live with an aunt in Angeles, the seedy home of Clark Air Force Base, a few miles south of Capas. Buscayno and his brother found jobs working in a restaurant and eventually drifted back to the sugarcane fields of southern Tarlac.[16]

Buscayno found work as a canecutter on Hacienda Luisita and on neighboring plantations. On a good day, he would cut 2 tons and earn the equivalent of about $2. More often, the amount would be less and the work sporadic. It was in the cane fields that the thin, quiet young man began to challenge local landlords and agreed to act as a spokesperson for canecutters demanding a 20-centavo raise. When the landlord refused, Buscayno led the workers in burning a field of uncut cane. The raise was granted. Buscayno's role in the dispute earned him the label of troublemaker, and local military officials ordered him to report weekly to authorities in nearby Concepcion, Benigno Aquino's hometown. Sometime in the late 1950s, Buscayno joined one of Commander Sumulong's Huk bands operating in southern Tarlac and adopted the nom de guerre Dante.

According to local legend, Dante made a name for himself in the Huk ranks in the late 1950s when he carried out an order to execute one of his own brothers, who was accused of being a military informant.[17] As the commander of a rebel band, Dante and his men lived with the peasants and survived by taxing the landlords, usually at the rate of 3 percent of each harvest. During this period in the early 1960s, Dante developed a friendship with Benigno Aquino, who at the time was Tarlac governor. As Aquino became more powerful, winning a seat in the senate, his relationship with Dante flourished. Dante was even a welcome guest at Hacienda Luisita, coming round to visit Aquino and chat with his wife. Years later, when I asked President Aquino about her recollections of Dante, she spoke fondly of the guerrilla leader. "I was so impressed by him. He was so thin, yet he spoke so forcefully. He was so articulate in Pilipino [the language native to the Manila area] even though that is not his native language."

Aquino warmed to the topic, and she went on to tell me about an incident in the late 1970s when both Dante and her husband were in a Marcos prison. Some friends had invited her to attend a court appearance of Dante as a way of showing opposition to Marcos. The next morning, Aquino was horrified when she discovered she was the only one there. When Dante was led into the courtroom, his face brightened upon seeing his old friend from Hacienda Luisita, and the celebrated New People's

Army commander waved a cheery greeting. Laughing, Aquino told me, "I remember thinking, 'There goes several more years on my husband's sentence.'"[18]

By the late 1960s, Dante had spent nearly half his life as an outlaw under the tutelage of Commander Sumulong. The authorities had attributed 25 murders to the guerrilla commander, several of them point-blank assassinations. But Dante was not a mere gunslinger. He had diligently studied Joseph Stalin's works in classes conducted in a crude "Stalin University" hidden in the nearby Zambales Mountains. He had excelled in political studies, carefully developing his own ideas and theories, and his intellectual achievements had won him the position of education chairman in Commander Sumulong's army. Dante had even begun reading Mao's *Little Red Book*, a gift from a Tarlac politician who had visited China.[19] The more Dante read and studied, the more uncomfortable he became with Sumulong's black market and underworld activities. In the countryside, the PKP had virtually ceased to function as an operational political party, and Dante, like other Huk commanders scattered around Central Luzon, was receiving minimal ideological or strategic guidance from the PKP hierarchy. All the while, Sumulong was growing rich running protection rackets in Angeles and selling U.S. goods smuggled from Clark Air Force Base.

Dante nurtured the dream of an agrarian revolution that would improve the lot of Central Luzon farmers, and he had been impressed by the KM activists who marched through the streets of Manila during the week and on weekends flocked to the barrios, quoting Mao. In the latter half of 1968, Dante had dispatched emissaries to Manila to establish contacts with the KM. On one occasion, Dante himself—with a 90,000-peso price on his head—had gone to Manila to join a demonstration of peasants and KM activists in front of the Congress building.[20]

Sometime in late 1968, Dante sought out Aquino's chief southern Tarlac lieutenant, Congressman Yap, and asked if he could arrange a meeting with Sison. By then, Sison was a savage critic of Marcos, and Yap was only too happy to oblige. The meeting was set for January 1969 in Dante's stronghold, Barrio Santa Rita (also known as Talimundoc), a poor village of Capas, near the place where the guerrilla leader was born. The peasants in this corner of Tarlac were completely loyal to Dante. Many were his relatives, and the barrio captain, Juanito Rivera, was one of Dante's unit commanders. Excited by the meeting but at the same time wary that he might be walking into a Lava trap, Sison left final instructions with his 12 Central Committee colleagues in the event that he did not return.

Later, Aquino would tell friends that he personally drove Sison to the meeting, passing through dusty barrios controlled by Dante's men.

Sison and Dante hit it off immediately, and they talked throughout much of the night about the possibility of merging their forces. They found they shared the same feelings of contempt for the Lava and Sumulong leaderships. Sison was impressed by the thin, taut peasant, who was obviously well read and expressed himself simply but intelligently. When they finally ended the meeting the next morning, they had reached an agreement in principle. Sison and the young Maoists had found their army. Dante had his party.[21]

3

A People's Army Takes Shape

Under cover of darkness on the tropical summer evening of March 29, 1969, Commander Dante and eight of his guerrilla lieutenants slipped into the sleepy Capas barrio of Santa Rita, where two months earlier the rebel leader had forged an alliance with Sison's Manila radicals. Dante and his men made their way to the largest building in the barrio, a simple, three-room frame house on stilts built from lumber the rebels had pilfered from the construction site of a nearby Voice of America relay station. Sison and four or five of his boyish Central Committee members were already waiting inside, and they greeted the peasant rebels.[1]

Sison had purposely selected the date—the twenty-seventh anniversary of the founding of the World War II Hukbalahap communist guerrilla organization—to formally launch the reconstituted communist army, the New People's Army. By doing so, the CPP leader hoped to lend credence to his claim that the new guerrilla movement was actually a continuation of the struggle for agrarian reforms Central Luzon tenant farmers and field hands had begun three decades earlier.

Santa Rita provided a fitting backdrop for the ceremonial launching of the new guerrilla war. The village was a traditional Huk stronghold and, as Dante's birthplace, had become the base for his rebel band. Although only 60 miles north of Manila, Santa Rita had been bypassed by government development projects. There was no running water or electricity. The barrio's sole link to the outside world was a poorly maintained dirt road, which became a swirling ribbon of dust during the dry months and a nearly impassable quagmire during the long rainy season.

On this momentous evening, Dante rigged a string of light bulbs to an automobile battery to illuminate the room. Sison began by delivering a solemn discourse on the historical significance of the occasion. The CPP chairman's impassioned rhetoric, laden with Cultural Revolution jargon, bewildered the poorly educated peasant guerrillas. One of them, a tough 19-year-old killer known as Commander Melody, giggled nervously.

Sison explained the revolution's goals as the liberation of Filipinos from the forces of U.S. imperialism and domestic feudalism. The NPA's responsibility was to win that liberation through people's war. Sison ran through a litany of errors and "crimes" committed by Sumulong and the "Lava clique," and he prescribed a remedy for the failures of the past: a strict code of discipline adopted from Mao's People's Liberation Army. Later, Sison led his army commanders in an oath of allegiance to the Party and NPA. In less than 90 minutes, the ceremony was over, and the rebel commanders drifted away into the night back to the safety of their adopted barrios, from where they would launch the war.

As NPA commander in chief, Commander Dante could muster about 50 men and an arsenal of 35 weapons: a few automatic rifles, several pistols, homemade shotguns, and antiquated one-shot rifles.[2] His army, if it could be called that, was a motley band of old farmers who had devoted their lives to Central Luzon's agrarian reform battles and hardened barrio youths, some of whom were inspired by the older generation's dream of better living conditions, and some of whom simply relished the power and excitement the rebel life offered.

The old generation was epitomized by Diosdado Layug, Commander Eddie, a weather-beaten farmer who along with other family members had joined the Hukbalahap's struggle against the Japanese. After the war, he had taken up arms against the government again in the PKP's People's Liberation Army rebellion for agarian reforms. By 1969, Layug was already in his fifties, a wizened veteran of countless battles in the war between Central Luzon peasants and landlords. Armed rebellion in the cause of agrarian reform had become a way of life to be bequeathed to serious young men such as Dante.[3]

At the other extreme were the young adventurers, such as Commander Melody, drawn to Central Luzon's rebel bands during the corrupt reign of Commander Sumulong. Melody, it was said at the time, had already killed "a truckload full of people," and he quickly would find life in Sison's rigidly disciplined communist army too demanding. By the end of the first year, Melody had deserted the NPA, under the shadow of a death sentence for impregnating two barrio girls and pocketing contributions from local politicians—acceptable practices under Commander Sumulong but scandalous breaches of the NPA's Maoist code of conduct.[4]

The blueprint of an army that Sison had drafted in early 1969 was an imaginative exercise in audacity that went far beyond any of his previous organizational schemes. Using the Chinese army as a model, he sketched out the framework for an armed force divided into conventional armies with corps and divisions all the way down to platoons and squads, supplemented by guerrilla units, militia, and "armed city partisans."[5] The main source of recruits and support for the army would be the peasantry, which Sison believed would be won over by an agrarian revolution waged by the NPA. On military matters, Mao's strategy would be faithfully copied: Retreat when the enemy advances, harass the enemy when it is at rest, and advance when the enemy retreats.

The strategy called for building a main army on the island of Luzon, while developing guerrilla units on outlying islands to force the government to scatter its troops throughout the archipelago. The protracted people's war charted by Sison would unfold in three stages: a strategic defensive stage, during which communist forces would be gradually built; a strategic stalemate, in which the NPA would reach parity with the government forces; and a strategic offensive, in which regular communist forces would attack isolated enemy units that had withdrawn to urban centers and fortified camps. In the countryside, the communist army would build "stable bases," multiply in strength, advance "wave upon wave," and gradually encircle the cities until final victory.[6]

The old communist armies had been notorious for their loose discipline and careless practices in the 1940s and 1950s. New recruits were usually accepted as members even before discussing the party's principles and rules.[7] But the CPP was founded on the Maoist principle of "iron discipline," and Sison decreed a puritanical code of conduct for the NPA. Drunkenness and gambling were strictly prohibited, and Mao's "Three Main Rules of Discipline" and the "Eight Points of Attention" were to be followed in all instances:

Three Main Rules of Discipline
1. Obey orders in all your actions.
2. Do not take a single needle or piece of thread from the masses.
3. Turn in everything captured.

Eight Points of Attention
1. Speak politely.
2. Pay fairly for what you buy.
3. Return everything you borrow.
4. Pay for everything you damage.
5. Do not hit or swear at people.

6. Do not damage crops.
7. Do not take liberties with women.
8. Do not ill-treat captives.[8]

Sison prescribed an intensive program of political education within the army to be conducted by Party cadres and commissars. The Party would control the army, and in both organizations, leadership would be by committee. CPP committees would decide issues by applying Lenin's principle of democratic centralism—the practice of decisionmaking by consensus, theoretically after a free and open discussion.

In May 1969, Sison convened the CPP Central Committee, which had been expanded to 22 members by the addition of Dante and his 8 commanders. For two days at the height of the scorching Central Luzon summer, the communist leaders met in a small hut surrounded by parched rice fields on the outskirts of Santa Rita. Dropping his usual seriousness, Sison tried to joke with the peasant guerrilla leaders, but they had difficulty understanding one another. Sison could not speak Pampango, the local dialect, and the peasants could not speak the Party chairman's native Ilocano. They could converse only in Tagalog, which the peasants had difficulty speaking and understanding.[9]

The plenum's most pressing order of business was how to expand the war beyond the flat, vulnerable barrios of Tarlac, which was within a few minutes' striking distance of several military camps. The rebels discussed opening fronts in the mountainous provinces of Zambales and Bataan on the western rim of Central Luzon and in the rugged Sierra Madre chain of Isabela province along Luzon's east coast. Within a few weeks, Diosdado Layug was dispatched to Isabela to recruit former Hukbalahap families to support a new guerrilla front.

That first plenum, like all in the years that followed until Sison's capture in 1977, was dominated by the CPP's founder. Dante faithfully voiced the sentiments of the peasants and field hands of Central Luzon, and he was no intellectual slouch, but invariably in discussions and debates, the others deferred to Sison.[10] Dante would remain influential as the army commander and would hold a seat on the five-member Executive Committee that ran the day-to-day affairs of the revolution, but Sison was the movement's founder, its chief ideologue, and its dominant force.

By March 1969, Sison and some of the Manila-bred Central Committee members had moved to the southern Tarlac barrios in an effort to supervise the movement's expansion beyond the area controlled by Dante's men. Military patrols frequently drove through the dusty barrios, but the existence of the new Communist Party was still unknown to authorities, and so Sison and his men were able to watch with casual amusement as the soldiers passed.

Dante, Co, and a few other Party members spent the weeks following the NPA inauguration translating the movement's founding documents from English to Tagalog, the language of Manila and surrounding provinces. They would work each day until 4 P.M., when Dante or one of the other veteran rebels would announce, "There will be no more operations today." It was an invitation to relax, for the old hands knew that the soldiers never failed to return to their barracks by that hour. Dante and Co would walk through the stubbled rice fields hunting doves and snipes with .22-caliber rifles.

From the beginning, the NPA established an ideological and ethical tone that set the movement apart from the indiscipline and political inertia that had characterized the old communist armies. Sison's personally trained cadres conducted intensive political education with the peasant fighters who filled the ranks of the NPA, and the classes were no casual affairs. So impassioned were the discussions of Mao's works that the young political officers conducting the sessions would often burst into tears when analyzing Mao's "Five Golden Rays."[11]

The revolution's main political training school was established in the compound of a Voice of America relay station in southern Tarlac, where some of Commander Dante's men worked as security guards. Dante and Salas, a native of neighboring Pampanga province, were permanent instructors at the school during 1969, and they would slip on blue security guard uniforms to look inconspicuous. Years later, Salas grinned with delight as he told me how new recruits were being schooled in Marx and Mao and the evils of U.S. imperialism, while a few feet away Voice of America employees went about their work.

Central Luzon gambling lords had always been able to buy protection from local politicians, law enforcement officials, and roving rebels, and they assumed that the new outlaws would have their price as well. After all, the Huks under Commander Sumulong had been content to collect their share of the profits each month. The gambling lords made the NPA commanders in Tarlac a generous offer of 6,000 pesos a month, but to their astonishment, the communist leaders flatly rejected the payoff. Nearly 20 years later, one of the Party officials who spurned the offer still recalled the incident with indignation. "It was unthinkable to us," he told me, his voice rising. "That money was dirty." The NPA's strict morality was extended to rebel-controlled barrios. In addition to banning drinking and gambling, the rebels even forbade peasants to attend cockfights.

The luxury of anonymity ended for the NPA on June 9, 1969, when a military patrol arrived in Santa Rita early one morning. Sison and Co sipped coffee as they watched the soldiers fan out through the village, and when the troops moved to another cluster of houses, the rebel leaders slipped away. Later that day, the soldiers returned to the barrio center and discovered an underground garage in which the peasants had hidden stacks of CPP documents. The capture of Sison's blueprint for revolution and its confirmation of a new rebel force operating in the Central Luzon countryside touched off a flurry of military operations in southern Tarlac. Helicopters and armored cars swooped down on suspected NPA hideouts, forcing the guerrillas to flee for their lives from barrio to barrio.

In late September 1969, the first battle between the government and the NPA occurred in the Pampanga barrio of Baluarte, outside the town of Mabalacat, a few miles south of Tarlac. An NPA contingent led by Juanito Rivera was in Baluarte when a government force of 300 soldiers surrounded the area. In the battle that ensued, the NPA gained its first martyrs: a young KM activist named Edgardo Payawal, who had been recruited from the U.S. Tobacco Company union; two peasant fighters; and a minor guerrilla commander named Benny.[12]

Later in 1969, progovernment death squads dubbed the Monkees, after the popular U.S. singing group, began terrorizing the Central Luzon villages where the rebels were operating. Soon, the area was gripped in a cycle of tit-for-tat killings between the Monkees and Dante's guerrillas, whom the Manila press nicknamed the Beatles. A majority of the killings were attributed to the Monkees, whose victims included politicians and policemen suspected of harboring NPA sympathizers and peasant organizers and leaders in NPA-controlled barrios.

Layug's efforts to organize support for the communists in Isabela had paid off by the latter half of 1969, and a new guerrilla front was opened in the villages of the Sierra Madre foothills of southern Isabela. He had begun by contacting a brother who had fought with the Huks in the 1950s and who had moved to Isabela to take advantage of a government resettlement program. Moving from one old Huk family to the next, Layug established a network of supporters from which an armed NPA unit could be built. Within a few months, pockets of support for the NPA had been organized around the towns of Jones and Cauayan.[13]

Back in Tarlac, almost daily military raids and patrols forced most of the Central Committee members to flee Central Luzon. Sison and Tubianosa moved to the northern mountain resort city of Baguio. Co returned to Manila and began conducting Party education classes among KM recruits in provinces surrounding the capital. Later in 1969, Co and other party leaders traveled to the newly opened Isabela front to give Marxist training to new recruits, most of whom were from Manila.

By the end of the first year, the movement was expanding steadily. Party membership, which was carefully screened, had risen to 300, and mostly comprised students and young workers from KM chapters. There were a few hundred guerrillas in the field, most of whom were deployed in the Central Luzon Front in Tarlac and Pampanga. Party cadres were hard at work organizing communist cells outside Manila to lay the groundwork for future guerrilla fronts. Salas was enjoying success organizing students and workers on Sumulong's turf in Pampanga. Nilo Tayag was establishing Party cells in the southern Luzon provinces of Batangas, Laguna, and Quezon. Another Central Committee member, Hermenigildo García, led a handful of activists and a small NPA contingent to organize a front on Negros in the central Philippines. García established a left-wing newspaper, the *Dumaguete Times*, to cover his activities among impoverished sugar plantation workers and small farmers.

Of Sison's lieutenants, only Arthur García remained behind in Tarlac. García was one of those closest to Sison, a former student at the Lyceum and an early KM recruit. He had dropped out of school to organize the U.S. Tobacco Company union, which was now providing the revolution with a stream of steady recruits. Physically strong and athletic, impetuous, bold, and self-confident to the point of brashness, García had taken to the life of a guerrilla. He relished remaining behind in the embattled Tarlac front with Dante's forces when the rest of Sison's inner circle pulled out.

García worked zealously at adding recruits to the guerrilla army. Sometime in late 1969, he recruited a mentally unstable young man from a Tarlac barrio over the warnings of the fellow's mother. The recruit was unprepared for the rigorous Marxist "criticism" and "self-criticism" sessions García loved to conduct. One night in late January 1970, while camped in an isolated corner of Hacienda Luisita, criticism of the young man by his comrades became more than he could bear.

The next morning, when the other eight or nine members of the unit went to a stream to bathe, the aggrieved man opened fire wildly with an automatic rifle. Calmly, García pulled his .45 pistol from his holster and ordered the others to take cover. García crept undetected to the space beneath the raised bamboo hut where the man had fled, but before he could fire, the crazed rebel spotted him through the bamboo-slat floor and fired several rounds from an M-14 rifle, killing García. The gunman then fled to his nearby home barrio with the unit's entire arsenal of rifles.[14]

A few days later, in February 1970, the movement suffered another blow when Dante's younger brother José was killed while leading a daylight ambush on two jeeploads of government paramilitary forces in a barrio near Santa Rita. Within weeks, that loss was followed by the arrest of Co, who was captured near Santa Rita after a meeting with Dante.

Co's arrest prompted Dante and several of his men to transfer to the Isabela front, where the NPA forces tried to avoid repeating the errors committed at Tarlac. Instead of recklessly ambushing government patrols, the rebels concentrated on educating and organizing the peasants, thereby slowly building a solid base of supporters. The young revolutionaries relied almost entirely on Mao's writings for step-by-step guidance in guerrilla warfare and political organizing.

One of Sison's Central Committee comrades later told me that Sison dreamed in those early years of establishing Mountain province, in Luzon's Cordillera range, as a sort of "NPA Yenan," a reference to the impregnable Shensi province base Mao built following the 1935–1936 Long March.[15] But for the time being, Sison and his lieutenants had their hands full building a refuge in Isabela, saving their beleaguered forces in Tarlac, and managing the fresh wave of demonstrations convulsing Manila.

In the late 1960s, Sison had written a widely read essay entitled "Student Power?" in which he contended that only by building a movement that attracted the peasants and "working masses" would students ever attain meaningful political power.[16] As the radical study groups in Manila grew larger, they became known as "teach-ins," after the antiwar movement gatherings being held on U.S. campuses. In the Philippines, the teach-ins fostered lively discussions about the Vietnam War, U.S. military bases, U.S.-Philippine relations, Marx, and Mao. At UP, the teach-ins produced such future leaders of the Communist Party as Rafael Baylosis, CPP secretary-general at the time of his capture in early 1988, and José Luneta, who by 1989 was the only founding Central Committee member still active in the Party leadership in the Philippines.

Sison's patient attention to the student movement had begun to pay big dividends by 1969 as radical activists held regular demonstrations denouncing U.S. imperialism, its local "puppet," Ferdinand Marcos, the Vietnam War, and U.S. military bases. Commander Dante's young, lean face began appearing on the posters that radical students carried, and the crowds echoed with chants of "Dante for president" of the Philippines. In the evenings, the demonstrators would gather in study groups and teach-ins, nurtured by accounts of NPA exploits filtering in from the countryside.

Against this backdrop of worsening political turmoil, in November 1969 Marcos became the first Philippine president ever to win reelection, in the most violent and fraudulent campaign the country had ever seen. The radical students, already disdainful of a political system dominated by elitist, ideologically indistinguishable parties, reacted to Marcos' tainted reelection with a vengeance. Student unrest peaked in January 1970 with the outbreak of three months of violent demonstrations that would become known as the First Quarter Storm. By spring, many of the students had graduated from attending teach-ins to conducting them in the slums and working-class neighborhoods of Manila.

The First Quarter Storm began on January 26, 1970, when Marcos and his flamboyant wife, Imelda, stepped outside the Congress building in downtown Manila following the president's delivery of his state of the nation address. A raucous crowd of 20,000 radical students, workers, and peasants jeered the shaken president and first lady and hurled rocks and bottles at their car. Afterward, police scattered the mob with batons.

Four days later, thousands of chanting demonstrators marched to the palace, where they commandeered a fire truck and rammed through the main gate. The mob spilled onto the palace grounds burning automobiles and cheering. Soldiers and police beat the demonstrators back with tear gas and truncheons, but six demonstrators were shot to death and several others wounded in sporadic clashes that continued late into the night outside the palace near Mendiola Bridge. On the following day, rampaging demonstrators attacked the U.S. Embassy, hurling Molotov cocktails, shattering windows, and ripping the U.S. seal from the embassy gate. In the days that followed, the radicals attacked the downtown Hilton Hotel and other perceived symbols of the U.S. presence in the Philippines.[17]

Marcos' accusations that the communists were responsible for the demonstrations in Manila from the late 1960s until the declaration of martial law in 1972 raises the question of how much, in fact, Sison and the Communist Party did orchestrate or control the protests. Some scholars have argued that ideology played little role in the protests, that the demonstrators were merely voicing discontent with long unattended social ills and the increasingly corrupt rule of Marcos or even mimicking the student demonstrations that were sweeping the United States and Europe. Many of the participants in the demonstrations were motivated by a combination of these reasons. Marcos undeniably manipulated the turmoil for his political gain by using the communist guerrilla movement as a political prop to be trotted out on stage when it suited his needs and ambitions.

Sison insisted that the CPP "inspired and guided" the demonstrations between 1970 and 1972, claiming that cadres involved in Party-controlled student organizations planned and supervised the First Quarter Storm.[18] One of his close aides, a former Central Committee member who was still involved with the KM at the time, told me that Party control over the protests was looser perhaps than Sison suggested. But this aide fully corroborated Sison's contention that the Party played a prominent role in secretly organizing and encouraging the radical upheaval.

Sison moved back and forth between the Luzon countryside and Manila during the period and fanned the urban unrest with a flurry of statements urging students and organized labor to continue their militant protests. When bruised and teargassed demonstrators decided that rallies were no longer a commensurate response to Marcos' rule, the Party was waiting to welcome the new recruits into Dante's army in the countryside.

The CPP cells within KM and other organizations were quick to capitalize on the angry mood sweeping Manila's campuses and factories. In an early essay, "Investigation of the Peasant Movement in Hunan Province," Mao stressed that a careful "social investigation" was needed to identify relevant local issues before political proselytizing could yield fruit. Committing Mao's words to heart, Filipino activists fanned out through Manila and the countryside conducting social investigations in factories, on campuses, and in rural barrios.

Julius Fortuna, who by the early 1970s chaired the legal left-wing coalition, Movement for a Democratic Philippines, recalled how a social investigation at Manila's conservative Far Eastern University enabled communist students to gain control of several campus organizations, which eventually supplied the underground movement with many recruits. "We came up with the plan of organizing layers and layers of organizations [to conceal their Marxist character]," he told me years later. Communist organizers would create new, seemingly innocuous clubs or infiltrate already existing organizations and then gradually establish control. In time, the activists were able to take over many of the school's influential organizations, which enabled them to tap into a new pool of potential recruits.

To the casual observer in 1969, there appeared to be little reason to fear a violent revolution in the Philippines. The country boasted all the institutions of a working democracy. Two political parties vied for power in elections, a president was elected every four years, and the military remained in the barracks. There was a bicameral congress and an independent judiciary. The United States liked to describe its former colony as Asia's "showcase of democracy," but in reality, democracy was an illusion for the vast majority of Filipinos. The two political parties, the Nacionalistas and the Liberals, and the elections they so vigorously contested, were dominated by rival factions of an elite that differed in self-interests rather than ideology.

More than 20 years of self-rule had done virtually nothing to solve nagging social and economic inequities, and in fact, the problems were worsening. Five percent of the population owned 50 percent of the wealth in 1969, and the median per capita income was about $50 a year. Real wages for those living in cities had fallen by 8 percent during the 1960s, and the combined rate of unemployment and underemployment was estimated as high as 25 percent. In the countryside, government agrarian reform programs were thwarted by intransigent landlords, and life for millions of indebted and impoverished tenant farmers and field hands had changed little since the rumblings of peasant rebellion in the 1930s.[19]

After the Huk peasant rebellion of the 1950s had crumbled, talk of social reforms largely had been shelved. The most pressing problem in the countryside continued to be that of landownership and the plight of landless peasants and field hands. Share tenancy had actually risen since the Central Luzon agrarian protests of the 1930s from 34 percent of all farmers in 1939 to nearly 50 percent by the early 1970s. In some areas of the country, such as Central Luzon, the tenancy rate among farmers was as high as 85 percent.

Since independence, one president after another had passed ad hoc agrarian reform packages—usually in reaction to peasant uprisings or the threat of unrest—but one after another failed to dent the problem. The reason was simple enough: From the barrio to the national level, political power was controlled by landlords. President Ramón Magsaysay's 1955 Land Reform Act, aimed at redistributing lands in areas of Huk unrest, succeeded in parceling out only 41 farm plots to landless peasants. By the end of his term in 1966, President Diosdado Macapagal's 1963 agrarian reform code, which sought to end sharecropping tenancy, had affected only 72,000 of the 1 million acres cultivated by rice and corn tenant farmers.[20] Before Macapagal's bill had ever cleared Congress, landowning legislators had gutted the land reform program with 200 amendments. Marcos managed to increase the number of leasehold agreements from 896 in 1965 to 6,340 in 1969, but his agrarian reform program remained scantly underfunded and soon succumbed to inertia.[21]

The tenancy problem was made more acute by an exploding population, which had tripled during U.S. colonial rule and doubled again between 1948 and 1970. In previous decades, the problems of overpopulation and growing concentration of land in the hands of wealthy entrepreneurs were eased by migration to undeveloped lands in the mountains or to outlying islands. But by 1970, there were no more frontiers, and those who had fled to the mountains had nowhere else to go. Population density grew from 166 persons per square mile in 1948 to 317 per square mile in 1970. In Central Luzon, the population density had risen to more than 500 persons per square mile by 1970.[22]

A government official who visited the Central Luzon countryside in late 1968 was appalled by the living conditions in the barrios: "The hospitals, the courts, the army camps are all in the provincial capitals and major towns. . . . Most of the poor peasants can't even afford the bus fare to see a doctor in town—if there are doctors willing to treat them for practically nothing."[23] Many tenant farmers and field hands, finding it impossible to provide for their families, flocked to Manila and other cities. Wretched slums of squatters living in lean-tos and flimsy shacks began proliferating around Manila and other cities, as the number of homeless rose dramatically during the 1960s.

By the end of the decade, the Philippines was a society that seemed to be careering out of control. Crime was rampant. Few men ventured about Manila without a gun. Corruption among government bureaucrats and politicians was rife. Poverty and unemployment were worsening, while the scions of the rich and powerful celebrated their wealth in lavish displays of bacchanalian revelry. Renato Constantino, the nationalist historian and writer, spoke forebodingly of a "sick" society and observed pointedly, "The urgency for thorough-going change has become so patent that even those who benefit most under the present system now attempt to pose as catalysts and champions of social reform."[24]

The large, violent demonstrations of 1970 shocked many Filipinos into taking at least cursory notice of the deteriorating society around them, and talk turned to the chilling topic of revolution. But in fact, the threat of revolution in the Philippines in the early 1970s was overstated. The Communist Party had managed to organize a few thousand students and workers, but the vast majority of Manila's 500,000 students remained either apolitical or unwilling to support an armed rebellion. Deepening dissatisfaction with Marcos could hardly be interpreted as support for revolution. A public opinion poll taken during the height of the First Quarter Storm reported that 8 out of 10 people still hoped to reform politics and society through existing structures. Fewer than 3 percent of those polled in another survey identified with the radicals' focus on imperialism and social justice.[25]

Given that environment, why was the communist movement that emerged in the late 1960s able to take root when similar attempts had failed so miserably? Francisco Nemenzo, the UP professor later shunned by the young radicals because of his links with the PKP, cited a confluence of factors: grinding poverty that underscored in human—rather than theoretical—terms the failures of Philippine society; a disenchantment with traditional politics that had eroded faith in the electoral processes and institutions; and the ideological inspiration of Mao Zedong.[26]

If Mao provided Filipino radicals in the late 1960s with the ideological cement to hold their movement together, Sison provided the vision. His energy, organizational talents, and unswerving devotion to the dream of revolution gave the movement an impetus that the old communist movement never had. Sison was a prolific writer, turning out revolutionary tracts, poems, and position papers under the pen name of Amado Guerrero and in the name of the CPP Central Committee. In 1970, in the midst of the chaos that was shaking the country's foundations, mimeographed copies of Sison's most important work, *Philippine Society and Revolution*, began to appear.

PSR, as the book came to be known, was Sison's Marxist analysis of Philippine history and society and a well-argued brief for the necessity of a Maoist revolution. It combined Agoncillo's and Constantino's nationalist accounts of Philippine history with Mao's concrete plan of revolutionary action. Many Filipino activists read Sison's work and were struck by what they believed were its profound truths.

Sison characterized the Philippines as a "semicolonial, semifeudal" nation in which workers and peasants—the vast majority of the population—were oppressed by foreign imperialists, domestic capitalists, and landlords. (This analysis was borrowed from Mao's description of prerevolutionary China.) He divided Philippine society into classes, with "big bourgeoisie landlords" and "big bourgeoisie capitalists"—the "local lackeys of U.S. imperialism"—at the top of the pyramid and the proletariat and peasants at the bottom. A protracted people's war would pit workers and peasants, and their allies from the "middle forces"—nationalist businesspeople, teachers, intellectuals, and students—versus landlords and big business. By practicing Mao's strategy of building a peasant army in the countryside, the revolutionary forces could gradually encircle the cities and "liberate" the country from "big capitalists" and "U.S. imperialism."[27]

Looking back nearly two decades later, with Sison's book still being hailed as the revolution's Bible, the significance of *Philippine Society and Revolution* probably cannot be overemphasized. PSR imparted Sison's confidence and sense of inevitable victory to those who read it. The blueprint that PSR offered a generation of Filipinos helped attract to the revolution a broad range of students and intellectuals as well as priests and nuns. "At the time PSR first appeared, it struck us as the most precise analysis of the Philippines' situation," Julius Fortuna told me years afterward. "Here was a book that gave not only a new analysis of Philippine society, but told us what is to be done. Constantino and Recto were merely criticizing. Joema offered a vision."[28]

4

Collapse and Retreat

By 1970, the New People's Army could field about 300 lightly armed guerrillas, most of them concentrated in Central Luzon and a few dozen in Isabela. Proselytizing by KM and SDK activists was producing a modest flow of recruits to the struggling communist army in the countryside. The First Quarter Storm of 1970 had been a turning point, the demonstrations and the government's violent response having pushed the entire student-labor protest movement toward the ranks of the radicals. "Morale was so high at that time that people were volunteering for the armed struggle," a student leader recalled years later. "They wanted to be sent to the countryside, though a number of KM people died because of lack of training." The problem for the communist leadership was how to transform the student protesters into savvy guerrillas.

Francisco was one of those who decided in the early 1970s that he was willing to give his life for the revolution. As a premedicine student at Manila's conservative Catholic University of Santo Tomás, he had joined the First Quarter Storm demonstrations. He and other premed students served as medics when the police moved in with clubs, cracking heads and breaking bones. By 1971, Francisco had become a full-fledged Party member, recruiting medical students and young doctors at universities for a CPP-controlled organization. On weekends, the organization would conduct free health clinics in Manila slums or in poor villages in the provinces surrounding the capital.

In April 1972, following a number of arrests in the student movement, Francisco was ordered to go underground. For three months, he worked in rebel "safe houses" in Manila treating wounded guerrillas who had been brought from the countryside. By the time many of the casualties arrived, gangrene had set in, forcing the rebel doctors to perform emergency amputations in crude underground "hospitals." Shortly before martial law was declared, Francisco was assigned to a nine-member NPA propaganda team in Batangas province, 40 miles south of Manila.

When I met Francisco 15 years later in a jungle NPA camp in Quezon province, he had spent roughly half his life in the communist underground. Except for a four-year stint in prison, which ended when Corazón Aquino released him in 1986, he had remained in the field since 1972. Although by the late 1980s he was in his mid-thirties, he looked much younger. His face was still boyish, and he had an easy grin and folksy style. The former medical student was now chief military commander of the Party's Southern Tagalog Region, a five-province area bordering Manila on the south and east.

Looking back, Francisco recalled how the transition from middle-class student to Maoist guerrilla had been made easy by his experiences as a medical school volunteer in the city slums and impoverished barrios.

> I would encounter sickness in the countryside among peasants and urban poor, and they would have no money. They could not buy medicine or afford to go to a doctor. In this type of society, only the rich could afford medical care. I told myself I would serve the people and join the movement.[1]

KM forays into poor rural barrios and urban slums had the same effect of driving home to young activists the stark contrasts and inequities of Philippine society. Others were radicalized in the street demonstrations, in which they or their friends suffered the blows of riot police. For some of the underground leaders with whom I spoke, the evolution was an intellectual process that occurred in the radical discussion groups in Manila.

Few political conversions were as dramatic as that of Victor Corpus. The son of a military surgeon, Corpus was a graduate of Manila's conservative Catholic De La Salle University. He was accepted into the Philippine Military Academy (PMA), the country's equivalent of West Point, and while there studied under radical history and political science professors. By his senior year, Corpus had been caught up in the fervor of nationalist passions sweeping Philippine campuses. In October 1966, Sison delivered a speech at PMA on nationalism in the armed forces. That encounter marked the beginning of what would become a close relationship between the impressionable military cadet and the radical nationalist. Later, as a constabulary officer, Corpus stayed in touch with Sison, sometimes dropping by in uniform to visit the communist leader at his apartment in the Manila suburb of Quezon City.

In 1970, after two years in the field, much of it spent training the private armies of pro-Marcos warlords, Corpus was sickened by his experiences and asked to be posted at PMA as an assistant instructor in political science. Corpus hoped to find peace at the academy, but instead he was appalled to discover widespread corruption and abuses of privilege. He earned the ire of his fellow staff members by posting a statement on a prominent wall inside the academy asking the unscrupulous officers to reform. Some of Corpus' idealistic students were equally dismayed by the corruption, and together they began plotting a cadet strike in late 1970.[2]

In the meantime, Corpus had gotten a message from his former mentor, Sison, who by then was underground leading the fledgling communist revolution. In October 1970, a courier guided Corpus to the Sierra Madre foothills town of Cauayan, in southern Isabela. There they met in a house owned by the Cauayan mayor, Faustino Dy. The CPP chairman and the military officer talked for hours, and finally Sison asked Corpus if he wanted to join the rebel movement. When Corpus indicated interest, Sison asked if he could steal the weapons from the PMA armory. A few weeks later, Corpus returned for another meeting with Sison and agreed to lead a raid on the armory.[3]

On the evening of December 30, 1970, while much of the PMA security force was guarding President Marcos as he vacationed in Baguio, where the academy was located, Corpus drove to the city's downtown Burnham Park. There he was met by 9 guerrillas. They returned to the academy, Corpus in his military jeep, the rebels in two cars, and they were waved through the gate. Inside, the rebels quickly tied up the armory guards and loaded 21 automatic rifles, 14 carbines, 6 machine guns, 1 bazooka, grenade launchers, and more than 5,000 rounds of ammunition into the cars. They drove all night to reach Cauayan, the entry point for the NPA base camp in the nearby Sierra Madre foothills. Corpus and the raiding team were escorted by Mayor Dy's police to a rendezvous point at the base of the mountains, where they were met by Dante and 10 guerrillas. After walking all day and all night, they reached the camp.[4]

Corpus' dramatic raid and defection were a tremendous propaganda coup for the communist movement which stunned the nation and sent shock waves through the government and armed forces. In one of a series of statements released to Manila newspapers, Sison announced that the communists had launched a "secret Victor Corpus Movement within the reactionary armed forces in order to disintegrate the principal component of reactionary state power." To sow further doubts in the minds of Marcos and his military commanders, the Communist Party issued several statements in the name of Corpus—written by Sison—casually referring to active coup plots within the armed forces.[5]

The Manila press reacted with a spate of stories and commentaries predicting an imminent coup or communist revolution. A jittery Marcos launched a "loyalty check" within the armed forces and beefed up security around his palace and the capital. While Marcos was worrying about the loyalty of his army, the communist leaders were preoccupied with expanding their own army beyond the precarious rebel footholds of southern Isabela and the Central Luzon provinces. In August 1970, the CPP Political Bureau ordered the acceleration of the cautious pace of Party recruitment, and by early the following year, with membership nearing 1,000, the Central Committee decided to begin forming regional Party committees and regional army commands. Within a few months, regional Party committees had been organized for greater Manila, central, northern, and southern Luzon, western and eastern Visayas, and Mindanao, covering the entire archipelago. Although the regional committees established regional army commands, in reality the regional CPP organizations and military commands outside of Central Luzon, northern Luzon (Isabela) and Manila existed almost entirely on paper.[6]

By 1970, the NPA had established a crude headquarters in the Isabela jungle. The camp was little more than a cluster of six bamboo huts atop a thickly forested ridge more than a day's hike from Cauayan, the nearest town. One of the huts served as a makeshift office with a typewriter and a rough-hewn wooden table. There were benches in the middle of the camp, at which the rebel leaders and their troops would sit around a fire after meals discussing political theories, strategy, and tactics.

For the first few months, the guerrillas in Isabela remained undetected. Porters carried rice to the camp from the town below, and the rebels relied on the forest to provide for their other needs. They fished with an improvised speargun in a nearby river, and they caught komodo-like lizards in small wooden traps. Occasionally, the fishing expeditions would land an eel, a delicacy that was cause for celebration. From time to time, Dante and Corpus would provide a wild boar or wild cat bagged on their hunting forays with a .22 rifle and a shotgun.

Their lives, later to become so precarious, were idyllic. The most life-threatening incident occurred when someone cooked up a batch of rare and delicious mushrooms. The entire communist leadership, Sison and Dante included, was almost wiped out when the mushrooms turned out to be poisonous. After a miserable day of dizziness, vomiting, and diarrhea, the communist command banned mushrooms from the camp's menu.[7]

The guerrilla force in Isabela at the time still remained small, numbering fewer than 100 men and women. While the leadership plotted strategy and discussed political theory deep in the forest, armed propaganda teams of 8 to 10 members moved through the barrios, enlisting peasants to support the revolution and searching for new recruits. In the meantime, Isabela had become the training ground for the Party's recruits from Manila, who were being schooled for assignments elsewhere in preparation for the opening of new guerrilla fronts.

Following a government crackdown on legal activists in August 1971, a stream of new recruits from Manila began flowing into the Isabela camps. Years later, Ariel Almendral, a former KM leader, recalled his flight to the underground:

> When the list of 63 students and activists wanted for arrest was published in the Manila newspapers and my name was on it, I asked to be sent to the NPA. I spent my last few days above ground with my family [near Manila], explaining my decision to go underground. A courier told me to bring three pairs of shorts, one extra pair of pants and three shirts, and meet him in front of a public building in Manila. We took a bus to Cauayan, Isabela, and after spending the night there, we walked all day into the forest until we arrived at a camp.[8]

The NPA forces in Isabela were careful to avoid attracting military attention, and raids and ambushes were conducted sparingly. The overriding goal of each "tactical offensive" was to capture as many firearms as possible to bolster the meager communist arsenal and to achieve maximum propaganda effect. New recruits from Manila underwent political and military training in a jungle camp; they studied political manuals prepared by Sison and the Central Committee and typewritten primers on guerrilla warfare written by Dante.[9] Corpus lectured on military strategy and tactics, as he had done at PMA. Whenever a group of rebels gathered, they would discuss their latest operations in an effort to learn the rudiments of guerrilla warfare from one another's mistakes and successes. After completing the training course, the new recruits were assigned to the guerrilla units scattered around the Isabela front. By 1971, the CPP claimed to have organized a "mass base" of 150,000 peasant supporters in Isabela.

An aggressive campaign of ambushes and raids by the NPA in Tarlac had swelled Central Luzon communist forces to several hundred fighters with more than 200 automatic rifles by the end of 1970. The army responded by concentrating several battalions in the region, and continual military operations took a heavy toll on the NPA and legal activists who were leading Party-organized peasant organizations. NPA forces in Central Luzon were dealt a crippling blow when a 60-person guerrilla company, the main fighting force, was surprised by the army and lost more than 30 new M-16 automatic rifles in a rout.[10]

In November 1971, the army turned its attention to the recently discovered Isabela front and poured nearly 2,000 soldiers into the province for a series of operations that lasted until May 1972. During that period, an entire 30-person NPA platoon was lost, its members killed, captured, surrendered or in hiding.[11] The rebels were badly outnumbered and outgunned by the U.S.-supplied Philippine army. The NPA arsenal consisted of the few dozen weapons Dante and his men had brought from Tarlac, Corpus' PMA spoils, and a handful of other firearms begged or borrowed from sympathizers. The weapons were an assortment of World War II–vintage carbines, Garands, shotguns, pistols, and a precious few automatic rifles. Ordnance was usually scarce, only six to eight clips per automatic rifle. Ammunition for the few Browning automatic rifles (BARs) in NPA hands was even harder to come by, although these weapons were treasured by rebel units. "We always gave our lone BAR to the most reliable guys," one NPA commander recalled years later. "In our [10-member] formation, when on a march, the BAR was always in the center, passed between only two or three guys. We wouldn't put it in the front because the casualty rate was too high. And we wouldn't put it in the back because it might not get in the fight."[12] In mid-1972, the guerrilla leadership in Isabela imposed a strict policy of avoiding military contact. The communists wanted the government to believe it had crushed the rebellion in Isabela because a shipload of Chinese arms and ammunition bound for the NPA was scheduled to be arriving off the Isabela coast in July.

Early in June, three NPA platoons totaling about 80 men commanded by Corpus broke camp in the Sierra Madre and began marching eastward across the rugged range toward Isabela's Pacific coast to meet the arms shipment. The rainy season had set in, and a steady downpour drenched the ill-equipped guerrillas and swelled mountain streams and rivers to treacherous levels. Guided by three tiny Dumagat tribespeople, the guerrillas struggled for 21 days through gloomy, leech-infested rain forests and jungles and over mountains that rose to nearly 4,000 feet. The guides killed wild boar and deer to feed the column. When they finally reached the coast, near the town of Palanan, the guerrillas were battered and exhausted. Their clothes were in tatters, and some of the men had little more left than their undershorts. They pitched camp and dug in on a ridge overlooking the ocean at Digoyo Point, at a spot where the narrow, rain-choked Digoyo River emptied its muddy waters into the blue Pacific. From their vantage point on the promonotory, the guerrillas enjoyed a commanding view of the rock-strewn, dirty-white sand beach and the sea beyond.[13]

A typhoon had just moved out of the area when a boat, a former Japanese fishing trawler renamed the *Karagatan*, arrived off the point in the predawn darkness of July 4, 1972. The *Karagatan* was loaded with crates filled with 1,200 automatic rifles, thousands of rounds of ammunition, bazookas, and other war materiel from China. A smaller craft capable of ferrying the arms up the river at Digoyo Point was supposed to have met the *Karagatan*, but it had gotten lost. Fearing discovery, the *Karagatan* skipper headed the 90-foot boat toward land and dropped anchor 300 yards offshore.

Around 7 A.M., the NPA forces began loading the heavy wooden crates into a lifeboat and two small outrigger canoes, known as *bancas*, and ferrying them ashore. One of the *bancas* capsized in the choppy seas, and its precious cargo was lost. At midmorning, a small plane passed lazily overhead, then circled around for another long look at the vessel anchored along the desolate stretch of coast. Later that morning, a logging company executive in the plane reported the mysterious boat to military authorities. Fearing that the operation had been exposed, the guerrillas guided the *Karagatan* into the mouth of the narrow river to speed unloading. By 4 P.M., all the arms and ammunition were ashore. The rebels were dragging the crates into the thick, forested jungle along the beach when two air force jets suddenly appeared overhead and buzzed the *Karagatan* from a few hundred feet. The guerrillas hurriedly scattered the crates in the jungle and covered them with leaves and palm fronds. As darkness fell, they prepared ambush positions along the beach for the soldiers they knew would be arriving.[14]

After nightfall, the crew hoisted the *Karagatan*'s anchor, and the captain began easing the boat from the river out to sea. But the tide had gone out, and the boat ran fast aground on a sandbar barely 100 yards offshore. Later that evening, when an unidentified vessel suddenly approached in the darkness, the rebel crew hurriedly abandoned the *Karagatan* and swam ashore.

The following afternoon, an army patrol aboard a tugboat appeared on the horizon chugging through the swells toward the *Karagatan*. The soldiers were preparing to tow the mysterious vessel away when the NPA forces opened fire from the ridge overlooking the beach. Corpus fired a few rounds from a Chinese-made B-40 rocket-propelled grenade launcher from the *Karagatan* shipment, but the tug was out of range, and the missiles fell harmlessly into the surf. The rebels' automatic rifle fire did wound the skipper and two soldiers aboard the tug and forced the patrol to turn back.[15]

The NPA forces were hoping to hold out until additional communist units could arrive to help salvage more weapons from the shipment. Bad weather and rugged terrain worked in their favor by delaying the arrival of the military for several days. When the weather broke, helicopters rushed fresh government troops to the area. But the soldiers were ambushed by Corpus and one NPA platoon as they approached the *Karagatan* along the beach from the north. Four soldiers were killed, and the column was forced to fall back and await reinforcements.

The following day, air force F-5 jets and helicopter gunships were called in to strafe and rocket the rebel positions. A navy gunboat arrived offshore and began shelling the guerrillas with 75-millimeter guns. Soldiers even tried dropping hand grenades from the helicopters onto the rebels, but these exploded harmlessly in the air overhead. The thick jungle canopy and poor aim of the military spared the NPA forces from casualties.[16]

On the fourth or fifth day, the northern Luzon regional Party leader, Melchor Canlas, finally arrived with 50 guerrillas, most of the remaining communist forces in Isabela. But under heavy attack from the growing government contingent, the NPA units were forced to withdraw inland two days later. The main NPA force broke into two groups of 50 to 60 guerrillas each and began retreating westward back over the Sierra Madre. A week later, they reunited on the far side of the range. They were able to salvage from the *Karagatan* shipment only about 200 M-14 rifles, several thousand rounds of ammunition, and a few rocket launchers. The rest fell into government hands.

Corpus and about 20 guerrillas were assigned to decoy the government troops while the main body commanded by Canlas withdrew over the Sierra Madre. One of the young men assigned to the perilous duty with Corpus was a softspoken cadre named Romulo Kintanar. Twenty-two years old, Kintanar was one of a half dozen men assigned to open a guerrilla front on the southern island of Mindanao and had been sent to Isabela for training. He had distinguished himself during the heavy fighting at Digoyo Point by rallying a group of rebels who were falling back under heavy fire and leading them back to their positions.[17]

Corpus and his men loaded themselves with ammunition and began their retreat around July 11. Marching southward, toward Quirino province, they continued walking for the next eight months, cut off from contact with other communist units. Their extraordinary trek took them through the rugged mountains of four provinces—Isabela, Quirino, Aurora, and Nueva Vizcaya—before finally linking up with other guerrilla units in early 1973.

The nearly year-long odyssey of Corpus and his tiny band of guerrillas is now counted by rebel veterans as one of the most extraordinary feats of NPA forces in the early years of the revolution. Throughout the tortuous, 200-mile-long march, the guerrillas were dogged by government troops. In early September, Kintanar contracted malaria and hepatitis and had to be carried in a hammock, which slowed the retreat. On the evening of September 5, the rebels pitched camp along a stream. Too weak to feed himself, Kintanar was laid in an abandoned bamboo hut. The following morning, as the rebels were cooking breakfast, army rangers attacked. Rifle fire riddled the hut where Kintanar was sleeping, but he managed to crawl outside and roll into a ditch. Nearly surrounded, Corpus and his men were forced to withdraw. One guerrilla was killed, and Kintanar was captured.[18]

As they continued southward, the communists tried to organize support in their path. In some barrios, they found a receptive audience and were given a place to rest for a few days. Their sympathetic hosts often contacted friends or relatives in neighboring barrios and invited them to come and listen to what the rebels had to say. Once the rebels had established rapport in a barrio, they would try to double back later to deepen support.

When they could not find a friendly village, Corpus and his guerrilla band survived by foraging in the jungle. They ate coconuts, bananas, and wild tubers. To avoid contact with government forces, they moved under cover of darkness. Occasionally, they ran into government patrols and were forced to fight. More than a dozen rebels were killed during the march, but they replenished their ranks with new recruits along the way.

Walking through the mountains and jungles of the Sierra Madre, the guerrillas had to contend with hazards other than soldiers. Corpus nearly died in 1973 when a rotten log bridge spanning a rocky gorge gave way and sent him plummeting onto sharp boulders. He broke his wrist and suffered a gaping puncture wound in his leg, which became infected. Bedridden for months, he was nursed back to health by Elizabeth Principe, a young UP nursing student who had joined the rebels in the countryside. She treated him by cutting the infected wound open with a razor blade and stuffing boiled strips of a T-shirt inside.[19]

In the spring of 1973, the forlorn guerrilla column finally straggled across the Sierra Madre and made its way westward into Nueva Vizcaya province. Circling back into their old Isabela enclaves, the rebels were stunned to find that the barrios that had once been the lifeblood of the NPA were now deserted. The peasants had been herded into "strategic hamlets" by the army. "There were no more barrios to organize," Corpus recalled. "The military had literally drained the pond."[20]

Years later, one Isabela guerrilla commander would recall the "eerie quiet" that settled on the province following Marcos' announcement of martial law on September 23, 1972. Radio stations, the only link to the outside world for the guerrillas and rural villagers, were closed. The rebels awoke to find their carefully constructed logistical network in shambles. The NPA Northern Luzon Command, headquartered in the Sierra Madre range of eastern Isabela, was cut off from the national leadership, which operated around Manila, 150 miles to the southeast. Politicians, merchants, and other middle-class townspeople who had been providing food, money and shelter, to the guerrillas were forced to break off all contacts, further isolating the rebels.[21]

On the eve of martial law, 7,000 troops had launched a massive offensive against the NPA in Isabela. Within a few months, the new offensive had wiped out the base areas and sympathetic villages the rebels had spent nearly two years developing. Large areas of Isabela were declared "free-fire zones," in which anything that moved was considered a target. Many leaders of peasant organizations and other groups sympathetic to the communists were abducted and summarily executed. Slowly, the army's cordon around the guerrillas in Isabela and surrounding provinces grew tighter and tighter.

In Isabela, martial law prevented the rebels from communicating with friendly units only a few miles away. The Isabela Plains Platoon, operating in the flatlands west of the Cagayan River suddenly found its lines of communication cut with the regional command, which was only 35 miles away in the Sierra Madre but on the east side of the river. In danger of being trapped by army battalions sweeping through the Cagayan valley, the Plains Platoon decided to try retreating to the Sierra Madre's forest region, where they hoped to reunite with other NPA units.[22]

For more than a month, the platoon edged northward along the broad Cagayan River, trying to slip across, but finding government troops blocking the way each time. At the end of October, the guerrillas found an unguarded crossing north of Ilagan. Under cover of darkness, sympathetic fishermen ferried the rebel unit across the river in dugout canoes, five to a boat. Almost immediately, the communist platoon was spotted by a government patrol, and at daybreak, two army companies with a combined strength of 200 troops attacked the 30 guerrillas. For hours, the rebels were pinned down by heavy fire unlike anything they had ever experienced. The platoon commander was seriously wounded by a bullet that shattered his thigh, and he ordered his men to withdraw, leaving him behind to be captured by the soldiers.[23]

Communist forces inside the forest region were not faring much better. The army's forced evacuation of broad areas east of the Cagayan River, where the NPA had built its strongholds left the guerrillas with two difficult choices: Either abandon the hard-won areas or try to survive in the jungle without civilian support. They decided to stay.

One of those rebels besieged in the Isabela forest in the weeks before the declaration of martial law was a dwarfish young activist from Manila named Tony. He had been a commercial art student in one of Manila's universities when he joined the KM in 1969. Two years later, lacking only one course to earn his degree, he quit college and asked to be sent to the Isabela guerrilla front. He was 19 at the time.

Life in the guerrilla zone changed drastically in August 1972, Tony recalled years later, when the army started forcibly evacuating civilians from the southern Isabela forest region. Sympathetic peasants left part of their rice harvest so the guerrillas would have food, but the stocks soon ran out. To survive, the rebels began competing with wild boars for wild vegetables. They supplemented their meager diet with whatever tubers and bananas they could scrounge. After a few months of subsisting on a meager diet and sleeping unprotected in the jungle, the nearly 100-strong NPA company was physically weakened and ravaged by malaria. Many guerrillas began deserting or surrendering to the army. By 1974, the southern Isabela company, the pride of the New People's Army, had been reduced to a pitiful collection of about 30 scrawny and sickly men and women hiding fearfully in the forest.[24]

If the Isabela NPA forces were beleaguered, they were better off than other rebel units outside the Sierra Madre. The army had formed two task forces in the region to destroy the communists. Total government strength in the campaign numbered about 10,000 troops backed by helicopters, jet fighters, armor, and artillery. They were opposed by fewer than 500 lightly armed guerrillas and 2,000 civilian communist supporters. An entire NPA platoon stationed along the border of Isabela and Ifugao provinces was killed by the military in September 1973. The NPA's Third Red Company, trapped in Aurora province, split into two groups and began retreating in March 1975. One group of 55 officers and fighters fled westward, walking more than four months and fighting nearly 50 engagements with pursuing constabulary rangers before stopping in Nueva Ecija province 80 miles away. An entire detachment of guerrillas left behind in Aurora to defend a few hundred communist civilian supporters who chose to stay in the province was killed, and about 100 civilian supporters died.[25]

The arrival of several dozen guerrillas and 200 civilian supporters from Aurora created more hardships for the three skeleton NPA companies hiding in the southern Isabela forest. Fear of attack and hunger were constant companions. Instead of trying to break out of the military cordon, the NPA units remained in the forest hoping that the tens of thousands of civilian supporters would return to their barrios. After three years of waiting in the harsh jungle, the NPA remnants were exhausted, their ability to fight weakened by constant hunger, sickness, and fatigue. Zealous young cadres like Tony had aged far beyond their years watching one comrade after another suffer and die. A Party cadre from Negros named Eddie Rodríguez died from an unknown ailment. A woman known as Ka Aleng, perhaps overwhelmed by fear, or hunger, or depression, hanged herself. One cadre ravaged by a burning malarial fever ended his agony with a bullet from his own gun. The list continued to grow.[26]

Years later, Sison criticized the Isabela NPA forces for disregarding Central Committee urgings to abandon their base in the forest. But one veteran of the besieged NPA forces said that communications with the Central Committee, broken in 1972, were not restored until 1975. Nevertheless, rebel forces in Isabela were reluctant to abandon their dream of creating a Philippine Yenan. But another military offensive began to take a heavier toll on the rebel army. By early 1976, 40 cadres and fighters had been killed, and the few barrios they had organized were razed. Demoralized by the latest defeats, leaders of the NPA survivors in the forest area ordered a retreat.

Tony was a member of an NPA unit that began the march northward. The rebels were nearly out of ammunition, and food was always scarce. "Sometimes when we were hungry," he remembered years later, "we would talk about nice restaurants in Manila where we would get certain kinds of our favorite foods."[27] Every day, they walked from 6 A.M. to noon and after lunch walked until dark. Their route took them through the heart of the formidable Sierra Madre, over forested, rock-strewn peaks and river gorges, through some of the most difficult terrain in the Philippines. Along the way, the rebels had to skirt a network of army outposts and 150 fortified villages. Several months later, Tony's column linked with other scattered NPA units in northern Isabela. Throughout 1976, most of the remaining Isabela force, now reduced to 200 guerrillas and civilian supporters, fled northward.

The final leg of the retreat began in January 1977, led by 100 guerrilla fighters with 70 weapons among them. The communist column snaked northward through the Sierra Madre, crossing the swift-flowing Pinacanayan River in southern Cagayan and then climbing to more than 4,000 feet as they threaded their way past Mount Cetaceo and the Twin Peaks. Falling rocks, mountain rivers, and the steep, perilous trail slowed the march, and many sustained broken bones and other injuries. Army rangers and air force helicopters posed still other dangers. The rebels suffered terribly from hunger and exhaustion along the way. Many children died, and others were delivered stillborn by weakened mothers. Rations were reduced to vines, roots, and small amounts of rice, which was sprinkled with rock salt for flavoring.

In latter 1977, the column pitched camp in Cagayan province, near Baggao. But before year's end, military operations forced the evacuation of villages in eastern Cagayan where the Isabela survivors had settled, and 40 guerrillas died trying to defend the new base areas. Another armed forces campaign in 1978 resulted in the deaths of more communist guerrillas and the forced evacuations of their civilian supporters. An NPA platoon escorted a group of unarmed guerrillas and civilian supporters further north over the Cagayan Peaks to the northernmost tip of the Sierra Madre near the town of Gonzaga. En route, 24 guerrillas and unarmed supporters were killed, captured, or executed by the military. It was the final, dispiriting chapter in the New People's Army collapse and retreat in northern Luzon.[28]

About 300 guerrillas, Party cadres and civilian supporters died in the northern Luzon campaigns of 1970–1978, a significant number considering the effective strength of communist forces in the region never exceeded 500 guerrillas and political cadres during the period. Those who survived had executed a series of retreats covering more than 220 miles through some of the country's most rugged mountains and jungles. The dream of an impregnable stronghold like Mao's Yenan had died, but the communist survivors formed the nucleus of a tough, experienced guerrilla army that by 1989 had sunk deep roots and enjoyed considerable support throughout 10 northern Luzon provinces.

5

The Ghosts of Plaza Miranda

It was the most shocking political crime the country had ever seen, an act that could be described as the Philippine equivalent of the assassination of President John F. Kennedy. "A day of shame," one Manila newspaper described it in a front-page editorial, and "an infamy the Filipino people will find hard to live down, if ever."

The scene of carnage remains etched in the memories of many Filipinos: Dying and wounded bodies litter a bloodstained stage and the asphalt below amid a tangle of overturned chairs and trampled campaign posters. On the platform, eight Liberal party senatorial candidates, the leading critics of Ferdinand Marcos, lie wounded. A few feet away, an award-winning Filipino photographer clutches his disemboweled midsection and stares blankly into the camera of a colleague as he bleeds to death. The lifeless bodies of a 10-year-old cigarette vendor and another victim are sprawled nearby on the ground, unattended.[1]

Ten thousand people had gathered that evening of August 21, 1971, in downtown Manila's Plaza Miranda for a Liberal party rally to proclaim the candidates for November's congressional and local elections. At 9:10 P.M., before a national television audience, at least three fragmentation grenades were tossed toward the speaker's platform, where the party's Senate candidates and other prominent Liberal leaders were seated. The first grenade clattered to the wooden stage and exploded, spraying the crowd with deadly shrapnel. Moments later, a second grenade arced through the air and exploded above the platform. At least one another grenade was thrown at the stage but failed to explode. Nine people were killed, and more than 100 were wounded.[2]

"It is not the ordinary breed of criminal that the law is up against in this case," the *Philippines Herald* editorialized the day following the

Plaza Miranda attack, "but a madman with an addled mind, or, at the worst, cool, calculating and devilish killers conspiring with others to wreck the established order." Marcos immediately blamed communist "subversives" for the savage crime, but his apparently unsubstantiated claim met immediate and widespread derision. The president's opponents widely believed he was the culprit, and this suspicion had hardened into the accepted version of the event nearly two decades later.

In 1988, several former top Communist Party officials—some of whom continued to maintain close contacts with the underground—told me the actual story of the Plaza Miranda bombing, which proved that Marcos had not been lying when he accused the communists of the attack. In separate interviews, these men provided never-revealed details of a plot to bomb the Liberal party rally conceived by the Communist Party leadership and carried out by Party operatives. Why had the information not come out earlier? Fear was the overwhelming reason. For those former rebels who no longer enjoyed the protection and anonymity of the underground, fear of retribution from former colleagues in the revolutionary movement or the threat of retaliation by right-wing extremists had enforced a troubled silence for nearly two decades. "Disclosure of the Plaza Miranda plan would destroy the prestige of the Party. And if you destroy the prestige of the Party, you will be six feet under the ground," one founding CPP Central Committee member explained. "When you seal a secret in the Party, you must not talk about it anymore."[3] Those who decided to challenge the code of silence have done so out of mixed motivations. Most had served time in military prisons and no longer viewed their former revolutionary activities as romantically as they did in their youth, and they appeared to have been genuinely troubled by their involvement in a bloody attack on innocent civilians. For some, long-simmering differences with José María Sison, described by several former senior CPP officials as the "mastermind" of the Plaza Miranda plot, led them to set aside their fears and talk about the bombing.

Nearly two decades later, the Plaza Miranda bombing stood as one of the pivotal points in the history of the Philippine revolutionary movement. More than one CPP veteran remarked that Sison had used the attack to force Marcos' hand, at a crucial moment for the communist movement. Marcos had played right into Sison's maneuver. The bombing considerably widened the gap separating Marcos from his moderate opponents, thus pushing the president further to the authoritarian Right and his opponents toward the Left. The suspension of the writ of habeas corpus and the accompanying repression that followed the bombing also pushed many liberals into alliances with the communist underground and at the same time opened the door to systematic military abuses against the citizenry, particularly in the countryside. Martial law brought wholesale state repression and forced into the communist movement many young Filipinos who otherwise might never have joined.[4]

By 1971, Sison was convinced that the Philippines was on the brink of revolution. It would take only a well-timed, traumatic incident to spark the great upheaval that would lead to an early communist victory, he believed. In early February, Sison met in Manila with three of his most trusted CPP Central Committee colleagues—secretary-general José Luneta, Politburo member Ibarra Tubianosa, and the Party's chief finance officer—and laid out a plan for Party operatives to attack an opposition Liberal party rally.[5] Such an incident, Sison maintained, was sure to speed up the revolution's timetable.

The CPP leader's logic for bombing the political rally appeared sound: The Liberal party would likely blame Marcos, its archenemy, for the attack and perhaps even retaliate. Marcos in turn would blame the communists. But with his credibility already sagging badly, few people would believe him. The resulting chaos and recriminations between Marcos' Nacionalista party and Benigno Aquino's Liberal party would heighten what Marx called the "contradictions" within the capitalist ruling class. If Marcos responded with repression, all the better, Sison reasoned. "Increased repression will result in increased resistance," he told his colleagues. This calculation became the keystone upon which the Plaza Miranda plot was fashioned. The conspirators were counting on a crackdown by Marcos to drive more people into the ranks of the radical movement and into the NPA in the countryside.[6]

It remains unclear whether any of the handful of CPP officials privy to the plan objected to the proposal to bomb a political rally. Only afterward would serious questioning occur. Nearly two decades later, a former CPP official, who at the time was a Central Committee member privy to the Plaza Miranda plan, said it was unheard of for anyone to oppose a proposal of Sison.

How could you question Joema? We had a very high respect for him as a leader. We had a very tightly disciplined party. Joema held very much power at the time. After he would make a decision, he would inform us. For example, he planned the PMA raid, and only after setting it in motion did he tell Dante. I got the feeling that Joema decided the Plaza Miranda bombing on his own, and then later informed the Central Committee members.[7]

In February 1971, Sison traveled to the NPA headquarters camp in Isabela where Dante and Corpus were staying. Later, they were joined by Luneta. During the course of the next several months, Sison and other Party leaders had long discussions about the political situation in the Philippines and about the strategy and tactics of the movement. The Party had a dilemma, Sison told his comrades. Hundreds of rifles and other weapons would be arriving from China in the months ahead, yet the NPA had only about 90 fighters in Isabela at the time. Somehow, the Party had to produce the conditions that would rapidly expand NPA strength. The rebels had to create one of history's "quantum leaps," as Marx described it. Sison gradually explained that they could create the conditions to achieve that quantum leap in membership. The key was intensifying conflicts between the opposing factions of the ruling class—in this case the opposition Liberal party and the ruling Nacionalista party. If the two ruling factions could be set against one another in a violent fashion, the ruling class as a whole would be weakened.[8]

On at least one occasion in those Isabela sessions, Sison said those conflicts could be intensified by creating a "disruption" at a Liberal party rally. "Joema explained that by forcing Marcos to be tyrannical, we could in fact push the Left as well as the more numerous moderate forces over to the side of the revolution," one of those present recalled. "If the moderates were pushed over to our side, that would solve our problem of manpower to match the thousands of firearms coming from China." But Sison never spelled out explicitly to his colleagues in the Isabela camp how he planned to provoke Marcos. Only later, after the Plaza Miranda bombing, did the rebel leaders in the Isabela camp understand that Sison had proposed an act of mass violence.[9]

Sison left Isabela after the onset of the rainy season and returned to the capital in June 1971. Back in Manila, the CPP leadership drafted a fiery cadre named Danny Cordero to carry out the bombing. Cordero had risen quickly through the ranks of KM in the late 1960s, and by 1971 was a powerful, charismatic Party leader in the suburban industrial belt on Manila's northern fringe. Cordero had built a strong underground network among students, factory workers, and fishermen in the suburbs of Valenzuela, Caloocan, Navotas, and Malabon, and his accomplishments had earned him a seat on the newly formed Manila CPP committee. His brash, confrontational style and hot temper reminded many of his colleagues of the late Arthur García. Some of Cordero's young KM recruits were intimidated by what they referred to as his "gunpowder temper," and by what one activist later recalled as Cordero's proclivity for "rash, violent tactics." But when it came to courage, Cordero was not lacking. He could be counted on for such a sensitive mission as the Plaza Miranda bombing.[10]

In mid-August 1971, CPP Central Committee member Reuben Guevarra arrived in Manila for discussions with Party officials. Guevarra was a member of the CPP's powerful Military Commission and was the political officer in charge of the northern Luzon region, which included the Isabela guerrilla front. At dusk on August 21, Central Committee member Manuel Collantes picked up Guevarra and drove him to a communist safe house in a comfortable middle-class subdivision of Parañaque, a Manila suburb. Guevarra was greeted by Sison, Politburo member Hermenigildo García, and another Politburo member who headed the Party's organizational department.[11]

Sison talked in general terms about something significant that was about to happen. "We are going to execute a delicate plan that will intensify the split between the ruling class to the point that they are going to kill each other," he explained to Guevarra. When Sison finished speaking, one of his Politburo colleagues took over. "Those people who will execute the plan will be assigned in your place [in Isabela]. You must take care of them ideologically and politically." The Politburo member closed with a warning for Guevarra: The plan was not to be discussed under any circumstances with anybody else in the Party, even with other Central Committee members. If anyone were found to have divulged details of the secret plan, he or she would be punished most severely.[12] Minutes after the meeting in the Parañaque safe house broke up, Danny Cordero and two accomplices carried out the "delicate operation," throwing at least three grenades at the Plaza Miranda stage filled with Liberal party officials.

Guevarra awoke the next morning to find newspapers filled with gory photographs and accounts of the previous evening's bloody bombing, but he was not particularly troubled. Although the bombing was bloody and violent, the Party's political line called for the seizure of political power through armed struggle. The Plaza Miranda attack was merely an extension of the armed struggle in the countryside, Guevarra reasoned.[13] His main concern was getting out of Manila before the Marcos crackdown Party leaders were expecting. After breakfast, Guevarra boarded a bus for Isabela and made his way to the NPA's headquarters camp in the Sierra Madre foothills.

Immediately after the bombing, Cordero disappeared from his district in the northern Manila suburbs. Three days later, he turned up in an NPA camp in Isabela. Cordero, his two accomplices in the Plaza Miranda bombing—Cecil Apostol and a Party activist named Danny—and a few other NPA recruits were assigned to military training under Corpus. Despite strict orders never to speak of Plaza Miranda, occasionally Cordero and the two accomplices alluded to their role in the attack. "It became common knowledge among the small group I was training that

Cordero and the other two were the ones who did Plaza Miranda," Corpus told me.

In mid-1972, NPA forces in northern Luzon were ordered to assemble in the Sierra Madre foothills to prepare for the arrival of an arms shipment from China. When the NPA units set out for the rendezvous in the northern mountains, Cordero was left in charge of a small contingent of guerrillas remaining behind to continue political work in the villages of southern Isabela. Unaware of the arms shipment already en route, Cordero began criticizing the order to pool NPA forces, which he thought was an overreaction to government military offensives. He became outspoken in his condemnation of Isabela Party officials and even floated the idea of deposing them. Cordero bragged that he had the confidence of the highest Party leaders and to prove it told some of his colleagues about his role in the Plaza Miranda bombing. He even demonstrated how he had tossed the grenade at the platform filled with Liberal party officials.[14]

Word of Cordero's insubordination quickly reached Reuben Guevarra. Guevarra was concerned with Cordero's rebellious talk, but he was far more disturbed with Cordero's disclosures about Plaza Miranda. He recalled the instructions he had been given during his briefing on the delicate operation: Anyone who spoke of Plaza Miranda was to be dealt with most severely. Guevarra immediately convened a military tribunal and drafted a list of charges against Cordero. Leading the bill of indictment was the accusation that Cordero had been inciting his command to rebel against the CPP leadership and that he had sabotaged the *Karagatan* operation. Most importantly, Cordero was slandering the Party by claiming responsibility for the Plaza Miranda bombing.[15]

The trial got under way in the Isabela forest near the town of San Mariano in early July. Ariel Almendral, at the time a political cadre assigned with the NPA, had been appointed to defend Cordero. Realizing he was fighting for his life, Cordero argued passionately in his defense. He swore that he had not been lying when he said he had bombed the Liberal party rally under orders from high Party officials. Of the tribunal members, only Guevarra knew that Cordero was telling the truth. Guevarra took no chances, packing the tribunal with his loyalists. Cordero's guilt was easily agreed upon, but the tribunal deadlocked when it tried to fix punishment. Four members argued that Cordero should be executed. Four urged a lesser punishment. Guevarra held the tie-breaking vote.

During a recess, Guevarra gathered the tribunal members and made his case: Cordero was dangerous to the revolution, a rebel who had broken the Party's sacred principles of iron discipline and democratic centralism; his execution would be for the good of the revolution.

Guevarra's lobbying swayed one of the members to change his mind, and the tribunal voted 6–3 (including Guevarra's vote in favor of death) to execute Cordero. In a gesture of Party solidarity, a juror who had opposed the death sentence, Elizabeth Principe, volunteered to carry out the execution. Cordero was led deeper into the forest. When they stopped, Principe pressed the muzzle of a .38-caliber Smith & Wesson revolver to Cordero's head and pulled the trigger.[16]

The secret of Plaza Miranda might have died with Danny Cordero in the Isabela jungle if not for the troubled consciences of a few young Party officials privy to the truth. Some of the CPP's Politburo members were horrified by the carnage at Plaza Miranda. They were supposed to be fighting a people's war against fascist landlords and greedy imperialists, not against liberal politicians. Indeed, the Party was secretly working with the Liberal party to undermine Marcos. How, these CPP officials agonized, could such an attack on civilians—on allies—be justified?[17]

Silently, some of the communist leaders nursed serious qualms about the bombing. It was not until some months later that one of the Politburo members got up the courage to discuss the subject with Sison. In a meeting of the Executive Committee, Hermenigildo García asked the CPP leader to admit that the Plaza Miranda attack had been a mistake. Sison vehemently defended the bombing and refused to accept any suggestions that it had been an error. García stubbornly insisted that Sison was wrong, the bombing was wrong, and they all should admit it.[18] Rarely had any of the young Party officials questioned Sison, and on the potentially devastating topic of Plaza Miranda, the Communist Party chairman was adamant: There was no mistake. Rather than force a showdown with their mentor, the others swallowed their misgivings about Plaza Miranda. The subject was laid to rest, never again to be formally resurrected within the Party.

Although the brief official debate died in the secret Executive Committee session, Plaza Miranda continued to haunt a few communist officials who knew of Party culpability. Most bore the truth in troubled silence. Only one was ever moved to act. The cadre who was the CPP Manila regional secretary at the time finally resigned from the Party in the mid-1970s because of his disapproval of the bombing.[19]

In a tactical sense, the Plaza Miranda bombing proved to be a brilliant tactical move by the Communist Party. Two days after the attack, Marcos responded with the repression that CPP leaders had anticipated. Citing a national emergency provoked by "communist subversives," Marcos suspended the writ of habeas corpus and began arresting radical student and labor activists. Playing the "red scare" card further, Marcos announced the discovery of a communist "master plan" to burn Manila and assassinate government officials and private citizens. Once again, Marcos warned that he might have to declare martial law.

The escalation of ruling class contradictions predicted by Sison also came to pass. A day after suspending the writ of habeas corpus, Marcos publicly accused Benigno Aquino and five other Liberal party leaders of having links with the New People's Army. He cited "overwhelming" evidence of Aquino's involvement with the communists, including supplying arms, ammunition, and food to Huk and NPA forces.[20] Marcos and his supporters even suggested that Aquino had prior knowledge of the communist plot, which purportedly explained Aquino's absence from the Plaza Miranda stage at the moment the grenades were thrown.[21]

A year later, after months of bitter wrangling with Aquino and other political opponents, Marcos made good on his martial law threats, and the Plaza Miranda incident seemed to recede into the mist of the nation's deepest mysteries. As years of ruthless martial law passed, and the nation was shocked by another sensational crime for which most people blamed Marcos—the 1983 assassination of Benigno Aquino—virtually all of the regime's political opponents became convinced that Marcos or his loyalists in the military had planned and carried out the bombing.

Through the years, various pet theories to explain the Plaza Miranda attack gained currency, but none suggested CPP responsibility. Former U.S. diplomats and intelligence officers who spoke with Raymond Bonner for his excellent 1987 book on the relationship between the United States and the Marcoses, *Waltzing with a Dictator*, dismissed outright the possibility of communist involvement in the bombing. These officials, noting that the grenades used in the attack had reportedly come from an army arsenal, said flatly that Marcos loyalists in the military had committed the crime, although they apparently offered no other evidence to support their claim.[22]

After Marcos fled into exile in February 1986, there were calls to reopen the Plaza Miranda investigation. But an unsolved 15-year-old bombing was scarcely a priority for a revolutionary government beset by crises, and the case remained in the archives until fall 1986. Then, overnight, the incident became entangled in President Corazón Aquino's worsening feud with Defense Minister Juan Ponce Enrile and his military supporters. In early November 1986, as rumors of an impending military coup swirled, Enrile's armed forces protégés leaked to the press copies of a letter by Victor Corpus, who had been captured by the government in 1976 and released from prison by Aquino earlier in 1986. In the letter, written to a movie scriptwriter preparing a film on his life, Corpus blamed the Plaza Miranda bombing on the communists, and said he was present when Sison and other CPP leaders had planned the attack. On November 8, Corpus held a press conference to confirm the authenticity of the letter and publicly alleged that the CPP had carried out the bombing.

Corpus' revelations seemed only to further complicate the mystery. After all, Corpus appeared to have a motive for smearing the communists. Recently released from 10 years in prison and out of work, he wanted to rejoin the armed forces. Two days before he told his story about Plaza Miranda, Corpus was reaccepted into the military as an active reserve officer at the rank of lieutenant colonel—three ranks above the one he held before defecting to the rebels. Some observers suggested that Corpus had implicated the Communist Party in the Plaza Miranda bombing to ingratiate himself with the military officers who were considering his petition to rejoin the armed forces.

Without supporting evidence from any of the past and present CPP principals who knew the truth about the Plaza Miranda plot, Corpus' disclosures fell on unsympathetic ears. The timing could not have been worse, coming amid the slow-motion powerplay Enrile and his military allies had set in motion. The coup plotters were hoping to manipulate Corpus' knowledge of Plaza Miranda to benefit their campaign to cripple President Aquino.

By revealing communist responsibility for the bombing, the right-wing plotters hoped to whip up support for a military move against suspected leftists and even against the government. A re-examination of Plaza Miranda would lead to new questions about whether Benigno Aquino had prior knowledge of the bombing. The military conspirators were betting that new questions about Aquino's under-the-table dealings with the communists would undermine his widow. From the perspective of the majority of Filipinos who supported the president in her battle with the military, however, to embrace Corpus' allegations would have been to side with Aquino's enemies in her hour of need. Furthermore, many Filipinos simply wanted to believe that Marcos was responsible for Plaza Miranda. It was far easier to cope with the staggering national ills by blaming Marcos for everything bad that had happened in the past 20 years.

Despite the rather indifferent public reaction to the new light shed on the Plaza Miranda bombing, Corpus' allegations rattled a skeleton that had hung quietly in the Communist Party's closet for 15 years. Reaction was swift. Sison, on a lecture tour abroad after having been released from prison by President Aquino, issued a statement denouncing Corpus as a liar and vehemently denying his former comrade's charges. Aboveground leftist leaders and organizations sympathetic to the revolution dismissed the Plaza Miranda allegations as right-wing-inspired canards. In the underground, CPP cadres suggested that Corpus was mentally unstable after 10 years in prison.[23]

Had the Plaza Miranda bombing not occurred, would Marcos have suspended the writ of habeas corpus or declared martial law? The answer is, in all likelihood, yes to both. Marcos was already scheming for ways to prolong his rule. He had floated the idea of martial law several times before Plaza Miranda and would undoubtedly have found another justification to impose it. Without the communist rebellion, however, Marcos might have found the public less acquiescent. As one former Party veteran remarked, "Marcos needed the communists, and the communists needed Marcos."

To this day, Plaza Miranda remains a troubling topic for older CPP veterans, some of whom entered the movement because of the government repression that followed the bombing and some of whom simply disagreed with the bombing on moral or ideological grounds. It is a topic rarely broached. One founding CPP Central Committee member described how he and another former top Party official have discussed the topic on a few rare occasions:

> The subject is so delicate that we don't even refer to it as the "Plaza Miranda bombing." We call it the PMB. Even though both of us know [that the Party was responsible], we play a game with one another. One of us will say, "I wonder who would have done such a thing?" The other will respond, "I don't know!" A part of our subconscious simply refuses to admit we were responsible for this.[24]

Another CPP official who had prior knowledge of the plan to bomb Plaza Miranda told me he suffered from nightmares about the incident. I asked another former top Communist Party official why Plaza Miranda had so traumatized Party members. "Because we viewed the Liberal party as our allies. They were against Marcos, and we were against Marcos," he replied, his voice rising. "And because of the treachery involved."[25]

Even the generation of Filipinos in their thirties who drifted in and out of the movement in the 1970s, many of whom now count themselves as liberals and progressives independent of the CPP, are uneasy when Plaza Miranda is resurrected. "People have blocked it out of their minds," one former Party activist said. "They don't want to believe that the Party could do such a thing."[26]

In the spring of 1988, near the end of a day-long conversation in Amsterdam, I asked Sison about the allegations of CPP involvement in the Plaza Miranda attack. "Vic Corpus is crazy," he burst out. Sison then contented himself with repeating the Party's public position on the bombing—that the Liberal party "at the time was our ally of sorts."

Although the Plaza Miranda bombing may have demonstrated Sison's tactical brilliance, achieving virtually precisely the effects he had predicted, the lasting angst it has caused in the movement—and Sison's own unwillingness to claim credit for what he might privately consider a brilliant stroke—also demonstrates something about the character of the Philippine revolutionary movement. It underscores the CPP's reluctance to engage in the terror tactics that have marked similar movements around the world and the idealism about their own motives that has led the Philippine rebels to the intense self-examination that has continued ever since the night Danny Cordero and his comrades tossed their grenades onto the Plaza Miranda stage.

6

Prisoners in a Gilded Cage

Shortly before noon on July 8, 1971, a sweltering summer day, an aging, dull-gray Mercedes Benz van pulled up outside a weathered hotel in the Portuguese colony of Macau. A 29-year-old Filipino communist and his wife ducked into the van with two young babies in their arms, and they sped off through the narrow, winding streets choked with bicycles and vendors. The van turned onto a deserted dirt back road and minutes later passed through a traditional Chinese archway that formed the international border. A few yards beyond, the van braked to a stop outside a small brick building. A cluster of smiling men in drab, high-collared Mao suits crowded around the Filipino travelers exclaiming at once, "Welcome to China!"

That passage to China marked the beginning of an extraordinary but tragic episode in the history of the Philippine communist movement. Details of the revolution's clandestine China project—its connection to the Plaza Miranda bombing in Manila, bungled Chinese arms shipments, rancorous disputes within the CPP leadership, and the broken lives of the young Filipino communists who spent 10 years in China—have remained under an impenetrable veil of secrecy. Even now, the Communist Party's leadership considers the China project too sensitive to discuss. Initially, a few former top Party officials provided me with intriguing bits of information about the clandestine project. Finally, in 1988, some members of the secret Philippine communist delegation to China in the 1970s and early 1980s agreed to reveal details of their mission. A portrait of the revolution's most mysterious chapter slowly emerged.[1]

From the beginning of the guerrilla war in 1969, José María Sison was convinced that the ill-equipped NPA would need a reliable rear area that could offer sanctuary and serve as a lifeline to the outside world. "We will win even without foreign aid," he told a friend around 1970, "but it will take a painfully long time."[2]

In an archipelagic country such as the Philippines, which has no contiguous neighbors, the lack of a friendly rear made life precarious for the fledgling rebel army. Never lacking in ideas or audacity, Sison decided that Chinese aid would be the solution. After all, the benefactor of numerous Third World revolutions was only 400 miles across open water from the Philippines. China would become the stable rear area for the Filipino guerrillas and a source of arms and other supplies. "Joe Sison wanted to open a 'Ho Chi Minh Trail' across the South China Sea between the Philippines and China. Those were his exact words," one of Sison's close Party associates who was privy to discussions of Chinese aid told me years later.[3]

Sison knew from his early 1960s contacts with D.N. Aidit and other Indonesian Communist Party leaders that China had generously funded that country's communist movement. The Filipino communists were further heartened by developments in neighboring Vietnam, where Chinese-supplied communist forces had managed to stall the mighty U.S. war machine by 1969. Support of offshore revolutions had emerged as the cornerstone of Chinese foreign policy under the direction of Cultural Revolution zealots. Sison was betting that the Philippine revolution would be able to take advantage of the radical winds sweeping China.[4]

He took the first step toward establishing a Chinese supply line in late 1968 by dispatching José Luneta to Beijing. Ostensibly, Luneta was there to work as a Tagalog language expert with Radio Beijing, but secretly he was to be the CPP's liaison with the Chinese government. Luneta broached the question of aid for the Philippine guerrillas with Kang Sheng, the Chinese Politburo member in charge of international relations. Kang Sheng agreed in principle to accept an official delegation from the CPP, which would be responsible for arranging any transfers of arms and other assistance. Luneta returned to the Philippines sometime in 1970, and Sison sent another trusted aide and Central Committee member, Carlos del Rosario, to Beijing in December to finalize arrangements for a CPP delegation.[5]

In early 1971, as the Philippines seemed to be edging toward upheaval, Sison began putting together a delegation to China. He chose nine trusted Party cadres, to be led by CPP Politburo member Ibarra Tubianosa.[6] Before the group departed, Sison gave pep talks to the young cadres reminding them that China was "the center of world revolution" and "one great revolutionary school" where they should "learn from the Chinese people." As always, he was supremely confident that his plan for channeling arms and aid to the NPA guerrillas would work. "Don't worry," Sison assured one of the cadres on the eve of his departure for China, "we will see each other in five years' time. It will be very easy to make the crossings."[7]

So secret was their assignment that members of the delegation were forbidden to tell even their parents and family members that they were leaving. Ricardo Malay, a Manila journalist, and his wife, Charito, were the first members of the delegation to enter China in July 1971, flying to Hong Kong as tourists before Chinese agents whisked them to Macau and then across the border into China. When they arrived in Canton after a rough six-hour drive from the border, they were feted at a banquet hosted by local Communist Party and military officials. Tubianosa and his wife arrived later in July, and within a few weeks, the entire delegation was assembled in Beijing.[8]

A few days after the Filipinos arrived in China, the bloody attack on the Liberal party rally in Plaza Miranda occurred. Word of the bombing reached Beijing a week later, with the arrival of newspapers from Hong Kong bearing grisly accounts and photographs of the carnage. A few members of the China delegation were horrified, because Tubianosa had been privy to the scheme and had told a few other members of the delegation about the plan to bomb Plaza Miranda—*a few weeks before the attack took place.*[9]

The China project was integral to the CPP's planning of Plaza Miranda. In order to make effective use of the flood of new recruits that the anticipated crackdown would trigger, the sparsely equipped guerrilla army had to have more weapons. Sison's handpicked envoys to China were to take care of that problem. But from its infancy, the China delegation labored under the pall cast by Plaza Miranda. At first, members who knew the truth kept private their misgivings about the bombing. Gradually, they began to discuss the troubling secret of Plaza Miranda among themselves. Only later, as its failures and frustration mounted, did the China delegation's knowledge of the Party's culpability for the attack contribute to bitter factionalism within the group. Eventually, the disputes would lead to violent confrontations and to a mutiny by some of the delegates against Sison's leadership.[10]

Sison's plans for the China project began to go awry almost from the beginning. The first jolt occurred when the Chinese insisted that the delegation would have to remain secret, scuttling Sison's plans to issue a dramatic statement announcing the opening of a CPP mission in China. The news that they would have to live a clandestine existence in Beijing was a blow to the Filipinos and added to their difficulties in adjusting to life in their new home. They were housed in a comfortable, two-story villa in a spacious compound reserved for foreign "fraternal guests"—representatives of revolutionary movements being supported by China—but they were discouraged from socializing with their neighbors and at first were even forbidden to reveal they were Filipinos. Furthermore, they were warned against having contacts with Chinese other than staff assigned to attend to their needs. Their hosts had given them a car and driver, but the delegation's movements were severely restricted.

If they were dismayed by their lack of freedom, the Filipinos were also dazzled by Chinese hospitality and by the exalted status they were accorded as representatives of Asia's fastest growing Communist Party. Chauffeured limousines shuttled them to and from official functions at which Tubianosa frequently found himself seated alongside China's top leaders. Nevertheless, life in China proved to be duller than the Filipinos had expected. Two members of the delegation with whom I spoke years later used the same words to describe their existence: "prisoners in a gilded cage."

The Cultural Revolution was still sweeping China when the Filipino communists first arrived, and they were not spared some of its milder hardships. Virtually the only programs Chinese television and radio were allowed to broadcast were eight ultra-leftist operas written by Chiang Ching. Two of the operas, "The Red Detachment of Women" and "White-haired Girl," aired every day without fail until the Cultural Revolution finally collapsed in 1976. "We got to know every song and every movement," one of the delegation members told me, finally able to laugh about what became an excruciating experience.

The Cultural Revolution was also hard on China's experienced chefs, who as members of the villified educated class were banished to the countryside to plant rice and raise pigs. Poorly trained Red Army cooks took over the culinary chores for China's elite and foreign guests. All of them, the Filipino communists included, suffered the gastronomical consequences.[11]

The Filipinos carried with them Politburo orders to get arms and supplies to the beleaguered NPA guerrillas, and the CPP leadership back in the Philippines was not in a patient mood. "We cannot wait for the liberation of Taiwan," Sison remarked sarcastically in an autumn

1971 memo to the Beijing delegation. On September 30, 1971, Sison's personal emissary, Fidel Agcaoili, arrived in Beijing bearing the first of several shopping lists from the CPP Central Committee. The Communist Party leadership asked for several hundred M-16 automatic rifles and ammunition, heavy weapons such as bazookas and mortars, and anti-aircraft guns. The Filipinos in Beijing and their Chinese hosts were amused by the request for antiaircraft guns, coming as it did from a tiny guerrilla force trying to stay one step ahead of the Philippine army.[12] After receiving assurances from the CPP delegation that its forces could manage such a shipment, the Chinese made their offer: 1,200 U.S.-designed M-14 rifles, which they had secretly manufactured from a purloined design, bazookas, mortars, communications equipment and medical kits. The Chinese flatly refused as too risky Sison's request that a Chinese navy submarine deliver the arms to the Philippines. The Filipinos would have to do it themselves.

With a green light from Beijing, sometime in late 1971 or early 1972 Agcaoili led a small team to Japan to buy a boat to transport the arms. Using a dummy corporation set up specifically for the arms project, the rebels found a 91-ton, 90-foot-long former fishing trawler named the *Kishi Maru*. The rusting boat was a candidate for the salvage yard, but it was relatively cheap, so the Filipinos bought it and hired a crew to sail the trawler back to Manila.[13]

At some point, CPP leaders in the Philippines decided that the arms project could be used to funnel badly needed cash into revolutionary coffers. As China was paying for the boat, the CPP Central Committee reported a purchase price several thousand dollars more than had actually been paid. The Chinese forwarded the amount without questions, but the deception was not appreciated by Tubianosa, who was left with the task of lying to his Chinese hosts.[14]

In the meantime, a former UP engineering student, Edwin Alcid, and two other Party cadres were sent to China for three months of maritime training in preparation for the arms transfer. A crew of six activists was assembled, and the boat, skippered by Alcid and rechristened the *Karagatan*, set sail for Fukien province on the southeast coast of China around mid-1972. In late June, ranking Chinese military officials accompanied Tubianosa to a Fukien port to supervise the loading of the weapons and other materiel, which were packed in wooden crates. Chinese officials warned that the shipment would be too heavy for the small boat, but Tubianosa, under strict orders from his superiors in the Philippines, insisted that all the weapons be loaded. A former CPP Central Committee member told me years later that the *Karagatan* nearly sank when the crates were loaded aboard.

The *Karagatan* set sail near the end of June 1972. Somewhere in the South China Sea, the overloaded, rickety old boat developed a hole in the hull and appeared to be in danger of sinking before the crew succeeded in stuffing chunks of a rug and pieces of plywood into the hole.[15] Finally arriving off Digoyo Point in the predawn darkness of July 4, the *Karagatan* searched in vain for the smaller boat that was supposed to ferry the arms to shore. When the craft did not appear, Alcid took the *Karagatan* closer to the beach, where small *bancas* were used to ferry the cargo ashore. That evening, as the *Karagatan* turned out to sea, the boat ran aground. Within a few days, government troops had recovered the bulk of the Chinese arms and ammunition.

It became known as the "mysterious boat," and, like the Plaza Miranda bombing, some Filipinos still insist that Marcos was behind the *Karagatan* incident. Public reaction to the *Karagatan* disclosures revealed much about the prevailing mood of cynicism and distrust that had settled on the Philippines by 1972. The nation's typically rancorous politics had become more hateful and personally vindictive than ever, perhaps a symptom of the chaotic times or perhaps an indication of the intensity of the rivalry between Marcos and archrival Benigno Aquino. For more than a year, Marcos had been hinting that he might hang onto power beyond the end of his term on December 30, 1973. By the time the *Karagatan* was discovered on an Isabela sandbar in mid-1972, everything Marcos said and did was read by his opponents as part of a Machiavellian master plan.

If his political opponents were unwilling to believe anything Marcos said, an increasingly jaded public was only slightly more benevolent. Not surprisingly, when Marcos announced to the nation on July 7, 1972, the discovery of the *Karagatan*—the "first clear evidence of any foreign vessel landing supplies, equipment and perhaps personnel in the Philippines in support of communist subversion"—much of the public and the press dismissed the news as a Marcos hoax.[16] Aquino led the legions of skeptics by suggesting that the boat was nothing more than an unfortunate fishing vessel washed ashore by a typhoon. Another Marcos foe, Liberal party Senator Ramón Mitra, echoed claims that the boat was harmless and to prove his assertion announced that the vessel was owned by the Karagatan Fishing Corp., with offices in the Manila port area.

In fact, the Karagatan Fishing Corp. was a Communist Party dummy. The radical activists who were listed as officers of the corporation tried to capitalize on the unexpected Liberal party support and released a statement that expressed "our deep concern over reports of alleged involvement of our boat, *M/V Karagatan*, with the New People's Army."[17] But the young "executives" did not wait around to be questioned by authorities.

The more details Marcos fed the press about the mysterious goings-on in an isolated corner of faraway Isabela, the more the beleaguered president found himself on the defensive. To a nation long used to endless political gimmickry, the whole affair began to look more like a partisan donnybrook between the Liberals and the Nacionalistas than the national security crisis of which Marcos was warning.

The Filipino delegation in Beijing first learned of the *Karagatan* debacle through an Australian shortwave radio broadcast.[18] Their Chinese hosts expressed concerns about the shipment being traced back to them, but they were sympathetic and encouraging to the demoralized Filipinos. Before the Central Committee could send an explanation, Marcos declared martial law, severing the lines of communication between the delegation and the CPP leadership. The China delegation was left to brood through a bleak, bitterly cold Beijing winter. "We were missing our families, our homes, our way of life, and the *Karagatan* failure deepened our sense of isolation and alienation, and our difficulty in adjusting to the shock of life in China," one of the Filipino communists recalled. "It was very depressing. And what outlets did we have? More Chiang Ching operas."

In spring 1973, a courier from the Philippines finally arrived bearing a Central Committee report on the *Karagatan*. Leaders of the China delegation were dismayed and angered by what they read. The CPP representatives in Beijing had been assured by their superiors, and in turn had assured the Chinese, that the landing site had been thoroughly reconnoitered and found to be deserted. It was, as the Central Committee had reported, a "perfect site" to receive the arms. In fact, the Beijing delegation was later informed that the Digoyo Point site had been selected by an examination of maps, with negligible reconnaissance. When the advance NPA force arrived at the site a week before the scheduled arms landing, they were surprised to find a busy crossroads for fishermen living along the coast.[19] Compounding the problems, the weapons were supposed to have been carried off in relays, but some of the NPA units did not arrive until a few days after the arms had been unloaded.

With Tubianosa taking the lead, the China delegation drafted a critique—the first in a series of contentious communications—of the Central Committee's handling of the arms shipment. Leaders of the CPP delegation blamed the failure on the impatience of Sison and other Party leaders and on what they criticized as hasty, amateurish arrangements for receiving the shipment. The China delegation had warned Sison that the *Karagatan* crew was inadequately trained, and the fact that the boat ran aground convinced them that they had been right. Their critique gravely implied that by seeking to infuse so many weapons so quickly into the countryside, the Central Committee was guilty of military adventurism—one of the charges Sison had made against the old PKP leadership. Finally, a majority of the China delegation demanded that Sison take responsibility for the *Karagatan* failure.[20]

Sison replied by blaming the failure on the NPA reception team and on other units in the field. In response, the China delegation insisted that the "central leadership"—meaning Sison—take responsibility for the botched arms shipment. Sison answered the latest criticism point by point and concluded with a caustic observation that the China delegation should spend less time complaining.[21]

Later in 1973, Sison formulated another proposal for an arms shipment, this time on the northwestern coast of Luzon, which was nearer to China. Even more ambitious than the *Karagatan* project, the plan called for a vessel to drop watertight tubes packed with arms off the coast of La Union province. NPA scuba teams would retrieve the weapons and ferry them ashore in small fishing boats.

Chinese officials approved the plan, and arrangements proceeded rapidly. In December 1973, Chinese military officials invited Tubianosa and his deputy, Ricardo Malay, to Hainan Island off China's southern coast to examine the weapons. Under a dreary Beijing winter sky blackened by the soot of the capital's ubiquitous coal stoves, the party of aging Chinese army officials and young Filipino revolutionaries boarded a luxurious air force plane bound for Hainan. Five hours later, the visitors stepped off the plane into the dazzling tropical sunshine. The Filipinos were whisked away to the VIP compound and then ushered to a dock for the show their hosts had prepared.

The Chinese had gone to extraordinary trouble and expense to ensure the success of the arms project. M-14 rifles, bazookas, and ammunition had been vaccuum-packed into dozens of specially made plastic tubes that could withstand the pressures of lying in the sea off Luzon. A Chinese scuba team demonstrated how the weapons would be dropped into the ocean and recovered safe and dry in their protective tubes. "We were very impressed," one of the Filipino guests said later. "We thought, how could anything go wrong?"

In fact, there were already signs of trouble. Noting Edwin Alcid's propensity for seasickness, the China delegation had protested the selection of the *Karagatan* captain as commander of the new boat, a small, former passenger liner renamed the *Andrea.* The Central Committee overruled the objections.

The *Andrea* set sail for Fukien province in late January 1974 with Alcid at the wheel supported by a crew of three former student activists and eight peasant guerrillas from Central Luzon who had never been to sea before. Before dawn on the second day, sailing in heavy winds and rough seas off the northwest coast of the Philippines and south of Taiwan, the *Andrea* ran aground on a mass of coral reefs.[22]

The *Andrea* crew was picked up later the same day by a salvage ship from Hong Kong, the *Oriental Falcon*, which deposited the hapless Filipino communists on a wreck that was being cannibalized by the ship. At one point, a flash fire broke out on the wreck and nearly killed three rebels. On another occasion, a Taiwanese naval boat decided to use the wreck for target practice and opened fire with machine guns and cannon. After two weeks, the *Oriental Falcon* returned to Hong Kong, where the *Andrea* crew was detained by immigration authorities. Five days later, the Filipino rebels were allowed to seek asylum in China.[23]

The failure of the *Andrea* project was a devastating blow to the China delegation, whose members had already begun quarrelling among themselves about political and personal matters. Tubianosa, an ill-tempered man who had never gotten along particularly well with his colleagues, became depressed and aloof. The others were in scarcely better spirits. Almost all were in agreement that Sison should bear responsibility for the latest failure.

Two years of anger, frustration, and self-pity were poured out in long letters to Party superiors in the Philippines. The letters condemned Sison for real or imagined ideological and political failures and attacked the entire CPP leadership on a broad range of issues: Why were CPP leaders so bent on Chinese aid when the revolution was purportedly based on the principle of self-reliance? Why had Sison denounced the Lavas for leading the guerrilla struggle from the cities when the CPP leaders were now doing the same thing? In a fit of passion, Tubianosa even revived the taboo subject of Plaza Miranda and denounced Sison as a "mad killer" for ordering the bombing the Liberal party rally.[24] The more disillusioned members of the group were bitter about the dreary lives they had been forced to live, and they were sick of what they felt were Sison's romantic, misguided notions about China and Mao. Three years of living amid Cultural Revolution chaos had convinced the Filipinos that China was not utopia, as comrades back home believed.

In late 1974, there was more bad news for the China delegation. A courier carrying the angry letters to CPP leaders, along with a $75,000 cash donation from the Chinese government to the Party, was captured crossing the Canadian border into the United States. (Copies of the letters eventually found their way into the hands of Philippine military intelligence officers, who showed them to imprisoned communist leaders to demoralize them.) Several weeks later, however, a second courier successfully delivered a new set of scathing letters to the Central Committee.[25]

For months, the China delegation's bitterness toward the CPP leadership had been deteriorating into savage infighting, and in March 1975, Tubianosa resigned as the group's head. He secluded himself in his room and refused to eat or speak with the others. In retaliation for Tubianosa's resignation and his harsh attacks on Sison, the Central Committee ordered that the rebellious Politburo member be placed under "super-vision"—in effect, under arrest—and he was forbidden to leave China.[26]

In the meantime, developments in internal Chinese politics were quickly overtaking the CPP's China project. Mao was dying and inca-pacitated, and the radical Gang of Four led by Chiang Ching was exercising effective power. By 1975, the Chinese radicals, increasingly preoccupied with their own internal power struggle, had grown tired of dealing with the bickering Filipino communists. They began pressuring their burdensome guests to accept a Cultural Revolution remedy for their personal and ideological ills: move to the countryside to join the peasants in manual labor. Sickened by their failures and the depressing life in the drab Beijing compound, the Filipinos finally agreed to accept the Chinese "advice."[27]

In late fall 1975, the Filipinos left Beijing for Hunan province, the revered birthplace of Mao. The Chinese had built a special compound for the Filipinos, surrounded by a high wall and a guard house, in a village 90 minutes southeast of the provincial capital of Changsha. The delegation was assigned two cooks and an interpreter and given the use of two jeeps. As another winter approached, the rebels settled into life in rural China.

The Chinese tried to make life in the countryside less dreary for their "fraternal guests" by showing movies every Saturday evening in the compound's dining hall. From this weekly ritual, the Filipinos were able to vaguely discern the shifting political winds swirling beyond the walls of their compound. At first, when Chiang Ching and the Gang of Four were still firmly in control, the movies were stern Cultural Revolution fare: shrill propaganda slavishly extolling Mao's political thought. Later, as the grip of China's radicals loosened, the menu was broadened to include films from like-minded communist countries. The triumph of Deng Xiaoping over the Gang of Four and the collapse of Cultural Revolution strictures resulted in movies from Japan and Hong Kong finding their way into the Saturday evening programs. But the high point for the Filipino communists came still later, in 1979, when Deng's campaign of "liberalization" filtered down to the Hunan compound in the form of a Charlie Chaplin movie.[28]

When spring 1976 arrived, the Filipinos threw themselves into their new lives as peasants. They planted rice in the paddies, grew vegetables, tended fruit orchards, and raised fish and pigs. For the moment, dark memories of Beijing were forgotten, and the group enjoyed a peace it had not known since arriving in China five years earlier. The delegates rose at 7 A.M., donned peasant garb—baggy cotton pants, blouses, and broadbrimmed hats—and assembled in the courtyard for group exercises. After breakfast, they headed to the paddies or vegetable plots for planting and hoeing. Later in the day, they met for political sessions in which they studied the works of Mao and engaged in "criticism" and "self-criticism." In every facet of their lives, they sought to transform themselves into model Chinese peasants. They made their own charcoal briquets for cooking and heating and collected their urine and excrement to be made into fertilizer—a routine that quickly lost its novelty during the hot summer months.

If the Filipinos thought they had finally found utopia, they soon realized otherwise. The old tensions and bitterness that had festered in Beijing resurfaced in the daily criticism and self-criticism sessions, which turned into rancorous personal attacks among rivals. Radicals in the group, who prided themselves on their slavish emulation of China's Cultural Revolution zealots, condemned others for "bourgeois" behavior, such as listening to classical music on Radio Moscow or Voice of America shortwave broadcasts. One member was castigated by his radical colleagues for making "nonproletarian jokes" and for buying two cartons of Marlboro cigarettes for the group during a trip outside China. The radicals recommended that they burn the "bourgeois" cigarettes and continue smoking their poor quality Chinese brand. There was little enthusiasm for the proposal, however, and the radicals wound up smoking their share of the U.S. cigarettes.

The disputes reached even more comical proportions when two of the more ideologically extreme Filipinos got into a fistfight during a basketball game. One of the protagonists wrote an eight-page proposal to the Central Committee requesting permission to engage his rival in a boxing match, with a referee, either ten or fifteen rounds, and "with or without gloves." For months, the two exchanged long, meticulously crafted ideological attacks on one another, which they distributed to members of the delegation—much to the others' entertainment.[29]

When Chinese officials offered the CPP delegation a new color television set to replace the old black-and-white model, the radicals objected on the grounds that if black-and-white television was good enough for Chinese peasants, it should be good enough for them. After a fierce two-week debate, the radicals prevailed, and the offer was declined. Only when their ruffled Chinese hosts suggested that there were others in the compound who might prefer color television—meaning the Chinese staff—did the embarrassed radicals accept the new television.

In 1977, the Chinese merged the *Andrea* crew—four university-educated Party cadres and eight peasants—with the official CPP delegation. Sison's leadership now became a point of fierce debates that pitted Tubianosa, Mario Miclat, and the peasant guerrillas from the *Andrea* against the rest of the group. The cadres who remained loyal to Sison in varying degrees found themselves in the uncomfortable position of having to defend the *Karagatan* and *Andrea* failures, the Plaza Miranda bombing, and other Party policies under attack by Tubianosa's faction. Efforts to thresh out their differences failed, and the feud spun out of control. One night in late 1977, one of the peasant guerrillas pulled a knife on a member of the rival group he had encountered in the hallway. Only the intervention of a Chinese interpreter prevented what might have been a bloody free-for-all.[30]

By September 1979, all the Filipinos had returned to Beijing. Deng Xiaoping's liberalization program was gaining steam, and the CPP delegation had become a political liability and financial drain on the Chinese government. By 1981, the status of the delegation had been so downgraded that the only official role for the Filipinos was to sit down occasionally with Chinese officials for briefings on developments in the Chinese Communist Party, and vice versa.[31] For practical purposes, the CPP's China project had died the moment the *Andrea* rammed a South China Sea reef.

A raw chill lingered in the sooty air when the delegation gathered together in Beijing for the last time in early April 1981. The occasion was the funeral of a member of the *Andrea* crew, a 59-year-old NPA guerrilla known to the others only as *Ka* (Comrade) Mon. The peasant had died of cancer only a week before the first members of the group were to begin returning secretly to the Philippines. Moved by the death of Mon, all the old adversaries from the delegation and *Andrea* crew, except Tubianosa, gathered for the funeral amid a spirit of joyless reconciliation. Each wore a white paper flower, a Chinese symbol of mourning, and they tearfully sang the "Internationale" as they took turns carrying the old man's coffin and shoveling the cold, wintry earth on his grave.

Immediately after the funeral, the first group of three from the *Andrea* project returned to Manila using fake Philippine passports, and by July, most of the crew had slipped back into the country. Later in 1981, most of the members of the original delegation left for Holland—the emerging source of funds for the revolution—for assignments with the CPP's National Democratic Front office. It was only after the fall of Marcos in 1986 that Tubianosa and Miclat, the rebels who dared challenge Sison, returned home with their families, 15 years after entering China.

Years later, bitter memories and disillusionment still lingered for some of those Filipinos who traveled to China in 1971 as young, committed communists imbued with the dream of revolution. One criticized the China project as an "adventurist" blunder. Another, recalling with anguish his years in China, described the mission as "the impetuous dream of an impetuous individual who wanted to take the shortest route to political victory," a cutting reference to Sison. Sadly, this former delegate told me, "The China project did more harm than good to the Philippine revolution."

That judgment may be too harsh. Political observers of all hues expected Marcos to declare martial law before the end of his term, and CPP leaders urgently felt the China lifeline had to be in place by the end of 1972. Viewed within that context, the postmortem offered to me by an *Andrea* crewman—a senior Party cadre by 1989—seems more appropriate: "People were young. The movement was young. We suffered from the frustrations of youth. It was all part of the revolution's growing pains."

7

Shaping the Revolution

With little more than Mao's *Little Red Book* and a vague notion of people's war, brigades of young activists began fanning out across the Philippines in 1969. Students who secretly had joined the Communist Party returned to their provincial homes to organize Party cells and guerrilla squads. By 1971, the revolutionary movement had taken on something of a national character, reaching far beyond the bounds of the Central Luzon communist-led Hukbalahap rebellions of the 1940s and 1950s.

The revolution spread to southern Luzon's Bicol region in a fashion typical of those first years. In October 1970, two Manila KM activists, Juan Escandor and Mila Ragos, organized some 15 students into a KM chapter in Legaspi, Bicol's political and economic center.[1] Their local contact was a popular student leader named Sotero Llamas, who had grown frustrated with the failures of the moderate Christian Socialist movement to which he belonged. The KM chapter took root in Legaspi, and new recruits carried the message of "national democratic revolution" home to the towns and villages of Bicol. KM chapters sprouted throughout the region.

In late 1971, national CPP leaders decided that a sufficient political base had been established in Bicol to launch guerrilla warfare. In December, the Party formed a 10-member armed propaganda unit and assigned it to the mountains of Camarines Sur province. Around March 1972, a tiny guerrilla unit was formed in southern Bicol, in Sorsogon province. Llamas had gone underground after Marcos suspended the writ of habeas corpus in August 1971. A few weeks later, Llamas and a handful of Party cadres went to the Albay countryside to launch the revolution there. "I started with a slingshot and a flashlight," he told me 17 years later. "I got my first gun, a pistol, when our group killed a cattle rustler."

After 17 years in the countryside as an NPA guerrilla, Tibbs bore the signs of great physical hardship. A scar on her neck was the reminder of a goiter operation, the legacy of years of poor nutrition. Emaciated, she weighed barely 100 pounds. Ulcers prevented her from drinking coffee and tea and restricted her diet. Her arms were scratched and scarred from long hikes through the Philippine jungles, her hands calloused and skin leathery from the hard years outdoors.

Yet with all the physical suffering she had endured over the past two decades, Tibbs remained as defiant and committed to the revolution as I imagined she must have been as a 16-year-old KM activist in 1970. I first met her late one evening in June 1987 reading and writing by the dim light of a homemade lamp in a peasant's house in southern Luzon. We met several times during the course of the next year, sometimes in remote guerrilla camps and villages in the countryside, at other times in Manila. Once, we spent an entire Saturday afternoon talking in a crowded McDonald's in one of Manila's busiest shopping malls. The intensity, energy, and sheer exuberance she radiated, whether huddled around a campfire with her comrades leading a "revolutionary sing-along" or sitting in a trendy Manila cafe discussing the latest political developments, always amazed me. Despite her physical frailty, Tibbs could walk for hours over rugged trails as nimbly as did the peasants whose lives she had embraced. But she was more at home delivering a lecture on the inevitability of a communist victory in the Philippines, and she was as fiery a speaker as any rebel I ever encountered.

By 1988, Tibbs had become the most powerful Communist Party official in the strategic region bordering Manila to the south and east, from where rebel leaders hope someday to launch a final offensive on the capital. In many ways, hers is a classic story of how the unlikely communist rebellion began so amateurishly and how it survived extraordinary hardships and setbacks to emerge as a force shaping the Philippines' political future.

For Tibbs, the path to revolution began in Sorsogon in a comfortable, conservative middle-class family. Her father was a local Liberal party boss, and as a teenager she idolized the party's rising star, Benigno Aquino. Years later, Tibbs would dreamily recall the time Aquino visited her home during his 1967 senate campaign. She worked tirelessly for Aquino as a volunteer, with an eye on a political career of her own someday. Secretly, Tibbs confessed to me with a laugh years later, she fantasized of becoming Sorsogon's first woman governor.

Her priorities were abruptly rearranged in 1970 as the galvanizing effects of the First Quarter Storm protests in Manila gradually filtered down to provincial campuses. Swept up in the passions of nationalism and the promise of political change, Tibbs and several friends joined a KM affiliate. After attending only three "discussion groups," she and her friends became convinced of "the necessity of a revolution." She rushed through her undergraduate degree program by the following year. A few months later, on November 3, 1971, 17-year-old Tibbs slipped away to the Sorsogon countryside to join an NPA armed propaganda unit.[2]

As armies go, the Sorsogon branch of the NPA was remarkably unimpressive in those embryonic days of 1971. It consisted of fewer than 20 inexperienced activists armed with a .45-caliber pistol, reserved for the provincial Party secretary, and a .22-caliber pistol. Later, one of the rebels showed up with a Thompson submachine gun she had stolen from her father. The others armed themselves with machetes, knives, and whatever else they could find. Tibbs settled for a hunting knife and an arrow, sans bow. Each morning, the commander would assign two "Red fighters" to "secure" the area around their camp and to scout for wild vegetables to eat. "When you were instructed to do that work, you felt proud because you had the precious weapons with you," Tibbs told me years later.

Although only a handful in number, the rebels created on paper an elaborate organization that recalled some of Sison's extravagant flights of fancy. To handle every conceivable task, they established a plethora of bureaus. There was a political bureau, military bureau, instruction bureau, women's bureau, even a cultural bureau. As they were so few in number, each of the young communists served simultaneously on several bureaus.

To expand their "guerrilla front," the activists set out alone and in pairs to establish "barrio organizing committees" in rural villages. The committee would include any local contacts the rebels had, along with those in the village deemed the most sympathetic and most capable of influencing others to support the movement. As the communists gradually gained entree to a village, they would organize farmers into associations that developed simple production and marketing cooperatives and sought better tenancy arrangements with landlords.

The rebels worked by trial and error, relying on Mao as their guide. They pored over the *Little Red Book* and over articles Mao had written on economic work, land reform, and "united front" tactics. "Mao's works were almost like a Bible," Tibbs recalled. "Everytime we had a problem, we would consult Mao." Fearful that they would repeat the mistakes of the old Lava party, they constantly tested one another for ideological purity using Mao's criteria. Was a particular decision dogmatist or empiricist? Left error or Right error? They fretted and analyzed and argued until they fell asleep at night and then began anew when they woke up in the morning.

By mid-1972, the KM activists who had taken to the Sorsogon countryside had achieved modest successes. Near the town of Barcelona, they had established a small base area where the villagers would give them food and shelter. In return, the rebels had organized a consumer cooperative that enabled the peasants to buy staples such as rice, salt, and sugar at stable, affordable prices. The political work had gone well enough to enable the communists to establish a local armed propaganda unit in March 1972, with weapons donated by a sympathetic con-gressman.[3] Other politicians and affluent families offered money or material assistance, some because they saw the rebels as a thorn in Marcos' side, others because they viewed the young radicals as harmless, well-intentioned nationalists. By fall 1972, the Sorsogon NPA Command consisted of two eight-member propaganda units with a few rifles and pistols and several three-person organizing teams armed with shotguns, machetes, and knives.

In Camarines Sur, rich landlords helped the struggling NPA armed propaganda unit survive the first difficult months by donating several rifles and handguns.[4] The landlords viewed the gifts simply as a means of protecting their interests. Armed with the donated rifles, the communist squad added to its arsenal and curried favor with local farmers by confiscating the weapons of a cattle-rustling gang. After several months of patient recruiting, the NPA contingent had multiplied to more than 30 fighters divided into four armed propaganda units, with another 50 unarmed activists broken into smaller organizing teams. On the political front, the results were less encouraging. Several months of recruiting efforts had yielded only a handful of barrio organizing committees, and government military operations were making further expansion difficult. By the time martial law was declared in September 1972, two NPA propaganda units in Camarines Sur had been wiped out by government forces.[5]

An AFP offensive in late 1972 brought NPA activities to a halt in much of the Bicol countryside. Soldiers dismantled the Party-administered farmer's cooperative near Barcelona and flushed the guerrillas out of their "safe" villages. The approach of an army patrol sent the lightly armed NPA squads fleeing for cover in the forest. "We had to run for our lives," Tibbs recalled. "We joked at the time that we didn't have automatic gunfire—we had automatic movement of the feet."

Martial law wrought a whole new set of problems for the novice guerrillas. Villagers were no longer able to provide food and shelter, and the rebels were forced to forage in the jungle. Rice, a three-times-a-day staple for Filipinos, became a rare luxury for the guerrillas. Instead, three times a day they ate *kamote*, a starchy native sweet potato.

Tibbs, who had been reassigned to Camarines Sur before martial law, was a member of an NPA armed propaganda unit that was surprised by a government patrol in November 1972. The men in the 10-member communist unit were able to run away when the firing broke out, but Tibbs and another woman were cut off. Finding themselves face to face with enemy soldiers, the women ignored an order to drop their weapons and opened fire with their tiny .22-caliber pistols. The soldiers responded with a volley of automatic rifle fire. Her companion was killed instantly, and Tibbs was slightly wounded in the abdomen. She rolled down an embankment into a stream, feigning death, and managed to run away. Fifteen years later, Tibbs was able to laugh as she recalled the encounter. "What I felt was shame rather than fear. Here were our little .22-pistols going 'pop, pop,' and the soldiers responded with the roar of their automatic rifles."[6]

Under increasing military pressure, the Camarines Sur rebels pooled their forces to form a guerrilla platoon in early 1973. The larger unit was able to organize 80 barrios by the end of the first year of martial law, but the government responded by deploying more troops to the province. The cordon grew tighter around the rebel force as one sympathetic village after another was occupied by soldiers. Low on food and ammunition and nearly encircled, the desperate NPA platoon launched a last-ditch attack on a government outpost in eastern Camarines Sur on November 27, 1973. The retreating rebels were caught by pursuing AFP troops near the town of Tiwi. Seven guerrillas—nearly half the remaining NPA force—were killed in the fierce battle, and several others were wounded. By December 1973, the Camarines Sur NPA Command was down to nine survivors, with seven rifles and 1 peso, 20 centavos among them. They began retreating on December 14, hoping to slip through Albay and reunite with communist forces in Sorsogon, 75 miles to the south, unaware that the Sorsogon front was besieged and under heavy attack by the AFP.

The ragged band of nine rebels was a defiant bunch, and to maintain their spirits they sang and joked as they walked. At one point, the oldest rebel, a farmer who had fought as a Huk guerrilla two decades earlier, clambered atop a large rock and christened the group "the last remnants of the old and glorious New People's Army." The others cheered.

They walked all Christmas day, then stopped the following day to celebrate the fifth anniversary of the CPP founding. Friendly peasants fed them boiled cassava stems, the best meal the guerrillas had eaten for days. In exchange, the rebels regaled the peasants with revolutionary songs and read passages from the *Little Red Book*. On December 27, the bedraggled group entered a village outside Oas, Albay, where two unarmed CPP cadres had been living for months and organizing the peasants. Upon seeing the armed strangers, the two cadres fled into the jungle fearing they had been discovered by government troops. The nine rebels sent a peasant into the jungle to explain that they were the survivors of the Camarines Sur front. Unconvinced, the two cadres sent a note back demanding that the strangers prove their identity by naming the Albay Party secretary. One of the group scrawled the name Sotero Llamas on the paper and sent it back into the jungle. Finally reassured, the two lonely rebels emerged from hiding and joyfully embraced their long-lost comrades.

The cadres wept when they saw the seven rifles carried by the Camarines Sur survivors. The Albay front had been organizing barrios for two years and still had not been able to form an armed unit. The jubilant cadres ran through the barrio shouting, "Mother! Father! We have an army! We have an army!" That night, the weary guerrillas stuffed themselves on plates of steaming *kamote*, and celebrated their escape. Four days later, January 1, 1974, the Camarines Sur contingent straggled into the Albay CPP headquarters camp, where they were welcomed by Llamas.[7]

By the late 1960s, Negros had become the country's prosperous sugar bowl, a boot-shaped island of rich, volcanic soil that descended gently from a rugged central mountain chain to the sea. Sugar accounted for one-fourth of the country's exports, and Negros was producing the lion's share of the nation's crop. Plantation owners, known as *hacenderos*, were assured of lucrative profits by a U.S. quota that guaranteed Philippine sugar growers prices as much as three times those of the world market. Negros sugar profits were also helped by the fact that the industry's workers were among the lowest paid labor in Asia. While the *hacenderos* became the most affluent of the nation's elite, Negros sugar workers became the poorest of the country's poor, a chronically malnourished and disease-ravaged underclass that struggled to survive from one harvest to the next.

Following the Cuban revolution, the United States had increased the Philippines' sugar quota. The Negros *hacenderos* responded by expanding output in the easiest possible way: They confiscated new lands from poor subsistence farmers, who usually did not have proper titles for their plots. The new wave of land grabbing came at a time when exploding population was already making land a scarce commodity around the country. On Negros, the dispossessed farmers at first moved further up the foothills, cleared new plots, and began anew. But by the end of the decade, they had been pushed far up the mountain sides to marginally productive lands. They were already struggling to feed their families, and there was nowhere else to go.

Simultaneously, the decades-old injustices of the sugar industry were beginning to stir new ripples of unrest among the desperately poor workers. The *sacadas*, the seasonal workers who harvested the ripened cane by hand, earned less than $1 for a 12-hour day. They were frequently cheated out of their wages by unscrupulous foremen. Typically, the *sacada* would go home with 30 pesos (about $10 in the 1960s) after spending the six-month harvest season cutting cane all day long in the tropical sun. Regular *hacienda* workers were hardly better off. During the months when work was available, they earned below the minimum wage, and the workers and their families averted starvation during the off-season by obtaining rice loans from the *hacendero*.

In 1969, Father Arsenio Jesena, a Jesuit priest from Manila, spent the harvest season with Negros *sacadas* and wrote a moving account of the exploitation in the sugar industry. He juxtaposed *sacadas* who earned 1 peso (about 25 cents) a day against *hacenderos* who dropped 120,000 pesos a day at the cockfights. "I saw the injustice of it all," Jesena sadly concluded, "and I began to understand why the communists are communists."[8]

When plans were made in 1969 to begin widening the guerrilla war beyond Central Luzon, Negros was chosen as the CPP's first target for expansion to outlying islands. Later that year, Central Committee members Hermenigildo García and Manuel Collantes led a small team of activists to Negros to launch the revolution. The group included a few of Commander Dante's Central Luzon guerrilla veterans led by a Tarlac peasant named Apolinario Gatmaitan.

Boy Gat, as he was known, and his small armed rebel band chose northern Negros as the target for the first guerrilla front. From the outset, the venture was doomed to failure. Boy Gat and his men did not speak the local dialect, and their Central Luzon accents made it difficult for them to move around inconspicuously. More importantly, their tactics were fatally flawed. Rather than concentrating on building a political base that would afford the guerrilla band a safe haven, the trigger-happy Tarlac guerrillas began killing local police. When authorities came looking for them, rather than run, the guerrillas fought a pitched battle near the town of Victorias on July 30, 1969. Two days later, Boy Gat's guerrilla squad clashed again with police, this time near the town of Cadiz. Shortly afterward, police caught Boy Gat and one of his men aboard a bus near the town of Escalante. The bodies of the two were later discovered, apparently summarily executed, although police later claimed the rebels had been shot while trying to escape. When García and his activist colleagues were subsequently arrested, the effort to open a guerrilla front on Negros was temporarily abandoned.[9]

Although the initial attempt to expand guerrilla warfare to Negros failed miserably, several secret CPP cells were formed and flourished amid a growing atmosphere of repression and polarization. Farmers displaced by land grabbers turned to the Catholic Church for assistance, and activist priests led by Luís Jalandoni, the scion of one of the island's wealthiest sugar families, took up the cause of poor farmers and sugar workers. Jalandoni's activism gradually led him into an alliance with the student activists who were building an underground network.

Martial law crippled the underground organization on Negros, and only five Party activists eluded the government dragnet, including Jalandoni, who by the time of martial law had secretly joined the Communist Party.[10] One CPP cadre recalled arriving in Negros in December 1972: "We did not have money to pay the rent for the house where we were staying. We did not have transportation fare for couriers to move around. We did not even have money for food or arms procurement. We began from scratch."

Sympathetic priests and nuns influenced by Jalandoni played a crucial role in rebuilding the CPP on Negros. Church people provided food and shelter for underground organizers, and priests ferried the fugitive rebels to the countryside in their personal automobiles. "Whenever we needed things and we had nobody to turn to, Luís would come through by getting what we needed from his Church colleagues," one Negros Party cadre told me.

For the first few months after martial law was declared, the Negros activists huddled in safe houses discussing Mao's political and military theories and playing chess. In late April 1973, the rebels launched another attempt to open a guerrilla front. This time, the poor, hardscrabble hill country of southern Negros was selected as the target. It was an area Jalandoni knew well from Church socioeconomic projects among the poor upland subsistence farmers. Four teams of two cadres each were assigned to zones in the area, given a budget of 150 pesos a month (about $38), and told to raise an army.[11]

By adapting their message to local issues, the NPA squads expanded rapidly and within a few months were turning down volunteers for lack of food and arms. In one barrio, the rebels found that residents were fond of cockfighting but that soldiers had banned peasants from engaging in the sport. The rebels began organizing cockfights for the villagers and posted guards to watch for government patrols. "It wasn't long before we had 100 percent support in that barrio," the CPP cadre who had suggested the idea told me years later, chuckling at the recollection.

The NPA strategy was to avoid contact with soldiers. The rebels would hide during the day, sleeping four or five hours, and meet at night with their contacts before moving to the next barrio. "We were so fired up, it was as though we feared being overtaken by time," one cadre recalled. After organizing several villages, the NPA squads would return to consolidate their earlier work. The process entailed what the Party called "cleaning operations," a euphemism for the execution of suspected military informants or others deemed "bad elements" in the barrio. The executions served as a compelling warning to those villagers who were less inclined to support the revolution.

In the early 1970s, CPP teams were simultaneously dispatched throughout the archipelago, and they formed organizations on the Visayan islands of Panay, Cebu, Samar, and Bohol. Cadres tried to open two fronts on Mindanao prior to martial law: a western front in the Zamboanga peninsula and an eastern front near the southern port of Davao. The first areas targeted by the rebels were barrios organized by militant activists of the Federation of Free Farmers (FFF) and Khi Rho, a radical Christian youth organization. The FFF had organized peasants to peacefully fight for their legal rights in land disputes. With the spadework done, the communists tried to convince the already politicized peasants that the limitations of legal actions necessitated an armed revolution.

After martial law was declared, many FFF and Khi Rho activists fled to the mountains to organize guerrilla resistance and joined the few CPP cadres already there. In Davao Oriental province, FFF and Khi Rho activists managed to establish an armed guerrilla unit. About 30 young activists—members of KM, FFF, and Khi Rho—gathered in the mountains of Davao del Sur and tried to organize villages to support the revolution. They gave up after a few fruitless months of bickering among themselves.[12]

On Mindanao, as on Negros, the galvanizing issue in the early years of the rebellion was land. Small farmers in southeastern Mindanao were being forced off their lands by banana plantations, some of them foreign owned. Frustrated by their defeats through legal methods, many peasants supported the rebels who came to their barrios promising "land for the landless." Despite some initial successes, an ambitious NPA expansion program on Mindanao collapsed in the months after martial law due to amateurish leadership and aggressive military patrols. By 1973, only two of five guerrilla fronts launched a year earlier remained open, kept alive by a skeletal force of activists. Front 3, one of the surviving fronts, had taken root in Davao del Norte province in eastern Mindanao. Because of heavy military operations, by 1974 the number of cadres and guerrillas in Front 3 had been reduced from 120 to 18, and their base of operations had been reduced from six towns to a single village. The survivors were forced to flee into the mountains, where much of their lives revolved around scavenging for food.[13]

Years later, one veteran cadre recalled that the communist squads encountered a host of internal problems as they tried to organize the countryside in the early 1970s. Rather than working with sympathetic Church people and tapping into the influential Catholic organizational network, as the Filipino communists would later learn to do so effectively, some cadres insisted on shunning the "clerico-fascists" and their organizations. Also frequent were what the cadre described as Left errors—extremism—on matters of Party discipline and tactics. On one occasion, the Davao del Norte cadres agreed to accept into their ranks four escaped convicts on the condition that if any one of the four committed a breach of NPA discipline, all would be executed. One did run afoul of Party rules, and although the other three had become exemplary "proletarian revolutionaries," they all were killed.[14]

By late 1974, a new wave of cadres who had been forced by martial law and the threat of arrest to huddle in safe houses in Manila were finally reassigned and fanned out through the Visayas and Mindanao. The cadres set to work building an urban support network; they organized professionals and Church groups to raise funds and provide logistical support for struggling communist units in the countryside. Gradually, the flow of support provided relief to the surviving rebel squads, and fresh cadres who found their way to the countryside breathed new life into the revolution.

8

Indigenizing "People's War"

In "Rectify Errors and Rebuild the Party,"[1] a brutal critique of PKP history, José María Sison argued that the earlier communist-led insurgencies could have succeeded had the proper strategy and tactics been adopted. Sison denounced José Lava for leading communist forces down the road of "Left adventurism" by attempting to seize power in two years. And he scorned the old leadership for its ignorance of Mao Zedong Thought and the Chinese leader's concept of people's war. The key to a successful revolution in the Philippines, Sison confidently declared, was a measured, stage-by-stage war led by a peasant army operating from "stable base areas" in the countryside and guided by the theories of Mao. The CPP's slavish adherence to Maoism preordained Party strategy and tactics in the early years of the war. Whereas the old PKP leadership had careened from one extreme to the other as it attempted to set the strategic and tactical course of the earlier rural rebellions, Sison maintained a firm, ideologically steady hand.

One key element of Mao's strategy that Sison adopted for the NPA was the development of stable base areas in the countryside. But neither Mao nor Sison offered a precise definition for the concept of a stable base area, resulting in various interpretations by cadres organizing guerrilla fronts in the early 1970s. Many cadres understood a stable base area to mean an economically self-sufficient communist enclave like the fortress Mao established at Yenan.

Years later, Sison denied that there ever was a "Yenan strategy" in the early years, although he and other cadres made it clear that Isabela was intended to be some kind of a central base in the early 1970s. The CPP chairman did dispatch cadres throughout the country almost from the beginning of the war in an effort to develop simultaneously several guerrilla fronts, rather than concentrating forces in a single base area on Luzon. The collapse of NPA bases in Isabela in the first two years of martial law convinced Sison and other CPP leaders of the folly of attempting to defend fixed positions at such an early stage of the war. By late 1974, the Central Committee had formally discarded the policy of building stable bases in favor of creating mobile guerrilla bases— that is, heavily politicized enclaves in the countryside within which communist forces could move safely but would not have to defend against military assault. The new thinking was reflected in an essay regarded as Sison's most original work, "Specific Characteristics of Our People's War," which appeared in December 1974 under his pen name Amado Guerrero.[2]

"Specific Characteristics" was in part an attempt by Sison to reassure his battered forces in the countryside that the strategic line of protracted people's war would ultimately lead to victory. He acknowledged that waging a prolonged guerrilla struggle in a country with so many scattered islands and without contiguous borders with friendly countries was "an exceedingly difficult and complex problem." But ever the optimist, Sison argued that the NPA could turn the initial weaknesses of fighting in an archipelago into long-term strengths.

The centerpiece of Sison's strategy called for the creation of a number of self-reliant, autonomous guerrilla fronts on each of the major islands. By conducting guerrilla warfare on multiple fronts scattered throughout the archipelago, the government would be forced to disperse its forces and would be unable to concentrate enough troops to destroy the rebels on any one island. Furthermore, the Philippines' mountainous geography could offer tremendous advantages to the NPA if exploited properly, Sison wrote. The positioning of guerrilla bases in the mountains, which usually marked provincial boundaries, would enable the communists to extend political and military influence over two or three provinces from a single base.

The most far reaching, innovative policy emerging from "Specific Characteristics" was that of "centralized leadership, decentralized operations." Sison recognized the difficulty of waging a war on simultaneous fronts in an archipelago. Communications with units in the field took weeks or even months. It was impossible to supply the guerrilla fronts from a central command, and the movement of personnel and weapons from one front to another was difficult and risky. To overcome the logistical problems inherent in the order to disperse forces, regional CPP committees and local cadres needed to be politically autonomous as well as materially self-sufficient. Local Party leaders and guerrilla commanders had to be able to interpret and react to developments in their immediate areas and innovate tactics without seeking Central Committee approval. Henceforth, Sison determined, the Central Committee would set general policies and guidelines for the conduct of Party operations and the war, but the actual implementation of the policies would be left to regional Party committees scattered around the country.

The granting of autonomy to local units was a bold break with the PKP policy of rigidly centralized leadership and was a move fraught with risks. Without the proper Party discipline, political supervision, and individual motivation, field commanders might develop into warlords. Sison minimized the risks by scattering scores of the most dedicated and talented cadres, trusted Central Committee members included, around the country. The Party's leadership by committee at every level also acted as a brake against warlordism or the development of local policies that deviated considerably from the national CPP line.

The new policy had a final significant effect on the guerrilla war during the latter half of the 1970s. The renewed emphasis on developing politically stable guerrilla base areas resulted in a marked decrease in NPA military activity in most areas of the country. NPA units, which from the beginning had been trained for education and propaganda tasks as well as combat, stepped up political organizing efforts nationwide. By the early 1980s, when the Party had grown to such a size that the NPA finally began concentrating almost solely on launching military operations, the sudden spate of guerrilla attacks stunned the Philippine military and political leadership.

The policy of decentralized operations proved to be a masterstroke that enabled the NPA to adapt to the Philippines' complex matrix of ethnic and linguistic diversity, which was so great that even adjacent barrios were sometimes cleaved by custom and language. Armed with the flexibility to discard unworkable tactics and experiment with new ones, leaders of the various fronts patiently developed the inept insurgency into a national movement of vast potential. Along the way, Communist Party cadres and guerrillas endured years of trial-and-error experimentation as they sought to build a rural revolution from scratch. Many of the efforts in the 1970s to set up "guerrilla zones" and build communist bases in the countryside ended in bitter failure, at a tragic cost in lives. But each defeat added to the sum of collective experience, and gradually the Philippine rebels indigenized the Chinese people's war.

Despite the difficulties wrought by martial law, the standing Central Committee order for regional Party committees in early 1973 was to build mountain guerrilla bases as rapidly as possible. The autonomy with which regional communist organizations operated led to quick success in some areas. But experimentation also resulted in failures, and none was more devastating than in Bicol in the mid-1970s.

Sometime in the first half of 1973, the Bicol NPA commander, Ramón Sanchez, received instructions from the Central Committee to establish a base near the region's mountainous northern boundary with Quezon province in southeastern Luzon. Upon receiving the order, Sanchez journeyed to Sorsogon province, at the southern tip of Bicol, to pick up rifles for his new command. He fell in love with the province, its picturesque, 4,800-foot-high Bulusan volcano, hot springs, and spectacular mountains. Without consulting the Central Committee, Sanchez decided to build the regional base in Sorsogon.[3]

Strategically, the decision had disastrous implications: Sorsogon was Bicol's smallest province, barely 75 square miles, located at the southern tip of a 150-mile long peninsula. Sorsogon was surrounded by water on three sides, and although rugged and mountainous, it was only 20 miles across in the area selected by Sanchez as the site for his guerrilla base. For a guerrilla force, there was precious little countryside in which to hide and maneuver, and government forces would never be far away.

Sanchez envisioned blending Mao's tactics and strategy with those of South Vietnam's communists. He hoped to establish a mountain base where peasants and guerrillas would build a self-sufficient bastion of revolution. According to Sanchez, the rebels' task was to emulate the struggle in South Vietnam by encouraging farmers to revolt and then to create liberated villages defended by booby traps and peasants armed with indigenous weapons.[4] NPA units set to work building a base in the mountains of southern Sorsogon near the towns of Matnog and Bulan.

In late 1973, military operations in Sorsogon resulted in the deaths of a few farmers and the arrests of several others. Many frightened peasants fled into the forest. Convinced that the peasant uprising they had been awaiting was at hand, Sorsogon communist leaders transplanted the refugees to three villages constructed around the NPA's mountain base. Hundreds of sympathizers and their families were moved to the rebel encampment. Booby traps were constructed along the trails leading up the mountain, making the liberated villages virtually impregnable. With fanatical zeal, the Sorsogon rebels set to work building a self-sustained, economically self-reliant bulwark of revolution. Communist leaders encouraged the peasants to manufacture coconut oil for cooking and lighting and to weave baskets and build rattan furniture to sell in local markets for cash. Adults and children underwent political training at Party schools and learned to read and write.[5]

By early 1974, communist strength in Sorsogon had mushroomed from a single armed propaganda unit to a force of nearly 250 cadres and fighters, more than 150 of whom were armed. Fired by their initial successes and rapid growth, the Sorsogon rebels forged ahead. Mao had emphasized that land reform must accompany the revolution, and so the Sorsogon rebels set out to fulfill this instruction. The Central Committee's national agrarian reform policy called for landlords to reduce the rent extracted from peasants by 40 to 50 percent of the harvest. Invoking Mao's radical agrarian revolution in China, Sorsogon Party cadres ordered landlords to reduce rents by up to 90 percent. In many cases, the guerrillas simply confiscated lands and redistributed them to their peasant followers.[6]

Some small landowners, trying desperately to protect the life savings they had poured into the land, offered the rebels 80 percent of their annual harvest—only to be rebuffed. The Sorsogon communists insisted on 90 percent. The confrontational tactics led landlords to close ranks and pool their money to help fund the operations of local military units. Undaunted, the rebels launched a series of reckless attacks and raids on government forces and as a result captured more weapons and attracted new recruits.[7]

In mid-1974, the AFP launched a massive campaign against the communist bases with 1,000 soldiers backed by fighter planes that strafed and bombed the liberated villages. A food blockade was implemented to prevent peasants who had been portering supplies to the communist bases from carrying large amounts of rice and other foodstuffs into the area. Laborers hired by the military destroyed the root crops that had become the primary source of food for the hungry rebels. Gradually, the soldiers tightened their cordon, and conditions deteriorated inside the NPA bases. A cadre serving in neighboring Albay province received two frantic letters from the bases pleading for bags of poisonous herbs for the booby traps hidden along the trails leading to the rebels' redoubts. As many as 80 soldiers, and several communists and their civilian supporters, perished in the bamboo traps.[8]

Life inside the Sorsogon base camp had become nearly unbearable. Bombardments and strafings from aircraft and artillery forced the inhabitants to spend entire days huddled in tunnels and foxholes. When stocks of rice, salt, and other staples were exhausted, the guerrillas and their peasant supporters combed the jungles for snails and edible roots. Many rebels and peasants, weakened by hunger and malnutrition, became ill from various diseases. Nevertheless, Party leaders exhorted the beleaguered communist forces to defend the bases. Eventually, the peasants began to desert the liberated villages, and demoralizing rumors of mass surrenders inside the Sorsogon cordon began to filter back to cadres in Albay province.

Too weak to break out of the enemy encirclement, the communist army in Sorsogon began to collapse at the end of 1974. Sanchez turned himself in to the military. As peasant supporters stood by the roadside crying, the commander of Sorsogon's crack NPA combat unit surrendered with a squad of armed guerrillas. By late 1975, only 10 of the once formidable force of 250 cadres and fighters remained. The others had died, deserted, or surrendered.[9]

The survivors abandoned the bases in September 1975 and straggled into Albay province led by a young guerrilla named Celso Minguez. When they arrived at the Albay NPA headquarters, they were half dead, emaciated, and diseased. Minguez was so riddled with hookworms that his comrades nicknamed him Commander Hook. He was so weak that it took him 30 minutes to put on his shoes or unroll his sleeping mat. For weeks, when he went to the latrine he would collapse from exhaustion. But Minguez recovered and by the mid-1980s had become the Bicol regional military commander, a deadly efficient guerrilla leader.[10]

In 1970, Sison dispatched one of his student protégés, Jorge Cabardo, to the eastern Visayas to open a guerrilla front. A few months later, Cabardo succeeded in establishing a front in southern Samar by coopting a local armed religious movement.[11] The rebels found the rugged terrain and thick jungle of Samar, one of the least developed Philippine islands, ideal for guerrilla warfare. Nevertheless, Cabardo was disappointed in the slow progress his forces were making.

A turning point in the CPP's struggle to organize Samar occurred in late 1974 when the Central Committee issued its policy ordering the development of major islands first in each region. Leaders of the CPP's eastern Visayas region, like virtually all the regional Party organizations at the time, had dispersed their limited forces on each of the islands in the region, which hindered the development of a single stronghold. "The idea of the Central Committee policy was to pinpoint a center of gravity in an area, and expand wave upon wave from that place," a ranking Visayas CPP official recalled years later.[12]

Hoping to develop a Yenan-style base as in Sorsogon, the Samar rebels gathered peasants who had been displaced by military operations and settled them in new villages carved from the jungle. The army soon pinpointed the communist settlements and in December 1977 began bombing the area in southern Samar. For three consecutive days, from dawn to dusk, artillery and planes pounded the jungle surrounding the communist base. "It was very, very demoralizing," a Samar cadre recalled. The rebels debated bitterly about whether to hold out in the new base or return with their peasant followers to the old villages they had fled. The Central Committee finally ordered the Samar command to abandon the jungle base and work on establishing mobile base areas.

Under the new effort, legal organizations for peasants—secretly controlled by the Party—were created to supervise political education and organizing. By strengthening support among villagers, the guerrillas were able to develop well-organized mobile base areas that did not require armed defense. If soldiers entered a barrio, the organized peasants became innocent civilians, while the guerrillas and cadres melted into the jungle. By 1979, Samar boasted the strongest communist organization, militarily and politically, of all islands.[13]

Sison had always envisioned Mindanao, the country's second largest island, as a theater where communist units would play a peripheral role by drawing enemy troops away from the main battlefield on Luzon. Positioned at the extreme southern end of the archipelago, 500 miles from Manila, Mindanao was a sprawling island cut by five rugged, heavily forested mountain ranges, an ideal environment for a guerrilla army. Yet after more than three years of proselytizing and attempts to wage guerrilla warfare, the NPA could muster only a skeletal force on Mindanao.

The Western Mindanao Front tried to revive the armed struggle in 1974. A single squad armed with fewer than 10 rifles was formed under the command of Romulo Kintanar, the young guerrilla who had been captured during the retreat from the *Karagatan* arms landing in 1972 and released a few months later. As government forces turned their full attention to a Muslim insurgency raging on the island, Kintanar prepared the tiny NPA squad to resume guerrilla warfare. Their first successful operation in February 1975 was a remarkably modest affair: Four enemy soldiers were ambushed and killed, and their weapons were confiscated.[14]

By the latter half of 1975, the Eastern Mindanao Front, encompassing Davao and the provinces of Davao Oriental and Davao del Norte, had a strength of 30 full-time cadres, including an armed squad of 15 guerrillas with one Korean War–vintage Garand rifle, one Thompson submachine gun, one World War II–era carbine, and a few handguns. A cadre arriving in the guerrilla camp that September brought the front's first automatic rifle, a U.S.-made M-16 bought in Davao on the black market.[15]

By 1976, whatever initial resignation or approval had greeted martial law had begun to wane. In the countryside, the Philippine military and its civilian "self-defense units" had become increasingly abusive and arrogant; soldiers routinely collected tribute in cash or kind from peasants. The NPA began to capitalize on the army's escalating abuses, and by 1976 eastern Mindanao cadres who had been afraid to move during daylight were busily organizing barrios day and night.

In 1977–1978, while the NPA developed a competent military force on Mindanao, internal political debates about strategy wracked the Party. In the western sector of the Eastern Mindanao Front, CPP cadres were emphasizing political organization and relegating guerrilla offensives to a secondary role. But the leader of the eastern sector, Magtanggol Roque, believed that rural communist forces should spend less time talking politics with villagers and more time building an army. Roque theorized that if the rebels had a strong army, they would win the support of peasants. The Party needed to organize just enough people to perform intelligence and support tasks, he argued.[16] Soon, the discussion about whether to emphasize political work or army building flared into an intense debate among Party cadres in eastern Mindanao.

The solution to the disagreement was finally provided by Sison's essay, "Our Urgent Tasks," which first appeared in July 1976.[17] Sison instructed communist forces in the countryside to strike a balance between organizing grass-roots political support and building a guerrilla army. In analyzing the CPP's past mistakes, he stressed the building of mass campaigns that targeted specific issues such as human rights violations, government corruption, landlord excesses, and foreign domination. To guard against military adventurism, Sison reminded NPA forces in the countryside to conduct only those guerrilla operations that they were assured of winning. Party cadres were exhorted to build an extensive political network in the countryside complemented by a strong underground organization in the cities. Years later, many Party cadres with whom I spoke described "Our Urgent Tasks" as a significant work that provided the widely scattered communist forces with firm ideological and organizational bearings as the revolution entered years of rapid growth and success.

9

Martial Law and
the Urban Underground

As NPA units struggled to build bases in the countryside, the protest movement galvanizing students and workers in Manila grew increasingly militant. By the early 1970s, the CPP had built a formidable underground organization in Manila, with a few hundred Party members scattered throughout legal student, labor, and youth organizations, and CPP organizing in the capital was moving ahead at a fast pace.

Omy, one of the emerging corps of teenage activists of that period, recalled that his path to the revolution began at the University of the Philippines High School, where he was a scholarship student. He started by reading radical writers in the university newspaper, *The Philippine Collegian*, and by his senior year had joined KM. In 1968, several prominent student leaders broke away from KM to form a rival Maoist organization, the SDK. Omy joined the new group and became well versed in Marx and Mao through regular discussion group sessions. By June 1970, he had become a candidate member of the Party and was assigned to the CPP's clandestine Manila youth and students bureau.[1]

Omy's first important Party assignment was to return to his home in the industrial suburb of Marikina and begin organizing local SDK chapters. He had grown up in a lower-middle-class neighborhood where his parents worked in local shoe factories, and he knew the people and their hardships. Omy spent the next year in his old neighborhood organizing poorly paid shoe factory workers. After the suspension of the writ of habeas corpus in August 1971, he was assigned briefly to help launch a Party-controlled civil libertarian group.

In September 1971, Omy was reassigned to UP to set up new Party front organizations. By then, the KM and SDK had become too radical for many students, and the Party needed fresh organizations to attract moderate students. Omy became leader of a new "moderate" student group. At the same time, he enrolled in other colleges in Manila's university belt, where many poorer students attended classes. He organized CPP front organizations at each of the schools in which he enrolled in order to attract students who were disinclined to join KM or SDK. Gradually, Omy was able to form Marxist study groups within the new organizations that set many students on the path to involvement in the rebel movement.

His next assignment took him to the slums of Manila and suburban Quezon City, where he worked at proselytizing unemployed youths. He used his university contacts to gain entree to poor neighborhoods, and then gradually won acceptance. Years later, Omy recalled how receptive the slum dwellers were to his message of armed revolution. Existing economic and political conditions provided the Communist Party cadres with all the teaching aids they needed. When Marcos raised oil prices, Omy explained to his slum audiences that U.S. imperialism and foreign domination of the country's economy were responsible. "It's very difficult to explain fascism, but the militarism and repression of the Marcos government made that easy, too. It was very easy to organize people for the movement in those days."[2]

Almost from the day Ferdinand Marcos won a bloody reelection victory in 1969, Manila had been rife with speculation that the ruthless president was poised to declare emergency measures that would enable him to seize power indefinitely. Marcos had been floating the possibility of martial law since the First Quarter Storm upheaval of 1970. A year later, following the Plaza Miranda bombing, he had suspended the writ of habeas corpus but reinstated it several months later amid a maelstrom of public protest.

In mid-1972, events once again began building toward a climax. Beginning in March, a series of mysterious bombings heightened tension in the capital. In July, Marcos announced to a skeptical public the discovery of a mysterious boat off Isabela, the *Karagatan*, which, he claimed (truthfully) was part of a foreign plot to supply the guerrillas. Before the debate about Marcos' fantastic charges had stilled, several more bombs were set off in Manila. Marcos and his defense secretary, Juan Ponce Enrile, attributed the bombings to a plot by communist "subversives" to sow confusion in the capital. But the opposition Liberal party, led by Senator Benigno Aquino, suggested that Marcos was staging the attacks to justify martial law.

Before midnight on September 22, 1972, military and police teams began sweeping through Manila arresting politicians, labor leaders, youth and student activists, journalists, businesspeople, priests, and others who were outspoken Marcos critics. Before the night was out, Marcos had succeeded in rounding up hundreds of opponents and in padlocking newspapers, radio stations, and television stations. The following day, he formally announced the imposition of martial law.

For months, Sison had predicted in *Ang Bayan*, the CPP newspaper, that Marcos was gearing up to impose emergency rule. Several veteran cadres with whom I spoke years later remarked, however, that they had expected Marcos to declare martial law sometime in 1973, rather than in September 1972. Nevertheless, the CPP responded fairly well to the sudden turn of events. The Party leadership kept in place in Manila many cadres who were members of legal organizations rather than transferring them to the countryside to join the NPA. Cadres with legal covers were ordered to exercise caution but to continue their activities. As a result, most urban Party cells remained intact.

Although martial law did not paralyze the CPP, it caused considerable disarray and tested the mettle of young activists. Party organizing activities came to a virtual standstill as attention focused on eluding the military dragnet. The beleaguered guerrilla zones in the countryside could absorb only a few of those forced underground by martial law, and so the CPP was faced with the daunting logistical task of hiding thousands of Party members and activists in Manila. The sudden transition to the underground took a heavy toll on young activists ill-prepared for the chronic pressures of life on the run. Some who managed to win immediate assignments to the countryside quickly decided they were not cut out for the work of a rural revolutionary, and they quit or asked to return to Manila. One prominent student leader sent to Central Luzon to organize peasants was so miserable that he was in tears much of the time, so he was sent back to the capital.[3] Others were not as lucky. Omy recalled that scores of radical classmates from UP went directly into NPA units in the countryside. Inexperienced and recklessly brave, many were killed.

Mila Aguilar was 23 years old and 7 months pregnant with her first child when she began life with her husband in the Party's Manila underground network a few weeks before martial law. She had been a talented leftist writer sympathetic to the radical movement, but not a Party member. Unbeknownst to her, her husband, Magtanggol Roque, was a CPP member who had become involved in the *Karagatan* arms smuggling project. After the boat was discovered, she and her husband were forced to go underground. During the next three years, they moved from one safe house to another, rarely staying more than three months in one place. It was a dreary existence with windows and shades always closed and the constant fear of arrest. Three weeks after martial law was declared, Aguilar gave birth to a son. Their shoestring existence in Party safe houses made it difficult to care properly for the baby, and he nearly died from severe diarrhea. Fearful that the child would die if he remained with her, Aguilar made the agonizing decision to give her son to her mother.[4]

At first, the exuberant activists who flooded the underground houses were filled with zeal. "They always had this idea that the movement would win in a few years," a CPP member in Manila at the time told me. As months, and then years, passed and they continued to languish in Manila scuttling from one safe house to another, demoralization began to creep into the ranks. Many cadres wrote position papers arguing for their reassignment to the countryside. "Everyone wanted to get out of Manila," Aguilar recalled. "Nothing was getting done. You couldn't go out. People were afraid for their lives."[5]

In early 1973, the Central Committee established the National Liaison Commission to oversee the orderly transfer of CPP members to the countryside. The decision was made to reduce by half the 1,500 Party members in Manila, in order to lessen the risk of arrest and strengthen the movement in rural areas. Working with regional Party committees, the commission determined how many cadres a region could absorb and then arranged for them to be smuggled to the guerrilla zone. In this fashion, hundreds of CPP members were transplanted to the countryside in 1973 and 1974.[6]

In the opening paragraph of presidential proclamation 1081, Marcos justified martial law to the nation—and perhaps more importantly, to his benefactors in Washington—by citing the threat of a communist takeover. Eighteen of 22 clauses in the declaration made reference to the insurgency, projecting the image of a life-threatening challenge to the nation. Through the years, Marcos' many critics have maintained that he vastly exaggerated the seriousness of the communist rebellion in order to perpetuate himself in power. This view is essentially correct— Marcos did grossly inflate the threat—but the communist revolutionary movement was not as weak in 1972 as some have suggested.

As would be the case nearly 15 years later when Marcos was finally routed from office, the communist political apparatus at the time of martial law was far more formidable than the communist military strength. Marcos' depiction of the NPA in 1972 as a serious *armed* threat to the government was pure hyperbole. According to the Philippine president, the NPA had at least 8,000 guerrillas, with as many as 10,000 rifles, supported by 100,000 sympathizers.[7]

While Marcos' detractors argue that the figures were rubbish, the one person who knows better than anybody the strength of the CPP and rebel army in 1972—Sison—maintains that the rebel movement actually enjoyed greater mass support than even Marcos claimed. Obviously, Sison's contention is self-serving and impossible to verify, but it does credibly suggest that communist political strength was broader in 1972 than has generally been credited. Sison agrees that Marcos considerably exaggerated the estimate of armed guerrillas, which the communist leader said totaled at most several hundred at the time of martial law, most of them concentrated in either Isabela or Central Luzon. The NPA arsenal consisted of 350 automatic rifles and a few hundred antiquated single-shot rifles, homemade shotguns, and handguns. The guerrillas were supported by a rural mass base estimated by Sison at 300,000, also concentrated in Isabela and Central Luzon, with a few smaller pockets of support in other regions of the country.[8]

On the political front, Sison contends, the communist movement was much stronger. By September 1972, the CPP had grown to 2,000 members. Sison estimates the movement had an "urban mass base"—sympathizers and hard-core supporters—of about 100,000 people, the bulk concentrated in metropolitan Manila and the rest scattered throughout 20 provincial cities. Most of the urban supporters were members of Party-led or -controlled organizations such as the Movement for a Democratic Philippines (MDP) and the Movement of Concerned Citizens for Civil Liberties. Sison readily agrees that the commmunists were hardly a military threat in 1972. But to dismiss the movement at the time as a disorganized collection of rabble-rousing students without significant support ignores the feverish political organizing activity that had been going on for more than three years in urban neighborhoods and rural barrios. These efforts had already enabled the movement to establish a sophisticated underground organization in Manila and sink roots throughout the archipelago.

If one of Marcos' motives for declaring martial law was his desire to destroy the communist movement, it is one of the great ironies of his remarkable political career that his gambit achieved the opposite effect. Although the CPP and rebel army had established a steady growth trend by 1972, the movement's survival was by no means guaranteed. A change in presidents, constitutionally scheduled for 1973, might have distracted and mollified Filipinos enough to stall communist expansion, at least temporarily. The U.S. disengagement in Vietnam had removed from public debate an issue that had galvanized the Philippine radical movement in the late 1960s. By 1972, "student power" worldwide was on the wane. In China, the "center of world revolution" for Filipino radicals, Mao's Red Guards were fading from the scene as the Cultural Revolution lost steam. Although Sison and hundreds of cadres had succeeded in developing some indigenous issues Filipinos could rally around, the Philippine communist movement, bred from the turbulence and idealistic activism of the 1960s, might have stagnated in the 1970s. Martial law changed the game.

The crackdown infused the already talented ranks of the CPP and NPA with a new wave of recruits who included many of the most brilliant and energetic students and young professionals the generation had to offer. Many of those who wound up in the underground had not been inclined to support an armed communist revolution. By declaring martial law, Marcos initially left reform-minded Filipinos with four choices: join his corrupt, discredited regime; accept imprisonment and possible torture by an increasingly arrogant military; retreat into non-involvement; or join the underground opposition.

The story of Nelia Sancho illustrates how young Filipinos were forced by martial law to make wrenching decisions they otherwise might not have made. Years later, Sancho characterized herself as having been reluctantly driven into the communist underground. "I didn't know what the underground was when martial law was declared," she told me 15 years later. "My going into the movement was totally because of martial law. It wasn't anything ideological. It was out of protest. I was not politically or ideologically prepared to go underground. But martial law left you with no choice."

Sancho, the 17-year-old daughter of a middle-class government auditor, had entered UP in 1968. She joined a popular sorority, won election as chapter president, and became a fashion model in her spare time. In 1971, she joined the raucous campus demonstrations more out of curiosity than conviction, and when hundreds of UP students built barricades at university entrances and renamed the campus the Diliman Commune (after the famous Paris Commune a century earlier), Sancho joined. At the barricades, left-wing student leaders conducted political teach-ins, discussing nationalism and U.S. imperialism, but carefully avoiding mention of Marxism. When police finally broke through the barricades, they chased the students into their dormitories and then tossed tear gas into the buildings. Angered by the incident, Sancho began regularly attending radical protests.[9]

In July 1972, a killer typhoon and heavy flooding ravaged the Central Luzon provinces north of Manila. Student brigades descended on rural barrios to distribute food, medicines, and leaflets blaming U.S. imperialism and local "fascists" for the "suffering of the people." The students were surprised to find highly politicized peasants in villages where the communist-led peasant rebellions of the 1940s and 1950s had once flourished. Fifteen years later, Sancho still vividly recalled sitting in a barrio listening to ragged peasants discuss their hardships. Few owned the small plots of land they farmed, and most shared half or more of each harvest with the landowner. They lived with their families in bamboo-and-thatch huts without running water or electricity and survived on a meager diet of rice and bits of fish.

When martial law was declared two months later, college friends who, fearing arrest, had gone into hiding began calling Sancho to ask if she could help them with food and clothing. In 1973, Sancho herself went into hiding after she discovered that military agents had come to her apartment asking questions about her. Gradually, she was drawn into underground work by acquaintances who had already joined the communist movement. At the house of a friend in a Manila suburb where she was hiding, she was reintroduced to two young college professors who had become CPP cadres. One night in October 1973, soldiers surrounded the walled compound outside the house. As the two Party cadres tried to climb out a window, soldiers burst into the room and gunned them down. Sancho and three college friends hiding at the house were taken to military headquarters for questioning, and she was released two weeks later. Afterward, her parents took her home to Davao, 600 miles away from the turbulence of Manila, where they hoped their daughter would forget about the revolution. But Sancho's experiences had deeply affected her, and like thousands of Filipinos radicalized by martial law, she did not forget. Two years later, she took up work as a legal Party organizer in a slum in the city of Cagayan de Oro.[10]

Martial law left the once-formidable legal protest movement in disarray, its leaders in hiding or in prison, its activists driven into the underground or cowering in fear. For months, CPP leaders and rank-and-file members were preoccupied with trying to remain one step ahead of military intelligence. Captured cadres, out of fear or torture, revealed the location of safe houses, and one arrest usually led to several others.

Omy, who had been arrested shortly after martial law was declared and released in early 1974, returned to UP to resume Party organizing work, only to discover that student activism was dead. Even intellectuals were afraid to voice dissent to the martial law regime. Undaunted, Omy joined innocuous campus organizations and created new groups that could become fronts for clandestine communist activities. He joined a popular fraternity and became president six months later. He organized a history club and immediately began sizing up the radical potential of the students who joined. Within a few months, he was forming secret Marxist cells within the organizations he had created or joined.[11]

Later in 1973, hoping that a resurgence of protests in Manila would distract military commanders enough to relieve pressure from beleaguered communist forces in Isabela and elsewhere, the Central Committee directed its forces in the capital to revive the urban protest movement. Lacking specific instructions, Manila Party leaders entered into secret talks with centrist anti-Marcos politicians. Marcos had dissolved Congress and suspended the U.S.-style 1935 constitution. The most prominent leaders of the political opposition, including Benigno Aquino, were in jail, while others had sought asylum in the United States. Many other Liberal party officeholders had cut deals with Marcos, agreeing to support his regime in exchange for remaining in power. Those remaining opposition figures welcomed the CPP offer to form an anti-Marcos front. Communists and moderates agreed upon a blueprint to rally the fearful enemies of martial law that called for a civil liberties campaign aimed at restoration of the suspended constitution.

Shortly afterward, in early 1974, Sison summoned the head of the Manila-Rizal Party Committee, former student leader Julius Fortuna, to the Central Luzon city of Angeles. The CPP chairman argued vigorously against a campaign with "bourgeois liberal" forces to bring back the old constitution. Instead, Sison suggested that Manila Party cadres conduct a campaign focusing on issues such as academic freedom, rising tuition fees, and the restoration of banned student councils and newspapers, or focusing on community and sectoral issues, such as living conditions in city slums or the difficulties of Manila Bay fishermen. If the "bourgeois politicians" raised the constitution issue, the Party could use the debate as an opportunity to discuss CPP propaganda and issues, Sison suggested. But under no circumstance was the Party to support such a "reformist" position as the return of a constitution that mirrored that of the United States.[12]

The guidelines laid down by Sison were followed, but not without some grumbling within the ranks of Manila Party cadres. Years later, one Manila communist leader lamented the Party's refusal to get involved in the constitution campaign as a golden opportunity missed. "Had we been allowed to raise the issue of the 1935 constitution," he said, ". . . we could have dictated the entire antifascist, anti-Marcos civil liberties movement during the early stages of martial law."[13] Instead, the CPP had to wait until 1983—and the assassination of Aquino—

before it again had an issue capable of unifying the urban anti-Marcos movement.

This disagreement between the Manila Party organization—the largest single unit in the CPP—and the Central Committee was the first of a series of confrontations between the two organs in the years that followed. At the heart of the problem were fundamental differences over what role Manila should play in the revolution. Mao had never accurately defined the role of urban forces in a people's war, emphasizing instead the paramount importance of peasant revolution in the countryside. Sison unquestioningly embraced this strategic line and ascribed to urban CPP organizations the secondary role of providing funds, recruits, and other support for guerrilla forces in the countryside.

By the late 1970s, against the backdrop of a weakening economy, communist efforts to rebuild an urban protest movement were beginning to bear fruit. Party cadres had organized communities of homeless squatters in Manila to fight the demolitions of their communities. Martial law had crushed the increasingly militant labor movement, but beginning in 1975, radical unions under the direction of Party cadres began challenging a strike ban imposed by Marcos.[14] The CPP even succeeded in reviving the student movement in 1977 by organizing protests to oppose a tuition fee increase and to demand reestablishment of student councils and newspapers.[15] Gradually, the strikes by militant workers and demonstrations by students and slum dwellers eroded the paralysis martial law had inflicted on Philippine society, enabling the revolutionary movement to step up its organizing activities in urban areas.

While the open urban protest movement was showing signs of recovering from the devastation of martial law, the underground CPP leadership was experiencing difficulties. The Manila Party Committee and the CPP's trade union and medical bureaus were decimated by arrests in 1974. These problems were compounded by festering differences on points of strategy and tactics between the Manila Party organization and the Central Committee.

In July 1976, Sison chastised the increasingly rebellious cadres in "Our Urgent Tasks." He accused Manila Party members of straying from the Maoist line and drifting perilously close to "bourgeois reformism." The Manila Party Committee was also guilty of "Right opportunism," Sison wrote, by virtue of its support of the moderate political opposition's demand for general elections.[16] Sison's reprimand did little to deter the young, independent-minded Manila Party officials. They had become convinced that the CPP chairman's insistence on relegating the urban front to a secondary role was a mistake, and they intended to press the issue. By 1977, the Manila cadres were on a collision course with the Central Committee.[17]

10

The Manila Rebellion

The successful student protests against higher tuition fees in mid-1977 encouraged CPP leaders to begin making plans for a sustained wave of demonstrations in Manila modeled after the legendary First Quarter Storm seven years earlier. The scheme called for widespread, coordinated protests by students, factory workers, and slum dwellers. Party leaders anticipated that the moderate political opposition would join the campaign and lend an air of mainstream respectability to the protests.[1]

Spearheading the secret planning of the campaign was the CPP's 13-member Manila-Rizal Committee, headed by a former student, Filemon Lagman, then in his mid-twenties. The Manila cadres were ecstatic about the plans for reviving the "parliament of the streets," which after five frustrating years of martial law, would again put them in the thick of the revolution. But the planning sessions resurrected a long unresolved issue: What role should urban areas play in the struggle? The guerrilla war seemed to be unfolding all too slowly, and Manila Party leaders became convinced that they could advance the struggle on their own. "We came to the conclusion that you need not wait for developments in the countryside to launch major political events in the city," a member of the Manila Party Committee recalled years later.[2]

That view of people's war, in the eyes of Sison and the leadership's orthodox Maoists, was virtual heresy. The strategic line they subscribed to in 1977 was unchanged after eight years of war: Surround the cities from the countryside; decisive developments would occur in the countryside, not in the cities. Manila Party leaders argued that by escalating legal and illegal protests in the city, the war in the countryside could be advanced. New cadres could be recruited and trained from the ranks of those joining Party-organized strikes, demonstrations and political education sessions in Manila. The recruits could be tempered and developed into experienced cadres before being dispatched to the countryside, ultimately strengthening NPA units.[3]

A number of Manila cadres had always viewed as too ambiguous the Central Committee's early 1970s commission to urban activists to create a "broad, antifascist, antidictatorship front." How, for example, were Manila cadres supposed to interact with anti-Marcos politicians—potential tactical allies—such as Benigno Aquino and his followers? The Central Committee offered no guidance. CPP leaders had little use for legal forms of struggle, a prejudice that stemmed from their contempt of the PKP's failed ventures in parliamentary struggle. More and more, the Manila Party organization differed with the Central Committee on what the tasks of urban activists should be. In 1974, the Manila cadres began quoting Sison's own words from "Specific Characteristics" about decentralized operations in an attempt to advance its argument that the Central Committee should allow the cadres the autonomy to determine urban policies and tactics.[4]

The tension worsened in 1975 when the Manila Party committee supported an opposition campaign demanding a new constitution and general elections. Manila cadres saw the campaign as a chance to build profitable alliances with noncommunist forces. Describing the proposed elections as the last step "before the majority of the masses understand and support . . . the armed revolution," the cadres even suggested that it might be possible to force Marcos from power through elections. At the least, CPP allies in a new legislature could "unmask the rotten nature of the reactionary regime and explain the uselessness of parliamentarism."[5] The Manila cadres supported the opposition campaign with their own similar drive, bannered by the slogan "Lift martial law; demand national, democratic, and antifascist elections!"

Sison retorted with a warning to the Manila Party organ against supporting what he scorned as "reformist" positions. Writing in "Our Urgent Tasks" later in 1976, Sison accused the Manila cadres of "Right opportunism" and chided the restless Party members that they "should not be flattered and should not remain complacent about being the biggest single party organization."[6]

Despite obvious fundamental differences with the Central Committee, the Manila Party Committee members reasoned in 1977 that Sison had given at least tacit approval to their theories by authorizing the coordinated protest campaign. Sison had even taken a direct hand in planning the demonstrations by joining the Manila committee in key sessions where plans were refined. "He did not oppose our plans," one of the Manila committee members recalled. "We interpreted his silence as approval."[7]

In fall 1977, Party planning for the urban destabilization campaign abruptly came to a halt when Marcos announced the scheduling of elections for a new National Assembly the following April. A few weeks later, on November 8, Sison was captured by military agents in the northern Luzon province of La Union.

Without waiting for Central Committee instructions, Manila Party leaders decided the communists should participate in the elections because (1) the CPP's participation would more deeply split the ruling elite between pro- and anti-Marcos politicians; (2) the election campaign would offer an unprecedented opportunity to conduct massive anti-Marcos propaganda; and (3) Party cadres would be able to conduct alliance work with noncommunist elements, which could enable the CPP to arrange financial and material support and thus improve logistics for communist forces in the field.[8] "While we had no illusions about participating in elections under the Marcos dictatorship, we believed we could use the elections to make gains," a Manila Party leader at the time said years later.

The Manila CPP leadership entered into indirect negotiations with anti-Marcos politicians led by Aquino, who remained in a military prison. Aquino was represented by his younger brother, Agapito, in a series of meetings with intermediaries for the Manila communists. The two sides soon reached an agreement: The communists would actively support the opposition in exchange for the inclusion of candidates recommended by Manila Party leaders. When the opposition Lakas ng Bayan party slate was finalized, it included five candidates approved by the CPP: Alex Boncayao, a labor leader; Charito Planas, a well-to-do political activist; Trinidad Herrera, president of the slum dwellers' Zone One Tondo Organization; Aquilino Pimentel, an Aquino protégé from Mindanao; and Gerry Barican, a former student activist.[9]

In the meantime, Manila Party leaders had become engaged in prickly discussions with the Central Committee about what role the CPP should play in the election. In a series of memos to the leadership, the Manila cadres sought permission to field Party-led union members, students, and other supporters to work as pollwatchers to thwart expected government election fraud. The Central Committee reacted coolly to the cadres' eagerness to plunge into the electoral fray. Top CPP leaders, led by Rodolfo Salas, Sison's successor, merely viewed the campaign as an opportunity to promote Party propaganda and issues. This view was forcefully articulated in a memorandum the Central Committee began circulating in Manila in January 1978. Conspicuously, however, the document did not directly address the issues of whether and how the Manila Party organization could support candidates in the elections.[10]

Accounts of what occurred in the weeks leading up to the election are conflicting. The Central Committee later contended that it had issued a boycott order two months before the elections but that the Manila-Rizal Committee had deliberately withheld the document from circulation among Manila cadres. One source with whom I spoke, who in 1978 was a young Party worker with access to communications between the Central Committee and Manila, supported the Central Committee version. According to this source, the Manila cadres had simply held the boycott order, later claiming the document had been lost. The former Party activist said he had tried to disseminate the order in Manila and was cashiered by his superiors.[11] A member of the Manila committee at the time offered a sharply divergent account. He insisted that the Manila Party organ lacked specific restrictions from the Central Committee, and therefore continued to play an active role in the campaign, organizing mass meetings for candidates and distributing anti-Marcos propaganda.

One week before the April 7 elections, the Manila Party leaders received an unmistakable directive from the Central Committee: They were to pull out of the opposition ticket and campaign for an election boycott. The five candidates annointed by the Communist Party were expected to withdraw as well.[12] On the eve of the elections, the Manila-Rizal Committee gathered for an emergency session in the town of San José del Monte, Bulacan province, 10 miles north of the capital suburbs. The meeting was harmonious, for almost all the Manila committee members were in agreement: The elections seemed to be looming as a turning point in their struggle. A defeat would radicalize the moderate opposition and bring them into closer cooperation with the communists, the cadres assured one another. If they managed to elect a few sympathetic candidates, the Party would benefit from the "democratic space" the legislators would carve out for dissident activities. Eleven of the 13 members raised their hands in a vote to defy the Central Committee boycott order and go ahead and participate in the polls.

In a last, frantic attempt to avert a confrontation, the Manila Committee dispatched a message beseeching the Central Committee to reconsider its boycott directive. But military operations prevented the courier from reaching the CPP leaders, who were meeting in the Central Luzon province of Nueva Ecija. After years of skirmishing, the battle lines between Manila and the Central Committee were drawn.[13]

In the final days before the election, the Manila Party organization made good its pledge of support by assigning radical student activists to the campaigns of opposition candidates. Party-organized activists even stood guard at polling stations on behalf of opposition candidates on election day.[14] It made no difference. As the Central Committee had warned, the opposition was crushed in voting marred by massive fraud. Not a single opposition candidate won in Manila. The "proletarian masses" did not take to the streets to protest government election fraud, as Manila Party officials had expected. Those who demonstrated against the election results were the "bourgeois reformist" elements that the CPP leadership despised.

Immediately, the Central Committee demanded an explanation from the Manila committee for its defiance of a direct order and launched an investigation of this breach of Party discipline, the first time ever in the movement's history that a CPP organ had defied Party policy.[15] The Manila Committee hastily drafted a self-serving analysis in which the cadres argued that the CPP had achieved concrete gains by participating in the elections. The Manila cadres maintained that the Party had been able to conduct massive propaganda and proselytize large numbers of people for the first time in its existence. Open mass meetings had been conducted under the guise of campaigning, and millions of pamphlets denouncing Marcos had been circulated. Furthermore, the Manila Committee reported, cadres were able to build alliances with noncommunist forces.[16] Filemon Lagman, the Manila-Rizal Party secretary, and two deputies hand-carried their defense to the Central Committee in mid-April still hoping they could persuade the CPP leaders to accept their arguments. Two weeks later, the Central Committee announced that the arguments were unsatisfactory. The Manila committee would have to answer for its insubordination.[17]

The Central Committee decided in May that the dispute should be resolved in a formal session, a "struggle meeting," which was scheduled for November 1978. In the meantime, the Party leadership moved against Lagman, who was viewed as the ringleader of the rebellion. The Manila Party secretary was confined in a safe house and forbidden to talk with other committee members as they prepared arguments for the November inquiry. The Central Committee assigned two handpicked loyalists, Edgar Jopson and Caridad Magpantay, to sit on the Manila committee and keep an eye on the rebellious cadres. (Magpantay at the time was the Central Luzon Party secretary and a close ally of Salas.) In July, Jopson, formerly a prominent student activist, was designated as the acting Manila Party secretary.[18]

Revolutionary work in the capital ground to a halt in autumn 1978 as the Manila Committee members plotted strategy. Ignoring the ban against contact with his comrades, Lagman began meeting with the other defiant Manila cadres to discuss their defense. He assigned two committee members to prepare a position paper arguing their case. The Manila cadres consulted every available work of Lenin, Stalin, and Mao and began to craft a lengthy ideological brief. Much to their frustration, they were forbidden to cite the Philippine precedent of PKP participation in the 1946 congressional elections through the left-wing Democratic Alliance. Sison had officially condemned the PKP as a rightist party, the "Lava revisionist clique," not worthy of CPP acknowledgment. The Manila Party officials found other precedents that appeared to support their decision to participate in the elections. Lenin, for example, had participated in municipal duma elections under the Kerensky government in 1917. There was also Lenin's directive to "use all forms of struggle," and a few supporting examples could be drawn from Vietnamese communists. But when it came to Mao and the Chinese model, the Manila cadres were stymied. They simply could not find a compelling parallel that would justify participation in "bourgeois elections."[19]

Seizing on this fact, the Central Committee, dominated by orthodox Maoists, quoted the Chinese communist leader extensively as it condemned the Manila cadres on multiple counts. The Central Committee arguments were compiled in a thick document, some 360 single-spaced, typewritten pages, which appeared in October 1978. Its chief author was Salas, who drew heavily from Mao's "On Contradiction" and "On Tactics" to support the leadership's rigid theoretical positions. The paper scored the Manila Party organization's decision to participate in the elections as shameless "reformism" and condemned the defiance of a direct Central Committee order as an unprecedented breach of Party discipline.[20] Too much emphasis had been placed by Manila cadres on the state of the revolutionary movement in the city without taking note of the steady expansion of communist forces in the countryside, the Central Committee argued. The scathing document included a bitingly sarcastic passage accusing the Manila committee of engaging in a "Russian" fantasy:

> Marcos is the tsar. The anti-Marcos reactionaries are the bourgeois Russian socialist revolutionaries and Mensheviks. Marcos' fall is the equivalent of the tsar's fall. Enter now the anti-Marcos reactionaries who function as social revolutionaries and Mensheviks. Then, the KT-MR [Manila-Rizal Committee] (like Lenin and other Bolsheviks) will call for the overthrow of the regime of anti-Marcos reactionaries (like the social revolutionaries and Mensheviks) because it is unresponsive to the demands and desires of the people. The party will then launch an insurrection in Manila-Rizal and throw out the reactionary regime (like in the October Revolution). Victory![21]

The ringleaders of the Manila rebellion—the Group of 11, as they became known—began holding secret meetings in a safe house unknown to the Central Committee or to its appointed loyalists on the Manila committee, Jopson and Magpantay. The group tried to line up support among cadres in the countryside in an effort to force the Central Committee to back down and also discussed the possibility of forming a breakaway party.[22] The Group of 11 was confident it would win a theoretical debate with the Central Committee when they met in November. But even more importantly, the rebellious CPP officials were confident they had full control over the huge Manila Party machinery, all the way down to rank-and-file Party members, some 1,000 in all. The sheer size of the Manila Party organization served as a forceful brake on Central Committee actions, a fact that bolstered the rebels' confidence. "That was our leverage," one of the Party rebels recalled a decade later. "That was why the Central Committee could not act drastically," such as ordering the execution of the rebellious Manila officials.

By this time, the dispute had grown much larger than a debate about whether to participate in elections. This was a theoretical discussion of what should be the movement's "mass line." The Central Committee believed the Manila cadres were guilty of serious ideological failure— they had emphasized an anti-Marcos, antifascist political line during the election campaign while ignoring what Mao had established as the equally important antifeudal and antiimperialist elements of the revolution. The Central Committee traced what it saw as the Manila failures back to 1975, when Lagman had become Manila Party secretary and spearheaded the "Lift martial law, call an election" campaign. The CPP leaders scorned the campaign as reformist and likened the Manila cadres to the much vilified "Lavaite revisionists," a slanderous pejorative.[23]

The rebels countered that the anti-Marcos movement was merely "the starting point" for communist propaganda work. "We were using the antifascist line," a Manila Party official said, "only as a starting point to discuss the deeper issues of imperialism and feudalism." The Manila Committee argued that it was crucial to establish alliances with noncommunist forces in an effort to build a broad anti-Marcos front that might bring about the victory of a liberal democratic government. Such a regime, the rebels said, would facilitate the victory of the revolution.[24]

Following a postponement of the struggle meeting ordered by the Central Committee, in mid-January 1979 the entire Manila Committee was summoned to a camp in the Sierra Madre foothills of eastern Nueva Ecija province. The Central Committee was represented by its Executive Committee: Salas; Secretary-General Rafael Baylosis; education chief Benito Tiamzon; Cordillera regional secretary Ignacio Capegsan; and propaganda chief Antonio Zumel. They were supported by three representatives of the Central Luzon Regional Party Committee who were staunch proponents of the Central Committee position.[25]

The dispute had been exacerbated by the fact that Manila cadres were leading a campaign to undermine the new CPP leader by denouncing him and his allies as "left-wing militarists," a reference to Salas' reputation in Central Luzon as an aggressive guerrilla leader. "We feared that Bilog [Salas], with his military background, would lead the movement more toward a military struggle with no emphasis on the urban struggle and politics," one of the Manila rebels told me years later. Adopting the slogan "Oust Bilog and call a national congress," the Group of 11 launched a campaign for a CPP congress at which new leaders could be elected. The Manila cadres believed that Salas and his allies were seeking to crush them because of their opposition to his leadership. The rebels even tried, but failed, to get an appeal for support to Sison, who was being held by the military in solitary confinement.

The atmosphere was grim and tense in the communist camp the morning the struggle meeting opened, and several in the Group of 11 believed they would be executed for their defiance. That ominous prospect seemed even more likely to the Manila rebels when Salas approached before the start of the first session and politely announced, "Comrades, you have to be disarmed." The reason, as Salas explained it, was to avoid any fatal outbursts of temper. The Manila comrades were hardly reassured.[26]

From the opening moments of the discussion, the two sides were bitterly deadlocked. They spent the entire first day debating what points should be placed on the agenda and how broad the scope of the exchange should be. Salas insisted that the lengthy Central Committee position paper should form the basis of discussion. A rancorous debate ensued as Salas began reading. Line by line, day after day, the rebels unrepentantly contested the Central Committee's bill of indictment and refused to budge an inch. Three weeks after beginning, they had covered barely the first 20 pages of the paper without reaching a consensus on a single point.

As the days dragged on, the Group of 11 grew increasingly pessimistic. The rebel cadres had believed that Tiamzon, a former Manila SDK activist, was sympathetic to their cause. They had banked on Tiamzon persuading his colleagues to show leniency toward them, but now it seemed that would not happen. Desperate, the Manila committee played its last cards.

Two of the rebels requested a private meeting with Salas and Tiamzon. One told the Executive Committee officials about the secret meetings of the Group of 11, the talk of forming a breakaway party, and the rebellious mood of Manila CPP cadres. Both rebels claimed they had broad support within the powerful Manila Party organization and concluded with a warning of the fragile situation the Central Committee faced. The message to the CPP leaders was unmistakable: Mishandle the affair, and the Manila rebels will split the Party.[27]

Stunned by the exchange, Salas immediately recessed the struggle meeting, and convened an emergency meeting of the Executive Committee. The CPP leaders hastily decided that the rebels must be isolated. Lagman and his two deputies were placed under de facto arrest in a tent away from the others. The Executive Committee then sat down with the rest of the Group of 11 and began questioning them about their plotting. The rebels freely admitted they had talked of forming a maverick committee to openly challenge the Central Committee's leadership. Having heard enough, Salas abruptly adjourned the gathering.

Before the Manila Committee was allowed to return to the capital, Salas and Tiamzon formed an ad hoc committee to take over administration of the CPP's national capital region. The six-member committee was to be chaired by Jopson and included Salas protégé Magpantay. Finally, the Executive Committee announced sanctions against the entire Manila Committee. Lagman was suspended from the Party for three years and his deputies for two years each. The remaining eight members of the Group of 11 were given six-month suspensions. Lagman and his wife, Lourdes Garduce, were reassigned to Party work in Nueva Ecija under the watchful eye of the Executive Committee. Four months later, Garduce was killed in an encounter with soldiers. Lagman endured his punishment and "reeducation" and by the 1980s had begun a quiet rise back through Party ranks.

The ad hoc Manila-Rizal Committee took power in March 1979 and immediately launched a rectification campaign to stamp out vestiges of the rebellion. Seminars were conducted for CPP cadres and activists that stressed the "inviolable" principles of Marxist-Leninism such as Party unity and "organizational discipline." On June 14, 1979, only a few weeks into the campaign, the entire Manila Committee was captured in a dawn raid on an underground house in the suburb of Las Piñas. Tiamzon narrowly avoided the military dragnet. He had visited the house the day before and was scheduled to return that afternoon.[28]

The arrests plunged the Party's Manila organization deeper into chaos. Among the booty captured by the military was a filing cabinet that contained detailed biographical data and the underground names of 80 percent of the Manila CPP members and the legal organizations to which they belonged. A series of arrests followed, forcing scores of activists underground.

The Manila rebellion was arguably the most serious crisis the CPP had faced in its first decade of existence. Never had the Party leadership faced such a direct challenge to its authority, and the threat of a crippling schism came perilously close to reality. Luckily for the CPP, the damage was largely contained within the capital region. In at least one region outside Manila, the Party leadership also chose to defy the boycott order and supported candidates in the election. Unlike Manila, the Bicol Party organization obediently accepted a Central Committee reprimand, and the crisis passed.[29]

Ironically, the Manila rebellion ended with the issue that ignited the entire episode—the boycott order—never having been discussed, much less resolved. An opportunity to carefully redefine CPP policies toward the prickly issues of participation in elections and alliances with non-communists was allowed to pass. Instead, the bitter debate was resolved organizationally—through a purge—rather than through careful analysis and broad-based agreement on policies. Seven years later, the failure to address the deeper questions underlying the rebellion would result in another decision to boycott an election and a disastrous CPP setback.

11

The New People's Army
Tastes Success

By the late 1970s, having experimented with tactics for much of their first decade, the New People's Army rebels had gained a measure of expertise in the tasks of organizing political support and waging guerrilla warfare. Those who had survived the years of running and hiding in the countryside were a hardy mix of former student activists, peasants, and lower-class urban workers. Gradually, they had melded into a tough, disciplined army. In Bicol, Mindanao, the Cagayan valley and Cordillera Mountains of northern Luzon, and the central islands of Negros and Panay—on virtually every major island in the archipelago—the plucky guerrillas painstakingly had built solid bases of support.

Throughout the decade, conditions had grown increasingly favorable for revolution. Martial law had not solved the nation's critical social, economic, and political problems, as Marcos had promised in 1972. His authoritarian "New Society" had merely engendered a new elite to replace the traditional landed aristocracy at the top of the country's social pyramid. Rural poverty and landlessness had scarcely been addressed, and the land tenancy problem had even worsened. Leaseholders on rice and coconut lands were still typically paying anywhere from 33 to 50 percent of each year's crop to the landlord.[1] Peasants continued to be forced off their lands by wealthy urban dwellers and foreign agribusiness concerns with well-placed connections in the government. Failing to solve any of the nation's pressing problems, martial law had managed to create new ones.

A negative product of martial law that had perhaps the single greatest impact on the country was the rapid rise of corruption in the military and thus the AFP's deterioration. Filipinos had traditionally taken pride in an armed forces that, unlike the armies of neighboring Southeast Asian countries, for the most part had remained out of business and politics and in the barracks. That changed dramatically with the imposition of martial law. Military officers suddenly found themselves in potentially lucrative government jobs with the political and economic power to lord it over those outside the armed forces. A growing number succumbed to temptation.

At the same time, Marcos reacted to the spread of the communist rebellion and the outbreak of a Muslim secessionist movement in the countryside by dramatically increasing the size of the AFP. The armed forces, whose troop size in 1967 was 45,000, had a strength of 164,000 soldiers by 1977.[2] AFP units saturated those areas where the communists were active, militarizing much of the countryside. It became commonplace for soldiers to treat virtually anyone living in an area of rebel activity as a communist sympathizer subject to threats, arrest, or summary execution.

The rapid expansion of the armed forces and broadening of their powers led to a breakdown of discipline within the ranks. Corruption became endemic, reaching to the highest levels of the AFP. On the local level, corruption often took the form of soldiers at a checkpoint extorting money or produce from peasants on their way to market, or patrolling troops expropriating a farmer's chicken. Public drunkenness among AFP units became a chronic problem and led to further abuses against the citizenry.

The covert torture and murder of suspected guerrillas and their sympathizers became standard practices in the AFP's war against the rebels; these practices led to the arrest and torture, and sometimes to the summary execution, of innocent civilians.[3] As part of the government's counterinsurgency strategy, Marcos authorized the formation of local militias known first as Barrio Self-Defense Units, and later as the Civilian Home Defense Force (CHDF). But the program was corrupted from the start by local mayors who created the units to act as bodyguards and to terrorize political opponents. The militia units, although armed by the government, were given little or no training. Frequently, village outcasts were recruited, armed with automatic rifles, and given virtual free rein to do as they pleased.

A CHDF unit I encountered in the northern Mindanao coastal town of Manticao in 1984 was led by a religious mystic named Nene Butak who claimed to have discovered the "lost books of Moses" and who led his men on nightly forays in search of communist guerrillas. The troops wore small homemade amulets in the shape of a Jewish menorah, which Butak and his men swore shielded them from communist bullets.

Traveling around the Philippines in the final two years of Marcos' rule, I heard numerous accounts of CHDF abuses, and the Manila press carried frequent accounts of extrajudicial killings and other excesses by militia forces against civilians. Perhaps the most shocking case was the April 1985 public murder of Italian priest Tullio Favali by a particularly notorious CHDF unit in the insurgency-wracked Mindanao town of Tulunan, North Cotabato province.

By the late 1970s, the effects of militarization and human rights abuses by government soldiers had become a primary, if not the single most important, reason that thousands of rural Filipinos joined or supported the NPA.[4] Capitalizing adroitly on the combined effects of steadily worsening economic conditions and an increasingly abusive army, the communist guerrillas gained entree and won acceptance in an increasing number of villages throughout the Philippines. For the NPA, the late 1970s marked a period of dizzying growth and success that carried into the next decade.

On a wilting tropical summer day in April 1988, in an NPA camp in the spectacular Cordillera Mountains of northern Luzon, I met a 28-year-old communist officer who was the product of that late-1970s matrix of economic misfortune and military abuse. The young man, who had adopted the rather unusual nom de guerre Ka Happy, was the commander of an NPA company operating in the provinces of Nueva Vizcaya and Quirino. We sat on the baked ground beneath a grove of scrubby trees, the brutal midsummer heat shimmering from the mountainsides, as Happy retraced his path into the revolution.

He had grown up in Barangay Naddungan, a barrio of the Cagayan province municipality of Gattaran, about 100 miles north of where he and his men were now operating. Naddungan was a typically sleepy Philippine farming village in which families lived in bamboo-and-thatch huts in the Sierra Madre foothills and along the fringes of rice paddies. The village was sandwiched with several others like it into a narrow valley between two outcroppings of the Sierra Madres bisected by the muddy Dummon River. Poorer families such as Happy's were forced to farm homesteads on the less productive hillsides.

Happy's father was a rice farmer who owned a hectare of land, rented another hectare, and paid the landowner one-third of each year's crop. Happy described a childhood of severe poverty, remembering one month when things got so bad that the family of nine had only a cup of rice to split among them each day. He attended classes through the fifth grade, walking two hours over hilly, dirt trails from the family's thatch hut to the nearest school. While clearing brush during his sixth grade year, he cut his leg very badly and never returned to school. In 1977, when he was 17, Happy met his first NPA guerrillas. The rebels stayed for a week at a time in the barrio conducting seminars. Happy became the NPA liaison officer for his village. Government soldiers first started visiting Naddungan in 1978 on occasional patrols and roughly questioned villagers about the presence of rebels. The soldiers took an even greater interest in Happy's village after the NPA ambushed an army unit nearby, killing four soldiers, and capturing several weapons.[5]

The turning point for Happy's flirtations with the communist movement occurred in 1979. One of his brothers had been helping set up a clandestine Party organization in their barrio. One day, the brother was detained by soldiers at a checkpoint and accused of being a communist. When Happy's brother refused to reveal the names of other villagers working with the NPA, the soldiers burned his mouth with cigarettes, submerged him in a barrel of water, beat him, then buried him in a pit up to his head. Word of his arrest reached the village, and his family and neighbors hurried to town en masse to ask for his release. Happy's brother was badly injured but still alive when his family took him home. He died a few days later.

Happy's parents had no legal means for demanding justice. Had they even attempted to bring the soldiers up on charges, they would have risked retribution. As was the case in many localities throughout the Philippines in the 1970s (and in the 1980s), the benefits of local government were virtually nonexistent in Gattaran for all but a privileged few. The mayor, who remained in office throughout the 1970s, was "greedy and corrupt," the local military commander recalled years later, and the police and militia forces were "abusive" toughs who acted on the mayor's every command.[6]

Another of Happy's brothers and six other youths from Naddungan later got a taste of the mayor's idea of law and order. The young men were arrested by the mayor's bodyguards one day in Gattaran and were accused of being communists. They were stripped naked and forced to march around town. Before releasing the youths, the mayor's police and CHDF contingent burned them with cigarettes. Afterward, all seven young men joined the NPA. As residents of Naddungan became more and more supportive of the rebels, government soldiers started putting up signs outside the homes of villagers listing the names and aliases of family members who had joined the NPA. In some cases, entire families joined the communist army.[7] By 1980, Cagayan province had become one of the fiercest battlegrounds between the rapidly expanding communist army and government forces. The war was played out in a savage fashion, with each side attempting to win the loyalties, or at least the acquiescence, of rural villagers. Nowhere was the war more hotly contested than in Barangay Naddungan.

When the NPA guerrillas began operating in the barrios, they killed the *carabao* thieves and other unpopular elements. "You could leave anything out and there was no more stealing," one resident recalled. "It was good." Later, the executions were extended to include suspected informers and outspoken anticommunists. Soon local vendettas were being settled. Civilians sympathetic to one side or the other became the victims in almost daily killings. In one instance in Barangay Calaoagan, about a mile south of Naddungan, an elementary school teacher alleged to have told the army about NPA activities was riddled with bullets during a lunch recess. The barrio captain and another teacher were also shot to death by rebels.[8]

Government soldiers and CHDF members contributed in no small way to the carnage by torturing and summarily executing suspected communist sympathizers and terrorizing villagers. The constabulary unit stationed in the area in 1982 was accused of committing many abuses against civilians.[9] Soldiers tried four times in 1980 to establish an outpost in Naddungan. Four times, the farmers who constituted the local NPA militia burned the outpost. When villagers were forced by the soldiers to rebuild the camp, they dumped feces around the perimeter. The stench became so overwhelming that the soldiers left the camp. As soon as they were gone, the villagers burned it again.[10]

The military tried to "win" Barangay Naddungan and break the resistance of villagers through a variety of heavy-handed tactics. The soldiers practiced "strategic hamletting," forcing families to move into more populated areas under army supervision. The army also burned the houses of suspected NPA sympathizers. But in their zeal to defeat the communists, the soldiers drove more people into the ranks of the rebel army. One classic example occurred in 1981, when government soldiers entered Naddungan at dusk looking for NPA rebels who were reported to have been resting in the village. Spotting the soldiers, a farmer ran to his house. The soldiers apparently mistook him for a guerrilla seeking cover and opened fire on the bamboo hut. When the shooting stopped, the man's wife and three of his children—ages three, five, and seven—were dead. The farmer survived but sustained a wound that required the amputation of one arm. When he recovered, he joined the NPA.[11]

By 1982, eastern Cagayan had become, in military parlance, one of the most "critical" areas in the country. The region supported as many as 300 full-time guerrillas. The regional CPP headquarters was based in the Sierra Madre foothills near the villages of Naddungan and Calaoagan. Teachers would ring the school bells to warn the guerrillas of approaching military patrols, and even town council members were working with the rebel army.[12] Eighty people from Naddungan—a barrio of 300 families—had joined the New People's Army. Happy had become an NPA propaganda officer in 1980 and a full-fledged guerrilla two years later. In the six years that followed, he fought in 20 battles across the northern Luzon provinces of Cagayan, Isabela, Kalinga-Apayao, Mountain, Ifugao and Nueva Vizcaya.

The government had finally regained effective control of the rural barrios of Gattaran by 1984, but at a staggering price. By the conservative estimate of the former local military commander, government forces had killed more than 30 villagers suspected of being guerrillas or CPP organizers. The former commander accused the communists of killing up to 500 people between 1977 and 1985.[13] Although the latter number may be considerably inflated, villagers remember the deaths of scores of civilians at the hands of the rebels and government forces. But of greater significance was the number of people driven by the excesses of arrogant local officials and soldiers to join the communist movement. Years after the armed forces had "pacified" Barangay Naddungan and neighboring villages, Happy, three of his brothers, and scores of other men and women from eastern Cagayan's rural barrios were carrying the communist revolution across the provinces of northern Luzon.

Whereas an ill-disciplined army and the failures of local government were the primary factors accelerating the expansion of the NPA in some areas, the harsh convergence of the issues of land grabbing and military abuses turned Mindanao into a fertile breeding ground for revolution in the late 1970s. CPP organizing teams that had struggled for much of the decade suddenly saw the number of recruits double, then triple and quadruple, while the number of guerrilla zones multiplied.

Victor Cambaya was living in a village in Agusan del Sur province when he first encountered the NPA guerrillas in 1976. His family was cultivating cacao, coffee, and coconuts on 20 abandoned hectares. Like most of their neighbors, the Cambayas did not hold the title to the land, and so they lived in constant fear of eviction. In 1977, 14-year-old Cambaya decided to join the rebels who spoke earnestly of improving the lot of peasant families. "When I joined the movement," he told me 10 years later, "I was convinced the objectives were good. They told me that if the revolution won, I could go to school free. Everything would be free. Life would be easy." In 1982, Cambaya's father and two brothers were beaten and hacked to death with machetes by soldiers from the Philippine Army's Thirty-seventh Infantry Battalion. Along with his dreams of a better life for his family and his children, Cambaya added revenge to his motives for joining the revolution.

By the end of the 1970s, the NPA had passed the initial test of survival. According to credible communist accounts, Commander Dante's band of 50 rebels had mushroomed to a force of 8,000 full-time and part-time farmer-guerrillas fighting in 43 of the country's 73 provinces. The communist fighters were supervised by 12 regional Party commands scattered from one end of the archipelago to the other. The Communist Party began martial law in 1972 with 2,000 members and by the end of the 1970s claimed 10,000 members.[14]

The NPA's first decade had been devoted to the opening of strategically placed guerrilla zones and larger fronts throughout the archipelago. Small, poorly armed forces struggled to develop communist mass organizations and local Party units. The NPA's standard formation in the 1970s was the squad, with anywhere from 6 to 12 members, operating as an armed propaganda unit. In some of the fronts that enjoyed early success, platoons and even larger formations were established, but these were the exception. Military operations in those first years were modest and targetted "local informers, bad elements, policemen, CHDF units" and squad-size regular government military units.[15]

As the NPA grew, the guerrilla commanders adopted more aggressive tactics that quadrupled the communist arsenal from 1,000 high-powered rifles in 1976 to 4,000 in 1980. In 1981, CPP leaders began a military buildup aimed at transforming the NPA from a scattered network of armed propaganda units devoted to political work into a regular guerrilla army primarily concerned with military operations. Political organizing work was turned over to Party mass organizations and local units, while the NPA devoted its energies to the development of regular squad-size to platoon-size guerrilla units.[16]

The revolution marked the beginning of its second decade under a leadership vastly changed from the one Sison had handpicked to attend the Pangasinan founding congress in early 1969. Turnover in the CPP's Central Committee was high as a series of arrests and defections kept the leadership in flux throughout the 1970s. The upheaval culminated with the 1976 arrest of Commander Dante and the November 1977 arrest of Sison. The CPP chairmanship was assumed by Rodolfo Salas, the former UP engineering student and KM activist who had been trained by Sison more than a decade earlier and who hewed closely to his mentor's staunchly Maoist orientation.

That the movement scarcely faltered following the capture of one top leader after another is a tribute to Sison's foresight and planning. He had insisted from the beginning that the Party develop a deep pool of cadres to replenish those who fell along the way. Strict adherence to the Leninist principle of committee leadership, as opposed to the PKP's tendency toward one-person rule, had further lessened the impact of the loss of high-ranking CPP leaders. By the time Sison finally fell into government hands, Salas was well prepared to assume command of the revolution. He had experience in the mass movement from his days organizing KM chapters in Central Luzon under the threat of assassination from Commander Sumulong's Huk forces; he also had been actively involved in the development of NPA guerrilla warfare and had personally planned and led ambushes in the 1970s.

However experienced he was in the political and military struggles of the revolution, Salas could not have prepared for the serious dislocation within the CPP hierarchy caused by Sison's arrest. "We had no money. We had no files. We didn't know the leaders in the other regions," he told me in 1988. The Central Committee had been reduced to five members, and Salas was the only surviving member of the Executive Committee, which was supposed to run the day-to-day affairs of the revolution. Using couriers, Salas contacted regional Party leaders around the country. Many of them, however, were reluctant to travel to Manila to meet the new chairman for fear of arrest. "We had to persuade them to please see us," he recalled. "Some came after two years."

By 1979, Salas had engineered the reconstruction of the Party hierarchy, including the election of a new five-member Executive Committee. But the leadership was still dominated by Sison's student radical protégés. Benito Tiamzon and Rafael Baylosis were from a younger crop of leaders, First Quarter Storm activists who had begun their careers as revolutionaries within the Marxist cells of KM and SDK. The two leaders least associated with Sison were Antonio Zumel and Ignacio Capegsan. Zumel had been an editor and union activist at the *Manila Bulletin* prior to martial law and his defection to the underground. Capegsan, a student activist in the mountain city of Baguio, was a member of one of northern Luzon's ethnic hill tribes trained in Isabela under Victor Corpus.

After surviving the challenge to his leadership posed by the 1978–1979 Manila region Party rebellion, Salas led the NPA to its greatest growth. By the early 1980s, larger guerrilla formations had enabled the NPA to launch more frequent and coordinated military operations. Support units were developed and military training improved. For the first time, NPA units began attacking town centers, municipal police stations, and isolated military outposts. Communist forces on Samar had expanded so rapidly by 1981 and were so effectively carrying out guerrilla operations that the Central Committee ordered the island command to curtail its military activities and transfer some of its military cadres to other Visayan islands.[17] By the end of 1983, the communist leadership reported the size of the rebel army to be nearly 20,000 full-time Red fighters, militia, and combat support personnel. A shortage of weapons, however, continued to slow the realization of the NPA's offensive desires.

By the early 1980s, the New People's Army was still a relatively small, lightly armed guerrilla force wedded to a hit-and-run war of nerves against a vastly superior government army. In Maoist terms, the NPA remained in the defensive stage of people's war. What made the rebel army a challenge to be taken seriously was the rapidly expanding communist political organization sinking deep roots in the countryside. More than a decade earlier, Sison had sketched the extravagant blueprint for a Philippine people's war in which a much weaker communist army would gradually force the government to spread its troops thinner and thinner to the point of exhaustion and eventual collapse. As the communists entered their fifteenth year of revolution in 1984, Sison's scenario of locking government forces in a stalemate loomed as a stunning possibility in the not-too-distant future.

12

The Battle for Davao

By the early 1980s, Davao was on the verge of becoming the Philippines' second largest city. The sprawling southern port was home to 700,000 people scattered over a vast incorporated area that ranged from densely packed slums to isolated rural villages. It was a rough-and-tumble place with a Wild West reputation where Japanese, Chinese and U.S. entrepreneurs had ventured to make their fortunes in timber and fishing prior to World War II. In the years that followed the war, tens of thousands of Filipino pioneers from Luzon and the Visayas had boarded ships for Mindanao, the "land of promise," as it became known. Many settled in Davao, while others fanned out across the fertile countryside. The city's importance as a vital center of trade and shipping grew as timber, bananas, pineapples, copra, corn, and hemp flowed from the island's interior through Davao on the way to Manila and foreign destinations.

The economic boom years of the 1960s and early 1970s gave way to hard times, due in no small part to the Marcos regime's neglect of Mindanao, and Davao was fast gaining a new notoriety. The city was on the cutting edge of the communist revolution that by the early 1980s had transformed Mindanao into the New People's Army's most impressive stronghold. The NPA had brought its war to Davao as early as 1977 when small squads—sparrow units—began carrying out assassinations and arms-grabbing operations targeting individual soldiers and police. By 1983, the urban attacks had been expanded to what the NPA called "armed city partisan" warfare, with rebel squads armed with automatic rifles assigned full-time to the city and based in slums where the guerrillas enjoyed considerable support.[1]

It had taken communist forces more than a decade of frustrations and failures to reach that point in Davao. During the first four years of martial law, the CPP maintained only a skeleton force of cadres and activists in Davao and other urban centers of Mindanao. Those Party activists who remained in the cities devoted their efforts to providing technical and material support for communist forces in the countryside. Resources were simply too precious for Mindanao's Party organization to risk squandering them on uncertain urban political ventures.[2]

Gradually, CPP cadres on Mindanao saw a need to upgrade the movement's urban activities. Cadres found that the rural population was highly mobile and that even peasants usually spent part of their lives living and working in urban areas. Thus, the cadres concluded, urban areas were more important in the Philippines than in prerevolution China or Russia, which made the development of a city-based mass movement a priority.[3]

An effort to revive Davao's legal mass movement as a principal form of struggle was initiated in 1976. Taking a cue from NPA armed propaganda units in the countryside, two- and three-person propaganda teams went house to house recruiting and organizing support in city slums.[4] Lucas Fernández, the nom de guerre of a Party cadre who arrived in Davao in 1977, was assigned to a CPP campaign that was developing the youth and student movement and building a united front with noncommunist elements. He recalled how the Party began rebuilding and strengthening its Davao organization:

> There were some legal organizations in Davao which we were able to sort of influence. In fact, there were some we took the initiative in setting up. One of the first organizations was a human rights organization. Then there were also certain Church organizations and institutions which we were able to influence. We were able to set up ND [national democratic] groups consisting of people who were involved in Church organizations and human rights organizations. We were able to influence, though not too successfully, a consumer organization. There were a lot of professionals involved in the human rights groups which were being established, and even the consumer group. We also had some contacts in the local media and even among government employees.[5]

Through the work of CPP activists within the consumer group, the Party was able to broaden its ties with Davao professionals, business-people and other influential elements of the middle-class who were being cultivated by the underground for possible material and logistical support. Far more successful, Fernández recalled, were the Party's efforts to influence and shape the agenda of the Church groups and human rights organizations that proliferated in the late 1970s. Nurtured by a fertile environment of economic crisis and mounting military abuses against civilians, the communists enjoyed rapid growth. Between 1978 and 1985, the urban Davao CPP organization saw its membership increase twentyfold from 50 to about 1,000 Party members.[6]

The communist successes in Davao were enhanced by the rapid growth of the NPA throughout Mindanao in the late 1970s and early 1980s. Under the leadership of NPA military specialist Romulo Kintanar and political strategists Edgar Jopson and Benjamin de Vera, the Mindanao Party organization aggressively experimented with new tactics in urban areas and the countryside. Bold offensive military actions using newly developed NPA platoons and companies of up to 100 fighters enabled communist forces to rapidly add recruits and arms while steadily expanding their area of operations on the island. By 1984, NPA platoon- and company-size units were operating in 16 Mindanao provinces.[7]

With Davao taking the lead on the political front, the CPP graduated from conducting local campaigns and mobilizations fashioned around popular issues to Mindanao-wide coordinated mass campaigns. The communists joined forces with noncommunist political opposition groups in a successful boycott of a 1981 presidential election called by Marcos. Mindanao Party leaders built on that success in 1982 and 1983, conducting more sophisticated island-wide urban campaigns that spotlighted issues such as human rights abuses and a deepening economic depression. By the time of the August 1983 assassination of Benigno Aquino, the CPP had developed a legal and underground urban network linking the cities of Mindanao.[8] When sustained protests broke out following the assassination, the CPP had the organizations and expertise to manipulate the ideologically diverse anti-Marcos movement.

Unable to catch the elusive sparrow units operating with growing impunity in Davao, frustrated military intelligence teams focused their fury on the communist underground's legal front organizations, which were expanding rapidly. Activists were arrested, and an increasing number were summarily executed. In one typical case, soldiers arrested three young men on November 13, 1983, and took them to the constabulary barracks for interrogation. One of the young men was 29-year-old Robertson Ignacio, son of the chairman of the Alliance of Urban Poor, a CPP creation for organizing slum dwellers. Later that evening, the three men were taken to the harbor front and shot to death.[9]

Avelino Ignacio, a weather-beaten fellow who looked much older than his 52 years when I met him in 1984, recalled going with his wife to the barracks to ask for the whereabouts of his son hours after his arrest only to be told that his son was not there. On a subsequent visit, Ignacio was told that, yes, his son had been arrested and accused of murdering a soldier. But there had been an accident. His son had been shot while trying to escape, a soldier said.

For more than a month, the military prevented the Ignacios from claiming their son's body, which had been buried in an unmarked grave in Digos, a town 30 miles south of Davao. Soldiers even prevented family members from entering the cemetery. It took the family more than a month to secure a court order allowing them to claim the body. Grave 3421 in the Digos municipal cemetery was opened on December 20, 1983. The decomposing corpse Avelino Ignacio identified as that of his son had a bullet wound in the head, a broken leg, and what appeared to be knife slashes on parts of his body.

Ignacio clutched his son's death certificate as he recounted this story the day before his family gathered for a private Mass on the first anniversary of his son's death. He had gone into hiding a few days after the funeral when arsonists burned his small shop, he explained. Now he did not hide his support for the revolution or his bitterness toward the government.

Strengthened by the support of people like Avelino Ignacio, NPA partisan units in Davao became bolder in their activities. They attacked soldiers and police accused of abusing citizens, assassinated alleged military informers, and punished—often by execution—local criminal elements. The NPA increased its base of support by providing protection to striking workers who faced harassment from business owners and to urban squatters who lived in fear of eviction from their makeshift homes. Communist-influenced organizations mobilized almost daily demonstrations or pickets somewhere in the city, while small guerrilla units harassed AFP forces on city streets and in rural Davao outposts.

The CPP's Mindanao leaders had good reason to feel buoyant as they gathered in the countryside of Agusan del Norte province in December 1983 to discuss plans for the coming year. The meeting brought together the full Mindanao Commission, led by de Vera, the political chief; Kintanar, the military commander; and Lucas Fernández, the urban strategist. Much of the discussion focused on a single topic: urban insurrection. Even before the Aquino assassination, Davao cadres had discussed the possibility that the surging protest movement could lead to a popular insurrection.[10] The cadres were encouraged by what they read about the Sandinistas' victory in Nicaragua and the integration of rural and urban political and military warfare in South Vietnam.

A leading proponent of the insurrection theory was Fernández, who had been elevated from the Davao Party Committee to the Mindanao Commission to supervise the island-wide development of the urban mass movement. Now, with the entire Mindanao Commission gathered, Davao Party leaders and their supporters on the commission raised the intriguing proposition: Might it be possible for the revolutionary movement to cut years off the war by fomenting urban uprisings?

Long days of contentious debates ensued. Gradually, the Mindanao Commission hammered out a rough consensus on a new strategic line that boldly advanced the notion of urban insurrection, rather than the long-dreamed-of NPA general offensive, leading the movement to victory. With unbridled excitement, the Mindanao Commission endorsed the "fast-track insurrection" strategy as the shortcut to victory.[11]

In January 1984, Fernández was summoned to Manila by the Central Committee to brief the national CPP leadership on the state of the urban movement on Mindanao and to receive instructions on plans to boycott the May 1984 parliamentary elections. Fernández used the opportunity to promote the fast-track insurrection theory. As Salas and other Executive Committee members listened, Fernández explained the insurrection strategy. "They just listened to me and then they didn't comment too much afterward," Fernández told me later. "They said we were still preparing for some sort of a strategic counteroffensive leading to a strategic stalemate. I was a bit disappointed."

If the CPP hierarchy was less than enthused by the insurrection strategy, the Mindanao Party leaders were undeterred. The Mindanao Commission issued a treatise declaring its acceptance of a Vietnamese-style "politico-military" strategic framework that differed from the Philippine movement's traditional Maoist model by emphasizing the equal importance of political and military tactics in the countryside and cities.[12] The Mindanao Commission statement exhorted Party cadres to "[prepare] our forces for armed uprisings of the masses in the future."

Mindanao Party leaders capitalized on the worsening economic crisis and labor unrest by organizing the first *welgang bayan*, or "people's strike," in Davao in August 1984. The CPP's answer to the general strike of more developed nations, the *welgang bayan* was a combination of work stoppages and coordinated demonstrations and rallies. With the Philippines lacking a strong industrial base that could be paralyzed by a conventional general strike, Party leaders expanded the targetted sectors to include public transportation, teachers, government employees, and other key areas in the country's economy and society.

Encouraged by the results of the initial Davao strike, the island's Party officials organized a series of *welgang bayan* and transport strikes in the final months of 1984, including a Mindanao-wide strike in

November. The actions were led by the Coalition of Organizations for the Realization of Democracy, a CPP-conceived united front vehicle that had succeeded in forging an alliance between the Party's legal elements and mainstream opposition politicians. The enormous success of the strikes led Party organizations on Luzon and in the Visayan islands to quickly adopt the *welgang bayan* as a new form of legal struggle against the Marcos government.

By 1984, the communist movement was mobilizing forces on several fronts and steadily consolidating its influence in Davao. Communist organizing teams conducted nightly political teach-ins in lower-class neighborhoods. Communist tax collectors filled Party coffers with "donations" solicited from businesspeople, some of whom were sympathetic, others simply fearful of reprisals. Communist-influenced trade unions paralyzed business operations, while armed sparrow units answered labor repression or abusive police and military actions with bloody retribution. Government propaganda in the local press and on radio was matched word for word by communist propagandists positioned in legal fronts and by sympathizers in the media. During the November *welgang bayan*, communist partisans in the sprawling Agdao slum district jubilantly hoisted the CPP's flag—a white hammer and sickle emblazoned on a field of red.

Alarmed government and military officials attempted to respond to the growing communist presence in Davao by stepping up police and military raids and patrols. AFP units conducted neighborhood sweeps known as zoning operations in areas suspected of supporting the communists. But the arrests and the growing number of summary executions—"salvagings," as the extrajudicial killings were dubbed—committed by security forces and their agents steeled resistance. "One of the most positive effects of militarization," a communist cadre told me in late 1984, "is that the people have become politicized. The NPA's intelligence comes from the masses."

The political killings spiraled out of control throughout 1984. The local authorities' preoccupation with fighting the NPA guerrillas led to a breakdown in law enforcement, and criminal syndicates operating with impunity added to the violence and chaos. Davao was swept by a rash of armed robberies and kidnappings for ransom. Prominent families began receiving extortion letters purportedly written by the rebels, although the communist leadership blamed most of the activities on criminal gangs masquerading as the NPA. In some cases, government soldiers and police were deeply involved in the criminal syndicates.[13]

The year drew to a close with a series of sensational attacks. In quick succession, communist assassins killed three AFP intelligence agents at noontime on a busy downtown street and a few days later gunned down three traffic police at point-blank range at a busy downtown intersection. On November 11, 1984, Father Allan O'Brien was midway through Sunday evening Mass at the crowded Redemptorist Church when a young man rose from his pew and fired two quick shots into the head of the man in front of him, Rodolfo Aquino, a Davao police officer. Aquino was the brother of Wilfredo "Baby" Aquino, the notoriously brutal, anticommunist *barangay* captain of Davao's Agdao slum, a communist stronghold. The NPA assassin calmly pocketed Aquino's service revolver, walked out of the Church, and boarded a passing bus.[14]

Government forces were just as active—and just as brutal. Twenty-six-year-old Mario Canello was picked up by soldiers during a zoning operation in his neighborhood of Davao's Toril district on December 8, 1984. Ten days later, Canello's headless body was discovered a few miles away. The body of a friend arrested with Canello, José Villano, was discovered 12 miles north of the city, his throat slashed. Canello and Villano were but two of 854 people murdered in Davao in 1984, most of whom were believed to be victims of insurgency-related killings.[15]

On a typically sultry tropical Sunday afternoon in November 1984, a CPP cadre working at a Davao human rights agency gave me a tour of the city. As we passed along Claveria Street, he pointed to the spot where a military intelligence agent was killed while walking his daughter to school a few days earlier. The city market area had became a haven for communist sparrows, and on this afternoon, the market was filled with vendors selling mangoes, jackfruits, watermelons, papayas, pineapples, fish, and shrimp. The military had made it a practice to sweep through the market area once a week hoping to snare, or at least flush out, the guerrillas. Poorly paid soldiers and police sometimes forced the vendors to pay extortion in kind or in cash.

Suddenly, my Party guide pointed to a cigarette vendor who brushed past us. The fellow, perhaps in his early thirties, clad in blue jeans, a striped polo shirt, and a plastic sun visor, blended effortlessly into the throng. The "vendor," my guide said, was the NPA assassin who had killed the intelligence officer the week before. We turned and watched the gunman stroll casually up the street with his wooden tray of cigarettes past a storefront constabulary outpost, until he disappeared into the crowd.

The unrest in Davao that facilitated communist organizing was exacerbated by a confluence of national ills: a deepening economic crisis, corrupt and inefficient government, an arrogant and ill-disciplined army and national police force. Local officials estimated that 20,000 Davao workers lost their jobs in 1984 because of the closure or retrenchment of city businesses. The Davao economy had virtually ground to a halt by 1985. The year began with 40 members of the Davao Chamber of Commerce announcing their intention to leave the city if the security situation did not improve. New construction and investment had slowed to a trickle. Three large companies were trying to close, and the local military commander was begging them to remain open, lest the layoffs worsen the deteriorating security situation.[16]

The economic crisis had deeply affected the lives of Davao's hundreds of thousands of slum dwellers, and made them easy targets for communist propaganda. The city's largest and most notorious slum, Agdao, had became so synonomous with violence and communist strength that local residents began calling the area Nicar-Agdao, after the war-torn Central American country. Actually a single *barangay*, Agdao was home to an estimated 125,000 people, nearly one-fifth of Davao's population in 1984, packed into a filthy, disease-ridden community of tumbledown shacks thrown up along the polluted Davao seafront. The slum had long been marked by tension between impoverished residents who had built shacks on vacant land and businesspeople who claimed ownership of the property. Once known for its criminal gangs, by 1984 Agdao had become known as the urban Davao stronghold of the NPA.

Communist success in organizing Agdao was due in no small part to the repressive administration of the slum's *barangay* captain. Although barely four feet tall, hunchbacked and grotesque looking, Baby Aquino struck fear in the hearts of Agdao's residents. He ruled the slum with an iron hand backed by a 40-member militia force armed with automatic rifles and the authority to terrorize and murder. Amid the grinding poverty of Agdao, Aquino's businesses—a massage parlor, disco-strip club, cockfight arena, and a motel specializing in rooms by the hour—prospered.

Communist cells also flourished amid the poverty, unemployment, and despair of Agdao, despite Aquino's brutal best efforts to block the underground organizers. By 1984, the NPA had gained the upper hand in the battle to control the slum. Urban guerrilla operations had decimated Aquino's once-feared private army, and only 3 of the original 37 Agdao militia members were still with the force by the end of 1984. The others had been killed by communist assassins or had fled. In fact, the government had effectively ceded much of Agdao to the NPA.[17]

As I wandered through the fetid, garbage-strewn maze of decrepit shacks in July 1985, Agdao residents spoke openly of their hatred for the government and the military. Some people just as openly expressed support and admiration for the New People's Army. Most told similar stories of misfortune at the hands of government soldiers. If there was dissatisfaction with the communist presence, it was muted by fear or acquiescence.

The Flores family was typical of those I encountered. Her husband was unemployed, so Lucila Flores, a middle-aged mother of seven, supported the family by peddling ears of boiled corn from a bucket. On a good week, she earned 100 pesos (about $5 in 1985) to support the family. Frequent military raids, an almost-daily occurrence in some parts of Agdao, had made life more precarious in the slum. Mrs. Flores recalled a typical military zoning operation that had occurred a few weeks earlier, on April 24, 1985. Soldiers had surrounded the neighborhood and fired their guns into the air before conducting a house-to-house search. Four young men were arrested, including Mrs. Flores' 17-year-old son, Henry. He was accused of being an NPA member, "without any evidence," she said, and was charged with subversion, a capital offense. Three months later, Henry Flores was still in jail awaiting a court date that had not been set. "I fear the military," Mrs. Flores told me, "not the NPA."

One of the Flores' neighbors, 70-year-old Mercedes Estella, described Agdao as "the place where the people are deprived of their rights." In 1985, Mrs. Estella had already lived in Agdao for 16 years and had given birth to eight children. Because her family and the majority of Agdao residents did not hold title to the plots where they had built their houses, the government had refused to provide water and other services to much of the slum. The Estellas and their neighbors had to pay 10 centavos for a gallon of water. "If we have no money, we have no water," she said. Her family's scrapwood shack was lit by a single 40-watt bulb jerry-rigged to an illegal electrical hookup.

Mrs. Estella recounted an incident in December 1984 when soldiers had entered Agdao and opened fire with automatic rifles on several houses where sparrows were believed to be hiding. "The military are the ones who cause problems," she insisted. Her neighbor, 40-year-old Hermando Calixijan, echoing CPP propaganda, blamed U.S. government policies for the poverty and oppression in Agdao. "People are 100 percent behind the NPA," he said boldly. Four months earlier, Calixijan's 20-year-old brother-in-law had been killed by soldiers during a raid in Agdao. He was the second of Calixijan's wife's brothers to be killed by the army.

The atmosphere in Davao by early 1985 was so politically charged that Mindanao's CPP leaders had begun to worry that the movement's supporters would rise up in a spontaneous insurrection and attempt to overthrow the local government. Party leaders were exuberant that the insurrection strategy appeared to be succeeding beyond their most ambitious calculations, but their sense of triumph was tempered by fears that they might not be able to control the rebellion.[18] Nevertheless, the CPP pressed the initiative with a series of protest marches, rallies, *welgang bayan*, and other mass actions. On May 2–3, legal Party forces carried out another successful Mindanao-wide *welgang bayan*. Three key leaders of the legal leftist movement were arrested while leading a general strike in Davao, and their detention sparked a new wave of protests. The political developments occurred against the backdrop of escalating violence by both the NPA and security forces. In March 1985, Davao set a single-month record for murders—107—most believed to be insurgency related.[19]

The soaring violence had grabbed the attention of AFP leaders and government officials in Manila as well as the media. Defense Minister Juan Ponce Enrile began describing Davao as the "urban laboratory of the NPA." In a desperate attempt to reverse the slide in Davao, the AFP leadership assigned a pair of tough, 51-year-old colonels to command government forces in Davao.

The officer assigned to the rural districts of Davao, Marine Colonel Rodolfo Biazon, was ramrod straight, more than six feet in height (unusually tall for a Filipino), articulate, and urbane—a cool, measured response to the chaos and violence of Davao. He sketched elaborate charts and graphs emphasizing the political aspects of the communist revolution. The war was a conflict between communism and democracy, Biazon declared, a point he drove home again and again in folksy presentations before civic organizations, schools, churches, and rural village gatherings.

In late 1984, Biazon moved 1,500 soldiers into an area of rural Davao heavily controlled by the NPA. The marines—the only branch of the AFP that had maintained a reputation for discipline—cautiously began patrolling the surrounding barrios. Biazon sat down for gripe sessions with the rebel-sympathizing villagers and coaxed them to air their grievances rather than continue supporting the guerrillas. With his earnest manner, Biazon gradually convinced Davao residents that he was genuinely concerned with their complaints. By mid-1985, a heavy-handed military offensive against communist forces in urban Davao and Biazon's effective campaign among the communist rural strongholds had contributed to an NPA decision to curtail activities in the city.

The year drew to a close with something of a lull in the bloodbath that had ravaged Davao for more than three years. The death toll for 1985 had reached 897, but the number of killings had dropped significantly in the year's closing months.[20] There were suggestions that the relative calm was less the result of government initiatives than of sheer exhaustion on the part of the communists' organized supporters in the city.[21] For three years, the underground had been mobilizing its forces for almost daily demonstrations, marches, rallies, pickets, and strikes. The level of militarization and government repression had continued to rise throughout the period, and the CPP front organizations had suffered heavy losses. The NPA sometimes controlled entire neighborhoods, but government soldiers controlled access to and from those neighborhoods, making it increasingly difficult for the communists to sustain their political and military actions. Furthermore, the attention of the city's communist leadership and AFP commanders had been diverted by dramatic developments in Manila: Marcos had announced the scheduling of a presidential election for February. For the moment, the protagonists in Davao took a respite from their savage war.

13

The Elusive United Front

José María Sison had never concealed his distrust of mainstream politicians. In "Rectify Errors and Rebuild the Party," he had warned that the national bourgeoisie (roughly the middle-class) would betray the revolution if given the chance and was strictly "an ally within a certain period of time and to a certain limited extent." Sison's idea of a united front was a CPP-led organization with a platform that corresponded to that of the Party and whose aim was to "win over the middle forces and elements in order to isolate the die-hard elements."[1] By 1980, these criteria had produced a popular front mechanism—the National Democratic Front—that was a collection of organizations created and led by Party cadres.

In the early years of the revolution, factionalism within the Philippine Left was a recurring obstacle to formation of a broad, enduring popular front. Bitter polemics raging among KM Maoists, the PKP faithful, and Social Democrats led to the 1967 demise of Sison's pre-CPP united front venture, the Movement for the Advancement of Nationalism (MAN). In 1972, the moderately successful Movement for a Democratic Philippines (MDP), a legal CPP creation, met a similar fate.

The declaration of martial law reshaped the political landscape and offered the CPP new opportunities to explore united front possibilities. Reacting shrewdly to the crisis of martial law, Sison proposed the formation of a "broad antifascist, antifeudal and antiimperialist united front." In April 1973, the CPP announced formation of a preparatory commission for the NDF and issued a united front program only to have other potential allies spurn the invitation for an alliance. Fears by other groups that they would be relegated to a meaningless role in a venture with the CPP were underscored by the proposed NDF program, which sounded strikingly similar to the Party's stridently Maoist Programme for a People's Democratic Revolution.[2]

The Central Committee did not share Manila cadres' enthusiasm for the burgeoning spirit of cooperation that existed between the CPP and the "anti-Marcos reactionaries" during the 1970s. Nevertheless, the Manila Party organization succeeded during the 1978 legislative campaign in forming the CPP's first functioning coalition with the estranged forces of the independent Left and political mainstream since the declaration of martial law. But the détente between the CPP's "national democratic" forces and noncommunists rapidly evaporated amid the bitter polemics that erupted between the Central Committee and Manila CPP leaders following the elections.

In 1980, the Party launched a new united front initiative led by a former Marcos administration official, Horacio Morales, who had excellent access to the Manila intelligentsia and upper classes.[3] Morales had been a rising star in the early years of the regime, serving as a presidential executive assistant and later as head of the prestigious martial law think-tank, the Development Academy of the Philippines. On the evening of December 26, 1977, Morales was scheduled to receive an award as one of the Philippines' "Ten Outstanding Young Men." Instead, he had a message read on his behalf announcing his defection to the National Democratic Front. Three years later, Morales was assigned to united front work under the guise of the NDF.[4]

Working within the CPP's strictures—which insisted that any alliance would have to "uncompromisingly be based on the wholehearted acceptance of nothing less than the 10 Point Program of the NDF"— Morales moved to give substance to the struggling front organization. He established a nine-member NDF coordinating committee that included the CPP chairman, an NPA representative, a member of the Marxist-oriented Christians for National Liberation, and representatives of Party-created organizations for academicians, businesspeople, and students. At the same time, Morales began meeting with groups outside the underground attempting to forge alliances with the urban intelligentsia, businesspeople, and other potential middle- and upper-class allies.

In early 1981, Morales, acting as the NDF's de facto chairman, began promoting a boycott of a June presidential election called by Marcos. Morales succeeded in persuading the expected opposition candidate, Gerry Roxas, a former Liberal party senator, not to participate in the election.[5] The boycott won widespread support among the mainstream political opposition, and the June 16 election was widely denounced as a sham in the Philippines and abroad. So buoyed was the CPP leadership that the leadership declared at the end of 1981 that the urban mass movements had made that year "the biggest strides since the U.S.-Marcos clique imposed fascist dictatorial rule in 1972."[6]

If CPP cadres hoped that the boycott success would be a springboard for the emergence of a broad-based front, they were frustrated once again. Morales was arrested in 1982, and efforts to organize the NDF as a functioning body floundered. Even if Morales had not been arrested, it is doubtful that he would have been free to expand the front much further. Salas shared Sison's narrow united front definition and continued to support the strategic line that urban areas should be developed primarily to support the war in the countryside. Salas had taken care to place the NDF under the direct supervision of the Executive Committee, which he headed, rather than allow the Party's United Front Commission chairman—who favored broader alliances with noncommunists—to oversee the popular front project.[7]

Mila Aguilar, who assumed leadership of the United Front Commission in 1980, told me years later that she had been shocked by the "rigid and narrow-minded" concept of united front that governed the Manila cadres and national CPP leadership. Only the basic masses—narrowly defined by Party leaders as lower-class industrial workers and poor and "lower-middle" peasants—were deemed reliable forces for the movement. Manila cadres assigned to united front work were fearful of broadening contacts within the middle and upper classes because the official CPP line emphasized the unreliability of these classes while exalting the lower-class "masses" as the "makers of history." Cadres disgruntled with the CPP leadership's narrow policy began to derisively describe the tenets of the united front program as *pera-bahay-frente* (money-house-front), a mocking reference to the Party's tendency to use middle-class contacts for financial support and shelter without building relationships of mutual interest and trust. "You talk to people only about what you need," one veteran Manila cadre recalled, "nothing more."[8]

Communist cadres were still struggling to build a viable NDF when the CPP received unexpected help from one of the anti-Marcos reactionaries the communists had so often scorned. Returning from three years of self-imposed exile in the United States, Benigno Aquino was assassinated at Manila International Airport on August 21, 1983, while in the custody of military escorts. Marcos blamed the shocking murder on the communists, a charge most Filipinos found ludicrous considering the 1,000-troop security force the AFP had deployed around the airport for Aquino's arrival. Marcos was the "no. 1 suspect," Aquino's widow, Corazón, declared, and millions of Filipinos readily agreed.

Overnight, Manila's streets exploded with angry demonstrations that evoked comparisons to the passion of the 1970 First Quarter Storm. What made these protests even more remarkable was the participation of hundreds of thousands of apolitical Filipinos, including large, influential segments of the middle and upper classes. Wealthy matrons, lawyers, bankers, and businesspeople joined with jeepney drivers, street vendors, and students in huge rallies.

In response to the demonstrations, the Central Committee issued an "Urgent Message to the Filipino People" in October 1983 notable for its accommodating tone toward noncommunist elements that had long been scorned as clerico-fascists and anti-Marcos reactionaries. In an even more jarring about-face, the Party applauded the Marcos Resign movement launched by Aquino's supporters and forces of the middle and upper classes. The newly politicized forces could "weaken the regime," the CPP declared, and "broaden and invigorate the anti-dictatorship movement by rousing and mobilizing . . . the politically timid and inactive sectors of society."[9]

Party cadres played leading roles in establishing legal organizations in alliance with the new political forces. One of the first such groups was Justice for Aquino, Justice for All (JAJA) led by former senator José Diokno, a nationalist and civil libertarian who had remained distrustful of the communists throughout his public life. Another was the Nationalist Alliance for Justice, Freedom, and Democracy headed by venerated nationalist Lorenzo Tañada. Sison's wife, Julieta, became a national council member of the Nationalist Alliance, which emerged as the CPP's strongest legal organization prior to 1985.

In January 1984, one of leading figures of the protest movement spawned by the Aquino assassination, Agapito Aquino, younger brother of the slain senator, spearheaded the formation of the Congress of the Filipino People (Kongreso ng Mamamayang Pilipino, or KOMPIL) as another anti-Marcos united front effort. Aquino invited Party-led forces to send delegates to the gathering and even asked Sison to send an address to the founding congress. Sison was elected in absentia as one of the 15 national council members of KOMPIL.

During two conversations we had in 1988, Salas disclosed extraordinary details of the interaction between the CPP and legal opposition forces during this period. Salas said that Benigno Aquino, prior to his return to Manila, had initiated an exchange of messages between them to discuss some form of alliance. But Salas' most startling revelation was the CPP's role in the formation of KOMPIL. According to Salas, Agapito Aquino turned to the CPP when plans for founding KOMPIL were sputtering. In early January 1984, Aquino met with Salas in Manila— one of several meetings they had following the assassination, Salas said—and they discussed the formation of KOMPIL as well as Aquino's views on upcoming National Assembly elections. They reached an agreement: The CPP would help Aquino launch KOMPIL if Aquino would allow the entire membership to decide whether to boycott the elections. Every organization that joined KOMPIL—even the CPP's forces—would be bound by the decision. "It was a gamble because the [CPP] had only 25 percent of the delegates. The bulk of the delegates came from the [moderate] political parties," Salas recalled.

In a telling demonstration of the CPP's considerable organizational skills, KOMPIL voted to boycott the elections. Salas grinned as he explained to me how the Party pulled off its coup: "When the conference came, the delegates of the political parties were old people. Their ward leaders were not so well versed on the issues." The Party's articulate activists and student leaders worked the crowd feverishly and dominated the floor debate with compelling speeches. Secretly, CPP forces cut a deal with a Muslim delegation from Mindanao. Party cadres supported the election of Muslim candidates to KOMPIL's national council, and the Muslims supported the CPP's candidates and the boycott position. The communists carried the day, and Agapito Aquino became a leader of the 1984 election boycott.

Unfortunately for the CPP's united front aspirations, Party cadres were far less accommodating toward noncommunists than the communist leadership's initial postassassination statements had implied. One veteran Party cadre with whom I spoke blamed the narrow united front views of top CPP officials for the collapse of a series of united front organizations. Gradually, the spirit of détente between the Party-led forces and others within the broad anti-Marcos movement faded to suspicion and mistrust. Afterward, the Central Committee described its moves to dominate the broad anti-Marcos front as an effort to "unify the newly activated elements and groups and provide direction for their efforts."[10] But when Party activists refused to compromise, the various united front organizations that had sprouted in the aftermath of the assassination split. Later, disgruntled Party cadres criticized the CPP's legal protest organizations in 1983–1984 for "unreasonable assertions" that resulted in "the opportunities presented by the Aquino assassination [being] lost."[11]

By late 1984, the Party had hardened its position toward the noncommunist elements that refused to submit to the National Democratic Front program. Those who dared questioned the Party's handling of the united front issue were taken to task for their dissent. A case in point involved Randolph David, a respected leftist UP sociology professor.

David wrote a paper suggesting that unarmed political resistance, rather than armed struggle, might be a more relevant method of opposing Marcos at that point in time. His thesis struck at the very heart of the people's war strategy that had been so assiduously applied for 15 years. For CPP true believers, David's suggestion was a vulgar heresy. Responding in the December 1984 issue of *Ang Bayan*, the Central Committee dismissed David as a "petty-bourgeois intellectual kibitzer" ignorant of the dynamics of the Philippine revolution.[12]

The CPP's hard-line position on the united front question seemed sharply at odds with the NDF's soothing talk of "no monopoly of political power by any class, party or group." In fact, a considerable number of Filipino businesspeople, lawyers, doctors, journalists, and liberal politicians continued to be attracted by the NDF's pledge of a "democratic coalition government" of all political forces. The NDF 10 Point Program had been revised in 1977 to tone down the shrill Maoist syntax of the original document. In 1984, after nearly two decades of corrupt, authoritarian Marcos misrule, and with no end to the regime in sight, frustration began to overwhelm those in the middle and upper classes who had never really taken the communist movement seriously. Inexplicably to many Filipinos, the United States remained staunchly behind Marcos. All the while, the NPA was gaining dramatically in the countryside, and it seemed possible that the communists might topple Marcos in the not-too-distant future. Against that backdrop, the NDF program began to look better and better to a widening segment of the country's intelligentsia. The NDF promised a coalition government that would "allow the free interplay of national and democratic forces during and after elections." The only criterion the NDF had set for participation in the government was a person's record in the drive to overthrow Marcos.[13]

Firmo Tripon was typical of those young, upper-middle-class professionals who in the Aquino assassination aftermath were attracted by the NDF's twin pledges of social revolution and political pluralism. The assassination was for people such as Tripon a "decision point," as he later described it. An executive in a Manila cordage company, he had grown increasingly uncomfortable with the martial law regime. Tripon had never been enamored by Aquino, but the brutal assassination touched a nerve. "It made you think that sooner or later the repression was going to reach your doorstep," he told me five years later.

Tripon began leading his employees to the frequent street demonstrations, and he caught the eye of Party cadres who had taken active roles in JAJA. The CPP was stepping up organizing activities on the labor front, and so the cadres persuaded Tripon to begin talking to labor groups. Tripon was soon speaking every week before gatherings of 100 or more workers. At first, he talked about the significance of the Aquino murder and the need to resist Marcos. Later, the activists who had drafted Tripon to speak began suggesting that his talks should also cover U.S. imperialism and the effect of International Monetary Fund–World Bank policies on the country. An attractive young woman in JAJA began cultivating Tripon and discussing politics. He was persuaded to join another fledgling anti-Marcos organization, the Nationalist Alliance for Justice Freedom and Democracy. A creation of CPP strategists, the Nationalist Alliance was more openly national democratic in its orientation.

The most militant members in JAJA had already begun discussing their national democratic ideas with Tripon while sizing up his political potential. They asked him how he felt about the NPA and the guerrilla war in the countryside and sought his opinions of the NDF program. Eventually, Tripon underwent a series of sessions with underground CPP organizers who lectured him on Marxism, labor issues, feudalism in the Philippines, the mechanics of revolution, and descriptions of life in NPA guerrilla zones.[14]

Tripon's business and upper-class contacts proved valuable to JAJA and the Nationalist Alliance. The radical activists leading the organizations came to him and asked for his help in raising money and other resources. Tripon called his Makati business district friends to line up trucks and sound systems for rallies and food and money for other activities. When Tripon came to the realization that his militant national democratic friends were the legal foot soldiers of the underground Communist Party, he was not overly concerned. "Up to a certain point, our objectives coincided perfectly," he later explained. Besides, he was deeply impressed by the energy and commitment of the NDF activists. They mixed freely with the lower classes, while Tripon's Social Democratic friends preferred to move in their more exclusive, upper-middle-class circles.

A growing number of Tripon's middle- and upper-class friends began dropping out of the protest movement as its leadership and agenda moved further and further Left. Their parting warnings to Tripon were that he would be "eaten alive" by the Reds. Tripon laughed off the suggestions. Later, after having broken with the NDF over the question of whether to support Corazón Aquino's government, he would ruefully recall, "I was the fool who thought I could moderate some of the communists' rough tendencies. Not because I was a communist, but because I wanted a fair shake for everyone."[15]

In early 1985, with the anti-Marcos movement's "parliament of the streets" beginning to sputter in Manila, the CPP leadership decided to try establishing an even broader united front. The new organization was to be called the Bagong Alyansang Makabayan (New Nationalist Alliance, or Bayan). Bayan's organizers hoped to forge an alliance of all centrist and Left-leaning anti-Marcos forces, a proposition that was as attractive to traditional politicos as it was to Party activists.

The lineup of Bayan founders was impressive. The centrist and independent left-wing forces included Tañada, the nationalist patriarch; Diokno, the civil libertarian; Agapito Aquino, the popular heir to his brother's large following; Emanuel Soriano, a prominent figure in the Social Democratic movement; and Jaíme Ongpin, president of the Benguet Corp., the country's largest mining concern. Representatives of the far Left included Rolando Olalia, chairman of the militant Kilusang Mayo Uno (May First Movement, or KMU) labor federation; Leandro Alejandro, leader of the radical League of Filipino Students; and peasant leader Jaíme Tadeo. All that remained to be decided was the ticklish issue of Bayan's leadership. After tedious negotiations among representatives of the various organizations and forces, a satisfactory formula was agreed upon. Those forces forming Bayan were divided into three groups: the NDF-led national democrats; the Left-leaning Social Democrats; and the centrist liberal democrats. Each faction would be awarded one-third of the seats in Bayan's national council.[16]

In May 1985, when the Bayan founding congress was convened to formalize the arrangement, the gathering turned into a disaster as the national democrats suddenly insisted that they be awarded a larger share of the seats on the governing council. Alejandro and other pro-NDF leaders argued that their organizations represented a larger constituency than either of the other factions. The Social Democrats and liberal democrats were presented with a *fait accompli*.

Outraged by what they viewed as treachery on the part of NDF forces, the majority of delegates belonging to the Social Democrats and liberal democrats walked out, led by Aquino, Diokno, Ongpin, and Soriano—some of the most prominent names in the anti-Marcos movement. Joining the walkout were the country's two most prominent human rights lawyers organizations and a group of radical intellectuals.[17] The rift quickly spread to the August Twenty-first Movement and other organizations within the anti-Marcos movement. When I talked with Aquino in early August 1985, he was still smarting from his clash with Party forces. The CPP, he charged, had dictated the composition of the Bayan national council. Before, he had allowed the communists to use him, "with my permission." No more, he vowed. "Diokno, Tañada and

I worked with them in trust. For us, that trust was broken at the Bayan national congress."

By August 1985, the protest movement that had once seemed capable of forcing Marcos from power had all but collapsed, a victim of the bickering between the NDF forces and the rest of the anti-Marcos elements. Corazón Aquino noted at the time that many of the "middle forces" who had been politicized by her husband's assassination had become involved in mainstream political parties or in other endeavors aimed at removing Marcos.[18] In fact, the moderate political opposition, Mrs. Aquino included, was immersed in intense negotiations aimed at forging a united front in the event Marcos called an early presidential election. When, in late 1985, Marcos did announce an election scheduled for the following February, the split within the anti-Marcos movement between the moderate Aquino "yellows" and the radical NDF "Reds" took on enormous strategic implications. A showdown with Marcos was looming, yet the CPP, by missing its finest opportunity ever to forge a broad united front, had played itself out of a position to influence the decisive events.

14

The Election Boycott and Strategic Debates: 1985–1987

To many CPP elements, from Rodolfo Salas on down through the ranks, there seemed no compelling reason to get involved in "bourgeois" elections. After all, while boycotting elections Marcos held in 1978, 1980, 1981, and 1984, the Party had enjoyed spectacular successes. The year 1985 had been one of impressive political and military triumphs for communist forces, and the revolutionary movement could legitimately claim to be a national political force with broad-based, grass-roots support.

CPP leaders maintained that this rapid growth was due to the soundness of the Party's "political line," which emphasized armed struggle over legal or parliamentary ventures. Unavoidably, the claim of a correct political line led the CPP leadership to downplay the significance of existing factors in Philippine society: the political arrogance, corruption, and indifference of Marcos and his government; the litany of military abuses; and the crumbling economy that had seen real wages drop significantly during the 20 years of Marcos rule and leave 7 of 10 Filipinos living below the poverty line—grasping for any hope of change.

If millions of people hoped that the country's first freely contested presidential election in 17 years would herald change, the CPP wasted little time in attacking the notion. The condescending tone of an NDF statement published in mid-November did nothing to foster an atmosphere of solidarity within the anti-Marcos camp:

> It is altogether possible that the dictatorship's mendacious propaganda may deceive the less politically sophisticated sections of the population

into believing that an "election" could lead to wide-ranging reforms. Our history has shown, however, that fundamental reforms can be brought about only with a complete overhaul of the present system, not through an "election."[1]

Responding in the December issue of *Ang Bayan* to opposition candidate Corazón Aquino's statements that the rebels would have to "ask for amnesty" and "lay down their arms" before she would talk with them, the CPP leadership depicted Aquino as the product of an elitist, "comprador-landlord class background" and scorned her advisers as "proimperialist[s]" from the business community and ultra-conservative and clerico-fascist Catholic priests and religious activists. Furthermore, *Ang Bayan* noted that Aquino admittedly had no program of government and had changed her positions on important issues, particularly on a December 1984 pledge to remove U.S. military bases.

The CPP conceded, however, that Aquino's popularity had split the anti-Marcos forces between radicals who favored a boycott and those who had cast their lot with the Aquino campaign. "Although convinced that a boycott is correct and conforms to principles and morality, many antifascists and progressives among the middle forces are worried that by boycotting they may be isolating themselves from the people," *Ang Bayan* observed.[2]

In fact, the boycott question was sparking serious debates inside the movement, particularly within the ranks of the CPP's legal allies. The radical KMU labor federation and the League of Filipino Students had almost immediately announced their intention to boycott the polls. But the legal umbrella organization Bayan, which counted as members many rural politicians and an influential slice of the urban middle class, was still grappling with the boycott issue.

A few days after Marcos called the election, top CPP leaders huddled with Bayan officials in an effort to thresh out the organization's official position on the polls.[3] The CPP Central Committee was represented by Rodolfo Salas, Antonio Zumel, Saturnino Ocampo, and Carolina Malay. Speaking for Bayan were Central Luzon's "three wisemen": José Suarez, a prominent lawyer and head of Bayan-Pampanga province; José Feliciano, former agriculture secretary and congressman, chairman of Bayan-Tarlac province; and José Pelayo, former social welfare secretary and Bayan official. Through late November and into December, the CPP officials and Bayan leaders met six or seven times. They gathered around a huge mahogany table in Feliciano's well-furbished house in the Manila suburb of Quezon City or at an Angeles safe house 60 miles north of the capital.

The Party leaders argued that it was "useless" to participate in the election, that Marcos would ensure his victory by cheating, as he had so often in the past. The Bayan officials in turn warned that Filipinos wanted more than ever to participate in an election. People continued to cling to the belief that they could oust Marcos with ballots rather than bullets. Feliciano, a longtime associate of Benigno Aquino and the survivor of four bruising decades of Tarlac politics, knew the CPP leaders from the rebels' early days in Central Luzon, and he spoke candidly: If he ordered his Bayan members in Tarlac, Aquino's home province, to boycott the election, he would be left standing alone. Everyone, Feliciano declared, from peasants to plantation owners wanted to participate in the election. Salas and his CPP lieutenants would not be dissuaded. Boycott was the proper position, they insisted. Their one concession was that Feliciano would be allowed to join Aquino's campaign rather than face isolation in his home province.[4]

Inside the CPP, the debate was becoming more intense. In early December, following the opposition's eleventh-hour unification behind Aquino's candidacy, the National Urban Commission urgently advised the Central Committee's five-member Executive Committee to cooperate with other "progressive organizations" in the campaign while "exposing" the elections.[5] On December 23, 1985, the Executive Committee—Salas, Secretary-General Rafael Baylosis, Military Commission chairman Juanito Rivera, Education Bureau chairman Benito Tiamzon, and United Front Commission chairman Zumel—gathered to decide the Party's official position on the presidential election. In the past, the Executive Committee had called the entire 15-member Politburo into session to discuss matters of such importance. On this occasion, for reasons that remain unclear, it did not. By a 3–2 vote, the committee ordered an election boycott.

In a 10-page memorandum to CPP cadres, the Executive Committee trivialized the election as "a noisy and empty political battle" between competing factions of the ruling class and a U.S. ploy to "give the reactionary opposition the chance to share in the power and privilege."[6] The committee argued that a boycott was necessary to expose the election as a sham. In response to those cadres who were warning of the disastrous implications of a boycott, the Executive Committee dismissed as "baseless" the "fear of a few that we might become isolated from the masses since, whatever we do, the majority will still vote."[7]

Nevertheless, leaders of the CPP's legal organizations saw the threat of isolation fast becoming a reality. Bayan was wracked by prominent defections to Aquino's camp. Lorenzo Tañada, the venerable old nationalist firebrand and Bayan's chairman, was at Aquino's side applauding as she announced her candidacy in early December, and Firmo Tripon, executive director for Bayan's metropolitan Manila chapter, took a leave to work in Aquino's campaign. In the countryside, where links between the legal national democratic forces and moderate political groups were more extensive, sentiments for participation in the election were running just as high.

In an attempt to stave off impending disaster, Bayan leaders offered organizational support in exchange for Aquino's adoption of some of the organization's "nationalist and pro-people" positions, including the immediate removal of U.S. military bases, in the opposition platform. But stung by CPP criticism and Marcos' red-baiting, Aquino's handlers brusquely rejected Bayan's overtures and contended that most of the demands were already incorporated in the opposition "minimum program of government."[8] Bayan's national council formally approved an active boycott position in an 84–6 vote on January 8.

By then, the wild enthusiasm surrounding Aquino's campaign was spreading throughout the country. Her campaign had shaped up as a moral crusade against the corrupt dictator, and it was inexplicable to Aquino's supporters how Bayan could undermine the opposition cause by campaigning for a boycott. While Aquino's campaign was attracting tens of thousands of fervent supporters, the boycott rallies were drawing embarrassingly small crowds.

In the campaign's final days, with Aquino obviously enjoying a groundswell of support, the CPP leadership scrambled to lessen the damage done by its boycott policy. The Executive Committee granted some Party-led legal organizations the flexibility to either support Aquino or at least avoid an active boycott campaign that would further alienate Aquino supporters. In late January, the committee directed CPP cadres and Party legal forces to change their focus from encouraging a boycott to thwarting election fraud by Marcos' political machine.[9] But the Executive Committee held firm on the boycott policy. While anticipating damaged relations with noncommunist forces, the committee was convinced that any negative effects from the Party's boycott would be short term.[10]

The unpopularity of the boycott order was not limited to the Party's legal front organizations. Without waiting for Central Committee instructions, the CPP's Mindanao Commission and some regional Party committees had voted to support Aquino or at least allow CPP supporters to "vote their conscience" in the election. Ignoring the boycott order, the Southeastern Mindanao Regional Party Committee urged its organized supporters to participate in the election if they desired and encouraged people to vote for Aquino.[11]

Not surprisingly to CPP cadres and legal Party activists, the boycott was overwhelmingly rejected by Filipinos on election day, February 7, 1986. But the extent of the rejection stunned some Party officials. In one Manila suburb considered by the CPP to be a communist stronghold, for example, 70 percent of the membership of Party-led unions disobeyed the boycott order and voted.[12]

Rather than fretting about the effects of the boycott debacle, the Party leadership took solace in its analysis that the movement stood to gain from the worsening polarization spawned by the fraudulent election. In all likelihood, the analysis would have been proven correct—if not for a failed attempt by military dissidents to depose Marcos. When on February 22, 1986, the exposed coup plotters launched a defensive revolt that was quickly supported by hundreds of thousands of Aquino supporters, communist forces around the country could only watch and await the conclusion of the dramatic events. In some regions, Party leaders discussed the idea of moving forces into nearby cities to help Aquino's forces win, but in the end they decided to wait in the hills.[13] Four days later, Marcos quietly fled the Philippines, and Aquino assumed the presidency.

For years, the CPP had insisted that patient armed struggle in the countryside was the surest way to oust Marcos. Now, Marcos' ouster in an urban popular uprising sparked by a fraudulent election was a stunning blow to the communist leadership and cause for demoralization in Party ranks. After having spearheaded the struggle against Marcos for 17 years, many CPP members and guerrillas could not understand how their leadership could have adopted a position that left them on the sidelines in the final, decisive confrontation with the dictator and resulted in the movement's exclusion from a share of power in the new government.

Overnight, the rise of Aquino and the burden of the discredited boycott policy forced the CPP to dramatically realign its strategy. NPA units were ordered to adopt a policy of "active defense" and drastically curtail tactical offensives against government troops. The Party's political cadres spent the rest of 1986 explaining the "boycott blunder" and subsequent events to supporters in the cities and the countryside and attempting to keep CPP's forces intact amid the euphoria that marked Aquino's rise to power. An even more urgent and difficult task for rural Party cadres was convincing their followers of the need to continue the guerrilla war.

In urban areas, a groundswell of criticism arose from Party ranks that unleashed pent-up discontent with fundamental CPP policies. A full-blown intraparty debate ensued with some veteran cadres for the first time in the movement's history suggesting that the CPP should discard the strategy of protracted people's war. A series of discussion papers written by middle- and lower-level Party cadres scored the

Executive Committee for "mechanical class analysis" and rigidity in united front efforts toward noncommunist opposition forces.[14]

One of the most outspoken CPP dissidents that emerged in the 1986 polemics was Marty Villalobos, the pseudonym of a veteran CPP cadre. In a discussion paper that began circulating widely in the days immediately following the ouster of Marcos, Villalobos argued that the strategic line stressing the primacy of armed struggle at the expense of urban political struggles was fundamentally flawed. He accused CPP leaders of having been "so fixated on the 'protracted people's war' strategy" that the Party was unable to make the necessary strategic adjustments despite "clear signs of an insurrectionary situation developing."[15]

Villalobos denounced the CPP's "serious tendency toward inflexibility and sectarianism" in dealing with potential noncommunist allies in Manila.[16] According to his analysis, the CPP's unyielding adherence to the Chinese model had caused the movement to miss its best opportunity to organize a broad popular front in Manila. He suggested that the CPP should have adopted the more flexible features of the Nicaraguan united front model, which allowed for strategic alliances with liberals and other noncommunist elements in opposition to the Somoza dictatorship.

In a subsequent paper, Villalobos made a case for the Party's adoption of an "insurrectional strategy" in which urban political actions would be the decisive form of struggle while rural guerrilla warfare would play merely a supporting role. Villalobos argued that the successful February uprising that Aquino rode to power had proven the feasibility of an urban insurrection. A key to developing such a strategy, he stressed, was a "flexible policy of alliances" with noncommunists.[17]

The CPP's National Urban Commission joined the critique of the people's war strategy in the inaugural issue of a new Party theoretical journal, *Praktika*, created in part to satisfy cadres' demands for a thorough discussion of the boycott decision and other strategic questions. The commission condemned the boycott as "an ultra-Left maneuver." Singled out for criticism was the Party's "dogmatic insistence" on dominating legal anti-Marcos groups that had arisen in the aftermath of the Aquino assassination.[18] The journal concluded with a somber appeal for an "effort at rectification" lest the movement be "ruined by major mistakes."

Forced to react to rising tide of criticism and discontent within the CPP, the Politburo issued a resolution on May 7, 1986, reprimanding the Executive Committee for committing a "major tactical blunder" in its "analysis and evaluation" of the situation and in its "understanding and application of the Party's tactics."[19] Significantly, the Politburo rejected arguments that the boycott decision was rooted in a fundamental flaw in the protracted people's war strategy; instead, the Politburo described the Executive Committee error as merely "tactical" rather than strategic in nature. The resolution took the committee to task for failing to call a full Politburo meeting to discuss the boycott issue and for disregarding and showing "lack of respect" to opposing views voiced by lower Party units. In chiding the committee for failing to give sufficient weight to the antifascist (anti-Marcos) struggle, the Politburo acknowledged shortcomings in the Party's united front work. Finally, the Politburo pledged to democratize Party decisionmaking by allowing greater input from lower units in the future, while ordering the Executive Committee to undergo self-criticism in a series of articles in *Ang Bayan*.

In late May, the committee responded to the furor and the Politburo reprimand with a resolution that was hardly repentant. The resolution argued that the boycott policy was not responsible for the CPP's disappointing position following the events of February 1986 and that the outcome was the reflection of the unfavorable balance of forces between the national democrats and the noncommunist forces.[20] Armed struggle, rather than political actions, would be the primary route to victory. Taking exception to calls within the CPP for an alliance with elements of the Aquino government, the Executive Committee depicted the new regime as dependent on "the counterrevolutionary military, the local and foreign big business, the conservative Church hierarchy and the U.S. government."

The Executive Committee's combative resolution fueled debate within Party ranks as "rectificationists" renewed demands for adjustments in the CPP's strategic line. The Politburo allowed the unprecedented venting of critical opinions to run its course through the first year of Aquino's rule. There were persistent rumors throughout 1986, given prominent play by the Manila press, that Salas and Baylosis had been removed from the committee for their role in the boycott blunder. In August 1988, I visited Salas in his cell in a suburban Manila military stockade and asked him about the allegations. He maintained that reports of his forced resignation were incorrect. Salas said he had resigned as CPP chairman in mid-1986 when a slim majority of the Politburo voiced disagreement with his analysis of the boycott policy and several other strategic questions. He indicated, however, that he and Baylosis remained in the Executive Committee.

Salas' resignation did not end the turmoil within the CPP. Party traditionalists who adhered to the committee's assertions that the Aquino government represented nothing more than a change in ruling-class faces were initially forced to accommodate CPP "reformists" as the movement sought to regain equilibrium lost in the boycott debacle and emergence of a popular president. In August, the CPP entered into cease-fire negotiations with the government while taking advantage of the new liberal atmosphere prevailing in the country—"democratic space," as it became known—to begin rebuilding the legal national democratic movement, which was in shambles because of the boycott. The boldest initiative was the formation of the Partido ng Bayan (People's Party, or PnB), a legal political party that was the brainchild of Sison and other communist leaders released from prison by Aquino.

Gradually, the debate about forging possible alliances with the Aquino government was overshadowed by the cease-fire negotiations, which generated new debates within the CPP. But the hand of those cadres and Party leaders defending the primacy of armed struggle was strengthened by existing realities in the revolutionary movement. The weakened state of the Party's urban organizations, both legal and underground, in contrast to the relative health and resiliency of communist armed forces in the countryside seemed to support a strategic line that placed its greatest emphasis on rural guerrilla warfare. The CPP leadership even more vigorously emphasized the primacy of armed struggle following the collapse of a 60-day cease-fire in February 1987.

During the campaign for legislative elections in the spring, the CPP Executive Committee again discouraged the movement's forces—legal and illegal—from expending too much effort on electoral politics. Party leaders claimed vindication in May 1987 when legal forces participating in the elections under the banner of Partido ng Bayan were crushed. A few days after the elections, Saturnino Ocampo revealed the CPP leadership's growing impatience with those elements in the Left who continued to question the primacy of the armed struggle. "We just want to reaffirm to those who think [participation in elections] is the alternative to armed struggle that they are wrong," Ocampo said.[21] While reiterating the primacy of armed struggle, the CPP leadership seemed to indicate its willingness to allow its legal forces to experiment further with electoral politics, although as a tactical, rather than a strategic, weapon.

In August 1987, the CPP leadership declared the period of internal debate over, and the Executive Committee issued a lengthy memorandum announcing the emergence of a consensus within the Party. The resulting strategy called for the revolutionary movement to direct its "most intense attacks on Aquino and her reactionary factions."[22] Moving quickly to enforce the "consensus," Party cadres unleashed a series of blistering verbal attacks on forces within the Left who either continued to question the strategic line or continued to critically support the Aquino government's "liberal tendencies." Bearing some of the harshest criticism were those national democratic elements who subscribed to an emerging concept of "popular democracy," one of the basic thrusts of which was cooperation on a more equal footing with middle- and upper-class elements who did not entirely accept the National Democratic Front political line or armed struggle.

The abrupt closure to the period of debate was met by continued defiance among some CPP units, and there were scattered reports of dissidents breaking away to form rival groups. The most serious schism occurred on Negros, where more than a dozen veteran Party and NPA veterans resigned to protest the CPP's decision to reject "critical collaboration" with the Aquino government and to escalate guerrilla operations.[23]

When the debate finally sputtered to a close in fall 1987, proponents of the protracted people's war strategy had prevailed. It appeared, however, that some concessions had been made to those Party members who argued for greater emphasis on political tactics, particularly in urban areas, with the aim of preparing the cities for future insurrectionary opportunities. Any doubts as to the movement's commitment to pursuing the protracted war strategy were erased in September 1987, when in the wake of a bloody coup attempt by government military dissidents, New People's Army units throughout the Philippines went on the offensive.

15

Talking Peace While Preparing for War

Throughout the election campaign, Corazón Aquino had pledged that one of her first acts as president would be to declare a six-month cease-fire and negotiate an end to the communist insurgency. Aquino and her advisers believed that most of the guerrillas had joined the rebel army because of military human rights abuses and poverty. The conviction was that the Filipino rebels were somehow "less ideological" than communist guerrillas in other countries, Ramón Mitra, a close Aquino adviser, later recalled.[1] Aquino's advisers were convinced that the armed forces were in no shape to wage an effective campaign against the rebels. A truce would give the government an opportunity to prove its sincerity by delivering reforms and reviving the moribund economy, while allowing the army time to retrain and refurbish its tattered image.

Staggered by the overwhelming rejection of its boycott policy and the sudden replacement of the "U.S.-Marcos dictatorship" with a popular government, the CPP leadership made a quick decision to accept the offer of political negotiations. Party strategists reasoned that a conciliatory response to the popular president would enable the movement to regain the moral and political high ground it had held during its years of steadfast opposition to the repressive Marcos and had lost in the disastrous boycott campaign.[2] Peace talks would also give the CPP time to thresh out the larger theoretical questions that by March 1986 were stoking intense debates within the movement's ranks.

CPP leaders saw negotiations not as a realistic manner of resolving the conflict but as a way to avoid further political isolation at a crucial juncture. The CPP also saw a chance to "test the extent, limit or capacity of the new government's reformism," while "keep[ing] the door open as much as possible for tactical alliances" with the government's liberal forces.[3] The CPP leadership made it clear to all its forces that the decision to pursue political negotiations in no way signaled a departure from the strategic line emphasizing armed struggle as the key to seizing political power. Nonetheless, significant political and military adjustments were necessitated by the new situation. Four weeks after Aquino took power, NDF chairman Antonio Zumel announced that NPA units were being ordered to limit their attacks to "remnants of the deposed fascist regime which are still in place." Furthermore, Zumel declared that the movement was "open to cooperation with other progressive forces" and would give the new president "time to carry out her promised changes."[4]

In the meantime, Aquino was having her own problems with the armed forces. NPA units had continued to conduct bloody attacks in most regions of the country, and AFP officials were beginning to blame the president's defensive reconciliation policy for the rising number of casualties. Military officials, led by Defense Minister Juan Ponce Enrile, had never concealed their skepticism toward the new insurgency policy. When a cease-fire was not immediately achieved, these officials began to question the policy. Aquino and her advisers did little to assuage military concerns and excluded the AFP leadership from cease-fire talks. The military did not join the negotiations until preliminary details for a cease-fire had been arranged.

By July, after nearly four months of secret communications between the CPP and the government, the two sides had agreed on acceptable panels for formal negotiations. Two CPP Central Committee members— Antonio Zumel and Saturnino Ocampo—were designated to represent the rebels; the government panel was composed of José Diokno and Ramón Mitra. In August, chief government auditor Teofisto Guingona replaced Diokno, who was suffering from cancer.

On the morning of August 5, formal negotiations began when Mitra met for three-and-a-half hours with Ocampo, Zumel, and another ranking CPP official, Carolina Malay. By the end of August, under increasing pressure from Enrile and his supporters in the military, Aquino and her advisers were becoming impatient with the communists' refusal to agree to a cease-fire until their demands for preliminary arrangements had been met.

The Philippine military establishment's campaign to thwart negotiations with the communists had won the encouragement of the Pentagon and the Central Intelligence Agency. Throughout the summer, Pentagon officials encouraged AFP opposition to the cease-fire strategy. U.S. assistant defense secretary Richard Armitage described the military situation as "serious and getting worse," and declared that Aquino's peace efforts had not produced results. He even sounded a sympathetic note for Aquino's military critics by telling Congress, "I'm sure Mrs. Aquino is going to have to let her forces take the proper action against the insurgents."[5]

Behind the scenes, the Reagan administration maneuverings were far more threatening. As AFP opposition to the proposed cease-fire intensified, the Pentagon and the CIA lined up against the State Department on the issue of Aquino's policy of negotiating with the communists. Armitage's statements were merely the sanitized public manifestation of the U.S. defense establishment's consternation. In the aftermath of a failed military putsch in July, the interdepartmental differences exploded into what one U.S. diplomat in Manila described to me as a "cable war" between the competing factions. Each group, attempting to be the decisive influence on policymakers back in the United States, bombarded Washington with cables arguing their respective positions. But the debate was no longer limited to the wisdom of Aquino's commitment to negotiations with the guerrillas. According to one U.S. diplomat, the CIA station in Manila had decided that Aquino's insurgency policy was a threat to U.S. interests, and that the Philippine military should be supported in a bid to overthrow her. "A lot of people back in Washington like Marcos," the U.S. diplomat, who was privy to the policy debates, told me at the time. In the meantime, while defending Aquino against her Pentagon and CIA critics, the State Department quietly drew up plans "for any contingency," the diplomat said, including the sudden removal of Aquino from office.[6]

By fall 1986, a consensus had begun to emerge among U.S. officials that Enrile's warnings of a worsening communist threat were timely and valid. There were, to be sure, concerns in Washington and in the U.S. Embassy in Manila that the defense minister's political ambitions and baggage from years of fealty to Marcos might dilute his effectiveness, and some U.S. officials had qualms about Enrile's polemical methods. "Johnny Enrile was Marcos' bagman. He was involved with every dirty trick they pulled for 20 years," a senior U.S. Embassy official knowingly told me one afternoon in October 1986. That said, the official generously credited Enrile with performing a valuable service for Philippine and U.S. interests. "Enrile's a point man for the anticommunist issue. The country needs that. They need to be told that the communists are at the door," the diplomat said. Whatever misgivings there were about Enrile's leading role in the debate about Philippine insurgency policy, as long as the wily defense minister did not actually try to seize power,

U.S. officials were willing to set their concerns aside for the task at hand. Reagan administration policy makers on both sides of the Potomac signed on to Enrile's campaign to thwart the talks.

The two negotiating panels were finally nearing agreement on a cease-fire when military intelligence agents arrested Salas as he emerged from the Philippine General Hospital in downtown Manila on the evening of September 29. Salas remained a key member of the CPP Political Bureau, and his arrest only hours after Mitra had announced that a truce appeared imminent was widely viewed as an attempt by the AFP to sabotage the talks. The NDF panel immediately announced that it would not continue negotiations unless Salas was released. Enrile's influential military protégés, who were already floating coup threats, countered by warning that the release of Salas would cause an armed forces backlash. With little other choice, Aquino congratulated the military for its accomplishment and appealed to the NDF to return to the peace table.

The incident exacerbated the polarization that had threatened Aquino's policy from the start. Communists, liberals, and even centrist supporters of the president accused the military of attempting to gain dominance over the government. The military accused Aquino of allowing communist influence, even within the government, to reach dangerous proportions. By October, it had become evident that more than Aquino's policy of reconciliation was at stake. Enrile's armed forces supporters were seriously discussing the need for a coup to "correct" what they viewed as Aquino's slide toward the Left.

Aquino tried to mollify the military by toughening her rhetoric toward the communists, warning that the hand she offered in peace was "soon to be clenched in a declaration of war" if negotiations failed. In late October, Aquino acceded further to demands articulated by Enrile and military officials; she announced that she would "soon" set a deadline for talks with the rebels and promised to implement a "comprehensive" insurgency program.[7]

The cease-fire talks resumed a few days after Salas' arrest against the backdrop of swirling coup rumors. On November 1, the NDF scored a propaganda coup by offering a truce to go into effect in early December. The proposal seemed to reflect new flexibility on the part of the rebel leadership. Previous demands for withdrawal of government troops from the countryside and recognition of certain areas as NPA controlled would now be only "talking points." The proposal reiterated NDF demands for the disarming of government militia units, private armies, and armed

PLATE 1. On the trail with my bodyguard, the irrepressible "Ka" (Comrade) Baldo, June 1987.

PLATE 2. Surrendered communist guerrillas construct a hut at Mindanao's Gambalay rehabilitation center.

PLATE 3. New People's Army guerrillas stand at attention while Communist Party officials and organizers raise clenched fists as they sing the communist anthem, the "Internationale."

PLATE 4. NPA guerrillas on patrol in the Bondoc peninsula of southern Quezon province take a break in the yard of a sympathetic farmer.

PLATE 5. Celebrating the revolution: Nearly 250 peasants and guerrillas from Barangay Rose and adjoining barrios in southern Quezon gather to celebrate the CPP anniversary on December 26, 1987. At left, Dante, a Barangay Rose peasant and deputy commander of the local communist militia, raises the communist flag, as the others sing the "Internationale" with upraised fists.

PLATE 6. CPP Central Committee member Sotero Llamas, the Bicol Party secretary, at work in his jungle "office" in a forward base camp in Albay province, February 1988.

PLATE 7. The revolution goes high tech: While rebel soldiers sleep barefoot beside him, the communist military commander for the six-province Southern Tagalog region bordering Manila on the south and east, punches a coded radio message he has just received into a hand-held Casio computer. Within a few seconds, he is able to read the message from NPA forces on the island of Mindoro, 100 miles away from his camp in Quezon province, informing him of military operations underway.

PLATE 8. Two NPA guerrillas, peasant women from southern Quezon province, share a communist newspaper as they rest in the house of Kulas in Barangay Rose on Christmas Day, 1987.

PLATE 9. A platoon of NPA regulars and communist militiamen from southern Quezon province gather in a forest clearing in a barrio adjoining Barangay Rose to celebrate the Party anniversary with peasant supporters, December 26, 1987.

PLATE 10. Kulas, a communist peasant in Barangay Rose, and his daughter, Yoly, home from her job attending to the house of Party cadres near Manila, prepare a chicken for lunch at their home on Christmas Day, 1987.

PLATE 11. Joy (*far right*), the Communist Party cadre who escorted the author on several trips to guerrilla zones, enjoys a meal with the peasant Dante (*center*) and his family in their house in Barangay Rose. Dante was killed by soldiers three months later.

PLATE 12. Office work in a jungle camp, Bondoc peninsula, Quezon, June 1987.

PLATE 13. Taking a break: Guerrillas in a Quezon province camp, June 1987.

PLATE 14. A guerrilla hangs laundry to dry in a Quezon province jungle camp.

PLATE 15. A jungle kitchen: Tin cups on tree limbs, water from a stream running through halved bamboo logs.

PLATE 16. Guerrillas on patrol stop for a chat with a peasant farmer, astride his water buffalo, taking a load of coconuts to market.

PLATE 17. The aftermath of Plaza Miranda: Blood and debris litter Manila's Plaza Miranda minutes after communist operatives hurled two fragmentation grenades onto the stage where a Liberal party political rally was underway on the evening of August 21, 1971. José María Sison had correctly anticipated that President Ferdinand Marcos would be blamed for the attack on his political rivals and would respond with repression. Immediately, Marcos began arresting radical activists, and two days later he suspended the writ of habeas corpus. (Photograph courtesy of the Lopez Museum)

PLATE 18. A young boy wounded in the stomach by grenade shrapnel staggers away from the Plaza Miranda stage seconds after the explosions. (Photograph courtesy of the Lopez Museum)

PLATE 19. The harsh life for workers on Negros sugar haciendas—among the lowest paid labor in Asia—is etched on the face of this grandmother and the ragged children who surround her. The NPA guerrillas had begun organizing support among the workers of this hacienda a few weeks before the author visited in March 1985.

PLATE 20. The faces of poverty in northern Luzon: a mother and her daughter in the doorway of their shack in the Cordillera Mountains of Nueva Vizcaya province. The family, which earned a bare subsistence living from slash-and-burn farming, was supporting New People's Army units in the area.

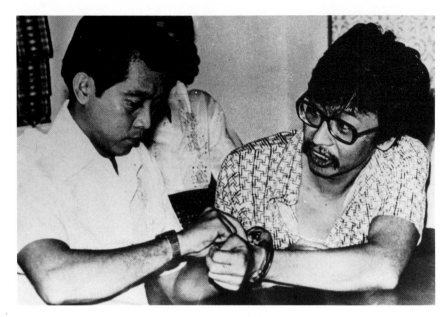

PLATE 21. A military escort removes José María Sison's handcuffs before the start of a court hearing on June 23, 1978. Sison was captured in the northern Luzon province of La Union on November 10, 1977. For the first 18 months of his imprisonment in a Manila army stockade, he was manacled and fettered to his cot. He was held in solitary confinement for five years. On March 5, 1986, eight days after assuming office, President Corazón Aquino released Sison. (Photograph courtesy of the *Manila Bulletin*)

PLATE 22. Rodolfo Salas, Sison's successor as chairman of the CPP from 1977 until 1986. Salas was arrested while leaving a downtown Manila hospital on the evening of September 29, 1986. This photograph was taken in August 1988 as the author interviewed Salas in his cell in the Philippine Constabulary stockade. (Photograph by Aleli Nucum-Jones)

WANTED DEAD OR ALIVE
₱150,000

BERNABE BUSCAYNO @ Dante

Commander-in-Chief, MA-MAO. Also known as Payat. 27-28 years. 118 lbs. 5'6". 2 gold teeth upper front, 1 full, other crowned; prominent Adam's apple; smooth and baby-faced; fair complexioned; nose slightly pointed. 3rd year high school at Holy Angel Academy in Angeles City. Cases involved: (1) Murder of Cpl Narciso Quiban and physical injuries of Pfc Florentino Rivera, 20th BCT, at Dapdap, Mabalacat; (2) Murder of Ladislao Bognot at Manibug, Porac; (3) Multiple murder of Ciriaco Santos, et al, at Barrio San Francisco, Concepcion; (4) Triple murder o f Cpl Alfonso Ponce, et al, at Barrio Libingan, Concepcion; (5) Murder of Martin Baking in Concepcion; (6) Murder of Sgt Igmedio Briones at Capas; (7) Murder of Cpl Federico Correa, et al, and physical injuries of others at San Miguel, Tarlac; (8) Murder of Police Chief Jesus Baluyut of Capas; (9) Murder of Sotero Bruno of San Roque, La Paz; (10) Murder of Arthur Apang at Sapang Tagalog, San Miguel; (11) Murder of Francisco Yalung at San Miguel; (12) Murder of Pat. Diosdado Basco, et al, at Concepcion; (13) Murder of Lt. Aquilino Cusi, et al, at Anupul, Bamban; (14) Double murder of TSg Marcelino Martin and SSg Juanito Tabamo at San Roque, Tarlac.

PLATE 23. Wanted dead or alive . . . Bernabe Buscayno, the founding NPA commander, better known as Commander Dante. The photo was taken sometime in the late 1950s or early 1960s. "MA-MAO" is a military reference to the Maoist nature of the new communist army, playing on the native word "mamao," which roughly means a "terrifying spectre." (Photograph courtesy of the Lopez Museum)

PLATE 24. Government soldiers inspect the Chinese-made rifles and ammunition from the *Karagatan* shipment, captured at Digoyo Point when NPA units were forced to withdraw into the Sierra Madre. (Photograph courtesy of the Lopez Museum)

PLATE 25. *M/V Karagatan*, aground on a sandbar off Digoyo Point, Isabela, after the crew unloaded Chinese weapons for Philippine communist forces in July 1972. (Photograph courtesy of the Lopez Museum)

PLATE 26. Life at the Hunan Province Commune: In a rare photograph, Filipino communists wash clothes at their Hunan province compound in April 1976. Those pictured are, from right, Ricardo Malay, vice-chairman of the secret CPP delegation to China; Rolando Pena, a crewmember of the ill-fated *Karagatan* and *Andrea* arms smuggling voyages; and Janos Sison, son of the founding CPP chairman. (Photograph courtesy of Ricardo Malay)

religious sects and the removal of police from counterinsurgency operations—but these demands had been championed all along by Aquino's
liberal supporters.[8]

Within a few days, the panels had agreed in principle on terms, but
before an agreement could be finalized, Aquino's deteriorating relations
with the military came to a head. On November 12, Rolando Olalia,
chairman of KMU and head of the fledgling Partido ng Bayan, disappeared.
Twenty-four hours later, his mutilated body was discovered in a suburban
Manila field bearing multiple knife and gunshot wounds. For weeks,
Enrile's military protégés had threatened to take action against Aquino
and the communists. Olalia, leader of the two largest legal organizations
allied with the underground, had expressed fear that he would be a
target.[9]

The NDF panel broke off talks following the discovery of Olalia's
body and said negotiations would not resume until Aquino ensured
justice for Olalia and gave "definitive evidence" that she could control
the armed forces. In the days that followed, the CPP's legal forces and
some of Aquino's liberal supporters took to the streets to denounce
Enrile and the military. Four days of Party-led strikes and rallies were
capped by a day-long funeral procession for Olalia attended by hundreds
of thousands, including NDF officials Malay, Ocampo, and Zumel, in a
dramatic aboveground appearance surrounded by bodyguards of tough
urban activists. Marchers shouted "Long live the National Democratic
Front!" as the rebel negotiators waved clenched, upraised fists.

The unprecedented displays of NDF strength fueled military concerns.
In the predawn hours of November 23, a coup attempt was thwarted
as Aquino's loyal armed forces chief, General Fidel Ramos, ordered
armed forces units not to accept any orders from Enrile's defense ministry.
Later that day, a grim-faced Aquino announced that she had fired Enrile.
To the communists, she issued a December 1 deadline for a truce
agreement, after which military operations against the rebels would
begin.

Enrile's meek acceptance of his removal momentarily chastened the
military and breathed new life into the peace talks. In a final session
on November 26, the panels resolved their differences. Later that evening,
the three communist negotiators gathered to celebrate the moment with
family members and friends. The scene was a small, airy bungalow in
a tree-shaded compound owned by Malay's family in Quezon City. A
friend of the NDF officials pulled out a pocket tape recorder and, quieting
the excited group, switched on a demonstration tape recorded earlier
in the week by the country's top pop group, the Apo Hiking Society.
It was a song entitled, "Cease-Fire." The communist leaders nodded
their heads in rhythm to the music and strained to catch the Tagalog

lyrics that spoke of a Philippines at peace. Outside, young peasant guerrillas with M-16 rifles stood guard in the darkness. The song ended, and after the communist negotiators offered polite applause and approval, the excited chatter resumed. I had never seen the rebel leaders so buoyant, although Ocampo confided that they had no illusions that the "substantive talks" scheduled to begin in a few weeks would lead to a peaceful settlement of the insurgency.

On November 27, negotiators for the two sides gathered in Club Filipino, an exclusive suburban Manila social club, to sign the five-page agreement, the first cease-fire in nearly 18 years of war. Outside, NDF supporters waved tiny rebel flags. Inside, hundreds of civilian and military officials, NDF followers, government supporters, and journalists packed the club to witness the ceremony, which was held in the same room where nine months earlier Aquino had taken her oath of office. Malay drew admiring gasps when she arrived in a pale pink tailored suit and black high-heeled pumps, a string of pearls dangling about her neck. Ocampo and Zumel were equally resplendent in crisp white, native embroidered shirts. After the representatives signed the truce, the crowd cheered lustily as Ocampo embraced chief government negotiator Ramón Mitra to consummate the ceremony.

Church bells pealed and festive crowds thronged streets throughout the Philippines as the cease-fire began at noon on December 10. In many towns and cities, ragtag NPA units paraded to the cheers of supporters and curious onlookers. Guerrillas reunited with families and friends, some for the first time in nearly two decades. In Bacolod, the Negros Occidental provincial capital, tens of thousands of people applauded as an unarmed rebel column marched to the town plaza. The promenade was led by two Catholic priests turned guerrillas wearing blue Mao caps and raising clenched fists. Later, they were warmly received by the provincial governor and the local Catholic bishop.[10]

I witnessed similar cease-fire festivities in Iloilo, the largest city on the neighboring island of Panay. Throughout the morning, radio stations aired interviews with the island's rebel leaders. The final seconds before the noon start of the truce were dramatically counted down by an overwrought disc jockey, and at the appointed moment, while church bells resounded around the city, the radio blared a scratchy recording of "Auld Lang Syne." On the edge of town, the NDF's local cease-fire representatives, two ranking communist rebel leaders, Concha Araneta and José Torre, a former Catholic priest, were the guests of honor at a church fundraising luncheon hosted by the local bishop and the flamboyant

Manila archbishop, Cardinal Jaíme Sin. Later that afternoon, the rebel representatives and 2,000 legal supporters—mostly peasants, fishermen, and students—gathered in a downtown park for a "peace rally" broadcast live by local radio stations. The stage was framed by two large NDF flags and festooned with the banners of leftist human rights organizations. The crowd sang revolutionary songs and held a "people's mass" conducted by radical priests. Throughout, Araneta and Torre signed autographs. For rebels long accustomed to anonymous lives in the hills, it was a heady moment.

That evening, I joined Araneta and Torre and several other rebels in their "suite" in the Hotel del Rio, Iloilo's finest. The rooms were a gift from the hotel owner, a former Marcos administration official who had languished in political purgatory since the flight of his leader and now hoped to curry favor with the communists. The rebels savored, sometimes awkwardly, the first night they had ever spent in a hotel. They puzzled over the menu, overwhelmed by so large a choice of food and uncertain how to order room service. Finally, they asked me to order, and the rebels feasted on plates of prawns, fried chicken, and rice.

Araneta was already arranging meetings with old friends from high school and college who had access to civic organizations and clubs where the rebels hoped to win new supporters. But she seemed equally thrilled with the prospect of indulging in family matters long neglected. Her children hardly knew her, and so she hoped to get reacquainted. There was Christmas to look forward to, the reunion of brothers, sisters, and parents; and there was the birth of another baby, her sixth, due in late January.

The euphoria that marked the beginning of the cease-fire quickly faded as the two sides staked out sharply contrasting positions for the next phase of negotiations aimed at ending the war. Ocampo listed as prerequisites for a lasting peace a new constitution, general elections, and the development of a new economic order. Although rebel negotiators stated that power sharing was not a formal demand, CPP officials proposed formation of a "transitional government" in which they would be allotted a voice. Furthermore, the rebels envisioned a settlement in which the NPA would retain its weapons.[11]

While emphasizing that the surrender of arms was nonnegotiable, the NDF further predicated a peaceful settlement on 10 demands that included sweeping land reform, an end to "unequal relations" with the United States, government-sponsored industrialization, the dismantling of civilian militia units, the repeal of "repressive" decrees promulgated by Marcos, and the formation of a propeople army. The government in turn offered the communists a settlement whose framework was (1) social and economic reforms within the parameters of a proposed constitution, which was to be submitted to a February 1987 plebiscite; (2) economic recovery activities with NDF participation; (3) 1 billion pesos for a "rehabilitation" program that included "amnesty with honor" for surrendering guerrillas; and (4) a rural "social amelioration program" based on government-assisted agricultural cooperatives. The government was hoping to coax as many guerrillas as possible to surrender during the cease-fire. As the substantive talks got under way, the government announced the 1 billion peso National Reconciliation and Development Program aimed at attracting rebels and their rural supporters. The program offered amnesty, job training, and other services to guerrillas who wished to surrender.

But the substantive talks stalled when the NDF rejected the government stipulation that further negotiations be conducted only within the framework of a new constitution. In desperation, María Diokno, a member of the government panel, sought her father's help in breaking the impasse. The elder Diokno, who was losing his 18-month battle with cancer, remembered a speech he had delivered during the Marcos years in which he had proposed a framework for national reconstruction that focused on "food and freedom, jobs and justice." It was vague enough that both sides might agree to it, Diokno decided, and so he drafted a formal proposal.[12]

Despite the acceptance in principle of Diokno's framework by both sides, the talks never reached the stage of serious negotiations. The remaining weeks of the cease-fire were spent trying to agree on unresolved details of the truce already in effect and arguing about what should be the subject of further talks. Two years later, María Diokno told me the talks had been all but doomed by Aquino's lack of vision for her government and the peace talks. The NDF became convinced, quite correctly, that the government merely wanted to keep it talking while trying to persuade rank-and-file guerrillas to surrender. Mitra, Guingona, and Diokno all told me that Aquino gave no instructions on how to proceed in the talks or on what the government's ultimate objective should be.

On the communist side, NDF negotiators had enjoyed impressive propaganda successes during the first weeks of the cease-fire, but the novelty of rebel leaders appearing on television or at speaking engagements was wearing thin. NPA forces in the field were getting restless, and rebel commanders were beginning to wonder if they could keep their forces intact if the cease-fire was extended.[13] The emerging consensus within the rebel leadership held that they had achieved all they could out of the negotiations, and now they had reached a dangerous point of diminishing returns.

On the morning of January 22, the two panels announced the indefinite suspension of the negotiations, citing death threats made against negotiators on both sides. That afternoon, as a column of leftist farmers, students, and workers demanding land reform attempted to force their way through police barricades near the presidential palace, security forces opened fire killing 18 and wounding scores.[14] Seventeen days later, the cease-fire ended with each side blaming the other for the collapse of negotiations.

Who won and who lost? Long after the war had resumed, communist leaders, government officials, military commanders, and the public debated that question. Both sides succeeded in projecting a willingness to peacefully settle their differences—no small matter considering the nation's powerful desire for normalcy after 20 years of Marcos rule. By displaying extraordinary resolve in staying the course with her policy of reconciliation, Aquino maintained her moral authority. The communists, who had entered the talks under the dark boycott cloud, regained some of the respectability they had enjoyed during the Marcos years. Some conservative critics suggested that by entering into peace talks, Aquino had enabled the CPP to escape the consequences of the boycott, but at the same time, many in the middle class were shocked to discover that the rebel leaders were, in fact, doctrinaire Marxists-Leninists. To others, the shadowy communist leadership succeeded in projecting a human face. In the countryside, rebel forces were given a free hand to conduct political and ideological education and organizing tasks among rural peasants. The AFP also took advantage of the break to conduct civic action work and to retrain troops.

The CPP leadership had determined that one of the greatest opportunities offered by the truce was the chance to address Filipinos' deep-seated fears of communism, and the Party unleashed a propaganda offensive toward that end. "Now it's a battle for each side to get the people to accept their program," Ocampo told me. "We have to try to get people to listen to what we are offering." Rebel leaders argued their positions on television and radio talk shows, before civic clubs and in public forums. The NDF opened an office in the National Press Club building in downtown Manila, feting journalists and other invited guests with beer, soft drinks, and roasted pigs. The communist propaganda blitz included field trips for reporters to guerrilla training camps, cultural shows, rebel weddings, birthday parties, and a steady stream of press releases.

For the rebels, in a nation that revolves around a network of personal loyalties, the cease-fire offered an opportunity to reestablish valuable contacts. I witnessed an example of the grassroots rebel campaign in the drowsy Central Luzon town of Santa Ana, in the heart of old Hukbalahap territory of Pampanga province. The local NPA commander surfaced during the truce to renew acquaintances with old friends, one of whom now owned a chicken farm in Santa Ana. When the rebel commander came calling, as he frequently did during the truce, the old school chum usually offered a few chickens for the rebel troops.[15] He was not a communist or even a rebel sympathizer in any real sense, but he enjoyed the guerrilla commander's visits and empathized with some of the rebels' grievances. Besides, it was wise to stay on good terms with the NPA.

Not surprisingly, a Defense Department postmortem on the cease-fire glumly concluded that NDF forces had achieved tactical and strategic benefits from the negotiations, including the improvement of NDF political machinery, which "later on might prove to be more difficult on the part of the government to address."[16] But what the paper did not mention was the intelligence bonanza enjoyed by the AFP when scores of rebel leaders surfaced to be photographed and followed, which ultimately enabled the military to arrest several ranking CPP officials in 1987 and 1988.

In the end, the cease-fire was not the turning point for the NDF in its battle to win public acceptance. In some respects, the truce was a victory for Aquino. The popular president fulfilled an important campaign promise and satisfied public demands for a brief respite from the 18-year war. However sincere Aquino was when she began negotiations—and I believe she thought a peaceful resolution was possible, although she never fully understood the motivations of the revolution—she could claim she had extended the hand of peace only to have it rebuffed by the communists. With her moral authority intact, Aquino renewed the war against the New People's Army rebels.

16

"Land to the Tillers"

"The magnitude of the land problem can be summed up here," the Communist Party official said, gesturing around us toward the bare, rocky mountains where *kaingeros* (slash-and-burn farmers) were losing their fight to scrape a living from the tired soil. "Look at these people, trying to cultivate this rocky hillside. They have no other place to go."

We were sitting in an NPA camp in the Cordillera Mountains of Nueva Vizcaya province in 1988 with a bird's-eye view of the desperate plight of Filipino peasants in this rugged corner of the northern Philippines. In all directions, the mountains had been almost entirely stripped of trees by logging companies owned by powerful politicians. Erosion was cutting deep grooves into the severe slopes and carrying away the thin remaining layer of precious topsoil. By night, the mountainsides twinkled with the orange glow of fires set by *kaingeros* as they prepared plots wrested from the hardscrabble for June planting. By day, an acrid pall of smoke and haze hung above the treeless hills, which shimmered like a desert mirage in the baking tropical sun.

Feudal landownership and agricultural practices coupled with the mountainous terrain that covered 86 percent of Nueva Vizcaya and neighboring Quirino province had produced harsh living conditions. The vast majority of the 370,000 inhabitants in the two provinces existed far below the official poverty line of 14,000 pesos (about $670) annual income. More than 8 out of 10 were tenant subsistence farmers and *kaingeros* living on rice and root crops. In the higher elevations, farmers grew coffee, stringbeans, and native sweet potatoes; rice and corn were cultivated on the lower slopes and narrow strips of plain and plateau. The peasants gave one-third to one-half of the harvest to the landowner for rent. Then there were the usurers to pay for crop loans that carried interest rates as high as 1,000 percent. Sometimes, peasants were required to pay 100 kilos of rice for every 100 pesos borrowed. Yields for upland farmers in the area were as low as 20 cavans (1,000 kilos) of rice per year, and so by the time rent and loan payments were settled, the farmer had only enough rice to last his family a few months. In between harvests, farmers would walk deeper into the mountains to gather rattan or pick guavas that could be sold to town merchants. Still, many peasants had to turn to usurers again to get money to buy enough rice to sustain their families until the next harvest, when the cycle of debt and misery would begin anew.[1]

By 1988, when I visited the mountains of Nueva Vizcaya, that harsh cycle had been eased for many peasants by a "revolutionary land reform" program being carried out by the NPA guerrillas. According to the NPA, in the course of one year beginning in 1987, 15,000 peasants in the Nueva Vizcaya-Quirino area were the recipients of agrarian reforms.[2] As a result, in the span of a few months the provinces had become one of the fastest growing areas of NPA strength on Luzon.

The initial phase of the rebel agrarian reform campaign targeted the 12 largest landowners in Nueva Vizcaya and Quirino, each of whom owned several hundred hectares of land. (A 1988 CPP survey showed that 3 percent of the population owned 85 percent of all productive agricultural lands in the two provinces.) The list included Nueva Vizcaya governor Patricio Dumlao, who had amassed several hundred hectares of land, and Congressman Carlos Padilla, another major landholder. Many of the 12 landowners had built what amounted to fiefdoms while serving as local or provincial government officials during the 20 years of Marcos rule. Their widespread holdings included piggeries, fish farms, cattle ranches, and prime agricultural land.

The ultimate goal of the rebel program was to distribute free land to farmers, and to do so communist peasant associations backed by the NPA simply took over several tracts of farmland. Rents had been lowered for some tenant farmers. NPA pressure, for example, caused landlords in five barrios of northern Nueva Vizcaya to reduce rents for tenant farmers from one-third to one-fourth of the harvest. In other cases, cattle, farm implements, hogs, and chickens had been seized by the NPA and distributed to peasants. Representatives of the communist peasant organization, the Pambansang Katipunan ng Magsasaka (National Farmers Movement, or PKM), had even "persuaded" town merchants to pay farmers higher prices for their produce. Subsequently, peasant minorities who had been paid 7 pesos per kilo for their stringbeans were paid as much as 15 pesos per kilo.

In one of the boldest displays of rebellion, 100 communist peasants backed by 23 NPA regulars hacked to death 95 cows owned by Governor

Dumlao and confiscated three barrels of fish from his lucrative fish farm.[3] The action had been timed for February 2, 1988, the day Dumlao was taking his oath of office. The farmers complained that Dumlao had let his cows loose to feed on their crops in an effort to force the peasants off their lands. Other peasants accused Dumlao of imposing harsh terms on his tenants and of even physically beating them.

Every aspect of the communist agrarian reform program was backed by the growing muscle of the NPA in Nueva Vizcaya and Quirino. The communist army singled out two or three prominent officials (including a former governor) and landowners in Nueva Vizcaya who had vigorously resisted the agrarian reform efforts and assassinated them. "The merchants know the NPA backs PKM," the Nueva Vizcaya-Quirino Party secretary explained. "They know that if we can get such important people, we can get them."[4]

In late 1987, communist farmers led by Party officials and NPA guerrillas in Nueva Vizcaya–Quirino convened a "people's parliament," which began issuing NDF "land titles" to landless peasants. What the NPA in Nueva Vizcaya–Quirino had failed to achieve in terms of support during 15 repressive years of Marcos rule, they accomplished under the democratic rule of Corazón Aquino—all attributed to the agrarian reform campaign.

During the Marcos years, landholdings in Nueva Vizcaya and Quirino had escaped the government's agrarian reform program because of the political power of the provinces' major landlords. Bing, the Party secretary, was confident that the same would hold true during the Aquino administration and beyond. His confidence appeared to be well founded. Most of the corrupt and repressive Marcos-era officials—the area's largest landholders—had simply switched loyalties and were now municipal and provincial officials representing the Aquino government.

"In our area, the people really don't mind who's in Malacañang [palace]," Bing said. "They still eat *kamote*. It's not a matter of whether its Marcos or Aquino. It's a matter of basic survival." He gazed out across the barren mountains before continuing. "As long as the government does not address the land problem and the needs of the peasants, it will never win. And we are sure they do not have the political will to address the land problem. For as long as the NPA continues to address the land problem, we will continue to grow."[5]

What was happening in Nueva Vizcaya in 1988 was hardly isolated. In virtually every province of the Philippines, communist peasant associations backed by NPA guerrillas were effecting agrarian reforms that went far beyond anything the country had ever experienced.

From the start, the revolution had been fashioned around the plight of Filipino peasants. "The main content of the people's democratic revolution," José María Sison had written in 1968, "is the struggle for land among the peasants."[6] The CPP founder had outlined a two-stage agrarian revolution to be carried out in the countryside during the course of the people's war. In the first phase, in areas where the NPA was still weak, landlords gradually would be forced to lower farm rents and curb usurious interest rates on crop loans. Later, once those areas were effectively controlled by communist forces, usury "and other feudal evils" would be wiped out. Lands would be confiscated from their owners and distributed to poor peasants, and landlords—the "parasites" of society—would be eliminated as a class.

One of the initial acts of the CPP Central Committee when it convened its first plenum in a sun-baked Central Luzon barrio in 1969 had been to decree lower land rents for local peasants. The gesture was largely symbolic, as the NPA at the time consisted of a few dozen poorly armed guerrillas who were more preoccupied with staying one step ahead of the military. But in time the CPP slogan "Land to the tillers" proved irresistible to many desperate peasants, and in the more remote upland areas, communist land reform was carried out.

By the late 1980s, the CPP agrarian reform program had improved the lives of tens of thousands of farmers living within reach of the NPA guerrillas throughout the archipelago. Land rents had been lowered. Usury had been curtailed or even eliminated. Farm laborers had been given higher wages and better working conditions. Agricultural production had increased, and peasant livelihoods had improved. In a few cases, land had been confiscated from landlords and distributed free to landless peasants.[7]

For the revolution, land reform had become an enormously effective means of winning the loyalty and support of peasants. In some areas, aggressive implementation of the agrarian reform program had helped the NPA counter the negative effects of Aquino's popularity. As 1987 began, CPP forces in Nueva Vizcaya and Quirino were being wracked by surrenders and desertions. A Party conference was called to discuss ways to stanch the hemorrhage, and it was decided that the movement's weakness in the area stemmed from a failure to deliver agrarian reforms to peasant supporters. An order went out to all NPA units in the two provinces to begin organizing barrio chapters of the PKM.[8]

Within a year, according to Bing, the NPA's territory had expanded from 45 barrios to 192 barrios in 20 towns. The population under varying degrees of rebel control rose from 7,000 to 35,000—about 10 percent of the inhabitants of Nueva Vizcaya–Quirino—during the same period. NPA troop strength in the two provinces had more than tripled from a single platoon to an oversize company of more than 100 guerrillas, all because, Bing said, the rebels had made agrarian revolution "the main program of the NPA and NDF in this area."

Although the results may not have been as dramatic in other provinces, the NPA's increased attention to land reform in the late 1980s had underscored the differences between the revolutionary movement and the government, both in policies and accomplishments. While Congress and the executive branch were bitterly debating the issue of agrarian reform, the NPA was carrying it out. For peasants long accustomed to neglect by the government, the communist program was welcome relief.

In the early years, the NPA had through force or persuasion carried out land reform in its areas of influence. But by the 1980s, to instill a sense of self-confidence and militance in the peasants, the CPP had shifted primary responsibility for implementation of land reform to the poorest farmers working through peasant associations organized by the Party.[9] The peasant association functions as a quasigovernmental body in the barrio and in its more developed stages maintains committees for production and economic development, finance, education, health, defense, and communication. Reducing usury, lowering land rents, providing irrigation, preventing livestock theft, lifting farm production levels, and even removing government military units in the area all fall within the responsibility of the peasant association. The associations also are effective vehicles for mobilizing people to participate in Party-organized demonstrations and for screening potential recruits for the NPA.

By the late 1980s, peasant associations in some areas had succeeded in establishing sophisticated cooperatives that had ensured farmers more affordable prices for pesticides, fertilizer, seedlings, and farm equipment. Cooperative farming techniques, such as "mutual labor exchanges" between peasants, had been introduced on a wide scale, and the sharing of expensive farm implements and water buffaloes had been promoted. (A Negros cadre told me the Party had abandoned communal farms on that island because peasants had become "too lazy.") Party-guided peasant associations had even constructed crude irrigation systems in some barrios that allowed farmers to plant three crops of rice a year rather than one or two. Still other cooperatives had been established to create livelihood projects such as pig- and poultry-raising ventures.

The measures had given peasants a genuine stake in the revolution, a fact that was driven home to me one day in May 1987. Without a communist escort or Party introduction, I ventured into a rice-farming barrio of the Bataan province town of Samal, reputed to be an NDF stronghold. Legislative elections were being held that day, and so several peasants were gathered on a bamboo bench under a towering mango tree. The surrounding fields of brownish rice stubble lay baking in the summer sun awaiting June rains and planting.

All the land that surrounded the village of bamboo-and-thatch huts, a place known as Barangay Ibaba, was owned by wealthy town residents, the peasants said. When I mentioned the NDF, a shirtless young man boldly piped up and informed me that the rebel political front was "the defender of the poor." The NDF was very popular in Barangay Ibaba, the young man declared. Another peasant explained that NDF organizers from the town proper had helped the farmers form a peasant association in 1985. Proudly, one of the farmers recounted how the association had succeeded in lowering the rent paid to the landowner from 16 cavans (800 kilos) of rice per hectare to 14 cavans (700 kilos), a decrease of more than 12 percent. (The average yield per hectare was about 70 cavans.) Another farmer volunteered that the NDF was also helping some of the peasants in their efforts to secure titles to mountainous lands in an adjoining barrio, which had been confiscated from a Marcos "crony" company.

How were unarmed peasants such as those in Barangay Ibaba able to win concessions from landowners, merchants, and millers? During the movement's early years, the CPP encouraged peasants to underreport the amount of the harvest. In other cases, peasants simply withheld the crop, daring the landlord to come and get the share he was demanding. Landlords quickly became aware that to challenge NPA-backed peasants was to invite retribution. As a matter of CPP policy, any landlord who resisted land reform was targeted for "punishment," which often meant assassination.

Those tactics continued to be employed by Party-guided peasant associations throughout the 1980s. But in a growing number of cases, peasants were able to win concessions from landowners, millers, and merchants through pressure tactics or even negotiations—although the threat of NPA coercion was always a backdrop to such discussions, a factor that encouraged an amicable settlement of differences with the militant peasant associations. "The local landlord class is afraid," a member of the CPP's Bicol Agrarian Reform Committee boasted.

The December 1987 issue of *Liberation*, the official NDF publication, recounted how peasants in a Bataan province barrio had persuaded thresher owners to lower fees for peasants and raise the wages of laborers by launching a strike and boycott.[10] Even without employing violence or the implied threat of coercion, communist peasant associations had become adept at wielding subtle pressure, including the threat of social ostracism, against "rich" peasants and small landlords actually living in barrios organized by the NPA.

A new tactic employed by the communist peasant associations following the fall of Marcos in 1986 was the occupation of idle lands and property belonging to alleged Marcos cronies. In Central Luzon alone, the Party's regional leadership reported that more than 3,000 hectares of land had been confiscated by PKM peasants and the NPA between 1986 and early 1988. Peasants in Bataan had converted 403 hectares of confiscated land into a communal farm supporting 150 PKM farmers.[11] The peasant association had given each farmer a cavan of seed grain at the beginning of planting season. Farmers were allowed to keep their harvest, although they were required to pay a 5-peso membership fee to the PKM and monthly dues of 2 pesos. Typically, beneficiaries of the land confiscations were asked to contribute 2 percent of their net income to the PKM chapter.

The NPA's role in revolutionary agrarian reform, although less conspicuous, remained critical to the process. Without the armed protection provided to peasants by the NPA, many small farmers would have fallen deeper into poverty and debt and in some cases would have lost their lands to usurers. In many cases, the threat of NPA attack had neutralized the private armies of bigger landlords and had intimidated smaller landlords and merchants.

The establishment of Party-guided peasant associations was a key step in the development of a core group of poor farmers who would assume militant leadership of the revolution at the village level. When the Party established a peasant association in a barrio, rich peasants were initially prohibited from joining so that poorer peasants might develop confidence and a sense of unity. Only later, after a strong association had been established, were rich peasants invited to join.

The CPP's pragmatic approach to agrarian reform sought to avoid alienating rich and middle peasants, and even some landlords, while the movement was still striving to win power. When possible, the Bicol Party agrarian reform official said, district Party cadres sat down with the landlord and explained in detail the communist program of revolutionary land reform. "We make it a point to build a basis of unity. In the process, we are trying to raise the landlord's political consciousness," the official said. Furthermore, "patriotic" landlords were given incentives to do business with the rebels. Friendly landlords might enjoy tax breaks and continued good health in the short term and favorable treatment and even possible compensation for donated lands if the revolution were to come to power. "Those who make alliances with us, those landlords who are enlightened and did not resist land reform will be allowed to own a certain amount of land after victory, perhaps 5 to 10 hectares," the Party cadre said. "But the ultimate aim from the Marxist point of view is to eliminate the landlord class."[12]

Overzealous implementation of the agrarian reform program by peasants in some areas had created complex problems for the Party. CPP officials noted instances in which interest rates charged by lenders were lowered too sharply by peasant associations and resulted in the withdrawal of loan capital. Rash efforts by Sorsogon Party cadres in the mid-1970s to reduce peasant land rents to only 10 percent of the harvest, or even the outright confiscation of lands, prompted landlords to pool their resources to support AFP counterinsurgency efforts. This led to the decimation of revolutionary forces in the province.

In the late 1980s, CPP officials appeared keenly aware of the strategic consequences of moving too quickly in the agrarian revolution and creating too many enemies in the process. The cash-strapped CPP was still largely dependent on the resources of rich peasants and small landlords to significantly expand production in the countryside, which was vital to fulfill the expanding demands of the growing communist army. So the Party found itself in the delicate position of having to attend to the needs of its poorest peasant supporters while not alienating rich peasants and small landlords.

There were also tactical consequences of moving too brashly, as one Party cadre ruefully recalled. Sometime in the 1970s, the NPA decided it was going to free peasants in a Pangasinan province village from usury. The peasants all agreed to stop borrowing from the local usurers. To provide the capital needed to finance each year's planting, the NPA organized the peasants into a cooperative to produce charcoal. The scheme worked well for a few years until the hills surrounding the barrio had become denuded from the chopping of trees for use in making charcoal. The local water table fell drastically and farm production plunged, throwing the peasants into financial crisis.[13]

Throughout the twentieth century, land reform had been a favorite topic among Philippine politicians and intellectuals. A series of government land reform bills had been enacted dating back to 1935, yet failure to enforce or implement the measures had resulted in little change in the lives of the great majority of Filipino peasants. By 1989, land issues and rural poverty were the twin engines driving the revolution.

Despite Aquino's campaign promises to effect sweeping land reform, nothing resembling an agrarian revolution had taken shape. Aquino had raised expectations with her oft-repeated 1986 campaign pledge to make her family's 15,000-acre sugar plantation an agrarian reform "model" for the rest of the nation's landowners to follow. But once in power, Aquino rejected pleas from farmers that she use her temporary powers of decree to legislate a sweeping land reform program. Instead, the president issued a nonbinding land reform decree, which was little more than a statement of intent, and left it to Congress—a body dominated by wealthy landowners—to thrash out the contentious issue.[14]

As a result, the agrarian reform bill finally approved by Congress and signed into law by Aquino in 1988 disappointed even the most moderate farmers organizations. The measure effectively excluded 2 million hectares of land—and about one-fourth of the intended beneficiaries—from the benefits of land reform, at least for several years.[15] Aquino's agrarian reform program did move slightly beyond the plethora of measures enacted into law during the previous 50 years. For the first time in the country's history, all agricultural lands—including sugarcane and coconut plantations—were targeted. The program aimed to redistribute farm plots to landless peasants and farm workers or implement production or profit sharing arrangements between landowners and their tenant farmers or plantation workers. At the end of the 10-year timetable established by the government program, landowners would be allowed to retain five hectares of land, plus three hectares for each child older than 15 who was tilling the land or managing the farm. But by 1989 landowners had found enough loopholes in the law to seriously—fatally, according to some critics—undermine the agrarian reform program. (In Central Luzon, for example, only 37 percent of landowners heeded the new law and registered their farms for eventual redistribution.[16]) Even though the land reform program enacted by the Aquino government was hardly revolutionary, intransigent landowners still denounced the effort as "communistic" and vowed to fight—with violence, if necessary— the implementation of agrarian reform.

While landowners were finding ways to circumvent the Aquino government's program, the NDF was forging ahead with a program that was giving tens of thousands of Filipino peasants unprecedented economic and political benefits. Party leaders were convinced that by giving a steadily increasing number of peasants a personal stake in the Philippine revolution, the movement was ensuring its ultimate success. "We have reached a level where the people are defending their gains," one ranking CPP official told me. "If the government cannot top our land reform program, they cannot win the people. The people have seen that our program works."

17

Barangay Rose:
Life in a Communist Village

On the day I arrived in Barangay Rose in October 1987, several dozen peasants gathered in a nearby forest clearing for a "people's court." A 23-year-old farmer had been accused of raping and killing an 11-year-old mentally retarded girl, and now he was to face the "revolutionary justice" of the de facto communist government in the interior barrios of southern Quezon province.

The trial began promptly at 10 A.M. under the supervision of a district NPA official and was attended by the father-in-law, grandfather and cousin of the accused.[1] Several witnesses testified that they had seen the defendant, who was drunk, carry the victim away from the barrio on the back of a *carabao*. Midway through the trial, the defendant was led before the gathering. Hanging his head in shame, he admitted his guilt but pleaded his drunkenness as an excuse. "My freedom depends on you," he pleaded before his friends and neighbors.

The NPA official asked the crowd to decide the man's fate by moving to one side of the clearing or the other. The vote was unanimous for conviction. Four communist militia members and four NPA regulars led the condemned man, blindfolded and hands tied behind his back, to a crude, freshly dug grave. A military outpost was not far away, so the execution was carried out with knives: three blows to the chest, two in the back. The victim groaned, fell to his knees, and collapsed in death.

The administration of "justice" was one of many ways in which the rebels had altered the lives of peasants in Barangay Rose, a typical Philippine farming barrio. It was also a measure of the pervasiveness of the CPP's control over the lives of the barrio's inhabitants and their acceptance of the sometimes harsh ways of the revolution. The trial and execution of the farmer would undoubtedly have seemed brutal to many ordinary Filipinos, but to peasants who witnessed the trial and who had long suffered from an utter failure of the government to provide law enforcement, justice had been served. My middle-class, college-educated Party guide from Manila, a 20-year-old former rock singer named Joy, spoke proudly of the moment, the first rebel trial and execution he had witnessed. "Justice is very expensive and very slow in the Philippines," he told me. "Justice belongs to those who have the money to hire the best lawyer. Revolutionary justice is fast and inexpensive. And it is very democratic."

The peasants in Barangay Rose whom I met viewed revolutionary justice as the first fruits of the revolution. "We had a *carabao* stolen in 1980 before the movement came here, and that [stealing] was eliminated when the movement arrived," a woman named Amy declared. Another peasant recalled that in 1981 the NPA had executed the leader of the livestock rustlers and "four other notorious criminal gang leaders." From the initial execution of *carabao* thieves and other "notorious" criminals, the communist system of judgment in Barangay Rose had expanded to become a rigid code of social and political behavior. By 1985, the local communist militia had taken over many of the duties of enforcing the new law. The militia investigated newcomers who moved to the *barangay* as well as strangers who were just passing through; in the eyes of the highly secretive communist underground, all were potential informers. The militia even began handling domestic disputes and other minor public order complaints, which were then referred to local Party officials for adjudication.

The severe communist administration of justice ran the whole gamut of offenses from breaches of the Party's strict moral code (excessive drunkenness or adultery, for example), to criminal violations (theft, rape, and murder), to the most serious "antipeople" and "antirevolution" offenses punishable by death (reporting NPA activities to the military). One district Party official, Claudia, said that in her barrio the NPA had executed 12 people, including a "gangster leaders with two wives," "informants," and others who "had criminal cases as well."

Since the 1970s, the dispensation of quick frontier-style justice has worked as a popular vehicle of expansion for the communist army. Francisco, the Southern Tagalog regional NPA commander, recalled that the Party's first social investigation team that visited southern Quezon's Bondoc peninsula in 1978 discovered that *carabao* rustling was a universal problem. According to Francisco, local government officials and the area military command helped transport the stolen animals. "So *carabao* rustling became the basis for organizing the peasants at the time," he told me a decade later. "It was the basis for propagandizing and for organizing the peasants to fight back. We expanded very easily because of that issue."[2]

During a visit to an NPA camp in the Bicol region of southern Luzon, I asked a CPP Central Committee member, Sotero Llamas, if he ever worried that the speedy, summary nature of the communist justice system was sending innocent people to their deaths. "There are shortcomings. We can't deny that," he replied, conceding that the summary nature of revolutionary justice "can lead to mistakes. But the mistakes are not a practice of design." By his estimate, more than 80 percent of the cases under the communist system are "quite well done."[3]

Barangay Rose was connected to the rest of the Philippines by foot trails that fed into an old logging path, which wound up a steep ridge and eventually widened into a gravel road that led to the nearest town more than 15 miles away. The road often became impassable for weeks during the rainy months, and reaching Barangay Rose became a difficult feat. Entering the barrio on one occasion during the rainy season, our motorized tricycle smoked and sputtered and finally ground to a halt in the quagmire that had swallowed the road. Joy, the Party cadre who had become my faithful guide to the southern Quezon guerrilla zone, directed me to grab my pack and abandon the tricycle. We would have to walk the final four miles to Barangay Rose. As Joy and I slogged along the muddy road in the cold, steady rain, we were joined by four young men whose faces I recognized. They were NPA guerrillas who had been to the nearby town buying food and other supplies and were returning to the communist camp in the roadless interior of Barangay Rose.

In its physical isolation and backwardness, Barangay Rose was not unlike thousands of Philippine villages. It was not a neat collection of little houses clustered around a village green but a sprawling expanse of rugged, coconut palm-studded hills, with primitive bamboo huts elevated on stilts scattered throughout the dank tropical forests and meadows wherever a source of water could be found. Distances between houses were sometimes considerable and measured not in kilometers but in rigorous minutes on the crude trails and streams that snaked through the hills. Although Ferdinand Marcos had brought electricity to thousands of barrios during his 20 years in power, Barangay Rose remained in darkness. The lives of residents were regimented by the sun, and the darkness of night was broken only with the dim light of crude homemade lamps fashioned from rag wicks and vinegar bottles filled with kerosene. Women cooked over wooden fires and washed clothes in streams that often were little more than fetid trickles of water. Men planted their rice and other crops by the the same century-old primitive methods of tilling the hillsides with water buffalos and simple steel or wooden plows. The land was so poor and the hills so steep and marginally productive that a peasant could farm 9 or 10 hectares of land and still be desperately impoverished. The only amenity the government had ever provided to the people of Barangay Rose was an artesian well constructed in mid-1987, but only a half dozen of the barrio's 85 families lived near enough to use the water.

Some of the people of Barangay Rose had great expectations that Corazón Aquino would end the government's neglect and solve the peasants' problems. Dante, the vice commander of the barrio communist militia, had told me that he and his wife had walked more than three miles through the forest to cast their votes for Aquino in the 1986 presidential election. "Some of Cory's statements in the campaign matched the program of the movement," Dante explained. But within a few months the Party line held that the new government was no different from the old regime, and this view had gradually filtered down to Barangay Rose. "There have been only small reforms," Dante noted bitterly in late 1987. By then, the peasants of Barangay Rose seemed to view the Aquino presidency with a sense of betrayal and with much of the same cynicism they had once reserved for Marcos.

Physically, Barangay Rose may have looked like thousands of other barrios, but the revolution had wrought remarkable changes for those living within its confines. In the decade that the communist rebels had been frequenting Barangay Rose, its inhabitants had been taught the basics of preventive health care and nutrition. Women had learned paramedic skills, and some could even perform minor surgeries. The NPA had helped residents construct sanitary toilets and taught men new farming methods.

One of the families that had benefited from the program of the revolution was that of Eladio and his wife, Amy. She was a weathered-looking peasant woman with close-cropped hair and large hands and feet rough and calloused from a life of hard work in the house and fields. When Amy smiled, she revealed a set of rotting teeth badly stained from the juice of the betel nut. Eladio was 51 years old, and he had lived in a far corner of Barangay Rose since 1963 supporting his family by farming almost six hectares planted with coconuts, bananas, rice, and corn. Eladio and his family lived in a large wood-frame house built in a rolling meadow dotted with a half dozen small bamboo huts and surrounded by sharp hills on all sides. His house was much larger and better constructed than that of the average peasant. The floor was made of wooden planks rather than bamboo, and there were four rooms— two almost-bare rooms for sleeping, a dining room with benches and a long, wooden table worn smooth over the years, and a small kitchen with an open-hearth stove.

Like virtually all of the peasants I met in Barangay Rose, he had stopped paying taxes to the government years earlier after trying un- successfully to obtain from the government a legal title to the land he had been cultivating. Eladio and Amy had cast their lot with the revolution in 1981 and had joined respective communist groups for peasants and women.

Rice is the lifeblood of Filipino peasants, and a few weeks before I had arrived Eladio had harvested his annual crop, which amounted to 30 pails (about 500 kilos). Eladio still had six children living at home— three others had married and had their own families in the barrio— and after contributions to the NPA, the rice would last his family only five months. From February until the next harvest in October, cash income from Eladio's other crops, primarily coconuts and bananas, would have to support the family. Eladio calculated that he earned 3,200 pesos (about $152) a year selling coconut meat. Many families in Barangay Rose ran out of rice during the rainy months between June and September, and their survival depended on gathering bananas to sell in distant town markets. For walking several miles over muddy trails carrying heavy bundles of bananas, a peasant might earn 10 pesos (less than 50 cents) per 100 bananas.

Most men I met in Barangay Rose confessed to having been heavy drinkers before the strict ways of the revolution were imposed, and Eladio was no exception. "When the movement organized us, I realized drinking was not the way to solve problems," he said. "I realized that when the comrades explained their policies and programs. The comrades told me to lessen my drinking habits. Little by little, I began to stop drinking."

I surmised that Eladio, having seen what the NPA did to the *carabao* thieves, must have been afraid of what the rebels had in store for him. Had the NPA warned him of the consequences if he continued drinking heavily? Eladio threw back his head and cut loose a gravelly laugh, revealing a huge wad of chewing tobacco and a set of badly stained and rotting teeth. There had been no threats, he insisted. "I assessed myself internally and decided it was bad for my health."

By the late 1980s, having firmly established control over Barangay
Rose, the Party turned its attention to improving the livelihoods of its
supporters. For years, the peasants had eked out livings by farming
small plots of rice and gathering coconuts and bananas to sell in town
markets. The hilly terrain was not very productive, and lack of crop
rotation further depleted the soil. Unlike the scarce, fertile lowlands,
where farmers harvest up to three crops a year, the farmers of hilly
barrios such as Barangay Rose were usually able to grow only one crop
of rice annually. During the remainder of the year, some farmers planted
corn, harvesting two crops in a good year. CPP cadres who supervised
the communist peasants association, to which virtually all the men of
Barangay Rose belonged, began the agrarian revolution by teaching new
farming techniques that improved output and raised incomes. Peasants
were taught to plant tobacco or corn between the rows of coconut
seedlings and to grow alternative crops to replenish the tired soil.

An integral component of the communist agricultural and economic
development programs in Barangay Rose and other areas had been the
formation of cooperatives and collectivized farming. The latter included
widely varying forms ranging from the collective cultivation of farm
plots to the communal use of farm implements and smaller-scale exchanges
of labor among farmers modeled after communist China's "labor mutual-
aid" societies. Through the various methods, the Party was gradually
conditioning peasants to the concept of collective work, laying the
groundwork for the cooperative and collective social and economic
activities envisioned by communist leaders in a post-revolution "people's
republic."

The boldest move toward collectivization in Barangay Rose occurred
in 1984, when under Party leadership 52 peasants began preparing a
one-half hectare rice plot to be farmed collectively for local NPA units.[4]
It took the men a year to construct the dikes and irrigation system for
the paddy, but by autumn 1985, the Barangay Rose peasants association
had harvested its first crop—25 pails of rice—for the rebel fighters. The
peasants took turns tending the paddy, working as much as two days
a week in the collective plot during the growing season. The harvest
was a collective effort aided by NPA guerrillas. In between rice crops,
the farmers planted coffee, peanuts, cacao, and pepper for the guerrilla
army. But in 1986, drought and disease cut the harvest to only 10 pails
of rice. The following year, asked by Party officials to boost production
for the growing NPA force in the area, the peasants expanded the
collective plot to three-quarter hectare.

The women of Barangay Rose were also mobilized to participate in
the economic development campaign. In 1986, under the supervision of
Party cadres, Amy and 55 other peasant women started a piggery to

improve the livelihoods of the barrio's poorest residents. Each of the cooperative members paid 10 pesos and, supplemented by Party funds, the cooperative bought a sow for breeding with other male pigs in the barrio. Rules for dividing the offspring were established: From each litter, three piglets would be reserved for the cooperative, three would go to the family who bred the sow, and one would go to the boar's owner. Eventually, the cooperative hoped to sell pigs at local markets and make the profits available to families who needed money for emergencies, such as the illness of a child. "If the comrades need money," Amy said, "then we will also help them."

By late 1987, the Barangay Rose piggery was still struggling to become established. The cooperative had added one piglet from the litter of a sow successfully bred by a peasant, but two other piglets had died. The survivor was being groomed for breeding by a boar owned by one of the poorest families in the barrio. "Our primary goal," Amy told me, "is to help the poor farmers uplift their economic situation and to raise funds for the organization. This is helping the revolution."

The revolution had brought further socioeconomic development to Barangay Rose, and other projects were in the planning stage. Communist doctors had given basic medical training to peasant women, and the peasants had been taught to make use of indigenous herbal medicines, acupuncture, and acupressure. A limited Party day care program was even available to peasant mothers, offering basic education along with political indoctrination for preschool children. A major project under planning at the end of 1987 was a community fish pond, which would improve the diet of Barangay Rose residents and, it was hoped, would eventually become a profit-making venture for revolutionary coffers.

Every farmer in Barangay Rose—even the poorest, according to Eladio—was expected to contribute one pail of rice to the movement each harvest. Barrio residents were also expected to pay "dues" to their respective communist sectoral organizations. Eladio said he paid 2 pesos a month to the peasants association, and his wife paid 1 peso to the women's organization. Sometimes, Eladio said, the guerrillas might ask him for supplies, or maybe bananas, rice, or coconuts, and he would give.

From the first days of the NPA's arrival in the late 1970s, politics had been the thread used by the communists to bind the peasants of Barangay Rose to the revolution. Politics became the medium by which all actions of the Party and communist army were explained and provided the framework for analyzing the poverty of Filipino peasants. The masses were poor because of the unjust semifeudal, semicolonial economic system imposed by the U.S. imperialists and nurtured by local big capitalists; the government neglected the needs of peasants because of its elitist and reactionary character. These and other explanations became truisms committed to heart by the peasants of Barangay Rose.

The communist political education of villagers began with the careful cultivation of a few trusted men and women in the barrio. Later, Party organizers convened larger meetings and gave longer political lectures. The process continued when the men, women, and children of Barangay Rose were organized into sectoral organizations. Instruction manuals used in the barrio classes summarized and simplified the teachings of Marx, Lenin, and Mao. The thrust of the Party's teachings was that the revolution was not merely about land or *carabao* thieves. The peasant families were taught that what was happening in their barrio was part of a larger cause—that of "national liberation."

Like virtually all the people of Barangay Rose, Eladio and Amy, who had only a few years of elementary schooling, had taken the Party's introductory basic mass course. They had also taken a course explaining the revolutionary land reform program. Curious to know how deeply the Party had imbued them with a vision of the future, I asked Eladio and Amy what changes they expected in their lives if the revolution won.

After some hesitation, both said they thought changes would occur, but they were not quite sure what. Then, as if remembering something she had been taught in the Party education sessions, Amy added, "The victory of the revolution will eliminate usury, land tenants and the people's misery."

I phrased my question in a different fashion: "Do you believe your lives will be better if the revolution wins?"

Amy answered, "If the revolution succeeds, equal rights will be implemented, because that is part of the program. Feudal relations for women will be ended." Eladio silently nodded his head in agreement.

Throughout the years the Party had skillfully molded various elements of Catholicism and traditional culture, and by the late 1980s an emerging revolutionary national democratic culture had taken shape in some barrios. Song was the most popular form of expression developed by the movement, and a book of revolutionary songs was widely distributed among units and supporters in the countryside. The guerrillas and Party organizers in turn passed the songs onto peasants.

In many barrios, the NPA and the Party had attempted to deepen political consciousness by forming cultural groups that performed revolutionary songs and short dramatic plays on holidays and special occasions. Typically, the songs and drama focused on the common problems of peasants and workers while extolling the revolution as salvation. The most memorable communist cultural presentation I witnessed occurred in Barangay Rose in 1987, on the eve of All Saint's Day, October 31.

That evening, I sat talking with Dante in his hut, surrounded by the melancholy isolation of the coconut forest, the darkness broken only feebly by the sooty light of a homemade lamp. Around 9 P.M., Dante's dog began to bark furiously at some unseen strangers in the darkness. We heard whispers and giggles, and suddenly sweet, melodic voices rose in song. We crowded into the narrow doorway as the Party's barrio cultural group sang a traditional folksong about the life of Christ. (The song was typically sung on such occasions, and, it seemed to me, held little religious significance for the peasant youths.) After we had applauded the performance, Dante held aloft the flickering oil lamp and introduced each of the singers. Some were already in their twenties, but most were teenagers, and some were even younger.

At Dante's urging, the group leader announced they would perform two short plays for their foreign guest. Dante and his wife scurried inside the hut and returned with two oil lamps, while the performers shuffled shyly to their assigned places. More whispers, and Dante rushed back into the hut, to return with an antiquated rifle, which he gave to a young man. Another fellow began strumming a battered guitar, and as Dante's speckled pig snorted happily at our feet, the performance began.

The first skit dramatized the effects of militarization in the countryside. The men posing as soldiers clutched sticks for rifles and pretended to get drunk before leaving on an operation. As they walked through an imaginary barrio, the "soldiers" stole all the livestock and other valuables from terrified peasants. At one house, the drunken troops knocked a farmer to the ground, and as he pleaded with them to leave, raped his wife. The young peasant girl who played the role of the rape victim cut loose a blood-curdling shriek as the soldiers wrestled her to the ground. (I wondered if Dante's neighbors might wonder what was happening and come investigate the noise, but no one did.) The skit ended with peasants fleeing their homes to become refugees.

The second skit told the story of an oppressed peasant named Tano. As a young man mournfully sang the story line, the others silently and with passion acted out the tragic tale. Tano, as the story went, worked hard in his field. One day, his daughter fell ill, just as the landlord demanded double the agreed rent. Tano begged for compassion, but the landlord demanded payment. Because Tano lacked money to buy medicine, his daughter died. He was forced to borrow money from a usurer and fell hopelessly into debt. In the end, Tano abandoned the land and ran away to the hills to become a Red fighter with the NPA.

Dante explained that to support itself the group had adapted a traditional Filipino practice of "soul hunting," roughly akin to the Western trick-or-treat practice. They walked from house to house singing songs in exchange for coins. Moved by the earnestness of the impromptu performance, I went back into the hut and dug a soggy wad of peso notes from my pack. It came to 45 pesos (about $2.25), which was more than the barrio youths could expect to earn in a few years of soul hunting. Excitedly, they thanked me, then disappeared along the trail leading into the dark forest.

The lives of Filipino peasants revolved around a constant struggle for survival, finding enough food and shelter to continue their harsh lives. Similarly, much of the energies of the NPA guerrillas and Party cadres were devoted to enduring the hardships of daily life rather than fighting the government. But in the course of this fight for survival, the lives of peasants and the communist rebels became inexorably intertwined. This process was underscored to me on many occasions but never so vividly as during a typhoon that ravaged the Bondoc peninsula in November 1987.

When word of the approaching storm was heard over a scratchy local radio broadcast one day at noon, I was in the well-built house of Eladio and Amy. Earlier in the day, 14 Party and NPA cadres who had spent the night in the house had left in the already steady rain to attend a regional command conference at a camp hidden in the forest several hours further down the peninsula. Later in the morning, a chubby-cheeked woman in her early twenties, an NPA guerrilla named Elvie, had sought momentary refuge under the raised house with her elderly parents. The family was from a barrio in a nearby town where vigilantes were active. Elvie had been unable to return home, so her parents had traveled over rugged trails to the NPA camp to visit her. Now, shivering and soaked, Elvie was guiding her parents back to the road, more than two hours distant, through heavy rain, rising streams and endless mud.

Throughout the day, despite the torrential rains and treacherous trails, kasamas (comrades) kept passing through the meadow, soaked and shivering but always cheery as they stopped to barter bits of news and gossip. Several school children, looking as though they had come from a swim, huddled under Eladio's house, their teeth chattering. Seeing the pitiful sight, three Party workers who had stopped for a respite offered the children an escort to their houses, and off they went.

Nightfall arrived early, and soon afterward six miserable-looking guerrillas clambered up the ladder into Eladio's house. The house was elevated on posts anchored in the ground, and the structure began to sway violently as the howling winds rose to more than 100 mph. By midnight, the wind had built to a terrifying roar that sounded like a freight train hurtling within inches of the house, and water was squirting through the spaces between the wall planks. Several leaks appeared in the thatch roof, and a woven thatch window blew out in the room where several of us huddled. We were sent scrambling for a dry spot as rain gushed into the room through the hole where the window had been. A section of roof was ripped off the back room where Eladio was lying with his wife and children, and they joined the futile competition to find a dry spot in the house.

As the housed pitched and rocked like a tiny boat in a raging sea, I huddled in a corner and locked my arm around an anchor post. One by one, the bamboo houses that dotted the meadow blew down, and Eladio's house began to fill with men, women, children, grandmothers, squalling babies, and frightened dogs and cats. The wind built to such terrifying fury that I expected any moment to be thrown out into the night with a splintering of timbers. But to my joy and amazement, the house held together, and by the time a tentative, gray dawn broke, the worst had passed.

In the dim light, I counted more than 30 people and an undetermined number of cats and dogs huddled in Eladio's battered house. Daylight also brought the first glimpse of the destruction wrought by the typhoon. The ridge that towered over the meadow looked as though a giant hand had swept angrily across it flattening everything in its path. Mud slides had left great brown scars across the ridge face. Trees and houses lay twisted and toppled in the meadow around us. Coconut palms that remained upright were badly damaged, their tops twisted and fronds ripped into shreds, and their ability to produce coconuts lost for two or more years. Eladio's banana trees, another source of food and income for the family, were snapped and their fruit scattered. Stoically, Eladio and his neighbors surveyed the destruction and began the enormous task of cleanup and reconstruction; they collected fallen coconuts and bananas and propped up battered walls and roofs.

The NPA camp a few miles to our south had barely survived the typhoon. Some of the crude bamboo-and-palm shelters were nearly crushed by trees, and most were battered and without roofs. While rebels and peasants had huddled fearfully in Eladio's well-constructed wooden house, the regional Party and NPA leaders had survived the storm in their flimsy lean-tos. At the height of the typhoon, they later told me, the indefatigable Tibbs, the regional CPP secretary, had led her colleagues in singing revolutionary songs. As they sang, they clung to the rickety sapling frame of their open-sided shelter trying desperately to keep their camp from being blown away. The heavy rains had soaked the collection of Party documents, including Tibbs' prized notebooks in which she recorded her thoughts on strategy, tactics and ideology. When I arrived two days later, dozens of soggy documents and notebook pages had been laid on fallen trees and bushes to dry in the sun.

At noon, Joy and I prepared to depart for the camp where a CPP conference was under way. Three Party cadres joined us on the soupy trail heading south from Barangay Rose. The hillsides were so slippery and soggy that at times we had to claw our way to the top with our hands. Tangled vines, thorny branches, palm fronds, and broken trees lay across the trail. We picked our way through the obstacles, and when that proved impossible, we abandoned the trail and hacked a detour through the surrounding jungle.

The heavy rains and fallen trees had aroused teeming colonies of stinging red ants, and we were soon covered by the maddening insects. While I groused aloud about the mud, the ants, the thorns, the fallen trees, anything that came to mind, my companions negotiated the trail without complaint and with unfailing good cheer. The closest any of the young communists came to complaining was a rather offhand comment that the trail was unusually *mahirap* (difficult). The camaraderie of the group was impressive as its members helped each other to navigate a patch of thorns or cross a dangerous gorge with the help of an outstretched hand. At one point, as we slowly wound our way through a stand of thick forest, one of the cadres spotted a tree laden with wild oranges. He quickly picked a handful and passed them around.

By evening, we were still several miles away from the NPA camp, and we searched for a place to spend the night. We spotted a small hut illuminated by the embers of a cooking fire. A sinewy farmer whose clothes hung loosely on his frail frame eyed us suspiciously as we approached. The hut was too small to lodge more than two of us, but he agreed, unenthusiastically it seemed, to allow Joy and me to spend the night. The others could stay with one of the farmers who lived on the ridge, he suggested, motioning toward a pair of flickering cooking fires on a nearly sheer ridge several hundred yards distant.

After a dinner of rice and a wild vegetable prepared by the peasant's very young wife supplemented by a small tin of potted meat and some crackers I was carrying, Joy borrowed the peasant's battered guitar and began singing Filipino and U.S. folksongs. Before joining the communist underground, Joy had played in a rock band that performed in Shakey's pizza parlors in Manila, and I joined him in a few melancholy Simon and Garfunkel ballads. Afterward, we talked for a while about our shared musical interests—the Beatles, Seals and Crofts, Simon and Garfunkel—and I wondered if perhaps Joy still preferred his secular music to that of the revolution.

The following morning, after a rigorous two-hour hike, we finally arrived at the NPA camp, a collection of bamboo lean-tos and larger shelters hidden in a forested gulch cut by a meandering spring-fed stream. Logistics for supplying the camp were still tenuous, however, and the food supply was meager. For lunch one day, we had what the rebels called heart of coconut palm, the hard white core of the coconut tree. It tasted somewhat bland and was the tough consistency of raw carrot, but when served with rice and eaten in large enough quantities, it was filling. On my final morning, there was no viand for breakfast, so most of the rebels ate heaping plates of rice sprinkled with salt. One by one, our perimeter guards came in, filled a plate with rice, poured a small tin cup of native coffee, and then returned to their posts in the forest around the camp.

At midmorning, two guerrillas arrived carrying a squealing black pig, which had been bought from a nearby farmer, hanging by its feet from a bamboo pole. The butcher was a ruggedly handsome, mustachioed deputy platoon commander named Rudy, who at 49 was reputed to be the region's oldest Red fighter. Nothing of the pig was wasted; intestines, liver, brains, ears, feet, tail, and blood were cooked to be eaten during the next two or three days. I had given the kitchen crew a bag of kidney beans to prepare with the pork, but, alas, having never seen them before, the chefs undercooked the beans and they were rather crunchy. The few rebels brave enough to sample the strange red beans politely expressed a preference for rice.

Our guide for the return trip was a strapping guerrilla in his twenties who had suffered from polio as a young boy. Although he limped badly, he moved swiftly and surely along the trails, which finally had begun to dry. I felt strengthened by the hearty meal of rice, beans, and pork, and we made excellent time.

A searing tropical sun was beating down when we reached a ridgetop clearing that offered a magnificent panoramic view of the Ragay Gulf. In the clearing, a peasant was sifting through the scattered wreckage of broken bamboo, clay pots, clothes, and other meager belongings— the sum total of his possessions. Four ragged-looking, malnourished children crawled through the remains of the hut. As the peasant worked in the hot sun on this late November afternoon, the Philippine revolution swirling without fanfare through the hills and valleys around him, an old transistor radio beside him played "I'm Dreaming of a White Christmas." It was a scene that filled me with a sense of irony and sadness, and it remains one of the most enduring memories of my travels through the countryside with the guerrillas and their peasant supporters.

Near dusk, after hiking for almost three hours, we arrived at a sturdy wooden house that was being used as a headquarters by Mike, the southern Quezon Party secretary. The balcony of the house, which belonged to an old farmer named Greg, was stacked with new boxes of M-16 ammunition. Greg clearly was proud to have such an important Party official staying at his house but, to my astonishment, could not contain his delight when he discovered he was to have a guest from the United States.

Greg was a gentle, courtly man in his sixties with an ample head of silver hair. He said that he had gotten to know several Americans during World War II, when he had acted as an errand boy for GIs operating east of Manila. Like most older Filipinos I had met, his memories of the United States were fond and nostalgic, and he was troubled by the image of the United States painted by the Party cadres as the root of his country's problems. He wanted to take advantage of my visit to ask all the questions he had stored inside him since the revolution had arrived in Barangay Rose. Oblivious to everyone else in the house, Greg squatted on the floor beside me and began to ask a torrent of questions.

Although his English was not bad, Greg was afraid he might miss something, and so he called for Joy to sit beside us and translate my words into Tagalog. I suspected that Joy, hearing some of the Party's teachings placed in doubt, shaped my answers to fit the movement's view of the world. Like virtually all the peasants I had encountered in barrios organized by the CPP, Greg was under the impression that the United States was poised to send troops to crush the NPA. Gently, I tried to suggest that this was unlikely. "The U.S. would not send troops here in the near future because Americans still remember the Vietnam war too clearly and painfully," I replied. Greg nodded his head slowly. The following morning, as I prepared to leave his house and return to Manila, Greg took my hand and shook it vigorously. As Mike and other Party officials stood by, the old farmer unabashedly declared, "I am so proud to have had an American stay in my house. You are always welcome to come back and stay here."

Of the 85 families living in Barangay Rose in 1988, 80 had at least one member who had joined the rebel movement. What was life like for those 5 families who had shunned the revolution? Unfortunately, I never met any of them. Tibbs, the regional CPP secretary, had spent much time in the barrio, and she assured me the movement did not impose its will on those families who had declined to join. They were not, for example, required to join farm labor exchange teams. On political matters, the Party was less benevolent. "They have to follow rules," Tibbs said. "They don't report to the enemy. They just keep quiet."

In late 1985, two brothers were accused of breaking those rules by revealing NPA activities to the local military command. One of the brothers, a tricycle driver, was arrested by members of the barrio militia and NPA regulars, tried by a Party tribunal and executed. Afterward, Tibbs went to the family's house to visit the man's widow and children. "I felt very terrible about it," she told me. "I could not imagine the children having lost a father and the wife having lost a husband." But, in the eyes of Tibbs and the communists of Barangay Rose, the victim had committed an unforgivable crime against the revolution.

The second brother was spared by the NPA and as of 1988 was still living in the barrio running a small general store across from the school, a stone's throw from the spot where Dante was killed. Long afterward, the execution of the tricycle driver and the pardoning of his brother lingered as a powerful reminder to residents: Beyond the matters of livelihood and culture and politics, the revolution held the power of life and death in Barangay Rose.

18

Revolution in the Church

Filipinos take great pride in describing their homeland as the only Catholic country in Asia. Nearly 9 out of 10 Filipinos identify themselves as Church members, even if most are only nominally so. Every barrio and town has a patron saint honored each year with an elaborate festival of religion and revelry. The Church permeates virtually every facet of society and cuts across class lines from the wealthy plantation owner with his lavish private chapel to the poorest peasant with a plastic Virgin Mary prominently displayed in his bamboo hut.

The Catholic Church was introduced to the Philippines by the Spanish conquistadors in the early sixteenth century and ruled in tandem with the crown's civil authorities. Parish priests not only controlled the spiritual lives of rural Filipinos; they also controlled the schools, courts, and elections. With the blessings of civil authorities, the Church steadily expanded its landholdings through royal decree and deceit, often by confiscating the plots of illiterate peasants ignorant of Spanish law.[1] Even after the end of Spanish colonial rule and a half century of U.S. rule, the Church had changed little in the Philippines. By the 1960s, the Church still had retained much of its colonial-era economic, political, and social power, and remained a bulwark of conservatism.

In 1965, the Second Vatican Council concluded in Rome with approval of a constitution committing the Church to a radical new mission: social justice for the poor. In the Philippines, Church "social action centers" sprang up to minister to the material as well as spiritual needs of poor peasants and urban slum dwellers, discarding traditional dogma that limited the Church's social role to pacifying believers. The Church threw reinvigorated support behind the Federation of Free Farmers and the Federation of Free Workers. Priests encouraged labor organizing and rallied peasants to contest land grabbing and the violation of tenancy arrangements by landowners.

Involvement in social protests invariably led some priests to encounters with Maoist students who were calling for a violent revolution. Initially, the two groups viewed one another with mutual disdain and distrust. "I thought the members of KM and SDK were just a bunch of misfits," a priest who later joined the communist underground recalled.[2] Student radicals in turn derided the reform-minded Church elements as clerico-fascists.

In time, the involvement of Church people in the revolution took a variety of forms, ranging from priests and nuns whose Christian commitment to addressing the injustices of society united them in common associations with the rebels, to the few hundred religious who disappeared into the underground and even took up arms against the government. The conversion of Catholic priests, nuns and layworkers from nonviolent social activists to armed revolutionaries occurred in two contrasting fashions. For some, the acceptance of a Maoist people's war was the result of frustrated efforts to give meaning to Vatican II's expressed concern for the poor. For others, the transformation was largely an intellectual process, the incendiary union of resurgent Philippine nationalism with so-called theologies of liberation.

Brendan Cruz, the nom de guerre used by one priest-turned-rebel whom I met, was one of the latter. As a young priest in 1968, he had joined a Church group demanding implementation of the Vatican II directives to minister to the needs of the poor. The group criticized the local Catholic hierarchy for not aggressively addressing social justice issues and questioned the morality of vast Church financial holdings. That involvement led Cruz in 1970 to join the Student Christian Movement, many of whose members had defected from KM and SDK when they failed to address Church issues.

Gradually, Cruz and other urban-based priests, nuns, and seminarians began to read Maoist literature and propaganda disseminated by Sison's underground Communist Party. Christian discussion groups, similar to the secular study cells founded a few years earlier, sprouted as Church activists read the works of European liberation theologians and debated the merits of nonviolent social protest versus armed revolution. Many Church activists embraced the fusion of Marxism and Christianity as "revolutionary ecumenism," and by 1972, they had reached two significant conclusions: first, that the goal of national liberation to which they subscribed could not be attained peacefully; second, that the institutional Church could not lead the liberation efforts.[3]

On February 17, 1972, radical religious activists were integrated formally into the CPP-led legal revolutionary movement with the establishment of the Christians for National Liberation (CNL). The occasion was the one-hundredth anniversary of the martyrdom of three reform-minded Filipino priests who were accused of rebellion and executed by Spanish colonial authorities. The CNL founding congress in downtown Manila's university belt was attended by 72 Church activists, including about a dozen Catholic priests and several Protestant pastors all dedicated to the concept of a national democratic revolution.[4] In the countryside, the CNL found a following among some priests and nuns who had grown bitterly disillusioned with the upper class' violent resistance to Church-inspired social and economic reforms. Cooperation between Marxist student radicals and provincial Church activists progressed, and by the time Marcos declared martial law that autumn, a Church-based support network for the NPA guerrillas was in place in a few areas.[5]

It was nearly 15 years to the day that Nick Ruíz had fled his Bohol province parish for the communist underground when we first met in Manila in September 1987. He had been Father Nick then, 30 years old, six years out of seminary, the first Filipino priest to join the NPA guerrillas. Now, at 45, traces of gray in his jet-black hair and wire-frame glasses served as gentle reminders of lost youth, and he asked to be called Nato, his underground nom de guerre. He did not wax nostalgic about the anniversary of his flight to the hills. There was too much work to do, he explained, too many problems to solve—right-wing vigilantes and Aquino's popularity, for starters—to dwell on the events of so many years ago. His career as a rebel had been a remarkable one, taking him from the comforts of a provincial parish to some of the harshest jungles and mountains, from a job as Bohol social action director to a seat on the region's Communist Party Executive Committee. Along the way, he proudly recounted, he and his comrades had brought land reform, health care, literacy, and "quick and democratic justice" to despairing peasants, things he had tried, but failed, to do as a priest.[6]

Ruíz had been ordained in 1966 as the impact of Vatican II was beginning to be felt in provincial parishes. Assigned to Bohol, he became a chaplain for the Federation of Free Farmers and director of the island's Catholic social action center. He was driven by his zeal "to give flesh and blood to the instructions of Vatican II, to make the Church relevant in modern times," he recalled.

In many areas of the country in the late 1960s, the most pressing social and economic problem was land grabbing by politically powerful families. Peasants often did not hold the proper title for lands they had been farming for years or even for decades. Prominent businesspeople, officials, and landowners frequently took advantage of the peasants' ignorance of the law by filing claims for productive lands and using political clout to gain proper titles. A common tactic was to get the Bureau of Foresty to declare an area unoccupied and then obtain a pasture lease on the land for 1 peso per hectare annually. Landowners fenced off their plots and hired armed guards to forcibly evict peasants. If they balked, a landowner might turn his cows loose to eat the settlers' crops or threaten violence. Occasionally, a landowner's security guards would kill a defiant peasant, and the others would invariably flee. In the past, peasants had acquiesced to the land grabbing by moving deeper into the forest or higher up the hillsides, clearing new plots of land, and cultivating rice or corn until forced to move again. Now, Church activists attempted to thwart the maneuvers of land grabbers through the courts by helping peasants win proper titles to their plots.

Other peasants were seeking better tenancy arrangements with their landlords. The Share-Tenancy Law passed in 1954 prohibited landowners from keeping more than 30 percent of a tenant's crop as land rent. But the law had never been enforced, and so after more than a decade the FFF and Church activists tried to force compliance. When landowners resisted, FFF activists encouraged farmers to simply withhold 70 percent of the crop—their legal share—regardless of the existing tenancy agreement. Angry landowners responded by filing criminal theft charges against the peasants, and many rebellious tenants were arrested.[7]

In case after case involving land grabbing, contested titles, and tenancy disputes, politically well-connected landowners won favorable judgments from the courts and government agencies. The results were hardly surprising to Church activists. After all, major landowners were usually prominent politicians, or at least they controlled local politics, including the appointment of judges. But recognition of existing political realities did little to ease the frustration. Failing to win redress through the courts, Ruíz and other Church social reformers began encouraging farmers to resist eviction from their lands and contest illegal or unjust tenancy terms. Compounding the frustration and anger of Church activists were the violent methods landowners employed against peasants. Ruíz recalled one case in Bohol in 1971 that was a turning point in his transformation from a priest committed to peaceful social reform to a communist guerrilla sworn to armed revolution.

A prominent Bohol landowner had filed a claim to land that several peasants had leased from the government for decades. The landowner, using his political connections in Manila, succeeded in winning title to the plot. The local Catholic social action center filed a court case on behalf of the peasants occupying the land, but the judge—a political appointee beholden to the wealthy landowner—refused to act on the case. In the meantime, the landowner attempted to enforce his claim by planting coconut seedlings on the disputed land. Warned by an FFF attorney that the landowner could cite the cultivation of coconut palms to support his claim for the land, Ruíz organized a truckload of peasants and Catholic student activists to uproot the seedlings. The landowner was enraged by the defiance, and he had the seedlings replanted. Ruíz again organized peasants and Catholic students. This time, armed guards hired by the landowner stood on a hill firing at the crowd as they plucked the seedlings from the ground. Eventually, the settlers were forced to leave the land.

By late 1972, Ruíz had filed on behalf of Bohol peasants 96 court cases involving land grabbing, disputes about ownership of land, and landlord-tenant arrangements. Some had not been reviewed by the court after more than a year. Not a single case was decided in favor of the peasants.[8]

Nowhere in the Philippines was the challenge to the Catholic Church greater in the late 1960s than on Negros. Sugar was king on the island, and a few wealthy families owned the vast majority of land, virtually every arable inch of which was planted to sugarcane. Luís Jalandoni had grown up on a Negros sugar hacienda, a scion of one of island's wealthiest landowning families. In the mid-1960s, he had walked away from the sugar baron's opulent lifestyle to become a priest.

Returning to the island in late 1967 from postgraduate theological studies in Europe, Jalandoni found fellow priests and nuns galvanized to address the daunting social and economic problems that kept the vast majority of Negrenses living in the harshest poverty.[9] Jalandoni was assigned to head a Church project to create a multipurpose cooperative for struggling subsistence farmers in the hardscrabble hills of southern Negros. The Church gave the farmers fertilizer to increase their production. A nurse was sent in to teach hygiene, sanitation, and preventive health care. The Kaisahan Settlement Project, as it was called, flourished, and within a few months the peasants had dramatically increased their output. As Jalandoni made plans to obtain two tractors to help mechanize the area, he and other priests involved in the project excitedly talked of making the Kaisahan experiment the prototype for similar efforts throughout the province.

In the meantime, Jalandoni had been appointed director of the Negros diocese social action center. He encouraged other priests to get involved in social projects—organizing unions for sugar workers, defending peasants against wealthy land grabbers, forming cooperatives to improve the livelihood of farmers and field hands. His activism catalyzed many young priests on Negros. One foreign priest described Jalandoni as "a John the Baptist figure who inspired us all."[10]

Around the same time, priests and nuns launched a campaign to improve conditions in the sugar industry. In 1969, Bishop Antonio Fortich of Negros issued a stinging pastoral letter in which he indicted the injustices of the existing plantation system. The bishop condemned the poor wages and housing provided to sugar workers, the lack of union organizing rights, and the land grabbing perpetrated against farmers. The Church began explaining Vatican teachings on labor and educating workers on their legal rights to demand the minimum wage and to unionize. Financial and technical support was given to the FFF and to a new union, the National Federation of Sugarcane Workers, formed to organize plantation workers.

A wave of strikes swept the Negros haciendas in 1971 as sugar workers pressed their demands for minimum wage and other reforms. Jalandoni witnessed the resulting repression in a strike in May in the eastern Negros town of Bais. The workers, who were earning only 2.75 pesos a day at the time, demanded that the plantation pay them the minimum wage, 4.75 pesos. One morning while Jalandoni was on the picket line with the striking workers, armed guards hired by the *hacendero* demolished the ramshackle shelters the workers had constructed. When the strikers immediately started rebuilding the shacks, security guards opened fire. Jalandoni followed the workers into a nearby canal, but the guards continued to charge. The strikers and the priest jumped into the next canal. The guards kept coming. Terrified, Jalandoni and the strikers fled into the cane fields. On the 10-hour bus ride back to Bacolod, Jalandoni concluded that sugar workers would have to arm themselves in order to force concessions from plantation owners.[11]

The Church's efforts to defend the rights of small farmers and sugar workers through the courts failed just as miserably on Negros as they did elsewhere. "The workers would put on their best clothes and borrow money to pay for the jeepney. When they arrived at the courthouse, the case would be postponed," Jalandoni bitterly recalled. A case involving a settler's wife who was raped and killed by a landowners' security guards was postponed more than two dozen times. In another case in which a farmer was killed by a landowner's guards, hearings were postponed again and again, while the victim's friends and family members were being threatened to drop the case.[12]

Jalandoni had read José María Sison's *Philippine Society and Revolution* and had gradually concluded that the national democratic revolution of which Sison spoke was the only alternative to the intransigence of the ruling aristocracy. Jalandoni recalled telling sugar workers:

We've made mistakes and we've suffered together. The thing is . . . it's like walking up the mountains and after walking for so many hours you find out you are on the wrong road. You have to go back and take the right road, which might be even steeper and more difficult, but it will lead to where you want.[13]

In 1971, reform-minded priests and nuns along with peasant leaders decided to press the cause of poor farmers through local elections. FFF leaders in the central Philippines picked the eastern Negros town of Bais as the place for their electoral debut. Traditionally, four prominent families had controlled the town's land and politics. But the FFF had been able to establish itself along the narrow strip of fertile coastal plain and in the surrounding hillocks of Bais.

Ruíz, Jalandoni, and other priests helped the FFF organize the Party of the Poor to challenge the four dominant families of Bais. The FFF's election platform was pure populism: better working conditions, improved social services, and higher wages for peasants, farm laborers, and workers. Forbidden by landowners to come on their haciendas, priests and other FFF leaders waited until nightfall to slip past armed guards and make their way to the bamboo huts of field hands, where they organized support for the new party. When the landlords found out about the organizing forays, they threatened the activist priests and FFF leaders, but the campaigning continued.[14]

On election day, the landowners crushed the challenge with their time-honored formula of "guns, goons and gold." Hired gunmen threatened some FFF supporters, while other impoverished sugar workers and tenant farmers were paid to vote for the landowners' candidates. In still other places, landowners simply rigged the count and in several precincts went so far as to credit the farmers' party with zero votes.[15]

The election disappointment had a shattering effect on some of the activist priests. "I realized then that parliamentary struggle could not be relied upon as a solution," Ruíz told me years later. Gradually, a number of rural Church activists like Ruíz and Jalandoni concluded that if peasants and social reformers had to follow the rules made by the landowners, they would never win. Meaningful change seemed hopelessly out of reach. "We began to raise the questions among ourselves," Ruíz said. "Is what we are fighting for valid? Is it just? Is it Christian? And the answers were—and still are—yes."[16]

Sometime before mid-1972, Ruíz, Jalandoni, and a few other provincial priests had agreed that if Marcos declared martial law, they would go to the hills and join the NPA guerrillas. When martial law was declared in September 1972, Jalandoni, who had already become a CPP member, went into the urban underground of Bacolod, from which he directed rebel activities on Negros and played a key role in trying to build a Christian-Marxist alliance in support of the guerrillas.[17] Ruíz fled to the hills of Bohol to join the guerrillas. There he was assigned to organize peasant support in preparation for the conduct of guerrilla warfare, and he began by trying to convince FFF members that nonviolent reform efforts had failed and the time for revolution had arrived.[18] From a nucleus of FFF members, Ruíz and the tiny communist force on Bohol slowly multiplied. As martial law dragged on, there were similar stories of Catholic priests and nuns embracing the revolution. Some were accused of subversive activities and jailed; a few fled to the hills and took up arms against the government.

While the Philippine Church hierarchy was preaching "critical collaboration" with the martial law regime, Catholic radicals were embracing Latin American liberation theology. By 1972, mimeographed copies of the English translation of Gustavo Gutierrez' *Theology of Liberation* were being devoured by Filipino Church radicals, who came to define the Church's mission as facilitating humankind's "total liberation." To some, this was an endorsement of the armed revolution led by the CPP. In the countryside, Basic Christian Communities (BCCs) based on Latin American models gave organizational form to the emerging liberation theology.

The BCCs were inspired in part by Vatican II's injunction to greater lay participation in liturgical and sacramental functions. In remote areas where there were only one or two priests for thousands of parishoners scattered across rugged, mountainous regions, the BCCs enabled the Church to maintain a presence through small prayer groups led by lay members.[19] Initially, the BCCs focused on spiritual functions. But in rural areas where land grabbing and military abuses were worsening, the BCCs gravitated toward political issues. Some Church social activists saw the communities as a nonviolent alternative to the NPA's growing influence in the 1970s. In some areas, BCC members were organized to help one another through cooperative planting and plowing. Livestock cooperatives, fish ponds, credit unions, and other projects were organized. Members were trained to be medics capable of providing a wide variety of health services. In the more politically active BCCs, peasants were taught how to organize themselves to resist land grabbing and military abuses rather than rely on Church-provided lawyers.

As the NPA expanded throughout the late 1970s, many BCCs fell into areas either controlled or influenced by the rebels. In some cases, BCCs became heavily infiltrated by Party members or their supporters, and priests organizing the communities were sympathetic to or even active in the rebel cause. But communist influence in the BCCs was uneven and varied from province to province and even barrio to barrio. BCCs could hardly be described without qualifications as communist fronts, armed forces claims notwithstanding.

The military focused on the BCCs as the fount of radicalism within the Church. Colonel Galileo Kintanar, writing in a 1979 intelligence survey of the Church, described BCCs as "the most dangerous form of threat from the religious radicals. They are practically building an infrastructure of political power in the entire country."[20] The military equated the teachings of the more politicized BCCs—for example, peasants should stand up to abusive landowners or soldiers—with communist subversion, ignoring the very explicit opposition to violence preached by many BCC proponents. Some peasants active in the BCCs were arrested and summarily executed as rebel suspects.

By the early 1980s, BCCs had been formed in about one-third of all Philippine dioceses. Some were devoted exclusively to spiritual matters, others encouraged social and political activism, and some were even allied with the NPA. But in many other areas, the BCCs continued to develop as a nonviolent alternative to the rebels.[21]

Despite the CPP's initial suspicion of radical Christians, the Party leadership shrewdly took account of the Church's vast resources and enormous influence and moved quickly to begin integrating radical Church elements into the revolution. Father Edicio de la Torre and other leading Church radicals played a prominent role in planning the NDF, and the NDF subsequently formed the Committee for the Participation of Christians, Chinese, and Moros aimed in part at increasing the participation of Catholics in the revolutionary movement.[22]

In the countryside, CNL priests and nuns who remained at their posts eased the trauma of martial law by providing desperately needed support services to the disorganized underground army of Party cadres and guerrillas. CNL members saved many activists from arrest and provided Church facilities and contacts—as well as badly needed financial and logistical support—for building an underground network.[23] Most of the CNL cadres who went underground were deployed to organize barrios to support the revolution. When enough peasants were organized to create and support a guerrilla squad, the CNL team would move on.

In the final years of Marcos rule, the Catholic Church tried to distance itself from the unpopular regime while stopping well short of withdrawing support. The architect of this policy was the politically astute Manila archbishop, Cardinal Jaíme Sin. Arguably the second most powerful man in the country, Sin was the spiritual leader of the Philippine Church. Upon assuming his post in 1976, Sin condemned military abuses and official corruption. When the regime responded to growing Church militancy by closing Catholic radio stations, raiding social action centers, and arresting priests and nuns, Sin held firm.

At the same time, he continued to maintain a polite, if sometimes strained, relationship with the Marcoses. To Church radicals and even a growing number of moderates, Sin's refusal to break with the repressive and corrupt regime was bitterly frustrating. In September 1985, Sin stunned even the most moderate Church elements by appearing at a nationally televised public mass celebrating Marcos' sixty-seventh birthday. Beaming and effusive, Sin embraced Marcos; then the two released doves to symbolize their "reconciliation."

Sin's actions might have led to a disastrous schism within Church ranks had Marcos not announced a few weeks later the scheduling of an early presidential election. It was Sin's skillful diplomacy that facilitated a compromise that united the opposition behind Corazón Aquino, and when Marcos tried to steal the election with brazen fraud, Sin and his bishops denounced the sham and questioned whether Marcos had the moral authority to retain power. As events rapidly hurtled toward a climax, the bishops finally broke with Marcos and announced support for a civil disobedience campaign called by Aquino.

In the decisive showdown with Marcos, Sin and the Church once again stepped in to play a pivotal role. The Manila archbishop responded boldly to a military mutiny by issuing a radio appeal urging the faithful to take to the streets to protect the rebels. Hundreds of thousands of people heeded the request, including priests and nuns who used their bodies to block the advance of loyalist tanks and troop carriers dispatched to crush the rebellion. Within four days, Marcos had fled the Philippines.

The fall of Marcos was a serious setback to communist organizing efforts within the Church sector. Many priests and nuns, even bishops, who had collaborated to varying degrees with NDF elements under Marcos overnight severed their links with the rebels. The sudden erosion of support stunned Party organizers. "We thought all along we had developed a strong antisystem, antifascist movement [within the Church]. But in fact the majority were only anti-Marcos," Brendan Cruz conceded. Although CPP organizing efforts within the Church were "picking up again" by 1988, Cruz made it clear that Aquino's popularity continued to limit the potential for dramatic expansion among religious rank and file. "The argument within the Church is to give Cory Aquino a chance," Cruz said. "It's been very hard to talk with those who gave us sympathy before."[24]

Viewing the Church as a possible key to a successful revolution, the CPP had made the religious sector a primary target for its organizing activities. Priests and nuns "can tip the balance," a CPP cadre told me. "They have credibility, and they are looked up to in the community." By 1989, the revolutionary movement's prospects within the Church had brightened. Aquino's popularity had ebbed somewhat amid the slow pace of social reforms, government corruption, and allegations of the type of human rights violations that had characterized the Marcos era, although on a lesser scale. Church moderates had been displeased with Aquino's sluggishness on agrarian reform and her support for anticommunist vigilantes. For some disgruntled clerics and seminarians, the argument of CNL organizers that meaningful change was not possible without the revolutionary restructuring of Philippine society had taken on a ring of truth.

After more than a decade of cultivating contacts and building clandestine cells, organizing within what the CPP called the "Church sector" (which includes Catholic and Protestant Churches) continued to be a laborious process. "It's so strenuous," a Party cadre complained good naturedly. "You have to be patient. You cannot easily convince them that hell is on earth and there is no God." Once they are in the movement, the cadre added, "Church people vacillate very easily because of their petty bourgeoisie class origin. Because of that tendency, we constantly sustain their political education and expose them to the masses."

Church sector organizing was usually the task of clergy who had already become CPP members. One of their duties was to establish five- to seven-member national democratic cells within churches and seminaries. Discussions of communism were avoided when recruiting within the Church "because of the equation of atheism with communism," one CPP cadre told me. "Usually, a priest or nun cadre presents himself as an NDF cadre rather than a communist because it is more acceptable to Church people." New Church recruits were usually assigned to legal human rights organizations or propaganda tasks before being elevated to more important assignments, the cadre said.

That most Church recruits preferred to remain in their legal positions rather than go underground to become full-time NDF organizers, the cadre said, slowed organizing. Church cadres were forced to divide time between religious duties and underground work. "It's so hard to get full-time organizers from the Church sector. But we don't pressure them. We recognize their traditional role in the community," the cadre told me. "We can utilize them in their role as parish priest, pastor, or nun."

In mid-1985, in an effort to speed recruiting work, the CPP established a new legal organization aimed at drawing Christians into the movement. By the end of the year, similar organizations had been established on the regional level to facilitate recruiting within the Church sector.[25]

In 1988, the CNL claimed a membership of more than 4,000 priests, nuns, pastors, and laity and even "a few" of the Philippines' 110 Catholic bishops.[26] CNL cadres were performing a variety of sensitive tasks within the revolution. Jalandoni held a seat in the CPP Central Committee and was director of the NDF's international office in the Netherlands. More than two dozen priests were guerrilla commanders and Party officials. Hundreds of other Church cadres were in organizing or administrative positions in the rebel underground, although the majority of CNL members remained in legal Church positions as parish priests and nuns, labor and urban poor organizers, and directors of social action programs and community development centers. Together, they formed an interlocking support and logistical network for the NPA guerrilla forces in the cities and countryside.

In the 1980s, legal CNL cadres assumed a greater role in the Party's legal efforts. A primary function of CNL priests in the provinces surrounding Manila, for example, was to work in the trade union movement.[27] During Party-organized strikes, CNL priests were assigned to lead protest masses "with a militant or political content" on the picket line. In another province near Manila, a nun who was a CPP member was running a community development center that provided primary health care to peasants and trained barrio medics. Under the direction of the communist nun, the center was building what a Party cadre described as an "alternative health system" in surrounding barrios stressing the use of herbal medicines, acupuncture, and acupressure. "We work hand in hand with the center," the CPP cadre said.[28] Other CNL cadres, working with Church liberals and civil libertarians, formed a network of human rights agencies, peace task forces, and relief organizations for detainees that were effective in highlighting military abuses. CNL priests and nuns in rural parishes helped facilitate the movement of cadres from towns to the mountains, provide care for wounded guerrillas, and provide underground courier services. CNL cadres also assumed responsibility for an ambitious program of community development under the auspices of "provisional revolutionary governments" being formed in rebel-controlled areas.[29]

The involvement of priests and nuns in the NDF helped overcome the strong anticommunist sentiments that underlay Philippine society. During the cease-fire and peace negotiations with the government in 1986–1987, the NDF consciously assigned rebel priests to public roles in order to project a moderate, human face and compete with Aquino for the moral high ground. Although not all CNL members were Party members, the dominant thinking among Church radicals was that Marxism and Christianity were compatible. Jalandoni, who was as tough-minded a revolutionary as any I encountered, described the relationship: "In the National Democratic Front the basis for unity is political. The Christian is not asked to renounce his faith. The Marxist does not have to be defensive about his being a nonbeliever. The important thing is that there is a program we are supposed to agree to and to implement."[30]

After adopting an anti-Church attitude for much of the 1970s, the CNL began talking in the late 1980s of a vision to radically transform the Philippine Church. Although the model cited by Church radicals was the Nicaraguan revolution, how the CNL would attempt to change the Church remained unclear. Brendan Cruz, the CNL spokesperson, told me that religious cadres envisioned "a new Church for the revolution, for the people," guided by a "Marxist-influenced" theology based on "Filipinized Marxism." CNL cadres were still at work formulating the new theology in 1988, he said, although it "is not anti-capitalist" and "we are not making demands for everyone to be socialist."

Church rebels acknowledged that their program was a prescription for conflict with the Vatican and the Philippine Church hierarchy, although Cruz insisted that the CNL was "not out to be schismatic" and had even formed a task force on Church and state relations to study and attempt to resolve potential points of dispute. Cruz said the CNL was hopeful that radical forces would be able to reach a meeting of minds with enough Church elements to avoid a divisive fight.

By the late 1980s, despite the CNL's inroads the radicals within the Catholic Church remained only a vocal minority. The bishops and a solid majority of the Catholic clergy were still supportive, in varying degrees, of Cardinal Sin's conservative-centrist leadership. But in their efforts to tilt the balance of Church forces toward revolution, Catholic radicals had given Filipinos a preview of the confrontation that would shake the institution to its foundations if the NDF were ever to come to power.

19

Inside the Labor Front

The CPP's strategy for seizing power calls for a "final offensive" launched by communist armed forces in the countryside to be accompanied by a series of insurrections in cities throughout the Philippines. According to the vision of communist strategists, hundreds of CPP-controlled labor unions with their membership numbering in the hundreds of thousands would spearhead the urban uprisings.

By the late 1980s, communist strength on the labor front remained far from the number needed to paralyze the Philippine economy, but the CPP had made impressive steps in that direction. Party cadres had managed to infiltrate and gain control of scores of unions in various sectors of the economy. Bus companies, garment factories, coconut mills, sugar plantations, electronics manufacturers, even public utilities in some provinces had fallen under the control or influence of the revolutionary movement. By military estimates, in metro Manila alone the CPP controlled 341 unions with a total membership of 106,000 by 1988.[1]

The primary source of trade union support for the revolution was the KMU, a legal national democratic organization in the lexicon of the underground. Founded in 1980 by uniting six national unions and labor federations, by the end of the decade KMU was comprised of 19 affiliated labor federations and claimed a membership of 650,000 workers, about half of whom were concentrated in the greater Manila area. While publicly denying military allegations that it was a "communist front," KMU did not attempt to conceal its revolutionary agenda or its support for the armed struggle. (It should be stressed that not all KMU members or leaders are communists.) Through strikes, demonstrations, and other political actions, KMU attempted to link the cause of workers with the national democratic revolution.

The CPP's operations in the labor sector have always been a closely guarded secret. In early 1988, I met a 28-year-old CPP cadre, Bani, whose assignment was to organize communist unions in several heavily industrialized provinces surrounding Manila.[2] In a revealing discussion of his work, Bani detailed how CPP-led unions had won the right to represent workers at hundreds of firms throughout the Philippines, and he talked candidly of the successes and failures of the revolutionary movement's trade union activities.

The process by which the CPP gains control of a union is careful and methodical, employing some of the same tactics Party forces in the countryside use to organize peasants. If the company has no existing union, Party organizers conduct a social investigation, a two- to three-month investigation of the factory owner and living standards of the workers. Cadres determine whether a factory is locally owned or multinational, and then check the political affiliations of the factory owner to see if he or she has any connections with the military. Even the source of raw materials and the identity of stockholders are traced. Next, Party organizers consult with a prearranged contact in the factory to determine working conditions. Workers' wages and possible violations of labor standards are noted. "After knowing those problems, we try to tell the people what they should receive as workers," Bani said. "When they become interested, we try to arrange an education seminar."

The introductory education seminar is known as the general trade unionism course (GTU), which seeks to politicize workers and lay the foundation for militant labor activism. Initially, Party cadres select those workers who are deemed most trustworthy and politically inclined to attend the three-day live-in seminar, with classes averaging about 15 workers. Although the course is legal in its content (the seminar skirts the issues of communism or the violent overthrow of the government), the GTU is conducted clandestinely. Seminar topics include an examination of capitalism and socialism. Party instructors lecture on "the role of government in exploitation of workers," the mechanics of trying to establish a "genuine" trade union, and the "alternative" socialist society the revolution is offering to workers. The course also attempts to link other common problems in the Philippines, such as malnutrition, disease among children, or prostitution, to unjust labor conditions. "We explain that women who are prostitutes would not be doing this if they had been given a chance to work at the factory," Bani said.

Bani's legal cover was as an organizer at a labor education center. The KMU's regional organization, according to Bani, served as the umbrella for "genuine trade unions," the underground euphemism for Party-controlled unions. The actual work of organizing CPP-sanctioned unions falls to one of several militant federations. These legal federations organize openly in nonunion companies or challenge what the CPP refers to as existing "yellow," or less militant, unions.

The process becomes more surreptitious when a challenge is being mounted to unseat an existing union. CPP organizers opt for one of two strategies. The Party's activists join the campaign for the election of union officers, "take control of the officers, transform the union, and try to disaffiliate with the yellow federation," or the activists choose to establish a rival union and attempt to have it recognized as the representative of workers at a factory.[3] In the case of the latter, the CPP must wait for the expiration of the existing collective bargaining agreement, which typically covers a three-year period. Sixty days before expiration, a "freedom period" begins during which workers are free to organize new unions. Prior to this, it is illegal to begin organizing a rival union at a company, and so Party workers have to "work quietly" as they lay the groundwork for a new union, Bani said. During the freedom period, if workers gather the signatures of 20 percent of the factory's work force—the minimum requirement to force a certification election—they can file a petition with the Labor Department for an election.

In factories in which there is no union or a yellow union, graduates of the general trade unionism course are asked to identify coworkers who might be interested in the course. Five to seven workers are chosen from the first group to become an organizing committee, which begins in earnest the work of building a radical union. Under CPP supervision, clandestine committees for education, finance, and propaganda are formed, usually with three members each. Even at this stage, some of the workers may have already earned Party membership, Bani said, but this is tightly guarded information.

As quickly as possible, the Party develops leaders within the factory and transfers the more general education and training tasks to the workers themselves. The ultimate aim of CPP-controlled unions is to develop workers into militant supporters of the revolution's political agenda. "We tell the workers they have to be involved in issues inside and outside the factories," Bani said. "For example, if we confine our activities just to union issues—such as higher wages—the company would just raise the price of its goods, creating a vicious cycle. That is the difference between us and the yellow unions, who tell their members not to get involved in things outside the factories."

Once the Party succeeds in capturing the union or winning certification for a new union, negotiations for a collective bargaining agreement with management begin. In many cases, CPP labor organizers find themselves plagued by an annoying irony: Their successes in winning concessions from management without a bitter fight actually weaken, rather than strengthen, commitment to long-term Party goals. "If they win concessions without a strike, and there is no military repression, it is difficult to convince the workers of the need to continue political actions," Bani remarked. "But if they experience military harassment in a strike, we can easily conduct political education." Another problem is that management concessions to Party-controlled unions sometimes raise the wages of workers to a level greater than that of yellow union workers in other factories within the same industry. "This sometimes causes our workers to become content, and they become less active," Bani said.

A classic case, according to Bani, involved an electronics components factory near Manila owned by a major U.S. corporation. In 1984, Bani took a leave from school to work at the factory in order to secretly establish a Party-controlled union. Management fought back, and after a few months, the radical union was busted and Bani was fired. Two years later, the CPP finally succeeded when its militant workers took control of a weak existing union and brought it under the KMU banner. Company management was fearful of KMU's militancy, and when in September 1986 the union filed a strike notice, management immediately granted the union's demands: a 15 percent salary increase every year for three years and a "fourteenth month bonus"—a month's bonus paid in addition to the traditional year-end bonus, the equivalent of one month's salary.

Bani was disappointed at the relatively easy victories. "We were not able to experience the hardships and military repression of a strike," he said. As Bani feared, the union triumph hurt communist political activities at the factory. "The workers have become complacent," he complained. "It's hard to involve them in rallies or demonstrations. We have to launch a GTU course, but if they're complacent, it's even harder to convince them to study."

Once a bargaining agreement is signed, the CPP continues its organizing activities under the guise of ensuring that management is fulfilling its end of the contract. But Party organizers simultaneously step up political education with underground classes. Workers are introduced to more revolutionary ideas through the basic mass course, which covers topics such as imperialism and feudalism. U.S. imperialism, for example, is blamed for the country's political and economic underdevelopment. Local capitalists are blamed for the "feudal conditions" that remain. The most promising graduates of the basic mass course are introduced to Marxist-

Leninist thought through the basic Party course. Workers who are already CPP members receive further political and leadership training in the basic cadre's course.

At the same time, an underground network parallel to the legal trade union activities is developed to accommodate any crackdowns on aboveground labor organizers. If legal union activities are shut down, the underground organization continues to function, Bani said. As the pace of underground political education quickens, aboveground labor training also intensifies. Special courses on leadership training, propaganda techniques, and financial administration are taught, and workers are instructed on how to pursue formal grievances.

The battle for the hearts and minds of workers reaches beyond the factory as well. CPP cadres conduct community organizing work in surrounding neighborhoods where most of the workers live. The motivation for such work, Bani acknowledged, goes beyond simple altruism. "During a strike, if the people living around the factory are hostile to us, that could undermine the strike," Bani said. So the CPP attempts to infiltrate homeowners associations and other groups in an effort to win community support and advance the Party platform and ideals.

The CPP's prime targets for union organizing and strikes are multinational companies. The Party tells workers that although their wages may be higher at multinationals, they are actually being cheated to a much greater degree because the "rate of exploitation"—a comparison of a company's profits with the wages it pays—is greater. Bani conceded that this explanation often means little to workers. "They just see that if they are paid less than other workers, they are exploited more, and vice versa," he said. "So we try to tell the workers that the struggle we are launching is not just for political gains or union gains, but for total human development."

Often the CPP has found it difficult to sustain labor actions because of pitifully small strike funds for workers, who live hand to mouth in the best of times. Sometimes, as in the case of the strike against three Nestlé plants in late 1987, the defeats were bitter. An antagonistic relationship between the Nestlé management and the KMU-affiliated unions steadily deteriorated in 1987, finally culminating in a strike in September. From the beginning, the strike failed to rally a majority of workers, attracting only about 10 percent to the picket lines, Bani recalled. The strike turned ugly at the Nestlé plant near Manila, which employed 600 people manufacturing powdered milk and noodles. Three people were killed when a Nestlé truck that was being stoned by strikers went out of control, struck a car head on, and killed the driver and two bystanders. Afterward, nine regional leaders of the KMU affiliate leading the strike were charged with murder in connection with the three deaths, and they went into hiding.

The strike collapsed in December when the union returned to work without the new collective bargaining agreement it had been seeking. Thirty union officers were fired for leading what the Labor Department ruled was an illegal strike. The decision to return to work was made "to save the union," Bani said, and the failure was "a big blow" to the Nestlé union in Laguna.

When I talked with Bani a few weeks later, he told me the Nestlé workers had expected the NPA to retaliate against the company. "But up to now, there has not been any," he said with obvious disappointment. A few days later, the Labor Department lawyer who served the return-to-work order on the striking Nestlé workers was assassinated as he left his office in downtown Manila. The NPA's Manila command claimed responsibility for the murder, saying the lawyer had been executed for "blood debts" owed the Filipino people.

Like work among peasants in the countryside, CPP efforts to organize workers were a story of mixed successes. The radical labor movement was not immune to Corazón Aquino's popularity. Catholic priests and nuns and lawyers who had helped the radical unions during the Marcos years were suddenly more reluctant to become involved, Party cadres said. Nevertheless, even the government conceded the revolutionary movement had become a major force in the labor sector. In the Southern Tagalog region, the number of KMU unions had soared from only 6 in 1984 to 70 in 1988. From single-factory strikes the CPP had progressed to coordinated strikes in some provinces and to even locally successful general strikes. Some of the Party unions boasted impressive strength. For example, a textile factory on the outskirts of Manila employed 900 workers, 50 of whom were CPP members.[4] By 1988, each department of the factory had its own clandestine Party core group.

As the number of CPP-controlled unions continued to grow, the challenge for the revolutionary movement was how to mobilize these large numbers of workers. Despite its expanding strength, the radical union movement had been frustrated in its attempts in the late 1980s to paralyze the country with general strikes. By 1989, the CPP had still not been able to weld its collection of sympathetic unions into a monolithic political and economic force. If the Party were able to accomplish that feat, the movement could find itself capable of crippling the Philippine economy and holding the government hostage to the revolution's political demands.

20

Inside the New People's Army

Death, capture, and serious injury are ever-present occupational hazards for those adventurous enough to join the New People's Army. There is always a danger of being caught at a checkpoint or stumbling into a military patrol while moving in and out of relatively secure communist zones. But beyond this, the hard life of a guerrilla trekking through the rugged, mountainous terrain carries its own more mundane perils. As I witnessed it, life inside the Red Revolution is one of frequent worries and tensions, to which the guerrillas respond with remarkable patience and good humor.

Exiting a communist area in the Cordillera Mountains of Nueva Vizcaya in northern Luzon, I got a vivid sense of the physical and mental rigors that are a part of the everyday lives of the rebels. The NPA commander assigned two of his toughest fighters, Nap and Reggie, to guide me on the long journey out of the area. The descent from the mountainside NPA camp was almost effortless, and in a half hour we arrived at the Matumo River, a silvery, swift stream that rushed through the craggy gorges. As we crossed the river, the sky quickly darkened and now a wind whipped through the river gorge as black and gray clouds swirled overhead. Lightning flickered above the mountains and lit the gorge in brilliant flashes. A macabre thought crossed my mind: It would be ironic to have survived six expeditions with the NPA guerrillas only to be struck down by a thunderbolt on Easter Sunday. We walked faster and faster as lightning cut jagged patterns across the sky and thunder resounded off the rocky mountainsides. By the time we reached the hut of a sympathetic peasant, we were nearly running.

My escorts and I had barely dropped our packs under the thatch eaves of the farmer's hut when torrential rains swept over the hillside.

As the deafening downpour and cracks of thunder continued, we shared a meager meal with the peasant and his wife and children—rice with *gabi*, the crunchy green stalks that were their only food. When the rain finally slackened after an hour, the peasant loaned us sheets of plastic to use as raincoats, and as darkness fell we set out again in a light, cold drizzle.

The trail climbed upward toward a narrow pass that opened onto the east slope of the Cordillera foothills and the busy National Highway beyond. Low-hanging clouds and a thick fog mixed with the smoke of the fires of slash-and-burn farmers and blanketed the mountainside around us like silent snowdrifts. The muddy trail disappeared into a dripping thicket of black jungle that concealed large rocks over which we slipped and stumbled. We shoved and clawed our way through the undergrowth only to emerge into a field of nearly impenetrable, razor-sharp cogon grass. The grass was taller than we were, and so there was nothing to do but put our heads down and push our way forward, folding our arms into our chests to avoid the cutting blades of cogon. Covered with dozens of tiny nicks, we finally reached the top of the pass and stopped only for a moment to catch our breath before starting down through the final few hundred yards of cogon and beyond to the house of a sympathizer.

We were now within range of the government patrols that were sent out almost nightly from the town below. Suddenly, a tiny light seemed to flash through the fog several hundred yards off to our left, on the side of the mountain facing the highway. Nap stiffened and drew his revolver. Was it a warning? A peasant's fire? Or was it a patrol? Behind me, Reggie clutched his pistol and cocked his head to listen for anything that might offer an explanation. The light flickered again, and Nap quickly smothered his flashlight. For perhaps four or five tense minutes, we stood absolutely still in the silence atop the pass, engulfed by the eerie fog, shivering in a strong breeze that cut through our wet clothes.

Nap began to wade carefully down the hill, his pistol leveled at whatever waited in the darkness ahead. Moving clumsily in the moonless night, I slipped on the loose soil, slicing several fingers on cogon grass as I tumbled to the ground. Nap motioned for me to be silent, his tension showing for the first time. My guides slowed their pace even more, their pistols pointed ahead as we broke from the swaying grass into a freshly plowed field, fragrant in the fog and drizzle. I could barely see Nap, a slow moving figure ahead of me, and then, only a few dozen yards away, a peasant's darkened house took shape. A dog began to bark frantically, a warning to its occupants of our approach. Now, Nap and Reggie were gliding in a half-crouch, and I prepared to throw myself to the ground if shooting started without warning. A dark figure materialized beside the house, and we froze in midstep.

"Hooo!" the figure called out hesitatingly. There was a moment of tense silence.

"Hooo!" Nap cautiously answered, taking aim as the figure edged toward us.

A few feet closer, and we could see that the shape approaching us also had a pistol leveled at us. Closer he came, as Nap and Reggie stood silently and absolutely still. The men's pistols were almost muzzle to muzzle now, until their faces took shape in the fog and darkness, and Nap and Reggie broke into sudden exclamations and relieved laughter. The man before us was a fellow member of the guerrilla company. "Oh! We thought you might be the military!" Nap exclaimed to the other man, whose name was Freddie. They exchanged handshakes and burst into conversation as though nothing had happened. Having survived the lightning and the "encounter," Nap decided it was enough for one evening. We would spend the night in the relative safety of the peasant's corn bin.

The NPA offered many contrasts to the armed forces, not the least of which were its superior discipline, morale, and will to win. During the Marcos years, the AFP earned a reputation for indiscipline, corruption, brutality, and low morale. By the late 1980s, it may have held the edge in troop strength and firepower, but when it came to the intangibles that are crucial to the success of any army, the NPA guerrillas appeared to hold a considerable advantage over government forces.

Discipline in the communist army was rigorous, and offenders of the strict Maoist code of conduct were severely punished. Several veteran cadres recalled that during the Cultural Revolution years of the late 1960s and early 1970s, a number of guerrillas and Party workers were executed for breaches of the disciplinary code. Although somewhat more relaxed by the 1980s, the NPA continued to make stringent demands of its troops. Drinking, gambling, and profanity were prohibited; frugality and hard work were demanded. Good relations with peasant supporters— without which the rebel army would wither—were assiduously cultivated, giving substance to the NPA's claim that it was a people's army. Political and ideological training inculcated high morale and the will to win in the peasant rebels. Despite a high rate of illiteracy, communist soldiers could explain why they were fighting and what they were fighting for. In contrast, most government soldiers were poor peasants or slum dwellers who enlisted in the government army not out of political conviction but because of economic deprivation.

I found life inside the "Red zones," in peasant barrios as well as NPA camps, to be remarkably egalitarian. Whereas most top-level officers of the AFP flaunted their privilege (and in some cases ill-gotten wealth) while enlisted men struggled to eat three decent meals a day, ranking CPP officials and NPA officers ate the same food and lived in the same accommodations as those of the communist rank and file, which usually meant sleeping on a raised platform of bamboo poles or wooden planks. "On a personal level, leaders and members are equal. A leader is assigned a task just like anyone else," a young Party cadre explained to me. "He can be asked to fetch water or cook a meal and he does it." The cadre was not exaggerating. To my surprise one day in an NPA camp in southern Quezon, I looked up after lunch to see the Party's front secretary washing dishes in a tin washbasin. It was his turn in the rotation of camp chores, and the fact that he was a senior Party official did not exempt him from the work. (To put this into perspective, even marginally middle-class families have domestic helpers in the Philippines. Few women of means—and certainly no men—would stoop to so plebeian a task as washing dishes.) NPA officers and ranking Party officials even washed their own clothes.

The strict egalitarianism was extended to virtually every aspect of life in the communist army. Scarce cigarettes, food, and delicacies were shared equally, even if it meant dividing the object into almost microscopic portions. In one NPA camp in northern Luzon, a chicken was bought from a peasant and boiled, and the cooks carefully apportioned the rare treat so everyone would get just about two bites. In other areas, when mangoes or wild oranges were found, the same occurred.

On another occasion, a camp in which I was staying in a remote rain forest of Luzon's Sierra Madre had run out of coffee. One chilly morning, a great cry erupted from the direction of the bamboo hut that served as the kitchen. Investigating the din, I was told that a *kasama* had been digging around in some leaves underneath the hut and had found a small plastic bag containing several precious teaspoons of coffee. A small celebration was under way, and already a great kettle of water was simmering on a campfire. Within minutes, steaming cups of the weak brew were ladled out to everyone in the camp and joyously savored by all.

The risk of death in battle notwithstanding, by the late 1980s members of the guerrilla army could in most places enjoy more secure lives than they had ever known. The NPA enjoyed the loyalty of thousands of sympathetic peasants who had become members of a great extended family that provided mutual support to all within its embrace, farmer and guerrilla alike. One of the lessons learned by the NPA leadership in the 1970s was that the guerrilla army was more effective when immersed in its peasant mass base as much as possible, rather than living in remote jungle camps. Veterans liked to describe their rapport with rural supporters by recalling Mao's analogy of fish swimming in water, and I found the metaphor appropriate.

The camaraderie and selflessness that characterized the guerrillas and Party workers I met were impressive. Outwardly, at least, the young rebels brimmed with enthusiasm, and that spirit was evident in the NPA camps and in individual members of the communist army whom I encountered in barrios and along jungle trails. It seemed that the hardships of their lives had become more bearable to the communist soldiers because of the shared sacrifice of all *kasamas*.

At most of the camps, the peasant rebels fussed over me, attending to my needs and trying to make my stay as comfortable as possible. (This hospitality was a characteristic of Philippine society at large, carried out with the zeal of a revolution's true believers.) Once, when I was returning from Barangay Rose to a nearby NPA camp after having hiked most of the day through three barrios, I reached the point where I did not think I could walk another step. Ahead of me was a treacherously steep, slippery, 20-minute downhill walk in darkness. Suddenly, a smiling young peasant guerrilla named Norma materialized along the trail offering her hand. I gratefully accepted, and she carefully guided me down the trail, her steely grip keeping me on my feet as we skidded and stumbled down the ridge. When we arrived in the camp, I was caked with mud and soaked from sweat and several downpours. I collapsed onto my assigned spot on the wooden sleeping platform, but before I could fall asleep several concerned rebels insisted that I change into dry clothes. Later that evening, several *kasamas* brought me soup and hovered over me massaging my aching legs and back to prepare me for my walk out of the jungle the following day.

From the beginning of the revolution, Sison had envisioned the NPA as a peasant army. A few urban workers and former students had been assigned to the army through the years, but the NPA was still built on peasant support 20 years later. Although many guerrillas had joined the NPA because of specific grievances against the government, many others had been drawn to the revolution simply because the communists were the first people who had ever come to their barrios and offered a blueprint for improving their lives. Many young men and women saw no future in meekly following in the footsteps of their desperately impoverished parents and grandparents, and so they joined.

One such recruit was Heidi, a shy and chubby-cheeked 18-year-old serving in the communist army in southern Quezon. One morning she came sauntering down the trail leading into the camp with an M-16 slung over her shoulder, her pony tail swishing and extra ammunition clips dangling from a belt around her waist. Curious to hear how such a pleasant, innocent-looking teenager had become a soldier in the communist revolution, I invited her to sit down, and we began talking through an interpreter.

Heidi's story, told with nervous giggles, could have been the story of any one of thousands of members of the NPA. She had grown up in a large, poor peasant family in southern Quezon who survived by cultivating a small upland rice plot and gathering coconuts and bananas to sell in the closest town. Like most of her brothers and sisters, she had not been able to go beyond elementary school. Soon after her home barrio had been organized by the NPA a few years earlier, Heidi had become a member of a communist organizing team that walked from house to house patiently explaining the revolution to the poorest farmers and their families. At the time, she was 13. Two years later, Heidi became a full-time guerrilla, and by 1987 she had been assigned to an NPA platoon that provided security to the Southern Quezon Front headquarters staff. Heidi's commitment to the movement had been further cemented by her engagement to a young guerrilla following a romance arranged by her colleagues, and she had been married in December 1987. At 18, her entire life revolved around serving the revolution.

One of the most striking characters I encountered in the communist zones was a peasant guerrilla named Baldo, a dwarfish fellow (just under five feet tall), who when I met him in 1987 was 38 years old and recently married. He had a kind, craggy face, and when he smiled, as he seemed to do most of the time, his eyes nearly disappeared and several teeth glistened with gold dental work. Baldo had been assigned as my bodyguard during my first visit to southern Quezon, and his inability to speak a word of English combined with my pidgin Tagalog led to some results that entertained the other rebels.

On my first morning in the communist zone, Baldo led me to a small stream that was used by the guerrillas for bathing. Wondering whether I should use the pool as a bathtub, I gestured to Baldo, pointed to the water, and made the motion of scrubbing myself. Baldo nodded his head and grunted loudly, so I waded into the pool and enjoyed a refreshing bath. Later, Mike, the front secretary, gently told me that several *kasamas* had complained that the water in the bathing/laundry pool had been muddy when they went to use it. I should have used a bucket to dip water from the stream for bathing, he explained, rather than sitting in the pool and roiling the waters. Baldo had misunderstood me. I sheepishly apologized to the other rebels for my faux pas, and explained the miscommunication with Baldo. For days afterward, the others took delight in teasing the good-natured peasant, imitating his hearty grunts.

Baldo had been a farmer in a neighboring province to the south, Camarines Norte. In 1982, he joined the NPA and spent three years in the area's main fighting unit participating in eight major operations against government troops. Only once in that period were they surprised by the army and forced to fight. Baldo was one of the hardest workers I met in the NPA, laboring from sunrise to sunset clearing brush, building new shelters, or portering supplies. Early one evening he strode into the camp with a flat wooden stick balanced on his right shoulder and his M-16 rifle in his left hand. A wicker bag filled with food and other supplies hung on one end of the stick and a jug of kerosene on the other. Sweat streaked his forehead and trickled down his face as he eased his heavy load to the ground and cheerily began greeting his comrades. Baldo never complained. He attacked even the most mundane chores with single-minded zeal, content to await his next order. In many ways, he epitomized the loyal, unquestioning peasant soldier the NPA sought to develop in barrios throughout the countryside.

Most of the rebels I encountered were between the ages of 16 and 25, although as Heidi's story illustrated, the CPP begins involving barrio youths in revolutionary work at a tender age. The oldest NPA regular I met, a peasant named Rudy who was a deputy platoon commander in the southern Quezon company, was 49. Though a growing number of members in communist fighting units had become equipped with combat uniforms, boots and other gear captured or bought from AFP soldiers, in general the NPA in 1989 was still a ragtag-looking army. Most rebel fighters wore T-shirts, cheap pants, and rubber flip-flop sandals.

The revolution had always placed greatest emphasis on political organizing, and in this arena the rebel forces were impressive. I watched the day's activities begin one morning at a peasant's house in Quezon province in which nearly 20 guerrillas had spent the previous night. After a breakfast of boiled rice and dried venison, the latter a rare treat bagged the day before by a guerrilla-hunter, the rebel contingent broke into three groups and set off to conduct political sessions with nearby peasants.

Only when preparing for operations or undergoing political and military training were NPA units assembled in camps. (Squad-size propaganda units were assigned full-time to political work and normally were not involved in military operations.) In between NPA offensives, which in some fronts were carried out only four or five times a year, combat companies of up to 100 guerrillas were broken down into three or four platoons and dispersed into the barrios. Guerrillas worked with peasants on their farms, growing rice and corn, planting bananas, and doing other production work. The Red fighters also helped peasant supporters during the harvest, for which the rebels received one-fourth of the crop. Apart from its economic importance, this farm work was politically important, an NPA regional commander said, because "it helps the fighters remember their class origins as peasants."[1]

"The Party leads the army" was the NPA's guiding principle, and as a result political and ideological instruction occupied a significant part of the lives of NPA members. Party committees were formed in each fighting company, and political officers, usually former students with some university training, supervised regular classes in Marxist-Leninist-Maoist teachings. A significant number of NPA members were Communist Party members, which required an advanced level of ideological training. (Half the members of the southern Quezon NPA company were Party members, the regional commander said.) Every NPA platoon had a Party branch, the smallest CPP unit, and the branch secretary was in charge of political instruction within the platoon. The Party branch also explained and helped analyze contemporary political developments, such as the 1986 presidential election boycott, Corazón Aquino's popularity, and the August 1987 military coup attempt. Each fighter was required to pass the Party's basic mass course, which was based on Sison's Maoist-oriented *Philippine Society and Revolution*. Political education averaged about two weeks a month for members of the southern Quezon NPA company, but sessions were irregularly scheduled. "More comrades want to join TOs [tactical offensives]," a 20-year-old, university-educated guerrilla explained. "The peasants get bored with the political sessions, but if we are talking about military tactics, they are very interested." Beyond political indoctrination, there were efforts to promote literacy within the NPA, the intensity of which varied from region to region. Illiterate Red fighters were given occasional instruction in reading, writing, and math. A member of the southern Quezon NPA company said most of his comrades were still only barely able to read and write.

A strong theme of the political education provided to NPA soldiers was that U.S. imperialism was largely to blame for the poverty and injustices in the Philippines. As I sat talking one morning with two young guerrillas, a rebel soldier named Roland suddenly looked up and with a puzzled look declared, "Ka Gregg, our revolution is against America." The expression on his face seemed to ask: Why, if the United States was a chief enemy of the revolution as his Party and NPA superiors had so often told him, was I there as a guest of his command? Although the better-educated and more sophisticated Party leaders and NPA commanders qualified that the revolution was against U.S. policies rather than the U.S. people, the distinction was too subtle for Roland and most of his peasant comrades to grasp.

Life in the camp was not all dreary political lectures, and I for one became a source of entertainment to the peasant rebels. They were delighted by my few Tagalog phrases, and they patiently tried to teach me more. After lunch each day, several of the young NPA members would settle under a tree or palm shelter and pass around a guitar as they sang melancholy ballads about the struggles of peasants, their frustrated search for liberation, and the certain triumph of the revolution. The sweet, soprano voices of the young women were haunting and reminded me of Catholic mass. Chess was a favorite pasttime for the men, as it is throughout the country. Most of the camps I visited had at least one well-used chessboard, and in the evenings men would congregate by the light of a lantern or candle for long sessions.

In lighter moments, the atmosphere reminded me more of a teenage slumber party than a war. During Party conferences, there were some afternoons when there was little to do. In one southern Quezon camp the women sat around a table shelling peanuts and giggling like school girls on a class campout. At other times the women gathered coconuts, mangoes, and jackfruit from the forest. One afternoon, improvising as the rebels often must, the women made a tasty delicacy by mixing a jar of peanut butter I had given them with peanuts and a wild tuber.

After two decades of guerrilla warfare, the NPA had learned to adapt well to jungle conditions and to use the remote and rugged terrain to its advantage. A typical guerrilla camp consisted of several small bamboo-and-palm shelters and at least one large frond-covered main structure with a table and raised bamboo or wood-plank platform that served as combination mess hall, conference room, and bunkhouse. Most of the camps were hidden in heavily forested, mountainous areas and were so well camouflaged with palm fronds that they were virtually impossible to spot from the air or even from the ground. The NPA placed a premium on mobility, and to keep the AFP guessing, in most cases the guerrillas moved to a new camp every few weeks.

Water supply was a primary factor for locating camps, and despite the tropical climate and heavy amounts of rainfall, potable water was sometimes scarce. Frequent cases of diarrhea in some camps I visited were attributed to the water. At one NPA camp in southern Quezon, the water supply was a shallow pit where runoff was collected from a hillside. Water for drinking and bathing was drawn from the pit, and on some mornings it was drained by midmorning before everyone had bathed. The alternative source was a "river" at the foot of the steep hillside several hundred yards below the camp. Envisioning a clear, swift mountain stream, one afternoon I joined several *kasamas* who were making their way down the hill to bathe. To my dismay, the river was a trickle of murky water. By the time I had negotiated the steep trail back up to the camp after bathing, I was drenched with perspiration and spattered with mud.

In contrast to most AFP installations I had visited, the NPA camps were usually beehives of activity: couriers coming and going throughout the day, porters arriving with supplies, and the constant construction of new shelters and better facilities. By 5:30 or 6:00 A.M., the camps were alive with *kasamas* doing chores like fetching water, sweeping the packed mud floors of their shelters, and doing laundry. Life inside the guerrilla zone was largely self-contained, and news from the outside world was sometimes limited. A *kasama* arriving from the outside world took pains to buy one or two newspapers, which were devoured at every stop along the trail by Party workers and literate guerrillas even as the papers grew steadily more out of date. Often, the rebels read articles to illiterate peasants. An effective, if sometimes slow, underground mail system had developed in the communist zones. Travelers coming from outside destinations usually carried letters from friends and loved ones of comrades living inside the zone. Anyone departing from a camp or from peasant houses that were popular rest stops along the jungle trails was handed letters folded into tiny "chiclets" and wrapped in clear tape.

The NPA units that I saw usually had enough to eat, and their diet was more nutritious than that of most peasants. The diet for rebels in a particular area also depended heavily on the degree of security of the surrounding barrios and the success of local Party tax collection efforts. Meat was rare in most NPA camps, and fish was not regularly available in most upland areas. Aries, a 20-year-old guerrilla with the southern Quezon combat company, estimated that his unit ate meat 10 times in a good month, "depending on our money supply." Sometimes, he said, his unit had only rice and salt to eat, and at other times "we go hungry." Wild vegetables and fruits gathered in the jungle were a primary source of food. My favorite was heart of banana, the sweet inner part of the banana tree blossom that tasted similar to artichoke heart.

Almost all the veteran CPP and NPA leaders I met suffered from health problems, most of which stemmed from years of poor diet aggravated by the inhospitable tropical climate of the jungles. In some areas, goiter was widespread because of the lack of protein and iodine in the diet. The most common maladies that plagued the rebel army were malaria, typhoid fever, dysentery, ulcers, and common colds. A veteran Party official who had spent 11 years in the Mindanao countryside told me that "almost all comrades have had malaria." A few, he said, had tuberculosis, one of the leading causes of death in the Philippines. Preventive health care and dental hygiene were emphasized in the communist army and to a lesser extent among its backward peasant supporters. A regional NPA commander in northern Luzon told me that an improved diet in recent years and greater attention given to health basics had improved the fitness of the communist army. Surprisingly— although it should not have been, considering the mountainous terrain— the most prevalent problem for NPA forces operating in the Nueva Vizcaya area was a high incidence of hernia.

Combat-related injuries posed more formidable problems for the NPA's crude health care system. The Southern Tagalog regional NPA commander told me that during a three-month military campaign in 1987, some of his units' combat deaths resulted from lack of adequate medical care.[2] Each NPA company was assigned a chief medic and deputy, who were supplemented by platoon and squad medics and their deputies. The medics were trained to perform acupuncture and acupressure treatments and were skilled in the use of herbal medicines. They also could perform minor surgeries (and even appendicitis operations) and could provide rudimentary dental care—an important function in an army of peasants who grew up with virtually no knowledge of dental hygiene. But the communist medics were severely limited in their battlefield capabilities. The NPA medics I met in southern Quezon, for example, could not handle gunshot wounds to the torso or head or broken bones. To improve health care in communist zones, both among civilian supporters and in the NPA, urban Party cadres were devoting greater attention to recruiting doctors, nurses, and medical students.

For city-bred Party cadres and guerrillas, the adjustment to the austere, physically demanding life in rural communist zones was usually a painful one, a fact I learned all too well. On my first visit to the southern Quezon communist zone, I met a Party cadre named Lisa who had been assigned to the guerrilla zone only four months earlier. Some of her efforts to cling to the comforts she had known in the city amused her peasant comrades and the veterans who had made similar adjustments years earlier. Conscious of her disheveled appearance in the morning after spending the night on a narrow platform of split bamboo poles, Lisa still made use of a small makeup kit. She also carried a red thermos bottle that she kept filled with boiled water for drinking or for coffee when it was available. When I arrived in the camp and donated to the communal kitchen a rice sack full of canned goods, noodles, raisins, dried mangoes, and other delicacies, Lisa conducted an immediate inventory. She squealed with delight as she dug her way through the sack, holding aloft one sorely missed item after another.

A fair-skinned woman in her late twenties, Lisa had grown up in an upper-middle-class family in Manila, attended an exclusive prep school, and graduated from an elite Catholic university. Lisa had worked for six years in Party-influenced Church and human rights groups before requesting a transfer to a Quezon guerrilla zone in February 1987. She still had not been able to bring herself to tell her parents that she had joined the communist underground. Instead, her parents believed her to be "working with farmers in Quezon," she said.

Less than a month after arriving, Lisa had participated in her first military operation, and she excitedly recalled the experience: For two days, more than 50 guerrillas had lain in wait near the town of General Luna for a military convoy. The ambush began when the NPA forces detonated a land mine beneath a U.S.-supplied armored troop carrier. Nineteen soldiers had been killed in the encounter; the NPA had suffered no casualties. Lisa said she had been struck by the sight of Red fighters bandaging the wounds of enemy soldiers. Even more exciting, she recalled, was the reception accorded the guerrillas as they retreated through a nearby barrio. Peasants greeted them with boiled corn, peanuts, and pails of water.

Late one brilliantly moonlit evening in November 1987, my NPA escort and I arrived at the home of a peasant in an isolated hollow of Barangay Rose. The hut was filled with the sound of a hacking cough, and peering inside, I saw Lisa lying on a straw mat on the bamboo-slat floor feverish and covered with a blanket. She complained of a headache, chills, and an upset stomach, but NPA medics were unsure what was wrong. Despite her illness, Lisa insisted on telling me about the military operation from which she had recently returned. The guerrillas had walked for several days over mountainous terrain to rendezvous with other communist forces. It had been a wonderful victory for the NPA and an exciting expedition, Lisa said, but she was afraid she had contracted typhoid fever.

Two days later, Lisa's condition worsened. Members of the barrio militia carried her several miles to a road and then took her by bus to the nearest hospital, a three-hour ride. That same day, I fell ill with severe diarrhea, vomiting, and a high fever. After a day, the regional CPP leadership, fearing I had contracted typhoid, decided to move me to a hospital in Manila. They put me on a *carabao*, and took me to the next barrio, where a jeepney was hired to drive me to the capital, seven hours away. The diagnosis turned out to be far better than it might have been. Like many urban cadres when they were first assigned to the barrios, I had contracted acute gastroenteritis from consuming some particularly disagreeable bacteria in food or water.

The Party and NPA exercised complete control over most aspects of the lives of members, even romance. Marriage was restricted to members within the movement, for obvious political and security reasons. Many rebels relished the role of matchmaker. "You come to the hills and we'll fix you up with a nice old-fashioned boy," I heard a rural Party cadre tell an urban cadre, the latter an attractive single woman in her late twenties. A cadre's Party superior had to approve courtship and marriage, and the same was true for divorce, which was not recognized by Philippine law. In fact, many underground marriages arranged during the movement's Cultural Revolution days of the late 1960s and early 1970s had ended in divorce.

The courtship process offered a study in Party discipline, particularly because couples usually were assigned to different areas and might see one another only every few months. A prospective suitor would approach the collective (Party cell) to which the woman belonged and convey his intention to court one of its members. Only after the woman and the collective had given their approval was the man allowed to begin seeing the woman. What followed was a six-month period in which "both parties size up the other, evaluate the other's characteristics, and develop the friendship," a 20-year-old Party cadre told me. At that point, if both agreed they were compatible, they were allowed to "go steady." After a year, if the couple desired marriage, their respective collectives would either approve or reject the request. A man had to be 21 and a woman 18 before getting married. During the ceremony, which was conducted by a Party official, the couple would stand with a CPP flag draped over their shoulders and pledge commitment to the CPP's concept of "class love," as opposed to the "personal love" of "bourgeois society." The Party's marriage guidelines stressed that "to work for your family instead of the masses is a feudal concept."[3] Party leaders were well aware that to force unhappy couples to remain married would negatively affect their work in the revolution, so divorce was allowed on four grounds: (1) if physical injury was inflicted by one spouse on the other; (2) if no communication from a spouse had occurred for at least three years; (3) if the couple pleaded incompatibility; or (4) if the lifestyle of a spouse was "veering toward the bourgeoisie, and the movement [was] neglected."[4]

Maintaining a marriage when one or even both of the spouses were living in a guerrilla zone was an emotionally draining task. Each spouse was allowed one annual leave for conjugal visits, which usually lasted only a few days. Many rebels were reduced to maintaining long-distance relationships via the fragile underground mail system. I was sitting in a peasant's hut in Quezon province one afternoon with several guerrillas when a rebel arrived with a letter for one of my NPA companions, a woman in her early twenties named Virgie. The letter was from her boyfriend, an NPA organizer in the next district, a two-day walk away. (It had taken a week to reach Virgie.) Beaming broadly, Virgie slipped away from the others to read her prized love letter. If there were not too many government military operations, Virgie said, she might receive two letters a month.

The movement had gradually loosened its harshly puritanical moral standards, which had been inspired by the Chinese Cultural Revolution. In the early days, public displays of affection between couples, such as holding hands, were strongly discouraged. Maya, a cadre from Negros, recalled that until the late 1970s, anyone who broke rigid courtship rules was punished with "hard labor," such as planting rice and digging irrigation ditches. Violations of the rules included premarital sex and even public kissing. Laughing, Maya said that there was such a high incidence of premarital sex within the movement by the late 1970s that the Party was forced to relax its rules.[5] Endorsing the swing toward greater sexual tolerance, a Manila-based Party cadre earnestly remarked, "You can't make love to Marx or Mao."

Maya had married a Party cadre named Roy when she was 18 years old. When I met the couple in late 1988, they had been married 10 years and had four children, the allowable limit in the movement, according to Roy. (The Party stressed strict family planning for its members.) The couple's children had posed something of a problem because both sets of grandparents had died—thus leaving Roy and Maya without close relatives who could look after their children. Usually, the rebels chose to leave their children with relatives or with sympathizers rather than subject them to the harsh life of running and hiding. Separation from children was a psychological strain for some NPA members and Party workers assigned to guerrilla zones. The former deputy CPP secretary for southeastern Mindanao, Froiland Maureal, explained to me a few days after surrendering in 1987, "It's not that I'm tired of armed struggle, but I want to raise my children. In eight years of marriage, we have not had the family together."

On each of my visits to communist zones, a network of farmers and shopkeepers, even minor government officials and politicians, fed and sheltered my guides and me as part of a well-traveled underground railroad leading from Manila to the rural rebel zones. The guerrillas called these people the *masa*, the "mass base," that gave lifeblood to the movement and enabled the rebels to elude government troops.

Despite the heavy concentration of soldiers in many areas, the rebels moved with ease in and out of the communist zones I visited. Once en route to the southern Quezon front accompanied by Joy, my CPP escort, our bus stopped for lunch at an open-air eatery near the town of Atimonan. As Joy and I devoured a plate of chicken and rice, our last hearty meal for a few days, another bus arrived from the Bondoc peninsula, our destination. Joy hurried outside and returned with four friends—three men and a woman, all in their twenties or early thirties, who were guerrillas and Party cadres returning from NPA units we would be joining. The only hint that the four had left an NPA camp earlier that morning was the mud caked on their pants and tennis shoes, and that was hardly incriminating evidence.

As we headed south from Gumaca, we left behind the paved, although badly pitted, National Highway for the heavily traveled gravel road that ran the length of the Bondoc peninsula. Since my first visit to the Southern Quezon Front and the brush with Captain Laudiangco at the army checkpoint in the summer of 1987, I had dreaded this final leg of the trip. But by late 1987, Laudiangco had been transferred, and his successor was far less diligent and aggressive. Checkpoints were only occasionally manned, and fewer army patrols were being conducted. I heaved a sigh of relief when our bus passed without stopping through the checkpoint where I had been briefly detained with my rebel escorts a few months earlier. It was 1 P.M., and the soldiers assigned to the checkpoint were either having lunch or were escaping the midday heat with a siesta. The NPA carefully took note of such habits, which could help them avoid a possibly fatal confrontation with soldiers at the checkpoint in the future.

21

People's War: The Third Decade

Shortly after dawn on March 20, 1988, nearly 200 NPA guerrillas aboard several stolen logging trucks sped into the town of Cabarroguis, the backwater capital of northern Luzon's Quirino province. The rebels paid no attention to government offices or local constabulary outpost, instead driving directly to the JPE sawmill complex on the outskirts of town. For a half day, the NPA force occupied the sawmill, then withdrew—after burning the sawmill to the ground. "We made our point," Bing, the regional NPA commander told me later with a satisfied grin.

A few days earlier, the manager of the JPE logging company and sawmill, a congressman named Junie Cua, had refused NPA demands to pay more than 1 million pesos ($50,000) in "revolutionary taxes." The attack on the sawmill was merely the rebels' way of reminding Cua that he was in arrears on his payments and that it was bad business in this remote area of the northern Philippines to antagonize the NPA.

Within the week, Cua sent a message to the NPA offering to settle his "back taxes," Bing said. Cua had already made his first payment by the time I arrived at Bing's camp in the Cordillera Mountains of Nueva Vizcaya a few days later. The communist commander confidently assured me, "We will collect more before the logging season ends in July."

The incident offered one measure of how far the NPA had progressed since its inauspicious beginnings in a dusty Central Luzon barrio. During the course of two bloody decades of warfare, the NPA had been transformed from a raw collection of several dozen student radicals into a savvy guerrilla army skilled in the arts of armed and political warfare.

The communist army had become entrenched in 60 of the Philippines' 73 provinces. It was collecting taxes from businesspeople and landowners, intimidating politicians and government officials, and controlling the lives of thousands in rural barrios. A sophisticated underground infrastructure was attending to the tasks of intelligence, logistics, communications, and medical work. By the late 1980s, the rebel army's battle-hardened veterans had grown confident that victory would be won within 10 years, barring "errors."

While triumph for the rebels was by no means certain, during eight expeditions with NPA units I saw little evidence that the government was seriously challenging the guerrillas in their strongholds. AFP operations in the 1980s had become more infrequent and in a smaller area, rebel leaders said. "We now have more time to consolidate and to organize the masses," an NPA regional commander in Luzon told me. Although never more than 10 miles as the crow flies from the nearest road, only once inside the communist zones was I reminded of the presence of an opposing army in the vicinity. One day while in the southern Quezon rebel zone an AFP UH-1 "Huey" helicopter flew several hundred feet overhead our jungle camp but quickly disappeared, unaware of our presence, as it continued on its journey.

Throughout the 1980s, as the NPA grew, the AFP was forced to spread its forces thinner and thinner. In 1981, for example, the army deployed three infantry battalions to combat the NPA in Cagayan province. By 1988, those three battalions were scattered over seven northern Luzon provinces. On paper, of course, the AFP continued to hold a huge advantage in personnel and weapons. But in the guerrilla zones I visited in the countryside, the AFP was capitalizing little on those advantages.

The war in the northern Luzon provinces of Quirino and Nueva Vizcaya underscored this. About 2,500 soldiers, vigilantes, and civilian militia members were arrayed against fewer than 300 armed guerrillas in 1988. But the mobility of the NPA forced the government to disperse its forces throughout the two mountainous provinces. An NPA analysis showed that government forces were able to effectively cover only 80 barrios scattered in 8 of 21 towns in the two provinces, leaving susceptible to communist control more than 300 barrios in 13 towns.

"The problem with the AFP," Bing said, "is they are using positional and conventional warfare against us. They have deployed most of their troops to protect lines of communication, town halls, electric facilities, sawmills. It is difficult for them to launch search-and-destroy missions."[1] The Nueva Vizcaya provincial constabulary commander, on whose shoulders fell much of the responsibility for counterinsurgency efforts in the area, was "good behind a desk" but was a poor field officer, Bing said.

(Bing also alleged that the provincial commander had a share in local logging operations, a fairly common practice among military officers.) The communist commander, on the other hand, had spent 10 years with the NPA in the northeast Luzon countryside. He knew the terrain, spoke the local dialects, and understood and empathized with slash-and-burn farmers eking out a living on the hardscrabble slopes of the Cordilleras.

When I visited a communist zone in Nueva Vizcaya in 1988, NPA forces in the area were under little military pressure. Every three months or so, the AFP would launch a Vietnam War–style search-and-destroy operation, dispatching three companies (about 300 men) supported sparingly by helicopters to comb the hills in search of the NPA for 7 to 10 days.[2] Bing said he would simply move his NPA units to another area out of harm's way and return to the affected barrios when the soldiers had withdrawn. "That leaves us more than two months to work before the next operation," the communist commander said, grinning broadly. Bing noted that the AFP occasionally launched platoon-size patrols, but these were "easy to avoid."

Mobility had become one of the keys to the NPA's military successes, and the speed and stamina rebel units displayed as they moved through difficult terrain were impressive. The rebels were tough and lean and traveled light. In addition to his or her weapon, the entire contents of a typical NPA soldier's pack was an extra pair of pants, one or two T-shirts, a change of underwear, and two rice sacks sewed together for use as a sleeping mat. The rebels usually carried no rations, relying instead on the hospitality of local peasants.[3]

The NPA adhered to the cardinal rule of guerrilla warfare: Fight only on your own terms and with a superior force, if possible. The growing strength of the NPA intimidated the army, and AFP officers seemed very reluctant to incur casualties. When an NPA force overran the town hall and constabulary outpost in the Bondoc peninsula town of San Francisco in early 1988, it took government troops several hours to relieve the beleaguered garrison. Fearing that guerrillas were waiting to ambush reinforcements (a frequent NPA tactic) the AFP dispatched a relief force by sea, which did not arrive until four hours after the NPA had withdrawn with 14 captured automatic rifles, 1 grenade launcher and 20 grenades, while suffering only three killed and three wounded.[4]

The dramatic growth of the NPA forced the military to make strategic adjustments. The AFP concentrated its forces in heavily fortified camps along provincial roads and in larger towns, and the troops ventured out only in platoon- and company-size formations. "Our task now," Francisco, a regional NPA commander in southern Luzon said, "is to drive the military off the provincial roads and back to the national highway." But to accomplish that feat, most NPA commanders I met believed that the communist army would require bazookas, mortars, surface-to-air missiles, and possibly other weapons. "We are unanimous in thinking that if we cannot get heavy weapons, we cannot win at guerrilla warfare," an NPA commander on Luzon told me in March 1988. "All we need now is heavy weapons."[5]

Although the NPA's growth through the 1980s resulted in greater military and political successes for the revolutionary movement, rapid expansion spawned a whole new set of problems for the communist army. Logistics became more complex and expensive. Sophisticated communications became essential. More reliable sources of funding had to be found. Additional political and military cadres had to be trained from a dwindling pool of educated recruits.

Rebel strategists hoped to escalate the war in 1989 and 1990, and toward that end the NPA was consolidating platoons and squads to create companies numbering 60 to 100 guerrillas. But the difficulty of moving undetected in large formations forced the NPA for the time being to abandon plans for battalion-size operations in southern Quezon, one of the NPA's most advanced areas.[6] Company-size units on Mindanao were forced to break into groups of 35 to 40 because of army shelling and food shortages, reassembling only to conduct military operations.

Additionally, the larger NPA formations created enormous financial burdens for the revolution. The cost of keeping a single NPA company in the field at the end of 1988 averaged 50,000 to 60,000 ($3,000) pesos a month. That figure swelled to 100,000 pesos a month when the guerrillas were conducting combat operations; the rebels' normally meager diet had to be supplemented with high-protein foods such as eggs, and assorted medicines had to be purchased for treatment of wounds.[7] The Bicol CPP secretary complained that the 50,000 pesos a month it was costing to maintain each of his region's four guerrilla companies in 1988 was too expensive. The Bicol budget was already stretched thin at the time because of much higher food expenditures resulting from a typhoon in late 1987 that had devastated the region, making it impossible for peasants to support the guerrilla army.

Even without typhoon damages, food was a more urgent problem for the movement with the formation of larger NPA units. AFP operations had hurt food production by sympathetic peasants in some areas, making shortages sometimes acute, a ranking CPP official told me. During lulls between military operations guerrillas were being organized to grow food and to work with peasant supporters on communal or single-family farms. Medical supplies also became more urgently in demand with the escalation of NPA military operations and the use of larger units. By 1988, the Southern Tagalog Regional NPA Command—1 of 17 regional NPA commands—was allotting 60,000 to 80,000 pesos ($3,000–$4,000) a month for medical supplies.[8]

By assembling larger forces and attacking larger military targets, the NPA managed to increase its arsenal of automatic rifles and other weapons more rapidly. But a shortage of rifles remained a chronic problem curtailing the growth of the NPA in many areas.[9] A veteran Negros cadre told me that one of the island's districts had a communist militia unit that had grown almost to battalion size (nearly 300 members), but that most of the part-time rebels were unarmed.

To make maximum use of the weapons and materiel that the NPA already had, the communist army continued to demand rigorous frugality and discipline. A standing order for NPA units prevented the rebels from firing M-16 automatic rifles on the full automatic setting in order to preserve ammunition. Red fighters were also strictly limited in the number of shots they were permitted to fire during raids and ambushes. During the postmortem conducted after every battle, a guerrilla was expected to account for the bullets he or she had fired.

Lacking a foreign benefactor, the NPA continued painstakingly to build its arsenal by ambushing and overrunning AFP units and even by purchasing weapons from corrupt (or impoverished) soldiers. The commander of an NPA unit I was visiting in the Sierra Madre region of northern Quezon province pointed to an M-14 rifle that a guerrilla was holding, which he said had been recently bought from a government soldier. "Our friends told us that if we had enough money, we could even buy tanks," the NPA commander told me, chuckling.

While hoping for heavier weapons from abroad, the NPA was making advances in developing homemade land mines and other weapons that were enabling the guerrillas to neutralize government armor. (According to a captured underground computer disk, the NPA allotted $100,000 for the purchase of "hardware and explosives" in 1988.) The crude but effective mines were fashioned from large cookie canisters packed with up to 90 sticks of dynamite. Other versions used homemade gunpowder manufactured from common fertilizers and pesticides. The mine was command detonated by a jerry-rigged device consisting of 12 size D batteries, which sent a charge through a wire connected to blasting caps inside the can. Another effective weapon against military trucks and armored personnel carriers was the *fugasse*, a steel or bamboo tube packed with black powder and scrap metal or a solid projectile. The device was positioned alongside the road and electronically detonated as the target vehicle passed. The mines were hazardous to the NPA specialists tasked with handling them, and I heard of several accidents.

On one occasion, an NPA platoon commander in Quezon was killed and another rebel had his hand sheared off when a land mine they were trying to defuse detonated.

Other attempts to develop a local weapons industry in communist areas were marginally successful. On Negros, for example, the NPA tried to manufacture crude hand grenades by packing explosives into bottles and attaching fuses. The grenades proved to be unreliable and somewhat hazardous for the guerrillas, so the project was abandoned, a Negros cadre told me. Underground gun factories were adding primitive shotguns and handguns to the NPA's arsenal, but most of these weapons were reserved for use by district rebel squads and militia units.

Communications was another area in which the NPA made enormous strides during the 1980s, improving the communist army's capability to carry out coordinated operations. By the end of the decade, the rebels had in place a sophisticated radio and transceiver network linking guerrilla units throughout the country with the central leadership in Manila. The NPA's radios and transceivers were bought, captured, or (I was told by CPP cadres in several regions) donated by sympathetic or opportunistic politicians or government officials. In some areas, the NPA's communications network surpassed the radio capabilities of opposing AFP units. Radio communications cut the relay time from the week a courier used to take to a matter of hours or even minutes. One afternoon in an NPA camp in the Bondoc peninsula I watched Francisco, the regional commander, decode a message he had just received from Mindoro, nearly 100 miles away, informing him of military operations on the island. In a few seconds the rebel commander had punched the coded numbers into a hand-held Sharp computer and read the message as it appeared on a tiny screen. Grinning, Francisco remarked, "This has become a high-tech revolution."

In the Bicol regional CPP headquarters camp, a crew of young women was manning a pair of radios that allowed Party secretary Sotero Llamas to maintain contact with his units scattered throughout the six-province region. A powerful high-frequency radio enabled the camp to communicate with the national command in Manila to the northwest and with other units scattered throughout the islands to the south. (The high-frequency radio was powered by a 12-volt heavy truck battery that had to be recharged every 18 days with a noisy gasoline generator.)

By the late 1980s, financing the revolution had in itself become a staggering challenge for the CPP and its NDF affiliates. A significant share of NPA and Party activities was supported by an elaborate system of taxation primarily targetting larger foreign- and Filipino-owned businesses, large landowners, concerns engaged in ranching, fish and prawn culture, logging and mining, and even government corporations—all of whom were categorized by the CPP as "class enemies."[10] Tax assessment on class enemies was generally pegged at 1 to 2 percent of gross income. Businesspeople or landowners who refused NPA demands were subject to economic sabotage or assassination. A communist commander in northern Luzon told me that in addition to the payment of taxes, the NPA demanded that companies "at least remain neutral" and "stay away from . . . the [government] counterinsurgency program." In 1986, the military reported that the NPA destroyed an estimated 163 million pesos (about $8 million) worth of property owned by companies refusing to pay rebel taxes.

Taxes on logging and mining companies were playing a crucial role in financing the revolution in several regions of the country, particularly on Mindanao, Samar, Negros, and in northern Luzon, and were helping the CPP at least partially solve a problem that arose as the guerrilla army rapidly expanded in the 1980s.[11] In its early years, the NPA had survived largely on contributions and taxes paid by peasants. This practice became unpopular with peasants in some areas and led to an erosion of support, Party officials admitted. By shifting the burden of financing NPA operations to big businesses (both Philippine and foreign owned), the CPP had eased demands on peasants.

Taxation was not limited to class enemies. Peasants and farm workers who had benefited from the NPA's revolutionary land reform program were taxed a percentage of net income from each harvest or, in the case of farm workers, a percentage of the wage increase. Agricultural taxes were usually collected "only after the second or third harvest under revolutionary land reform," according to the NDF tax policy document.

The rapidly escalating cost of financing the revolution also led the NDF to devise more innovative ways of raising revenues for its political and military activities. CPP computer disks captured by the military in 1988 showed that the world's stock markets were a major, if not leading, source of funds for the revolution. CPP-run businesses such as fish farms and interisland shipping companies were other sources of income for the underground.[12]

Aggressive NPA taxation activities also had the effect of helping to spread government military forces dangerously thin, as AFP units were deployed to protect private businesses and vital industries. The provinces of Nueva Vizcaya and Quirino offered a classic example. The regional AFP command deployed the Forty-eighth Infantry Battalion to the Nueva Vizcaya–Quirino border area in June 1987 to keep lucrative logging areas controlled by local political warlords free of the NPA. Within a year, the guerrillas gradually forced the dispersal of the battalion by launching attacks in other parts of the two provinces. A company was sent to the northern Nueva Vizcaya town of Dupax to respond to increased NPA activities. Another company was sent to the town of Villaverde following a rebel attack there. A third company was sent to the town of Bagabag, leaving only one company in the border area where the entire battalion was originally deployed.

Despite the military presence, the NPA continued to collect hefty taxes from local logging companies. Each piece of heavy equipment was assessed a flat tax: 50,000 pesos for a large bulldozer, 30,000 pesos for a small bulldozer, and so on. Sawmills were taxed 500,000 pesos ($25,000), and on top of that, logging companies were taxed anywhere from 10 to 25 percent of net income.[13]

Bringing the war closer to a stalemate, as the NPA was striving to do, required expanding the movement's political base, and that was proving difficult in the late 1980s with a popular president in office. In thousands of barrios the NPA was struggling to consolidate its control. One morning in 1988 in a fishing village along the remote Pacific coast of northeast Quezon, I met an NPA organizer, an outgoing woman in her twenties, who was experiencing the new difficulties.

Sandra was a member of an NPA armed propaganda unit assigned to establish communist organizations and attract recruits in the coastal barrios of northeast Quezon. She had been a rebel mass organizer in Laguna province during the time of Marcos, and she had found it much easier work then. Now, she sighed, the pace of organizing "is very slow. The people are no longer convinced that armed struggle is the way to end their poverty." It was more difficult to convince villagers to contribute food and shelter to the NPA. "Sometimes," she admitted, "we do not feel welcome."

The southern tip of the rugged Sierra Madres where they sliced down into northern Quezon was only about 50 miles east of Manila as the crow flies, and CPP strategists viewed the new guerrilla zone as a potential staging point for future attacks on the capital. Most of the barrios were accessible only by sea, and we reached the place after a five-hour sail through rough seas in a 15-foot pumpboat, a motorized outrigger canoe. We put in at a village built along the beach, at the foot of the foggy Sierra Madre that rose spectacularly just beyond a thin, palm-covered ribbon of coastal plain. When we arrived, the beach was teeming with armed guerrillas who were preparing to return to the Bondoc peninsula, more than eight hours by pumpboat.

The coastal barrio that was the entry point for communist forces in the area had been organized by the NPA within the last three or four years. In 1985, the NPA had consolidated its hold on the barrio by executing three people accused of being military informants. After that, villagers who may have been uncomfortable with the rebels had at least acquiesced to their presence. A squad-size communist militia unit had been formed to police the barrio, provide intelligence, and conduct patrols.

The NPA fighting unit assigned to the area was a 30-member guerrilla platoon commanded by a former Manila student activist who had adopted the nom de guerre Ivan (in admiration of Ivan Koniev, the aggressive Soviet field marshall who captured Berlin at the end of World War II). I met him and several regional CPP officials after a nearly vertical two-hour walk up the Sierra Madre overlooking the fishing barrio. Carved from the mountainside overlooking the Pacific Ocean, the camp was hidden in a magnificent rain forest filled with wild orchids, rhododendron, ferns of all sizes, and huge hardwood trees that formed a thick canopy overhead.

Ivan noted that the NPA had progressed far from the days in the mid-1970s when he had been sent to the countryside armed with a homemade pistol and a machete. As late as 1984, his platoon was armed with one M-16 automatic rifle, one automatic carbine, and the rest shotguns. By 1988, Ivan was able to issue new recruits M-16 rifles and military packs.

The NPA had first pioneered urban guerrilla warfare in the 1970s as a tactic for capturing badly needed weapons, but by the late 1980s, assassinations in Manila and other urban areas had become a key component in the NPA's armed strategy and an effective political weapon. Urban guerrilla teams were killing police involved in breaking strikes, outspokenly anticommunist government officials, conservative business-people, factory owners, even an occasional right-wing journalist. NPA assassins were also responsible for the October 1987 killings of two U.S. soldiers and a retired GI outside Clark Air Force Base.[14] The CPP subsequently declared a policy of targeting U.S. citizens who were linked in any way to counterinsurgency activities and even suggested that U.S. development officials would be potential targets for assassination. On the morning of April 21, 1989, the rebels made good on their threat by assassinating U.S. Army Colonel James N. Rowe, an adviser to the AFP, as he was being driven to his Quezon City office.

The urban killings were used to demonstrate to supporters the NPA's capability to punish its enemies and implement revolutionary justice even in areas where the government and AFP were strongest. The threat of death had become a powerful deterrent to factory owners engaged in labor disputes with unions linked to the rebel movement. But the urban NPA killings had alienated many middle-class and professional elements in Manila, and even left-wing human rights advocates appealed to the communist leadership to halt the attacks. The NPA finally acceded to public criticism and restricted operations in the capital. At the height of the campaign in 1987, more than 120 soldiers and police were killed in Manila in the NPA's first major effort to bring the war to the capital. One of the NPA Manila commanders said the objectives of the killings were to open a new front in the war effort and to organize residents of Manila, "especially the workers in the city, into higher revolutionary forms of struggle."[15]

The NPA's Manila urban guerrilla unit is known as the Alex Boncayao Brigade, named for a labor leader who joined the NPA in the late 1970s and was killed by the military in a 1983 encounter in Nueva Ecija province. The first five-member "partisan" unit was formed in early 1984 in the slums of Malabon, an impoverished seaside suburb on Manila's northern fringe. In late May 1984, police Brigadier General Tomás Karingal, commander of the capital's northern sector, became the first victim of the brigade. Karingal had been singled out for "antilabor activities" stemming from the violent dispersal of striking workers in the city's northern industrial belt. In late 1987, a member of the NPA Manila regional command placed the strength of the Alex Boncayao Brigade at 50 guerrillas (a credible figure) working from 12 bases in metropolitan Manila.[16]

In addition to boosting the morale of radical workers and sympathetic slum dwellers, the Manila NPA attacks tied down additional AFP troops in Manila. Police swept through poor neighborhoods suspected of harboring the urban guerrillas and detained hundreds of men. Although the sweeps succeeded in hampering NPA activities, the repressive measures alienated residents of the neighborhoods subjected to the raids, and the Aquino government's image of tolerance suffered.

Outside Manila, in provinces where the war had been a bloody reality for years, the response to urban NPA operations was far more benign. In many towns and cities, communist assassination activities had become an effective means for intimidating anticommunist government officials and for winning favor with farmers and fishermen who were often the victims of abusive police and soldiers. One morning in late 1987 in a peasant's house in Barangay Rose, I met the commander of the NPA's Southern Quezon Front Partisan Unit, a 16-member urban assassination squad that was waging a relentless war against opponents in the towns and villages of the Bondoc peninsula. His was name was Aga, and he was 24, an elfish-looking fellow with a thin mustache and scraggly goatee.

Aga had grown up in a barrio of southern Quezon and had joined the NPA in 1983. Before his assignment to the southern Quezon urban partisan unit in 1984, he had spent one month in the countryside undergoing basic military instruction and a special course for sparrows that included intelligence training. At the end of the course, Aga was given a .45-caliber pistol and assigned his first target: a constabulary sergeant who was accused of involvement in the murders of several farmers suspected of having communist sympathies. Aga waited for the soldier one Sunday afternoon outside a cockfighting arena and gunned him down when he stepped outside. Aga grabbed the dead man's pistol and ran away. By NPA standards, the operation was amateurish: In his nervousness, Aga had fired five shots, three more than the NPA textbook procedure of shooting the victim once in the head and once in the chest.

In the three years that followed, Aga participated in 17 of his unit's 27 operations. The targets were determined by the CPP front committee and were based largely on complaints from sympathizers and rebel intelligence, I was told. Twenty soldiers, police, government officials, and civilian militia members had been assassinated, and seven weapons had been confiscated. One of the victims was the mayor of Lopez, whom the NPA accused of establishing an intelligence network in the barrios. He was killed in his house in 1985. In the week before Aga and I met in late 1987, his men had assassinated a police officer accused of establishing an antisparrow unit and killed two members of a right-wing vigilante organization in a nearby town.

I asked Aga how he felt about the AFP's characterizations of sparrows as terrorists. He took a long drag on a cigarette before replying: "It is our job, and the masses ask help from us to eliminate these bad elements. Following most of our operations, we explain to the people, verbally and written, why this person was executed, what specific crimes against the people he was guilty of."

Despite the movement's considerable support at the grass-roots level, NPA commanders acknowledged that the communist army was not infallible and that many mistakes had been made during the course of 20 years of war. An NPA commander in the Southern Tagalog region, for example, noted that the rise of vigilante groups in some rural barrios of Lopez (Quezon) was due in part to NPA heavy-handedness. The rebel commander recalled there was "too much taxing" and that "some of our comrades mistreated some of the people. That opportunity was taken by the military." The NPA had tried to rectify its mistakes, the commander said, by "asking the forgiveness of the people," a practice he said was a policy of the Party and NPA. "We even pay the people if we come to know what our comrades did was bad."[17]

There were other occasions in which NPA tactics in the countryside had provoked a widespread negative response. Most notable was the destruction of four bridges in Bicol in the fall of 1987, which severed the region's only rail link to Manila and closed the National Highway leading to the capital. The destruction of the bridges sparked a popular backlash, as prices of basic commodities soared and farmers found it difficult to transport their produce to town markets.

The destruction of the Bicol bridges marked an effort by the NPA to develop infrastructure sabotage as a new tactic. In the NPA's previous two decades of struggle, the guerrillas had spared power lines, bridges, and other infrastructure targets in all but a few cases. While defending infrastructure sabotage in a long article in *Ang Bayan* in September 1987, the NPA once again proved responsive to public criticism. By 1989, although NPA forces were continuing to target government facilities and equipment and private businesses for sabotage, the CPP appeared to have at least temporarily abandoned plans to pursue infrastructure sabotage as a tactic.

Disagreements about other matters of strategy and tactics, particularly the decision to escalate armed attacks against government facilities in August 1987, precipitated a split in the Negros underground. Several veteran cadres led by then-Negros CPP secretary Nemesio Dimafiles resigned from the Party and formed a breakaway group. The split caused the collapse of the Party's underground network in Bacolod, the Negros Occidental provincial capital, but NPA operations in the Negros countryside appeared to be only slightly affected.[18]

As of early 1989, the NPA faced the prospect of a war that could go on and on for years with no victory and no defeat. The thought, while sobering to communist political and military leaders who were not getting any younger, appeared to be a price most NPA veterans were willing to pay. "We are getting older. Our health is not as good, and we talk about this going on and on—particularly if we do not get the heavy weapons that we need now," one veteran NPA commander said. "But we are very optimistic. We were able to survive the first 10 years, the most difficult years. That was the survival test. Now, we cannot be destroyed by the enemy."[19]

22
The Faces Behind
the Revolution

After 20 years of carefully cultivated anonymity, the men and women who headed the Philippine revolution remained mysterious shadows even to most of the Party membership. No charismatic figure such as Ho Chi Minh or Fidel Castro had been allowed to rise to lead and give the movement a face. Who were the prominent figures of the movement by the late 1980s? What were their backgrounds? How had they risen to the top of the revolutionary leadership? Most of the attempts to answer those question had come from government intelligence and was either false or intentionally misleading. Through the years, many leading figures in the rebel underground had been reduced to frightening caricatures.

From relaxed conversations in prison cells to tense, disguised meetings in underground safe houses, I met many of the anonymous rebel leaders, and found they were not the one-dimensional, impersonal murderers as so commonly depicted by military propaganda. To be sure, they were dedicated Marxist-Leninists, sophisticated, well-educated, and committed to violent revolution. But they viewed their cause as in the patriotic tradition of the world's revolutions, the French and American included. Obviously, I could not journey inside the psyche of the rebel leaders. The sketches that follow should be viewed less as a comprehensive inventory of the rebel hierarchy or psychological profile than an attempt to give flesh and blood to some of the most prominent faces behind the Philippine revolution.[1]

Flashing a broad, bucktoothed grin, the bespectacled face in the big picture window peering down at me was unmistakable. The figure waved his arms furiously in greeting, and I knew I had finally found José María Sison. It had taken me more than six months to track down the man who almost single-handedly had conceived the revolution and helped nurture it to self-sufficiency. Our rendezvous was finally arranged for an apartment on the outskirts of Amsterdam, and it was there where I met Sison on a raw April day in 1988.

Sison and his wife, Julieta, warmly welcomed me into the second floor apartment. He had shaved his scraggly mustache, which had always given him a sinister appearance. Cleanshaven, his jet black hair well pomaded, wearing thin wire-frame glasses, and dressed in well-pressed gray woolen pants, a light pink button-down shirt, and black leather dress shoes, Sison had the severe look of a conservative college professor.

In the nearly two years since they left the Philippines in late 1986, a few months after Corazón Aquino had released him from prison, Sison and his wife had been crisscrossing the globe. Their travels had taken them to Australia, Singapore, Japan, India, Greece, Central America, and virtually every country of Western Europe. They had just returned from a trip through Latin America highlighted by stops in Nicaragua and Mexico. Along the way, Sison had spread his gospel of Marxist-Leninist revolution, damning Aquino and predicting economic and political disaster in his native land.

By 1988, the Sisons had established a comfortable, if hectic, existence. They spent much of their time moving between the Netherlands and West Germany, where they were feted by European radicals as the First Couple of the Philippine revolution. It had been dizzying for Sison, particularly after nine years of isolation in prison. Through it all, he appeared to have lost little, if any, of the fire that had driven him to audaciously plot and lead a Maoist revolution.

Despite his self-exile 6,000 miles away from the Philippines, Sison was still a key player in the revolution. AFP intelligence suggested he had reassumed the chairmanship of the CPP, an allegation that cadres in the Philippines coyly declined to confirm or deny. Whether he had formally reassumed leadership—and it seemed doubtful to me that he had as of early 1989—his influence and stature within the movement remained enormous. His old writings still constituted the Party's basic readings, and one former protégé assured me, "The older comrades don't consider any other authority than Joema." After his release from prison, Sison had been hailed as a cult hero in the Philippines. Savvy political activists and giggling coeds who had not been born when the revolution began besieged him for autographs. At parties, fans and followers lined up to have their pictures taken with the legendary Amado Guerrero.

Aquino had tried in vain to wrest a pledge of support after releasing Sison from prison. Wearing a yellow shirt (Aquino's campaign color), he was escorted to the president's temporary office along with Bernabe Buscayno, the founding NPA commander whom Aquino released at the same time. An old Aquino family acquaintance, Buscayno promised to support the president. Turning to Sison, Aquino pressed him, "I hope you're going to help me, Joema." He sat quietly.[2] Within days, it became apparent that Sison had no intention of supporting the new government and remained dedicated to revolution.

Now, nearly 50 years old, Sison clearly reveled in his freedom. For eight hours, we sat and talked about the revolution to which he had devoted his life. I was treated to a tour de force of mood and emotion, charisma and bombast. One minute Sison was a mischievous gossip regaling me with whispered stories about the byzantine politics of the old communist party and the secret love affairs of the Lavas, the next a fire-breathing revolutionary lecturing me on the political correctness of the CPP's disastrous boycott of the 1986 presidential election and on why Aquino was "a much weaker opponent than Marcos." He harangued and reminisced, parried and dissembled as he set forth his version of the movement's history.

As we talked, Sison nibbled at orange slices, mixed nuts, and *hopia*, a bean paste–filled biscuit popular in the Philippines. When that was gone, he chain-smoked cigarettes. Occasionally Sison jumped up to accept phone calls, at least one of which appeared to be from the Philippines. Ever the leader, he crisply gave instructions over the phone. Before leaving, I asked Sison if he would ever return to the Philippines without a change in government. He grinned impishly. "There's a lot of coastline, and if the NPA reaches 25,000 rifles, there would be a lot of areas in the countryside."

While Sison was attracting the attention of military intelligence back in Manila, the revolution was being led by a once-obscure student activist named Benito Tiamzon, who was in his late thirties by 1988 and something of an unknown quantity even to many prominent members of the movement. He had studied engineering at UP, where he became involved in the radical student movement. Assigned to trade union work, he led a 1970 strike at the General Textile Company in Manila. That same year, he helped establish an SDK chapter in the Manila suburb of Marikina and became the vice chairman.[3]

After going underground at the time of martial law, Tiamzon had been captured in 1973 and jailed in Fort Bonifacio, the army headquarters camp. One colleague who had served in prison with the softspoken Tiamzon recalled that he had shunned the often intense ideological debates among the CPP detainees. While there, he helped organize a hunger strike among prisoners.

After his release from prison in 1974, Tiamzon rejoined the underground and played a key role in organizing the communist army in Samar, which by the late 1970s had become the revolution's most advanced stronghold. Following the arrests that depleted the CPP leadership in the mid-1970s, Tiamzon was brought into the Central Committee. By the end of the decade, he had been given a seat on the Executive Committee and put in charge of the CPP's education department.[4] Following Salas' resignation in 1986, Tiamzon assumed the top CPP position. During his rise through the ranks, Tiamzon had made few enemies and impressed few people. "He's a very balanced cadre, but he's not that exceptional. He has mostly practical experience," said one former ranking Manila Party official who knew Tiamzon from their student activist days and from prison in the 1970s.[5] But the fact that he had been a relatively obscure student leader had saddled Tiamzon with something of an image problem as the CPP's paramount leader. Privately, some Party cadres spoke nostalgically of Sison's "stature" and "sense of vision," characteristics that many veteran cadres felt were lacking in the young CPP chairman.

If Tiamzon remained a figure of mystery to most of the CPP rank and file, Rodolfo Salas was the revolution's fallen star. Having spent his student days organizing other students and workers in his native Pampanga province, Salas had built a formidable CPP organization in Central Luzon during the early years of the movement. When Sison was arrested in 1977, Salas assumed leadership of the Party.

Under Salas' tutelage, the CPP and NPA tripled in size and became bolder in the military and political tactics. A 1985 *Commentary* magazine article described Salas as "ruthless and brilliant" and as the architect of a "campaign of terror, assassination, and torture in the Philippine countryside."[6] His harshest critics within the underground would later say the NPA grew in spite of Salas' leadership, that he was a dogmatic and unimaginative figure who led the movement to the brink of disaster by insisting on a boycott of the 1986 election. One former Central Committee member who resigned after a series of disagreements with the Party chairman said Salas was "paranoid and obsessed with compartmentalization" and accused the chairman and his close ally, then-CPP secretary-general Rafael Baylosis, of never having grown "beyond their Cultural Revolution background."[7] When Salas was arrested in September 1986, the attitude among some Party cadres was hardly one of sorrow. There was the feeling that a delicate problem had been resolved.

The short, squat man who greeted me at the doorway to the communist cell block in suburban Manila's Camp Crame stockade was not what I had expected of Rodolfo Salas, the celebrated Commander Bilog. He was barely taller than five feet, although his arms and legs were well muscled from manual labor and long walks in the countryside. His hands and feet were large and calloused like those of a Filipino peasant, badges of honor for a revolutionary. He was clad in shorts, T-shirt, and rubber thongs. His curly hair was mussed, and he rubbed his eyes as he adjusted to the sunlight of the narrow, dusty sliver of yard between the rectangular concrete cellblock and the 15-foot high wall topped with concertina wire that enclosed the compound.

Salas greeted me with a sleepy, gap-toothed smile and apologized for his disheveled appearance, saying he had stayed up much of the night finishing *Whirlwind*, the James Clavell novel. By then, August 1988, he was approaching his second year in prison, and Salas was starved for books and conversation. "You get tired of the same faces all the time," he noted dryly.

The military had housed several ranking CPP leaders in the compound, and Salas introduced me to a who's who of the rebel leadership: NPA commander Romulo Kintanar, CPP secretary-general Rafael Baylosis, Executive Committee members Benjamin de Vera, and Juanito Rivera, the latter Salas' closest friend and a onetime Huk commander under Dante in Tarlac in the 1960s.

I was the first journalist to be allowed inside the stockade with all the arrested CPP leaders, and the feat was entirely the accomplishment of Salas' resourceful wife, Josefina. She was a physically strong, gregarious woman who had worked as a Party labor organizer. With guile and charm, she had persuaded a reluctant constabulary colonel to allow a foreign journalist to visit her husband.

Salas' cell was uncomfortably stuffy in the midday tropical heat. The room, 15 by 20 feet, had been almost entirely furnished by friends and family members. In one corner was a steel bunk bed. His small library of tattered paperbacks was strewn across the top level and included Clavell's *Shogun*, which Salas said he had read three times, and David Stockman's *The Triumph of Politics*. Another corner of the room was occupied by an IBM-compatible word processor, which Salas used to write letters, memos, and political essays.

In two sessions, Salas and I spent nine hours talking about a wide range of subjects. Although he was softspoken and at times struggled to express himself in English, Salas was hardly the cold, aloof individual I had expected after talking with some of his critics. His gaze was steady and self-confident, and he was personable and at times witty. When he laughed, as he often did, his narrow eyes vanished below bushy eyebrows. He was indeed devoutly orthodox in his Marxist-Leninist beliefs and proud of it. But I found little to support the caricature of Salas as a psychopathic killer. Although Salas was depicted by the military as a hard-liner, on several issues facing the revolutionary movement Salas struck a stance considerably more moderate than others I had heard in the underground.

Salas may have lost some of his influence because of the boycott controversy and his arrest, but he continued to be a major force within the movement, and so I asked him about his reputation as an ideological extremist and militarist. He seemed eager to finally address the issue. "I always let the record speak for itself. In my case, it's my nature. I would prefer to work quietly. [Executive Committee member] Tony Zumel asked me, why don't you answer that [*Commentary*] article? I had other more important matters. I just dismissed it."

"Doesn't it bother you?" I persisted.

"Personally, it doesn't bother me," he said. "I know that, in a way, it gives a bad image to the movement. But it's to be expected. We were saying in the movement, to be attacked by the enemy is a good thing."

But a different issue was nagging Salas as he languished in prison. He was convinced that his arrest had been a betrayal from within the Central Committee. He had even written a letter to Juanito Rivera confiding his suspicions and complaining bitterly that his allies were being removed from leadership positions.[8] The Central Committee investigated Salas' complaints, which focused on a critic within its ranks, Ricardo Reyes. The investigation subsequently cleared Reyes of any link to Salas' arrest.[9]

Compounding Salas' unhappiness was the intense criticism that some CPP elements had directed at him during the theoretical debates of the underground during 1986 and 1987. Was he disappointed that some members of the movement to which he had given the best years of his life had turned on him? "I've tried to be philosophical about it," he said. "I've seen the movement up and down, in ebb and flow. At the time [the boycott decision was made], without wanting to sound self-righteous, I felt that time would bear me out." By 1988, he felt vindicated by the rightward drift of the Aquino government, its slipping commitment to human rights, and its failure to deliver basic social reforms. But he was nagged by doubts, wondering if his quiet style of leadership had contributed to his downfall.

"I really wanted to avoid that personality cult building. Other movements have, but in ours, no. That was one of the weaknesses of the old movement and even in our movement before"—a surprisingly critical reference to the Sison years—"building up these people. I realize now in prison, it's a different situation. What you need now is high projection. Makes me question, did I do the right thing?" He laughed, somewhat bitterly, I thought, then mused aloud, "Was I correct?"

When the NPA went on the offensive throughout the countryside in September 1987 and urban guerrillas stepped up assassinations of civilians and authorities in Manila and other cities, military analysts blamed the outburst of communist violence on one man: Romulo Kintanar. Inside the movement, Kintanar was credited with pioneering the NPA urban assassination squad techniques in Mindanao. His prowess as a military leader was rewarded in the late 1970s with a seat on the Central Committee. Following Rivera's arrest in 1987, Kintanar was believed to have assumed command of the NPA.

Other than Salas, no leader of the movement had been singled out for vilification in the fashion that Kintanar had. The military had depicted him as a "psychopathic" killer, a gunslinging warlord who cared little about ideology and knew even less. In one of the few published descriptions of the NPA commander, an anonymous source quoted in the *Commentary* article described Kintanar as "a psychotic . . . who loves to put a bandanna around his forehead and then go out and kill people."[10]

After talking with people who knew Kintanar well and after two brief personal encounters with the NPA commander in prison, I still could not find a shred of evidence to support that image. Every single person I met who knew or had worked with Kintanar—even those who had become critical of the movement—spoke of him with varying measures of respect and affection. When I finally came face to face with Kintanar in August 1988, I understood why. Whatever his proclivities for political violence—and he certainly was not ashamed of his role in the Philippine revolution—I found him personable, with a shy, almost self-deprecating air. At 39, he was exceptionally large for a Filipino, barrel-chested, tall, and muscular, and he appeared to be in excellent condition.

Kintanar was staying in shape by playing hours of ping-pong every day. Once as I was leaving the stockade, he shook my hand and asked cheerily, "Do you play ping-pong? We'll have to play ping-pong the next time you come." He explained that the CPP prisoners were practicing for a tournament against renegade soldiers who had participated in coup attempts against the government and were being held in an adjacent compound. Occasionally, the communists and right-wing soldiers were allowed into a yard where they competed in friendly games of basketball. When I remarked that I had heard he was an accomplished classical pianist, Kintanar bowed his head shyly. I told him that I looked forward to talking with him on a future visit, and Kintanar grinned as he replied, "I'll be here."

In fact, he would not be there for long. Kintanar used his charm to befriend his jailor, a constabulary major. On November 12, 1988, a few weeks after my last visit, the NPA commander persuaded the guards to allow him and his wife to take a birthday cake to the major. While the party was in progress at the major's home just outside the stockade, the rebel couple slipped away to a waiting car and made their escape.

Kintanar was the chief architect of the phenomenal NPA successes in Mindanao during the late 1970s and early 1980s. As a guerrilla leader, he earned the respect and affection of his peers. He was aggressive and outspoken in his demand for action but never abrasive, a cadre who served with Kintanar on the CPP's Mindanao Commission told me. The cadre recalled Benjamin de Vera, the CPP Mindanao secretary, once saying of Kintanar, "When Rolly Kintanar says something, everybody listens, everybody follows."

Kintanar had earned this respect leading his poorly armed guerrillas into combat against AFP soldiers, and he became a legendary figure in the underground by virtue of his exploits of derring-do. Once in 1981, Kintanar and virtually the entire Mindanao CPP leadership were riding in a car when they were stopped at a military checkpoint near Cagayan de Oro on Mindanao's north coast. Soldiers opened the trunk of the car and asked the communist leaders to open cartons, which contained CPP propaganda and documents. Kintanar jumped from the driver's seat, thrust his hands on his hips, and insisted that the soldiers not open the cartons. But the government troops would not be dissuaded. Feigning exasperation, Kintanar told the soldiers, "Ok, you can open the boxes, but you'll be responsible to Colonel _____," naming a senior AFP officer in Cagayan de Oro to whom Kintanar claimed to be delivering the boxes. The other communist officials could only watch in amazement as Kintanar convinced the soldiers that they would be committing a grievous mistake if they disturbed the boxes. The CPP officials were allowed to proceed.[11]

In 1984, Kintanar, de Vera, and the entire Mindanao Commission staff were in a safe house in Cagayan de Oro when a military raiding party surrounded it and shouted for the rebels to surrender. Kintanar leaped into action, ordering one of his men to turn off the lights while leading the others into the basement. As gunfire crackled, one by one the rebels crawled out a basement window. Kintanar and de Vera tossed grenades at the soldiers and clambered over the wall of their compound. De Vera crawled to safety, then walked several miles to a rural village. Barefoot and clad only in a pair of shorts, Kintanar headed toward the beach. It was after 2 A.M., and he was nearly three miles from the urban center where he hoped to find refuge in another communist safe house. Kintanar scoured the beach, found a stick, and put an empty tin can on the tip. All the way into the city, he walked along the beach twirling the can on the stick, passing himself off as a hopeless mental case. Before dawn, he reached the safety of another rebel house.[12]

At some point, Kintanar developed a passion for playing classical piano. He was also fond of U.S. folksongs. One of his Mindanao comrades told me about a trip he and Kintanar had made to the countryside in the late 1970s. "I found it quite weird because we were out there in the countryside in a poor peasant's hut, singing American folk songs—Bob Dylan, Peter, Paul, and Mary—as I played the guitar," the CPP official said, laughing heartily at the recollection.

Like many of his colleagues, Kintanar had endured his share of tragedy. During a CPP Mindanao Commission meeting in December 1983, Kintanar learned that his wife and several other Party cadres had died when an interisland ferry, the *MV Doña Cassandra*, sank en route from Manila to Mindanao.[13] Later, he married Gloria Jopson, a Party colleague and the widow of a senior Mindanao CPP official, Edgar Jopson, who was killed in 1982. By the late 1980s, Kintanar was widely respected as the CPP's top military strategist. Under his aggressive and innovative direction, the NPA entered its third decade of war.

———

During one of my sessions with Salas, I was distracted by a commotion outside the window. Through the steel bars, I could see a game of ping-pong mixed doubles in which one of the men was contesting the score. The chunky protagonist held the ball as he insistently argued his case. He knew what the correct score was, if only his opponents would admit they were wrong. Finally, after a spirited debate, he won.

Viewing the zeal with which Rafael Baylosis argued his point in a game of ping-pong with his comrades, I felt relieved that I did not have to face him in a debate on matters of Marxist-Leninist ideology. By most accounts, there was only one Filipino communist who could match Baylosis in sheer doggedness and intensity: Sison. Baylosis had been the CPP secretary-general until his arrest in March 1988, and in underground circles he was known for his uncompromising ideological orthodoxy. His sometimes abrasive intensity had earned Baylosis his share of critics during the course of his rise through CPP ranks.

His ideological zeal was not dimmed by imprisonment in 1973. The CPP prisoners had an English-language copy of *Quotations from Mao Zedong*, at the time the Bible for Filipino radicals. Baylosis took the book and excised references to Lin Piao, the Chinese general who had attempted to overthrow Mao in 1971, writing "do not read" across the offending pages. "It was a measure of Baylosis' dogmatism," one former communist cellmate told me. "He wanted to be accepted as the ideological guru."

At UP, Baylosis had majored in political science. Francisco Nemenzo, the UP political science professor, recalled Baylosis as one of his top students, very articulate, "one of those students who dared to argue with the teacher."[14] In 1970, at his college graduation, he had organized students to hold up antigovernment placards during commencement ceremonies. Afterward, he underwent political and military training in China and disappeared into the underground. Following his release from prison in 1976, Baylosis went underground again and was inducted into the Central Committee the following year. He rose to the CPP's number two position, which he was holding at the time of his arrest in 1988.

The 1986 cease-fire negotiations offered the revolutionary movement its first opportunity in 20 years of struggle to publicly project its views. For the crucial role of conducting the negotiations—and perhaps even more importantly, giving the movement a human face—the CPP leadership selected three former journalists: Saturnino Ocampo, Carolina Malay, and Antonio Zumel. By 1989, Ocampo and Malay occupied positions of considerable influence within the revolutionary movement. (Zumel was suffering from serious health problems that had forced him to curtail his activities.)

Born in 1939, Ocampo had grown up in a Central Luzon barrio in Pampanga province, 1 of 12 children born to a poor tenant farmer. While working evenings, Ocampo put himself through two years of college at the Lyceum in Manila, where Sison was a professor. In 1964, Ocampo became one of the charter members of KM. After taking a job as a reporter at the *Manila Times* that same year, he joined a group of reporters sent to South Vietnam to cover Philippine troops serving in the war. While being shepherded around Saigon with his group, a young Vietnamese reporter whispered to Ocampo, "Would you like to see a guerrilla zone near Saigon?" The following day, Ocampo slipped away to meet the Vietnamese reporter, and they were led by a Vietcong guide to a communist-controlled area near the capital. The Vietnamese reporter could speak little English, so Ocampo used hand signals to communicate with the communist peasants. The experience evoked memories of his own impoverished childhood in a Central Luzon peasant barrio. "It was very touching meeting with them," he told me years later.

In 1967, Ocampo wrangled an invitation from the Xinhua news agency to secretly visit China, and he spent 14 days visiting collective farms and factories. He was deeply impressed by the experience and what he felt were the positive effects communist revolution had wrought on China.[15] Back home, Ocampo became more deeply involved in radical political activities. In 1971, he stunned colleagues at a formal dinner by announcing that he was "going back to my roots." That evening, he disappeared into the rebel underground. By the time soldiers captured him in a house in Olongapo outside Subic Bay Naval Base in 1976, Ocampo had become one of the leading theoreticians of the revolutionary movement and held a seat on the Central Committee. He spent the next nine years in jail before escaping in 1985 while attending ceremonies at the National Press Club on a temporary pass.

In her brown wig, gray pants, loose black shirt, and cheap slippers, the moon-faced woman with the blazing red lipstick and huge, tacky-looking man's silver watch dangling from her wrist blended in easily in the seedy Manila tourist district. "Do you recognize me?" Carolina Malay asked with a coquettish laugh. "You should see me when I wear my false busts."

Although I had spent hours with Malay on several occasions, I would not have recognized her. The cease-fire in which she had served as NDF chief of staff had ended a few days earlier, and Malay had returned to the cloak-and-dagger world of the communist underground. As we met in a downtown apartment, she was visibly tense. She shook the last cigarette from her cheap straw handbag and fumbled for a lighter. Drawing deeply on the cigarette, she seemed to relax. For the next two hours, she patiently and deftly fielded a barrage of questions.

I found Malay one of the most fascinating of the rebel leaders I met, an exceptionally sophisticated, multifaceted changeling whose shifts in mood and demeanor could be surprising. She was a gifted writer, Paris educated, fluent in French, and flawless in English—a language she used, as a matter of principle, only as a last resort. She could be bluntly outspoken and belligerent—"I stopped believing in God a long time ago," she declared once—as well as soothingly softspoken. She could be stern and icy, convictions on her sleeve as she insisted that there were no hawks or doves within the revolutionary movement: "We're all the same." At other times, she could be enchanting, girlishly charming, and gregarious.

It was the latter Malay I saw in May 1987 in a quiet town in Bulacan province a few weeks after the encounter in downtown Manila. She had discarded the wig (which made her look much younger than her forty-seven years), and she looked radiant in a pastel print dress, her doe-like eyes wide and flashing, her hair flecked with wisps of gray. When she saw me, she waved a cheery greeting. She was unusually effervescent, swirling and shifting from one foot to the other as she talked. "Do you have a baby yet?" she asked me almost flirtatiously. "That's so Filipino of me. But I can't resist asking."

"I talked with your mother and she was worrying about you," I replied. "She said you had left your clothes behind when you returned underground at the end of the cease-fire."

Laughing, Malay exclaimed, "My mother! She's always worrying about my clothes, what I eat." She laughed again and confessed, "I enjoy being underground again. You can be any name you want. You can be anybody you want."

Growing up in a fashionable neighborhood of Quezon City, the only daughter of an accomplished journalist and a writer, Malay could have been anybody she wanted. At UP, she had studied English literature and showed little interest in politics. After graduation, she worked as a newspaper reporter and wound up at the *Manila Times* covering foreign affairs.

She traveled to China with other Filipino journalists in 1965 and was unimpressed. Later that year, she accepted a scholarship to study in Paris, where she dabbled in art classes at the Sorbonne. Although not well versed in radical politics, Malay fell in love with a radical student activist from Morocco who immersed her in leftist political thought. She met other students from newly decolonized countries, and that marked the beginning of a period of soul-searching.[16] Gradually, Malay developed strong anti-U.S. and nationalistic sentiments.

In early 1968, Malay attended her first political protest, joining students rallying against the Vietnam War in the wake of the Tet offensive. In May, she joined other students at the Paris barricades. By the time she returned to the Philippines in 1969, shortly after the NPA founding, Malay had already made up her mind to join the underground. Back home, she began writing for a Filipino-language newspaper. She met

Ocampo, and they fell in love and were married. In 1971, she joined her husband in the underground. Years later, her mother tearfully recalled a friend of her daughter's coming to the house shortly afterward. The friend explained that Carolina was in need of money and had given instructions to sell her prized collection of English literature classics and paintings to raise funds.[17]

Malay vanished into the anonymity of the communist underground for the next 15 years. During the early 1970s, Malay and Ocampo became involved in CPP propaganda work and were responsible for founding the Free Philippines News Service. Malay gave birth to two children during the early years of martial law, then was forced to leave them with her parents to be reared. Years later, she recounted to me how her revolutionary convictions were tested to their limits following her husband's arrest in 1976, and her subsequent assignment to the countryside. It was nine years before she was reunited with her husband following his escape in 1985. By then, Malay had developed into a tough, experienced revolutionary, establishing her position in the CPP leadership and earning the respect of her rebel peers.

In the wake of Baylosis' arrest in early 1988, Ocampo was rumored within leftist circles to have been elevated to the Party position of secretary-general. The other most likely choice for the post was José Luneta, one of Sison's early student protégés who was in his mid-forties by 1989. Luneta had also been a UP political science student of Francisco Nemenzo, and the professor remembered Luneta as not very articulate or assertive but possessing a keen mind and a talent for writing.[18] Luneta was the only remaining active member of the original Central Committee, and he was viewed within the movement as a loyal ally of Sison. Imprisoned in the late 1970s and early 1980s, Luneta escaped and reassumed a leadership position in the underground.

23

"A Terrible Time"

On March 16, 1986, Fely, a frail-looking NPA guerrilla with mournful eyes, stood in the forest of North Cotabato province and watched as several rebel companions shoveled dirt from a shallow, unmarked grave. One by one, the bodies of five guerrillas were pulled from the pit. Fely instantly recognized the clothes of one of the badly decomposed corpses. This was her husband, a rebel platoon commander. His hands and feet were lashed tightly together, and handcuffs bound his wrists.[1] The guerrillas were not casualties of a battle with government troops or of disease. "My comrades in the movement told me it was other comrades who killed my husband," Fely softly recalled two years later. Accused by their comrades-in-arms of being military spies—deep penetration agents (DPAs)—the rebels had been executed.

The five guerrillas were victims of an NPA purge so terrifying and brutal that hundreds of guerrillas and perhaps tens of thousands of civilian supporters deserted the formidable communist organization on Mindanao between 1985 and 1987. Eyewitness accounts and other available evidence suggest that hundreds of CPP members and guerrillas were executed as suspected military agents, and thousands others deserted in fear for their lives. One CPP official told me the purge had cost the movement "one-half of all organized [civilian] masses and cadres" on Mindanao. Another Party official who had to flee Mindanao at the height of the purge later recalled, "It was really a terrible time. I myself did not know who to trust anymore. Some of my friends who had so much potential turned out to be DPAs."[2]

The seeds of the purge were planted in the NPA's dizzying expansion in the late 1970s and early 1980s. The rapid growth had put a strain on the movement's ability to screen recruits as carefully as in the past, and lapses in discipline and other problems started to occur.[3] Less rigorous practices in recruiting and political indoctrination spelled even more serious problems on Mindanao, which by 1982 was riding the crest of a wave of expansion that established the island as the revolution's most advanced stronghold. "We were so engrossed with the rapid development of both the military and political aspects of our work that certain aspects, for example consolidation [of areas under rebel control] and security check-ups, were not given that much attention," a member of the CPP's Mindanao Commission during that period later told me.[4] As a result, the Party official said, the AFP was able to infiltrate the NPA through the use of deep penetration agents.

According to CPP officials, only a few recruits were military agents when they actually entered the underground. The rest were enlisted by the military in the early stages of their involvement in the CPP or rebel army. Once inside the movement, the military spies enlisted more agents, usually recent recruits or members who harbored grievances against comrades. Often the association with the military would begin innocently enough. An agent would suggest to a new recruit that it might be a good idea to have military contacts in case of a crackdown at their school or factory. The agent would explain that a military friend might be able to work out an early release or prevent torture. A meeting would be arranged, and eventually the activist would be asked to provide information. Often there was no turning back.[5]

Sometime around late 1984, CPP leaders in northern Mindanao began to grow suspicious after the failure of several NPA operations and other internal problems. In some instances, the military was able to anticipate and force the cancellation of rebel operations. At other times, raids and ambushes were botched by NPA units. When regional Party leaders read an underground account of how the military had infiltrated rebel organizations on Luzon in the 1970s, they were convinced they had the same problem.

An investigation was launched in northern Mindanao's Bukidnon province in mid-1985, and several NPA members and supporters were taken into custody by their rebel comrades for suspected spying. According to separate accounts from two former senior Mindanao Party officials, some of those arrested claimed during interrogation to have knowledge of military agents working in the Party's labor and student organizations in the northern Mindanao city of Cagayan de Oro. Suspicions that agents had succeeded in infiltrating the city's underground were reinforced by the Cagayan de Oro Party Committee's history of arrests and failure to expand. The allegations quickly multiplied. There were reports of DPAs operating in the nearby province of Lanao del Norte, then Agusan del

Norte, and the island of Cebu to the north. The investigation broadened and eventually led to suspected spies in every city and region of Mindanao.

By the end of 1985, paranoia generated by the fear of infiltration had swirled out of control, paralyzing operations and leading to the "arrest" and detention in jungle stockades of hundreds of guerrillas and Party activists, even ranking officials. Frantic investigations led to hasty trials and, in most cases, executions. CPP officials would later admit that many innocent people were killed or forced to leave the movement. Party officials would blame virtually all the excesses—the shoddy investigations, executions, torture—on other agents who had infiltrated the investigation and judicial processes. "DPAs were able to cause the execution of people who were in fact entirely innocent," a Mindanao CPP leader said.[6]

Although the CPP and communist army had purged its ranks of suspected infiltrators on several occasions during the 1970s, the Mindanao purge was unprecedented in scope and lives lost. Due to conflicting accounts on the extent and duration of the purge, by 1989 it was still difficult to determine accurately how many people had been killed. Senior CPP officials downplayed the extent of the purge, placing the number of NPA members who had been executed at 60. A former Mindanao Commission member told me the figure was higher, but he declined to be more precise. Military officials, on the other hand, periodically reported throughout 1986 the discovery of mass graves on Mindanao filled with the skeletal remains of those who were purportedly killed in the purge. The military claimed 800 people had been executed in the purge and began calling parts of Mindanao "the killing fields."

Although Party officials suggested that the purge had ended in 1986, there was evidence that the investigations and killings continued through 1987 and into 1988, although at a much diminished level. Australian journalist Louise Williams conducted extensive interviews with NPA and CPP members in northern Mindanao in mid-1988 and reported that in one region alone—centered around Surigao del Sur province—executions and desertions had reduced communist forces from seven companies (about 600 men and women) to a single company of fewer than 100 rebels. She added that the purge was still continuing at the time of her visit in mid-1988.[7]

In January 1988, I spoke separately with three former guerrillas in Davao del Norte province, all veterans of at least five years in the NPA who had left the movement during the purge and had applied for government amnesty in 1987. Collectively, the former guerrillas claimed either to have witnessed or to have personal knowledge of a total of 80 executions of comrades suspected of spying for the military. Their information was limited to only two of Mindanao's six regions and covered the period between 1985 and 1987. According to their accounts, the victims included several NPA platoon commanders who were investigated following failed raids or ambushes they had led.

By all accounts, damage to communist forces on Mindanao was devastating. Morale plunged as panic swept the ranks, and hundreds of guerrillas deserted, fearing they might be suspected next. Other cadres were asked to voluntarily leave the movement. "You didn't know who to trust," a ranking CPP official recalled. "It really cost us."[8] Eddie Aroma, a rebel who ran away from his unit in southeastern Mindanao after 10 comrades had been executed as suspected DPAs, said the rank-and-file guerrillas "were not really told what had happened to those who were killed," he said. "That's why many had defected, especially those who were not sure. Those who had made mistakes in operations or quarreled with their commanding officer got scared. Many of them defected."[9]

In the aftermath of the worst of the purge, it was impossible to determine to what extent the military had actually succeeded in infiltrating NPA ranks and to what extent paranoia had been responsible for the bloody affair. AFP officers were vague in their explanations and obviously delighted by the chaos and internecine bloodshed within the rebel organization on Mindanao. A CPP official from Mindanao who had taken part in the Central Committee's investigation of the purge later told me that the total number of infiltrators probably numbered no more than 100 throughout Mindanao but that some of the agents had risen as high as regional Party committees. "There was one guy who was really quite good, and we were trying to develop him for united front work," the Party official recalled. "I participated in the investigation of this guy. For a while, I myself was wondering if there was enough evidence to arrest him. But later on, the investigation showed exactly how he was recruited into the DPA network. I was shocked. He was executed."[10]

––––––––––

When I returned in December 1986 to Agdao, the Davao slum district that had become a bulwark of the revolution during the 1980s, I was stunned by the transformation that had taken place. I was escorted into Agdao under the watchful eye of the anticommunist vigilantes of a group calling itself Alsa Masa (Risen Masses). On the surface, at least, the people of Agdao had turned against the revolution they had nurtured only a few months earlier. Many residents readily admitted they had welcomed the guerrillas as liberators. "Every night they held lectures in my house," Arceli Arevalo, a portly matron proudly told me, pointing to a shack fronting one of the muddy paths that wound through Agdao. "The communists had good ideas before. But they became worse." Other slum dwellers spoke of unfulfilled promises of jobs and equality, forced tax collections, and rebel "abuses"—usually a reference to communist executions. Arevalo's 18-year-old son, George, told me he had been an NPA assassin and had killed 14 people in four years. One of his victims was a 16-year-old boy who had allegedly talked to the military about rebel movements. Two others were women who had a penchant for gossip. Now, Arevalo, George, and their neighbors had joined Alsa Masa. They conducted patrols through the slum searching for communists and carrying weapons supplied by the military.

According to local legend, the birth of Alsa Masa stemmed from the 1986 murder of a popular Party cadre, Victorino la Morena, who lived in Agdao. La Morena, friends and relatives said, had voiced opposition to some of the NPA killings and refused to carry out more executions. On the evening of March 22, 1986—as the DPA hysteria swirled through the Davao underground—guerrillas dragged la Morena from his house and killed him. Fearing they might be killed next by their comrades, Party activists and NPA sparrows in Agdao began surrendering to the military and offering to work against their former colleagues. A few weeks later, the growing number of rebel defectors banded together with Agdao toughs and formed Alsa Masa. Armed and encouraged by local military commanders, Alsa Masa chapters soon spread to nearly every neighborhood and rural barrio of Davao. The communist military and political organization quickly collapsed, and even legal left-wing groups in Davao were virtually driven underground by the intense anticommunist sentiments whipped up by Alsa Masa and the military.

How could such a vaunted communist stronghold crumble so quickly? Lucas Fernández, one of the Mindanao CPP leaders at the time, told me later that the communist organization in Davao was vulnerable because the intense nature of the political and military war through the early 1980s had left little time for deeper political and ideological training of organized masses. The rise of a popular president, the Party's responsibility for the election boycott, and internal disputes stemming from the DPA hysteria and theoretical debates all contributed to the collapse. Dismissing suggestions that excessive taxation and violence had led to the communist demise in Agdao, Fernández saw the problem as one of successful government propaganda rather than rebel mistakes. The Davao front had been "temporarily lost," Fernández conceded, but the Party machinery had been reestablished by the end of 1987. For the time being, however, cadres had been ordered to lie low.

A central question remained: Had the people of Davao actually embraced the revolution in the early 1980s, or had they reluctantly acquiesced to its rule? In search of an answer, in 1988 I traveled to a remote corner of Davao that only a year earlier had been touted as one of the revolution's showcase communities.

At first glance, Punta Dumalag seemed an unlikely spot for a decisive battle in the Philippine revolution. Three decades after landless settlers descended on a sun-baked spit of land jutting into the Gulf of Davao, the village remained a cluttered collection of ramshackle huts built on stilts and scattered haphazardly along a badly rutted dirt road, spilling over into the murky, garbage-strewn waters of a shallow cove. One hundred sixty families made their homes in the barrio, one of Davao's poorest communities, eking out subsistence livings by fishing and working in a nearby sawmill.

CPP cadres first organized the squatters of Punta Dumalag in the late 1970s when the land's legal owner tried unsuccessfully to evict the settlers to make way for the construction of a seaside resort. By 1985, the Party had transformed Punta Dumalag into a model revolutionary community. A clandestine barrio revolutionary council acted as a shadow government, administering social, economic, and political activities, collecting taxes, and imposing a severe brand of law and order. The communists established a health clinic, organized a cooperative to provide water and electricity, and formed a fishing cooperative where barrio residents shared their income. In return, every resident of Punta Dumalag was expected to serve the revolution, from the men and women assigned to attend rallies and demonstrations orchestrated by the underground to children organized into spy brigades to monitor the comings and goings of strangers.[11]

In the months preceding my visit to the village one balmy afternoon in early 1988, yet another political cataclysm had swept Punta Dumalag. The communists had been forced to abandon their once impregnable stronghold, and a fiercely anticommunist autocracy led by Alsa Masa vigilantes now ruled the barrio. The sawmill, closed for nearly two years by a communist-led strike, was now bustling with the whine of saws and the clatter of freshly cut lumber being stacked in the yard. The barrio water pump built during communist rule was now daubed with Alsa Masa slogans scrawled with thick blue print, and a crude sign reminded residents of a new curfew, midnight to 4 A.M., that was slightly more liberal than that imposed by the communist regime. Stopping at a shack with a hand-printed sign that identified it as the Alsa Masa outpost, I asked three young men why Alsa Masa had replaced the communists in Punta Dumalag.

"The killings," one of them replied.

"Did the NPA kill many people in Punta Dumalag?" I asked.

"No, in Davao."

"But didn't the NDF give you livelihood projects that helped the people of Punta Dumalag?"

"They were fakes. They were made to deceive the people," the fellow declared without elaboration.

One of the other men added, wistfully it seemed, "When the NDF was here, many foreigners—Australians and others—visited here. They gave three to four million pesos [$150,000 to $200,000] for the NDF livelihood projects. But when the NPA left, the money stopped."

Inside the shack, four men hovered over a game of mahjong, a popular form of gambling in the Philippines. Arquilino, a slight fellow seated at the mahjong table, introduced himself as an Alsa Masa member. He was in his thirties and unemployed, he explained over the clatter of mahjong tiles, as were many of the men in Punta Dumalag.

Alsa Masa had closed the health center after alleging that wounded guerrillas had been brought there for treatment. The vigilantes had also forcibly dismantled the fishing cooperative and a soap-making venture established by the communists. A few residents of Punta Dumalag, including those who had been members of the NDF barrio council, had fled when Alsa Masa was organized.[12] But most of the settlers remained, and now they too professed allegiance to Alsa Masa. If Punta Dumalag residents were secretly unhappy with Alsa Masa, as Davao NDF faithful suggested, it appeared that the poor squatters at least had adjusted to life under the new order. As I left the village that afternoon, a giggling woman invited me to return that evening to attend an Alsa Masa discotheque fundraiser.

When I returned at 10 P.M., a cool breeze blowing off the gulf wafted through the maze of shacks filling the air with the sweet smell of sawdust. The steady "whump, whump, whump" of a driving disco beat grew louder in the darkness, and suddenly a surrealistic scene came into view in a burst of light and color. Gaily colored streamers had been hung over the barrio's cement basketball court, which was filled with people gyrating to the scratchy sounds of well-worn disco records. Overhead, a shimmering silver mirror ball spun in the breeze bathing the dancers in a kaleidoscope of colors.

Isidro, a sawmill worker and self-described Alsa Masa "adviser" whom I had met earlier, appeared out of the shadows. Noticing my amazement, he shouted above the din, "This is the first time for people to enjoy themselves like this since the NPA got out. Under the NPA, we had one freedom: to kill a man."

Although Isidro may have been exaggerating, the contrast to the ordered life under the communists must have been startling to the inhabitants of Punta Dumalag, and those in attendance clearly seemed to be enjoying the festive evening. Unfortunately, I never got the chance to mingle and talk freely with the disco-goers. Isidro saw to that, hovering over me until I left, insisting that "everyone here belongs to Alsa Masa."

"What if somebody does not want to join?"

"We will talk to them," he replied cryptically.

It seemed to me that the residents of Punta Dumalag were less than free to reject Alsa Masa, just as they had been less than free to refuse the NDF. Had the people of Punta Dumalag genuinely embraced the goals of the revolution, or had they supported the rebels out of fear and economic desperation? Had Punta Dumalag thrown the NDF out, or had Alsa Masa organizers from outside the barrio imposed the new anticommunist order on a fearful community? Did the impoverished squatters now support Alsa Masa, or were they merely tolerating a new armed administration? Given the politically charged climate that engulfed Punta Dumalag in early 1988, it was impossible to obtain unvarnished answers to these questions from within the community.

Father Jaíme Afable had taken over the sprawling southern Davao parish that encompasses Punta Dumalag in November 1985, when communist control over the squatter colony was at its peak. He had never felt particularly welcome visiting the village during the tenure of the communists. Now, nearly a year after the rebels had fled, Afable had formed definite opinions about the forces and events that had buffeted Punta Dumalag. "If there were people who supported [the communists], it was intimidation or accommodation," he told me flatly. Although willing to concede that the NDF livelihood projects were genuinely welcomed by the settlement's desperately poor inhabitants, Afable suggested that living under harsh communist rule was the price many people felt they had to pay in order to make ends meet. He was convinced that his parishioners in Punta Dumalag were "definitely happier now than in 1985" when the communists were in control. To support his contention, Afable recalled that Punta Dumalag residents had told him that the communists had forced them to join antigovernment rallies and demonstrations. Now that the communists were gone, "you see the sense of freedom" among the people of Punta Dumalag.

Did that include the right to refuse support to Alsa Masa?

Afable politely sidestepped the question, instead relating that some of his Christian community leaders had joined Alsa Masa, and were even participating in its nightly patrols. His only advice to those parishoners was to avoid bearing arms.

Offering another perspective, Carolyn Arguillas, a Davao journalist with unabashed leftist sympathies, suggested that the "conversion" of Punta Dumalag and other neighborhoods to Alsa Masa was largely motivated by fear. The end of communist rule in Punta Dumalag in early 1987, according to Arguillas, came as the result of the anticommunist tirades of a local radio commentator who threatened rebel-controlled communities with destruction unless they pledged support to Alsa Masa. Punta Dumalag had been specifically singled out as a target. "People were panicking," she told me, and so they joined Alsa Masa.

Arguillas drove home an even more fundamental point: The Aquino government and military were deluding themselves if, as it seemed in early 1988, they believed the vigilante strategy was a key to defeating the rebels. "In a year or two," she remarked late one evening in a Davao coffee shop, "people could say, 'Yes, we supported Alsa Masa because they had guns.' Those who hold the firearms, whatever they say goes. But what's the guarantee that the loyalties of these people are on their side? The point is, this still isn't the solution to the insurgency."

The greater significance of the communist setback in Davao was not that the NPA had been uprooted from a stronghold, but that the collapse had marked the emergence of a phenomenon that almost overnight changed the complexion of the war. Encouraged by the military, Alsa Masa became the prototype for vigilante groups that by spring 1987 were proliferating throughout the Philippines. In many areas, the military actually took the lead in forming vigilantes, while disingenuously describing the groups as "spontaneous" responses to communist depredations. Civilian vigilante groups became the cornerstone of the government's strategy against the guerrillas. Aquino gave her blessing to vigilante groups in 1987, and U.S. officials encouraged their spread by applauding the groups as valid "local responses" to the rebel threat. But before long, the vigilantes became a public relations nightmare for Aquino, at home and abroad, as evidence of human rights abuses by the vigilantes mounted.

In her state of the nation address in July 1988, Aquino ordered the disbandment of vigilante groups and the organization of military-supervised Civilian Armed Forces Geographical Units (CAFGUs) in their place. She maintained that the CAFGUs would be better trained and more accountable to the military and therefore would be less inclined to commit abuses. But by the end of 1988, few vigilante groups had been disbanded, and it seemed likely that the groups would continue to hold sway in many isolated areas where the writ of Manila simply failed to run. The rough brand of justice dispensed by the vigilante groups seemed sure to produce more of the abuses that would fuel support for the guerrillas.

The same weekend that I visited Punta Dumalag in January 1988, Representative Stephen Solarz, the New York Democrat and influential shaper of U.S. policy toward the Philippines, was in Davao and stopped in Agdao to visit the birthplace of Alsa Masa. He repeatedly asked the slum dwellers what their needs were, and the reply each time was, "Jobs."[13]

It seemed almost certain to me, as it must have to Solarz, that communist influence would rebound in Davao if the fundamental causes of the poverty that gripped Agdao, Punta Dumalag, and other communities were left unaddressed. There was little to suggest that these issues were being given more than perfunctory attention by the government, and so it seemed only a matter of time before the violence would begin anew. The communists would again capitalize on poverty, unemployment, injustice, and government neglect.

Aside from the internal damage, the Mindanao purge hurt the revolution's largely favorable image with many Filipinos, who had viewed the NPA as a benign movement of Robin Hoods. Military propagandists who had struggled for years to depict the rebels as bloodthirsty Marxist killers cut from the same cloth as the Khmer Rouge reaped a windfall from the bloody tragedy. Coincidentally, the Mindanao purge was beginning just about the time the popular image of the guerrillas was being challenged in the foreign press. A December 1985 article in *Commentary* authored by Ross Munro, a *Time* magazine correspondent, depicted the movement as "arguably the most brutal Communist insurgency in the world today" and further suggested that the Philippines was facing the specter of "a Pol Pot future" should the rebels come to power.[14]

The comparison to the Khmer Rouge was quickly dismissed by most foreign observers, U.S. diplomats included, as rhetorical overkill. Even some AFP officers with whom I spoke in the months that followed found the characterization rather farfetched. True, the NPA did not hesitate to kill its enemies, but even many committed foes of the rebels found something principled and disciplined in their violent ways. NPA violence seemed far more selective and directed than the brutal killings being carried out by security forces. There were no known acts of indiscriminate terrorism or systematic sabotage aimed at creating chaos and destabilization. The NPA may have been killing civilians and government officials in the countryside, but to U.S. Embassy officials who had served in Vietnam, there was no question that the Vietcong had been far more brutal and ruthless.

24

"People's Republic of the Philippines"

We expect many from the ruling class to get out of the country. We expect there will be saboteurs. We expect there will be U.S. imperialist agents doing their best to destabilize. We also expect it will mean hard work for us. We have started talking to several Nicaraguans, and they all told us how hard the work is after the revolution is won.[1]

The Mindanao purge gave chilling grist to government and military propaganda mills, which suggested that the fratricidal killings were a portent of things to come should the New People's Army ever come to power. Was the Philippines staring into "a Pol Pot future," as the movement's most outspoken detractors suggested? Or would victory herald the birth of a truly democratic and egalitarian society, as supporters of the revolution insisted? Hysteria and hyperbole aside, how would a National Democratic Front government govern the Philippines?

The CPP has never concealed its goal of altering Philippine society in a most radical fashion. The initial draft of the Programme for a People's Democratic Revolution was a shrill blueprint for Maoist revolution.[2] It envisaged the sweeping nationalization of industries and collectivization of the peasantry on state farms and held up as models the world's most radical communist societies: China, North Korea, and Albania.

The first NDF program issued in 1973 hewed closely to the CPP line and was hardly a vision to hearten many middle- or upper-class Filipinos. But beginning in the late 1970s, a series of NDF programs suggested a considerably more moderate, pluralistic revolution. Predictably, skeptics maintained that the CPP has merely tried to moderate its image in order to attract enough noncommunist support to seize power, while supporters insisted the changes reflected a genuine broadening of the revolution.

Like most revolutionary movements, the Philippine rebels have been so preoccupied with their struggle to seize power that the particulars of how they would rule have not been resolved. By the late 1980s, the CPP had dispatched cadres to Vietnam, Nicaragua, and the Soviet Union to study how revolutionary changes had been carried out in those countries.[3] In 1987, NDF committees began extensive studies of various postvictory questions that the movement would face. International law, justice systems, economics, and other questions were among the topics being discussed. Other issues under study included how brutal the consolidation would have to be, who would be put on trial, and who would be put to death. The NDF had pledged to invite noncommunists to participate in a coalition government, but one national Party cadre told me in late 1988 the movement was still debating where to draw the line.

The NDF program states that upon victory a "political consultative conference" of all revolutionary forces would be convened to form a council that would govern the country for a "short but reasonable span of time." A constituent assembly would be elected to draft a new constitution, which would be followed by general elections. "Elected representative assemblies" are planned "at every level" to enact laws.

From the outset of any postvictory scenario, a prickly issue would be the delineation of powers between the Communist Party and the NDF, which by 1989 included a not inconsiderable number of noncommunists. Even if the most orthodox Marxist-Leninists within the NDF were to dominate the new government, the results would likely be something closer to Nicaragua rather than to, say, North Korea (or Pol Pot's Cambodia). The Spanish colonial heritage, Roman Catholicism, and other shared cultural traits have led many Filipino rebels to substitute Nicaragua for China as the more favored model for the revolution to follow. Every ranking CPP official with whom I spoke professed a preference for at least a nominally pluralistic political system rather than a one-party state dominated by the CPP.

"Political pluralism is a necessity in our country. Even with a socialist economic system, a one-party system is impossible and is not advisable here," Rodolfo Salas, depicted by comrades as a rigid Marxist-Leninist, told me in late 1988.[4] Salas said three factors—a relatively large middle class, the country's "long democratic tradition," and the identification with Western culture and political systems—discouraged creation of a Soviet- or Chinese-style system.

The extent of the society's pluralism, according to Salas and other ranking CPP leaders, would depend on several factors, including the progress of efforts to consolidate the victory. The rebels expect massive U.S. efforts to destablize a revolutionary regime, as has occurred in Nicaragua. Such a scenario would strengthen the hand of the more doctrinaire Marxist-Leninists who favor strong centralized controls over politics, the economy, and other aspects of society. Political pluralism in the Philippine revolution would probably mean a strong ruling party (either the CPP or a government party dominated by the Communist Party) and several relatively weak traditional parties. One CPP official suggested that the more liberal parties existing in the Philippines in the late 1980s—the Philippine Democratic Party–Lakas ng Bayan, a member of Aquino's ruling coalition committed to the removal of U.S. military bases, for one—would be allowed to continue in existence.

A question I asked every senior CPP official I met was how harsh they expected the initial period of consolidation would be. The NDF program explicitly provided for the creation of a people's tribunal to "try those who have committed crimes against the people" and pledged to "escheat properties and ill-gotten wealth amassed by the ruling elite of the previous regime." The program also promised "severe punishment of those guilty of grave crimes and reeducation of those who deserve leniency."[5] Would this foreshadow a bloody purge as occurred in Cambodia or a massive campaign of reeducation as was conducted in Vietnam?

One regional CPP secretary told me there would have to be an extensive campaign of reeducation "to raise nationalist consciousness and for ideological development." Several CPP officials expressed their hope that the process of consolidating victory would not be bloody, but they did not rule out the possibility. Salas noted that victory after a long, bitter military struggle (such as in Cambodia) would increase the risks of a harsh peace. Another factor in consolidating the revolution would be the outcome of likely conflicts between rural Party and NPA units that had fought the war and borne the brunt of military violence and repression and urban cadres whose perspective was much more moderate and conciliatory.

In the late 1980s, the NDF appeared to be taking genuine steps to avoid the type of debilitating outflow of capital and people that had characterized the revolutions of China, Vietnam, and Cambodia. Saturnino Ocampo and other leading CPP figures pledged flexibility in post-revolution economic and political policies, at least in the short term. Party leaders were hoping to appeal to the bulk of the middle class, the "national bourgeoisie," whose support in the quest for power and in a postvictory setting was deemed crucial. "We don't forsee the middle class fleeing the country after victory, since there is provision for their participation in national rebuilding," Ocampo said.[6] But other Party leaders made it clear they would not mind if the wealthiest landowners and businesspeople and other "reactionaries" fled the country, thereby lessening the chance of organized resistance within the Philippines.

The economic future of the Philippines represented some of the most difficult questions for NDF strategists. What should be the degree of state involvement? What industries should be nationalized? How much foreign investment should be allowed? Should land be confiscated immediately from landlords? What form should the agrarian revolution take—collectivization, cooperatives, or the distribution of small farm plots to individual peasants? These questions and many others were being studied and debated by NDF policy committees in the late 1980s.

In the short term, the NDF had committed itself to a mixed economy led by a strong government sector with a substantial degree of private enterprise. The immediate goal of the revolution was to establish a "national democratic program" that would nationalize key industries, distribute land to peasants, and develop a national program of industrialization. (The NDF program called for the nationalization of most foreign businesses with the promise of compensation to owners who had not engaged in "antipeople and antirevolutionary activity.") Land would be distributed to landless peasants in stages, and the government would promote the organization of cooperatives in the fishing and agricultural sectors. Creating a socialist state was the ultimate aim of the revolution, but Party leaders said first the Philippines would have to go through a long period in which some features of capitalism were more fully developed.

The most detailed description of the revolution's economic plans for the future was offered to me by Brendan Cruz, the former Catholic priest who had become a ranking Party cadre. According to Cruz, the first stage of the revolution would be marked by a transitional period lasting five to ten years. During this stage, "limited capitalism" would be allowed "so we can develop the means of production," while the beginnings of a socialist state were gradually moved into place. "Strategic industries" would be immediately nationalized, and the gradual nationalization of other selected industries would occur, "probably within five years. Then you start implementing more socialist elements," Cruz said, until the socialist state is fully in place.[7] The Party official said the Philippine revolutionary movement had learned an important lesson from Cambodia: "They moved too fast."

Even the so-called hard-liners expressed a preference for initial economic policies that would set revolutionary change in process without needlessly antagonizing middle-class businesspeople and landowners.

Salas spoke of the need for a "compromise" in which the revolution would provide landlords whose lands had been redistributed to peasants an opportunity to "invest and participate in economic life. That's why we are not going on an all out confiscation of landholdings. We have a program of compensation either in direct compensation or incentives to shift to industries." Salas expected that the bigger landowners would "really resist," but he was convinced that "small landlords and even the medium landlords would agree to a compromise."[8]

Foreign investment, once anathema to the movement, would be welcome within certain limitations, CPP officials said. "Before, we used to look at foreign investment as totally evil to Philippine society," Joyce, a Negros Party cadre, said. "We still view it as inimical to economic growth, but a necessary evil." Salas said he believed the revolution could do business with investors from Japan, Western Europe, and even the United States.

Invariably, skeptics will doubt the sincerity of the CPP when it talks of economic flexibility and compromise. Cruz, in fact, told me that assurances given to businesspeople and other middle-class Filipinos that capitalism would be allowed to continue for a while after the revolution had improved recruiting among these groups. (He described these assurances as a "clarification" of the NDF's political line.) But despite the movement's skillful exploitation of its moderated economic language to attract middle-class support, it seemed clear to me that the economic disasters of Vietnam, the trauma of Cambodia, Deng Xiaoping's market-oriented economic experiments, and Mikhail Gorbachev's *perestroika* all had offered sobering lessons to leaders of the Philippine revolution. That China, the Soviet Union, and even Vietnam (which in 1988 adopted one of the most liberal foreign investment policies in the world) were courting economic contacts with the noncommunist world did not escape the attention of NDF economic policymakers.

Nevertheless, the temptation to impose a rigidly controlled economy would be great for those men and women leading the revolution who had cut their political teeth on Lenin, Mao, and even Stalin, and who had struggled for so many years to achieve victory. On economic matters, like other major policy issues facing the rebels, I sensed there would be intense debates as they determined what role the state would play in the new Philippines.

The social agenda of the NDF called for the eventual implementation of a cradle-to-grave welfare system offering guaranteed health care, housing, education, and employment. The NDF had pledged to maintain

"all the basic democratic rights contained in a liberal democratic constitution," including rights to property, due process, free movement, free
assembly, free speech, and a free press. Would the revolution try to
impose on society at large the sort of puritanical discipline that had
characterized the CPP and NPA? How committed would an NDF
government be to protecting the rights of those who did not support
the revolution? These crucial questions could be answered only after
the new government had assumed power.

The paramount concern of most Party leaders with whom I spoke
was carrying out the revolutionary program, and their attitude was that
individual freedoms and civil liberties were secondary concerns. Several
CPP officials stressed there would have to be limits attached to freedoms
of speech and the press, among others. Some newspapers would have
to be shut down, CPP officials suggested. But even the most zealous
Party cadres were resigned to the fact that there would have to be "some
newspapers operated by the middle forces."[9]

While guaranteeing religious freedom, the NDF had made it clear it
would not tolerate Catholic Church involvement in political affairs.[10]
Efforts by radical Catholics to create a "people's Church" supportive of
the revolution would likely lead to disputes with the relatively conservative Philippine Church hierarchy and the Vatican. While asserting that
an NDF government hoped to maintain good relations with the Vatican,
a 1988 *Liberation* article noted that a revolutionary government "will
not allow the Vatican or any other religious center to interfere in the
internal affairs of the Philippines."[11]

Whether the revolution would attempt to confiscate Church properties
(a matter that was under study by the NDF) or lift the tax-exempt status
of the vast network of Church-run schools (also under study) were
prickly questions that could quickly lead to an open breach between
the new government and the Catholic Church. CPP cadres viewed the
education system as a primary vehicle for inculcating the values of the
revolution among the next generation of Filipinos. This would create
yet another area of competition between the revolutionary regime and
the powerful Catholic Church.

On matters of foreign policy, the NDF had pledged to remove U.S.
military bases from the Philippines and cancel most treaties and agreements with the United States. A "revolutionary, independent, nonaligned
and peace-loving foreign policy" would be adopted; the government
would also reserve the right to support "other people's struggles for
national and social emancipation." The NDF held out the possibility of
"cordial diplomatic and trade relations with the U.S."[12]

As for fears of a bloodbath on the scale of what occurred following the victorious revolution in Cambodia, several factors seemed to preclude replication of such a brutal scenario in the Philippines. In general, the educational level in the Philippines, even among the peasantry, was considerably higher than had existed in pre-1975 Cambodia. Consequently, the CPP and NPA were better educated and more sophisticated as of 1989 (although some independent leftists expressed concerns that the emergence of a more peasant-dominated leadership could eventually increase the possibility of excesses). Another mitigating factor was the importance Filipinos placed on the family and its ties. During the first 20 years of the movement, family ties had been played both ways, helping legitimize the rebels among a broad section of society and at the same time moderating some of the more radical policies of the Party and NPA. The accommodations that a significant number of the country's economic and political elite had established with the NPA by the 1980s appeared to further lessen the likelihood of a harsh revolutionary transition, at least in the short term.

As much as the CPP and its guerrilla army had forged a revolutionary path in Philippine society, through 20 years of brutal war the movement had still demonstrated considerable appreciation and respect for traditional values and customs. The Philippine rebels had studied most twentieth century revolutions, and a significant number of CPP officials had expressed commitments to avoid the excesses and mistakes of the past. Ultimately, of course, only the victory of the NPA will answer the question of how benign or brutal the Philippine revolution really is.

25

Red Christmas

The most important date on the Philippine revolutionary calendar is December 26, and for months, Party acquaintances and peasants I had encountered in Barangay Rose had asked if I was planning to attend Christmas and the CPP anniversary festivities in the barrio the following day. Lisa, a Party cadre, had even invited me to her wedding, which she hoped would be held on the anniversary of the CPP's founding. It did not take much to pique my curiosity, so I made arrangements for my wife, Aleli, and I to return to Barangay Rose for the celebrations.

Our rainbow colored minibus was crowded with travelers returning to their home towns as we headed down the Bondoc peninsula on the afternoon of Christmas Eve 1987 accompanied by Joy, my Party guide. Several miles south of Gumaca the bus braked to a stop at an army checkpoint that had not been there on my previous trips. Fatigue-clad troops jeeringly ordered "all men and queers off the bus," and two soldiers boarded and searched for weapons while the men milled about outside. I pressed against the bus trying to look as inconspicuous as my light skin would allow. I heaved a sigh of relief when the soldiers did not ask any questions, and we arrived at our jumping off point without any trouble. We had difficulty finding a jeepney that was still plying the secondary road that ran into the hills near Barangay Rose. But finally we crammed into the back of a 28-passenger jeepney along with 34 other people and squeezed even tighter as the driver loaded a vat of frothing coconut milk, six cases of beer, two cases of soft drinks, and several boxes of dry goods into the aisle. After a bumpy, 20-minute ride, we reached the end of the run and set off walking the final miles to Barangay Rose.

The December weather was as close to comfortable as could be expected in the tropics, and after a 45-minute hike we arrived in the beautiful meadow at the entrance to Barangay Rose. Outside the first house we approached, nearly a dozen men, women, and children were clustered around three men armed with long banana stalks stirring a sticky brown mass in a big black pan. The concoction was *bibingka*, a sweet rice cake served only on Christmas and a few other special occasions.

Supervising the operation was the grizzled peasant Punding; one of his daughters and her husband, an NPA company commander, were among the curious. It was decided by Joy that we would spend the night with Punding's family. There was a festive air as children scampered about and visitors came and went. Both of Punding's older daughters were home, having gotten time off from their NPA duties to spend Christmas with their family. Punding had slaughtered a pig for the occasion, and so we feasted that evening on roasted pork.

Punding was what the communists classified as a "middle peasant"— a farmer who was well-off compared to the average southern Quezon peasant. He had earned enough money from growing rice and coconuts to open a small general store in the downstairs of his handsome, tin-roofed, two-story wooden house. Punding and his wife, Meding, continued to farm a few hectares of hilly land in an adjacent barrio, a two-hour hike away.

Punding was viewed as something of a problem by CPP officials. There was no arguing the fact that he had given considerable support to the revolution—support that had certainly made life easier for the communist army in Barangay Rose. Punding's home was a well-used rest stop and shelter for guerrillas entering and leaving the barrio, and his contributions of food and money helped sustain the local rebel organization. But, as Party officials recalled, Punding had not rushed to join the revolution when the NPA first began visiting Barangay Rose. Actually, his daughters had persuaded the shrewd, hard-working peasant and his wife to support the movement.

Twenty-year-old May, Punding's middle daughter, recalled that her first encounter with the NPA was at school when a communist organizer came to talk with her and her older sister. "All I had heard about the NPA were scary things," she told me. "They were supposed to be killers, rapists, criminals." But May found the goals of the revolution, as explained by her NPA visitor, to be "reasonable and very good. I found them not the monstrous people we were made to think. My sister and I met with the person very often until we finally decided to join the movement."

Punding and his wife were horrified by their daughters' decision to join the communist movement, May recalled. "My father offered to work harder so that we both could go to any college of our choice. But we knew that we would learn more in the movement than in school, so we stuck to our decision. My parents were very sad." May begged her parents to understand. "I explained to them that I had to do this for the service of our nation, that I had to give whatever I can to the movement." The two daughters finally convinced their parents to support the revolution, and by Christmas 1987, May was a full-time NPA organizer and Shirley was working part-time for the movement.

The rub between Punding and the communist hierarchy was what important Party officials viewed as his impertinent habit of questioning the decisions of local rebel leaders. One time when regional CPP officials had decided to transfer May away from Barangay Rose to the island of Mindoro, nearly 100 miles distant, Punding and his wife initially cried and pleaded with their daughter not to go and then registered their forceful objections with CPP officials. Punding even wrote a letter to a Party cadre, whom he had guessed correctly was the ranking regional official, asking for reconsideration of the transfer. Laughing about the episode later, the regional CPP secretary told me she had asked Punding why he was writing her. She was only a "responsible" person in the movement, she had told him. But Punding persisted, and finally the Party grudgingly relented. May stayed in the Southern Quezon Front, and Punding continued to faithfully, if sometimes cautiously, support the revolution.

The hills of Barangay Rose resounded on Christmas Eve with the booms of the bamboo "cannons" that peasant families used to celebrate Christmas and the New Year. The cannons were actually bamboo tubes in which lighter fluid was squirted, then ignited through a hole bored at the closed breech end. As darkness fell, we could see muzzle flashes twinkle throughout the valley and hear the muffled explosions a few seconds later. The children who lived in the cluster of houses in the meadow had their own cannon, and they squealed with delight each time the flames and smoke belched from the bamboo tube with a deafening roar. The cannonade lasted late into the evening.

Punding's house was the largest and most comfortable place that I visited in Barangay Rose, and one of only two or three with a concrete foundation and ground floor. My wife and I were shown to a small upstairs bedroom in which sacks of rice were stored. The night air was cool and pleasant, and I fell asleep listening to Christmas carols on a BBC shortwave broadcast.

Christmas morning was heralded with the booming of bamboo cannons and the excited chatter of the children who filled Punding's house. The playful imps had a toy cap gun, and they added their modest "pop, pop, pop" to the barrage as they ran shrieking. At 8:30, the young children and teenagers began leaving in groups for the barrio school, a half-hour walk through the jungle, to attend a Christmas program. Some of them clutched coins and tiny gifts from parents and relatives. Punding's youngest daughter, Marybelle, rushed through her chores, fetching pails of water from a nearby well, slopping the pigs, and washing breakfast dishes. She hurriedly washed up, slipped on a fresh blue-and-white calico dress, and joined three girlfriends for the hike to the school.

Joy, Aleli, and I set out for the house of Kulas, a member of the Party's barrio revolutionary council. The first thing I noticed upon our arrival was that Kulas had shaved his thick mustache. "The demons [soldiers] might recognize me," he solemnly explained. Then breaking into a grin he confessed another reason for parting with his mustache: A local candidate for mayor had been giving away razor blades— "Gillettes," as Kulas called them—and so he decided to give them a try.

Four rebels were sitting around the bamboo hut, including Baldo, my amiable bodyguard on a previous trip, and Claudia, a plump district Party official. Another guerrilla busied himself by trying to fix the spring on Claudia's pistol. Kulas' wife, Guring, and his daughters brought out plates of Christmas treats: *bibingka* and thin, fried rice noodles called *pancit*. Throughout the morning and afternoon, guerrillas and Party officials came and went offering greetings of "Merry Christmas," and stopping to rest and chat and savor Guring's delicacies.

The occasion was even more festive for Kulas and Guring because of the homecoming of their eldest daughter, Yoly. Six months earlier, 15-year-old Yoly had left the barrio to work as a domestic helper for several urban CPP cadres who lived near Manila. She took care of the baby of two married cadres, cooked, and did housework, for which she was paid 250 pesos a month (about $12). She sent most of her earnings back to her family. Now Yoly had returned home for the first time, and she reveled in the opportunity to dote on her younger brother and sisters and help her mother in the tiny kitchen.

Yoly had belonged to the communist youth organization in the barrio before she was sent to Manila. She and her 12-year-old sister, Lerma, had attended school in an adjacent barrio about an hour's walk each way over difficult trails. "The school is so poorly run," Yoly said softly. "Often the teachers are absent because they do other things to augment their incomes. I know some of them do laundry for others. Sometimes they do not have classes on Monday and Fridays because of outside work, which leaves classes only Tuesday through Thursday." Now Yoly's education was under the auspices of Party tutors.

My wife and I joined Kulas by the cool stream that looped around his hut and watched as he plucked and dressed a chicken killed for the joint celebration of Yoly's homecoming and Christmas. He squatted at the water's edge, a dog and a pig prowling hungrily at his side, and deftly chopped the chicken into pieces with swift swings of his machete. As Kulas worked, he talked about his commitment to the revolution— "the movement," as he reverently called it—that had so changed his life.

Kulas had been living in a nearby barrio when he first came into contact with the NPA around 1981. He joined the movement "because there were many bad elements in my barrio. There were many drinkers, many cattle rustlers and robbers." But the crime and lawlessness of which most peasants spoke had touched Kulas in a way more personal than most.

In 1981, a *carabao* had been stolen from his father-in-law. The prime suspect was a local landlord. After confronting the man, Kulas' father-in-law was murdered by one of the landlord's sons. Kulas went out and bought a .45-caliber pistol to avenge the death, but before he could act, he was approached by the NPA.

> I told them about my father-in-law's death, and they told me to forget my revenge because the NPA will take care of the problem. The NPA had received a lot of other complaints about the same person. When I heard about the death of this person, I was glad I didn't have to kill my fellow man. I was impressed by the NPA. After several months, I joined them.[1]

The revolution had wrought many changes in Barangay Rose, he added. For example, "before the NPA came here, I would buy animals and shortly afterward they would be stolen. The thieves were supported by the military, so we couldn't do anything to get them back. Now, we can tie the animals anywhere and they won't get stolen."

Kulas spoke about his decision to join the movement as though he had undergone a religious experience that had changed his entire outlook on life. "Since I was enlightened, I learned not to be greedy and not have vices, especially gambling and drinking," he said. "Now, instead of using money to buy liquor, I give the money to help my family. It becomes a matter of self-discipline, realizing that drinking is not only a waste of money; it's not good for the health either." (Drinking is prohibited mainly for security reasons, Kulas said. A person might start talking about the underground organization when drunk.)

"Before the NPA came, we looked down on women as second-class citizens and as objects of pleasure," he continued. "But after you become aware you look upon them as partners, and they have the same rights as men, so you respect them; you don't step on their humanity." His "enlightenment" had made him further realize, Kulas said, that "all I need is a small piece of land to support my family, have my children finish grade school so they can read and write and do arithmetic, and the movement will take care of the rest."

His devotion to the cause had earned Kulas the confidence of district Party officials. He served in the barrio militia, joining patrols, helping transport food and other materiel to NPA units in the area, and performing other valuable services for the revolution. Kulas had been arrested in April 1986 at a military checkpoint in Batangas province, south of Manila, carrying four M-16 rifles hidden in a jeepney. The rifles were intended for the Batangas NPA Command. His military captors beat him and struck him in the chest with their rifle butts, Kulas said. "I was tortured very badly before they allowed me to see my lawyer," he recalled. "I knew my rights—the Party taught us human rights courses, so the military could not pressure me into confessing." He was held in jail for six months on subversion charges, then suddenly released without ever facing trial. "The enemy is bad," Kulas said as he reflected on the experience, "but there are some military men who are nice and we remember their names. Too bad in combat bullets cannot choose their targets."

Kulas was less benevolent in his attitude toward President Aquino, and he repeated Party rhetoric condemning the new government as worse than Marcos. "We are very disappointed with Cory, endorsing vigilante groups and all," he said. "She had the farmers killed in Mendiola"—a reference to the 1987 killings of 18 leftist agrarian reform protesters outside the presidential palace—"and workers [killed] in the factories. Marcos used to imprison us. We have to be more careful now because they kill instantly, with no questions asked."

But in reality, the government in Manila had little impact on Kulas. He had stopped paying government taxes in 1981, and now he recognized the National Democratic Front as his government. At 36 years of age, the doting father of four children, Kulas seemed content with his life, supporting his family by growing coffee, spices, bananas, and coconuts on a five-hectare plot that was a one-and-one-half hour walk away. And he seemed particularly content with his role in the communist revolution.

That night, as my wife and I settled down to sleep on a straw mat laid across the bamboo floor, Kulas apologized for the humble accommodations. "I'm sorry all I have to offer you to sleep on is a bamboo floor, but we're in the middle of a revolution," he said. "If we win, I'll pick out a nice apartment in Manila. Maybe I'll become wealthy, and I'll be able to offer you cushions to sleep on." Kulas chuckled at the thought.

Guring prepared a tasty lunch of roasted chicken and a dish of chicken boiled with papaya. As we ate, Laya, a jovial, 20-year-old NPA cadre whom I had met on previous visits, arrived.

"How are you?" I asked.

"Sad," she replied forlornly, "because my husband is not with me." Laya explained that her husband was in the next district helping conduct a month-long training course for guerrilla recruits. Her first wedding anniversary was the following day, December 26 (a favorite date for underground weddings), and the occasion would pass without her getting to see her husband.

Laya was one of a few peasant recruits from the Bondoc peninsula who had begun to rise through the ranks of the regional underground organization. One of twelve children, she had been forced to quit school after the sixth grade. CPP organizers had taken notice of her, and she had been trained to become an NPA cadre, an elite status. Laya was now an army political instructor who taught the basic Party course for prospective CPP members and the basic mass course for newer recruits. She carried with her a pastel blue children's school satchel bulging with her textbooks, a blackboard eraser, and a single piece of chalk.

Laya traveled throughout the front conducting classes, although lately she had been spending most of her time teaching the basic Party course to NPA members. The course lasted 15 days, and then Laya would move on to another area to teach a new batch of students. Christmas and the CPP anniversary offered a break from classes, but Laya wished aloud that she could see her husband.

Anniversary ceremonies were scheduled around the country in every district where the revolution had sunk roots. After lunch, Kulas and a few other peasants and CPP cadres set out for the designated site in our district. Relishing his assignment as security for our group, Joy buckled on an ammunition harness and threw a borrowed M-16 rifle over his shoulder. The trail at times broke out of the dripping, gloomy jungle, and we wound along the slippery dikes of rice paddies and climbed bare hills and ridges where peasants were cultivating fields of upland rice, coffee, and peanuts. The NPA's efforts to teach crop diversification appeared to be winning adherents.

As we passed bamboo huts along the way, our column swelled, and soon we were nearly two dozen strong. Our destination was a small clearing alongside a spacious bamboo house, and by the time we arrived, the place was already bustling with peasant families, armed guerrillas, and Party functionaries. Dante was wearing a military fatigue cap and an ammunition belt with several automatic rifle clips about his waist. Noticing the bewildered stares my arrival had prompted, Dante strode over to me, smiling broadly, and shook my hand. He gave an effusive welcome to Aleli and asked us to spend the night in his house.

A bamboo flagpole was raised in the clearing and an antiquated public address system hooked up. The ceremony began with two cadres singing a song about AFP depredations against the peasants. Then, on cue, a platoon of communist militia and NPA regulars, men and women, armed with automatic rifles and a few old World War II–vintage carbines marched into the yard. Most of the 25 guerrillas were barefoot or wearing rubber thongs and clad in T-shirts and cheap trousers or blue jeans. As they marched, the 250 peasants gathered for the occasions raised clenched fists and sang the communist "Internationale," anthem of the revolution. Dante, looking solemn and standing ramrod straight, slowly hauled the Communist Party banner up the bamboo flagpole.

A few peasant women did a brisk business hawking candies, cigarettes, and coconut juice, and children frolicked and climbed the trees surrounding the clearing, but for the most part—in contrast to traditional barrio fiestas—this was a staid affair, heavy on stern speeches. Claudia, the portly district CPP official with a .45-caliber pistol hung in a black leather holster, offered "warm and red greetings to all" and with a dramatic flair declared, "We are not sure if we will be alive to celebrate the next anniversary." Another long-winded Party official promised that "our victory is not far. Our comrades are working hard. Our army fights. The enemy is getting weaker. The unbearable sorrow of the farmer is almost over."

The speeches quickly began to bore many of the peasants, and a few stood up and wandered about the clearing. Unperturbed, the speakers lectured passionately about such sundry topics as the treachery of the Aquino government, the foreign debt, commodity prices, the curse of anticommunist vigilantes, and the need for everyone to redouble efforts on behalf of the revolution.

The restive audience was finally recaptured by the cultural segment of the program. Several CPP members performed a short play about an anticommunist vigilante group in the area, the Solo Brothers. The vigilantes were depicted as hard-drinking, heavy-gambling louts who stole, raped, and murdered their way through rural barrios as part of Aquino's "total war" policy against the revolutionary movement. Rich in humor and drama, the play ended with the NPA guerrillas killing the vigilantes and liberating the barrios. The peasants, clearly gripped by the performance, lustily applauded its triumphant conclusion.

The speeches began anew with a district Party official delivering a shrill 45-minute discourse on the low intensity conflict counterinsurgency strategy that, she charged, was being foisted on the Philippines by the United States. "Cory is no different from Marcos. There are no changes because the economic system is rotten," she railed. "Why can we not go to school? Why can we not eat?" Relating how the United States was defeated in Vietnam, she nearly shouted, "Whatever war the U.S. starts, as long as people are united, they won't win."

Again, the audience grew noticeably restless. This time the moment was saved by a young peasant boy, 10 or 11 years old, who recited several poems extolling the revolution and beckoning peasants to "join the fight." After a final speech, the long afternoon drew to a close with one more rendition of the "Internationale" and a burst fired from an aging AK-47 rifle.

The tedium of the speeches made little difference to peasants such as Ka Adam, a smiling, bucktoothed old man wearing a blue cap, blue shirt, and new-looking camouflage fatigue pants tucked into black rubber boots. We bumped into one another after the ceremony, and he held out his hand in greeting. He was 65, had been in the movement for eight years, and was a member of the revolutionary council in a barrio adjacent to Barangay Rose. He pointed out his wife, Betta, a comical-looking old woman wearing a Russian-style fur hat who had been selling candy and cigarettes during the ceremony. Proudly, Adam announced that three of his children—two boys and a girl—were serving in the NPA's southern Quezon fighting unit.

Dusk was approaching, and it was time for both of us to get on our way, so we wished each other well. Betta gathered up her basket of wares, and the old peasant couple ambled over to join the procession of peasants, Party officials, and guerrillas trudging off along the muddy trails to their homes and camps primed for another year of war and revolution.

Caught in a polite, but awkward, tug of war between Kulas and Dante over who would have the honor of hosting us on our final night in Barangay Rose, Aleli and I decided the most diplomatic course was to return to Kulas' house. As we relaxed later in the cool dusk, I dug some teabags from my pack and Kulas put a pot of water on the fire. He had never seen a teabag before, and he marveled as the small white pouch turned the steaming water a reddish brown. Kulas gulped it down. "Delicious," he pronounced.

Kulas' wife and his two eldest daughters had left earlier in the day for another barrio where they were to attend a wedding. Before we went to sleep, Kulas announced that he would fix us a farewell breakfast of chicken and newly harvested rice. Kulas did not own a watch and usually woke with the crowing of the cocks and the first light of dawn. But with his foreign guests, he spent a restless night of anticipation. Suddenly, in the middle of the night, Kulas awoke with a start, and fearing it was nearing dawn, he began to ready the pans in his tiny kitchen. When my wife stirred, Kulas whispered, "Ka Aleli, what time is it?" It was 3 A.M. Sheepishly, he settled back down on his straw mat. Before 5 A.M., he was up again killing and boiling two more scrawny chickens and cooking a big pot of new rice. The meal was memorable— the chicken was delicious, and the rice, as Kulas had promised, was more flavorful than any I had ever tasted.

After breakfast, we walked to Dante's hut, but he had gone hunting. Disappointed, I left some cans of beans and Vienna sausages with his wife. In return, she insisted I take a sack of candy she had made. After asking her to extend to Dante our apologies for not spending the night, my wife and I promised to return to visit them. But six weeks later, Dante was killed, and his widow and children abandoned their home and fled Barangay Rose.

26

Facing the Future

"The end game," the veteran Communist Party official paused for effect as she wrote the words on a battered black board, "the end game is a general insurrection."

Some of the dozen district and provincial Party officials sitting on the rough board floor of the palm-covered jungle classroom had been dozing in the midday tropical heat, but the speaker's words jolted them. The communist cadres sat up, eagerly waiting to hear more.

In the years ahead, the revolution would come to a dramatic climax, the lecturer declared. Political, economic, and social crises would overwhelm the government. Strikes and demonstrations would begin to paralyze the cities, while NPA guerrillas would reach parity with government forces in the countryside. Massive civil discontent would explode into insurrections throughout the Philippines. Simultaneously, the NPA's Red fighters would launch a final offensive, overrunning camps of the "puppet army" and occupying provincial cities. Finally, communist troops would march triumphantly into Manila, and political power would fall into the hands of the revolution.

Despite this heady talk of stalemate, final offensive, and victory, the communists remained far from seizing power in the Philippines as 1989 began. The CPP and its guerrilla army had survived the first three years of Corazón Aquino's six-year term, offsetting its casualties and defections and even territorial losses with new recruits and expansion into untapped areas of the countryside. Party unity had been stretched to its limits in sometimes rancorous internal debates, but in all but a few isolated cases, it had held. The movement had achieved much in 20 years and effectively governed hundreds, if not thousands, of rural barrios. But the dream of seizing national political power—the end game of the CPP's political and military forces—at best appeared to be years from fulfillment.

Would the New People's Army ever defeat the U.S.-backed Armed Forces of the Philippines? Were the political forces of the National Democratic Front on a course for an eventual share of power? Or was the revolution ultimately destined to fail in its dream of creating a socialist People's Democratic Republic of the Philippines and fade away into oblivion? As the the CPP and its guerrilla army entered a third decade of political and military struggle, the movement had reached a crucial juncture with these questions hanging in the balance.

The revolution was faced with several vital strategic and tactical questions as 1989 began, and a serious misstep on any one of several issues threatened to undermine its chances for success. When and how the NPA should escalate the guerrilla war, how much emphasis should be placed on legal urban struggles and electoral politics, and whether the controversial tactics of urban guerrilla warfare and economic sabotage should be expanded were all contentious issues awaiting resolution. Internal problems—described to me by former CPP chairman Rodolfo Salas as "theoretical, political and organizational"—were other critical variables that would have a bearing on the movement's future success.

The problems facing the Philippine revolutionary forces were magnified by the considerable disappointments and setbacks suffered by the CPP in 1988. Several senior Party officials at the national and regional levels were arrested, raising fears within the underground of extensive military infiltration. In the countryside, anticommunist vigilantes organized by the government forced the NPA to withdraw from some secure barrios, denying the guerrilla army its protective mass base, restricting rebel operations, and shrinking the potential pool of communist recruits. The news was equally grim from Manila and other major cities, where steady communist advances on the labor front stalled and the CPP's once-flourishing urban mass organizations struggled to revive legal protests against the government. There was also the nagging challenge of a popular democratic president enjoying considerable international support.

For most of its first 17 years, the movement had enjoyed ideal conditions for a communist revolution: a corrupt, authoritarian ruler backed by an abusive military and a martial law government in an impoverished, Third World nation. Victory had seemed within grasp as recently as 1985, only to be denied by Aquino's dramatic accession to power. In 1989, CPP strategists were still groping to find the formula that would again set the revolution forging ahead. A sort of back-to-the-Marxist-basics movement swept the Party, resulting in a redoubling of theoretical training in the hope of recapturing what one cadre nostalgically referred to as "the spirit of the Cultural Revolution," that galvanizing force that had inspired the movement in its formative years. Private fears within the CPP that the movement was adrift even sparked talk of recalling Sison back from voluntary exile in Europe to lead the Party once again and breathe new fire into the ranks.

Outwardly, at least, virtually every CPP and NPA official, even rank-and-file Party activists and guerrillas with whom I spoke, were still remarkably confident that they would prevail. I got the sense from many that if necessary, they were willing to spend the rest of their lives fighting. But a growing number of senior CPP leaders had begun to fear by the late 1980s that the patience of their supporters was not boundless and that a victory had to be achieved sooner rather than later. "It's a protracted people's war," a member of the CPP's Southern Luzon Commission told me in 1988, "but we realize it's a matter of time before people will start to ask if we can really win this war. So we have to move faster." That feeling had further changed the quotient in the Philippine insurgency by 1989 and was fueling an international search for heavy weapons that could dramatically change the complexion of the war.

For all the revolutionary movement's problems and setbacks, the CPP and its guerrilla army still had much in its favor. Pronouncements by Aquino and military officials in 1988 that the insurgency had been "broken" were hardly grounded in political and social realities. The military estimated NPA strength at the end of 1988 to be more than 24,000 guerrillas operating in 60 of the Philippines' 73 provinces and supported by considerably more than 500,000 civilian sympathizers. It was a national movement anchored on a broad base of support scattered throughout the archipelago, cutting across barriers of local language and ethnic background. The NPA had become strong enough in many areas of the country to demand, and receive, cooperation and even material aid from landowners, officials, politicians, and businesspeople.

Despite its professed Marxist-Leninist orthodoxy, the CPP had demonstrated through the years its ability to adapt to national political conditions and local situations. Theoretical rigidity was shelved for a pragmatic politics of survival inside the rural guerrilla fronts. Perhaps the most significant example was the foresight that led the CPP to forge an alliance with Church radicals, a bold rejection of the old PKP's anticlericalism that had paid enormous dividends.

The movement's flexibility and responsiveness had led the CPP to respond to criticism and acknowledge the Party's fallibility and, when necessary, to modify or even scrap unpopular or unworkable policies, such as a bloody assassination campaign in Manila in 1987. The revolution's collective leadership had enabled the movement to survive scores of top-level arrests during its 20 years of existence. Without question, the arrests in 1988 of key regional leaders from Central Luzon and the Visayas along with three prominent members of the CPP Central Committee had caused temporary dislocation and created logistical and security problems. But during the course of two decades a chain of executive committees had been painstakingly built at every level within the Party and NPA, from the barrios up to the Central Committee and its more exclusive Executive Committee, enabling the movement to withstand the death and capture of leaders.

Another inherent strength was the CPP's policy of decentralized operations, which had encouraged innovation and creativity within the semiautonomous regional organizations. Despite the predictions of AFP observers and other skeptics that the NPA would eventually degenerate into a collection of regional communist warlords with their own fiefdoms, with few exceptions decentralization continued to work successfully as of the late 1980s. Although regional Party units continued to enjoy flexibility, the acquisition of sophisticated field radios had enabled the NPA command to exercise closer control over its units scattered throughout the islands.

Still another source of the movement's strength was the policy of concentrating energies on political indoctrination rather than military operations. The CPP's founders considered this policy a necessity because of what they perceived as the country's geographical disadvantages. Lacking a friendly border across which the guerrillas could flee for sanctuary or an easy source of foreign aid and weapons, the CPP leadership decided that a politically enlightened peasantry would have to provide that sanctuary. The Party's careful campaign of political "enlightenment" had shown peasants that they could exercise some control over their lives. In the process, the movement's almost complete reliance on peasant support had kept it closely attuned to the needs and desires of its chief constituency.

The armed forces had begun to challenge NPA hegemony in a few areas with small special operations teams (SOTs) trained extensively in civic action and propaganda techniques. If deployed on a wide scale, the SOTs could restrict NPA movements and even force the guerrillas out of some rural barrios previously ceded to communist forces. But the ultimate success of the program depended on the subsequent delivery of government services and measures to improve the quality of life in rural barrios. On this count, after three years in power, the Aquino government seemed to be making precious little headway. Communist organizers were making the argument to impoverished peasants and slum dwellers that Aquino had been hailed as the best democracy had to offer Filipinos and that even she was failing to improve their lives. How could they expect anyone else to do better?

That the revolutionary movement did not disintegrate after the fall of Marcos and the installation of an enormously popular president in 1986 is further evidence of the inherent strengths of the CPP and the New People's Army. Aquino's rise to power did not send hordes of NPA defectors pouring from the hills—as many officials of the new government had envisioned in 1986—although the restoration of democratic rule in the Philippines had a chilling effect on the revolution and slowed the growth of rebel forces.

A source of concern for CPP officials in many regions was the proliferation of anticommunist vigilante groups organized and armed by the military. The vigilantes were proving to be "quite effective in some ways," a senior CPP official assigned to the Luzon countryside told me in 1988. They had forced the NPA to temporarily abandon barrios in many regions. The most celebrated successes of the anticommunist vigilantes were on the southern island of Mindanao, which in 1986 had been the area of greatest strength and support for the revolutionary movement. The rapid proliferation of vigilantes had forced the NPA to flee many of its formerly secure barrios in 1986 and 1987.

But there was a flip side of the coin that worried many Filipino observers and heartened CPP strategists: Abuses committed by the vigilantes in rural barrios and even urban areas were beginning to create victims who, if not already sympathethic toward the guerrillas, were now inclined to support the NPA and the protection offered by the rebel army. Much like the government's notoriously abusive Civilian Home Defense Force militia units during the Marcos years, the vigilantes were in many areas spreading a new wave of terror through the countryside that, if left unchecked, in the long term could significantly boost the fortunes of the revolutionary movement.

The strategy of the CPP leadership by 1988 called for strengthening communist forces in the cities and the countryside with an eye toward a decisive confrontation in 1992. While continuing to stress a Chinese-style protracted people's war aimed at encircling the cities from the countryside, the forceful arguments by many Party cadres on behalf of a Nicaraguan-style "insurrectionary" strategy had resulted in greater emphasis being accorded to the development of communist political and military capabilities in urban areas. Unfortunately for the revolutionary movement, the CPP was experiencing some of its greatest problems on the urban front.

In 1989, the NDF's legal mass organizations in Manila and other cities were still struggling to regain the ground they had lost since the end of the Marcos regime. Efforts to revive urban protests in 1988 were crippled by the capture of ranking members and staff of the CPP's United Front Commission.[1] At year end, CPP-guided legal organizations were not able to muster the crowds that three years earlier had numbered in the tens of thousands in Manila, Cebu, and Davao. The legal movement's losses included many prominent business and professional elements; some accepted positions in the Aquino government, and others simply parted ways with the NDF over questions of tactics and objectives in the new atmosphere of democratic space that developed after the departure of Marcos.

One of the biggest disappointments for CPP leaders was the decline of the student movement in the late 1980s. Party documents spoke bluntly of falling membership and waning influence within the student movement.[2] In a sign of the times immediately following Aquino's rise to power in 1986, a Center-Right student party at the University of the Philippines succeeded in ousting the entrenched radical student government, which had supported the NDF political line. The struggling radical student movement suffered a further crippling blow in 1987 with the assassination of Leandro Alejandro, a charismatic Bayan leader who had continued to be a driving force in the student movement. Ruefully surveying the flagging fortunes of student radicalism, a veteran CPP cadre who had been a product of the 1960s student demonstrations remarked to me, "Before, there were more student activists willing to engage in revolution work full-time. Now, students seem to worry more about parking space than politics."

The CPP had been able to partially offset the loss of student recruits by building a radical, community-based youth movement in Manila and other cities. Kabataan para sa Demokrasya at Nasyonalismo (Youth for Democracy and Nationalism, or KADENA) an organization openly sympathetic to the revolution, had organized more than 100 chapters in factories, schools, and mostly lower-class urban communities by the late 1980s. Among the functions of KADENA and militant student organizations was the coordination of a campaign against renewal of the lease on U.S. military bases in the Philippines, which was to expire in 1991. But anticommunist vigilante organizations in Manila and other cities had begun targeting members of KADENA and the League of Filipino Students, and by 1988 scores of activists had been reported missing or murdered. Membership in the militant organizations had become a risk that many middle-class students and youths were unwilling to accept.

The revolutionary movement's most successful legal mass organizations by the late 1980s were the Kilusang Magbubukid ng Pilipinas, a national federation of peasant organizations claiming more than 500,000 members, and the Kilusang Mayo Uno, which claimed a membership of more than 650,000 workers. Militant peasants supported by NPA muscle confiscated agricultural lands in the countryside and organized demonstrations in Manila and other cities. At the same time, the Aquino government's relaxation of restrictions on labor activities in 1986 resulted in an explosion of strikes and other militant actions by unions influenced or controlled by the CPP. The radical unions made formidable inroads in Cebu, metropolitan Manila, and the Laguna industrial belt southeast of the capital and succeeded in paralyzing various key sectors of the economy with strikes. Recruits from the ranks of labor even helped offset the revolutionary movement's loss of support among the middle class and professionals.

But advances on the labor front stalled in 1988, in part because of government cuts in oil prices and transport fares and in part because of disarray in the Manila underground caused by the arrest of several ranking CPP leaders.[3] Tougher government action against illegal strikes, right-wing vigilante harrassment of union members, and extrajudicial killings of labor organizers and activists by suspected military agents were also factors contributing to the curtailment of militant union activities in 1988. Despite the relative lull on the Philippine labor scene in early 1989, the war was far from over. Filipino workers remained among the poorest paid and most exploited in Asia, and labor unions continued to be the victims of the same acts of repression that had earned the Marcos regime international condemnation. As a result, communist strategists planned to make the nation's factories and industries a key battleground in the years ahead. In the process, the CPP hoped to sabotage government attempts to revive the country's long-suffering economy and build a force of committed workers who would be able to paralyze the nation with strikes and demonstrations when the order for a general insurrection came one day in the future.

The movement's problems on the urban front were exacerbated by continuing debates on how much of its resources the CPP should devote to developing support in the cities and on what tactics should be used. The emergence of electoral politics as a possible new front for the revolution had set off contentious discussions that seriously strained relations between the communist underground and NDF forces in legal urban organizations. The CPP had never viewed electoral politics as a key to victory, and as of 1989, the movement's leadership still placed little stock in elections as a viable avenue for advancing the revolution. Poor showings by a CPP-sanctioned political party, the Partido ng Bayan, in legislative and local elections in 1987 and 1988 respectively had merely reinforced the belief of the revolutionary leadership that armed warfare would continue to be the primary route to power in the Philippines.

Perhaps the greatest failure of the revolutionary movement after two decades of struggle was its inability to build a broad popular front like that which propelled the Sandinistas to power in Nicaragua in 1979. By 1989, despite limited successes by radical Christians and others tasked with attracting noncommunist elements to the cause, the revolution's political umbrella organization, the National Democratic Front, remained largely a collection of groups formed and led by the CPP. The movement's insistence that noncommunists accept the NDF's Marxist-based program had hampered efforts to forge a functioning alliance on a national level with a decisive number of middle-class and business elements.

Inside the movement, a growing number of ranking CPP officials and cadres were dissatisfied with the efforts to build a broader popular front. Sotero Llamas, the CPP Central Committee member, remarked to me in 1988 that "a military victory alone is not enough. We need to build alliances with intellectuals, politicians and businessmen. More serious efforts must be given to this sort of work." Llamas and other Party officials said the NDF's demands—Llamas cited in particular demands that noncommunist elements seeking an alliance accept CPP leadership and the validity of armed struggle—precluded the building of a broad popular front.[4]

CPP strategists were resigned to the fact that it would be difficult to rebuild a successful open mass movement or develop a strong national united front under a popular democratic president such as Aquino. Even with the favorable conditions of the corrupt, repressive Marcos years, the revolutionary movement had managed to develop little more than a tenuous alliance with noncommunist elements at the national level. The CPP and NDF elements had been more successful on the provincial and local level, and they were slowly enlisting middle-class and professional support for the revolution.

By the late 1980s, the NDF claimed to have developed popular fronts that included middle-class and professional elements in the Cordillera Mountains and other parts of northern Luzon, Samar, and the Mindanao provinces of Agusan del Sur and Agusan del Norte.[5] The NDF was attracting professionals by offering them a chance to shape their futures. Lawyers active in the NDF, for example, were given an opportunity to draw up an alternative legal system for a revolutionary government. Doctors, teachers, bankers, and economists were all given similar opportunities. Although the elements of a popular front appeared to be taking shape by 1989, the NDF's growth beyond the revolution's traditional peasant and working class-foundations was still slowed by the CPP's insistence on a dominant, vanguardist role in any alliance.

The CPP's cautious approach to a popular front was a deliberate policy grounded in the lessons of Philippine history. The country's turn-of-the-century elite had betrayed the 1896 revolution to U.S. colonizers. In 1946, the PKP and its peasant Hukbalahap guerrillas were lulled into laying down their arms to participate in elections, only to be stripped of six congressional seats and to have peasant supporters gunned down in the Central Luzon barrios. A more recent reminder could be found in 1972: When Marcos declared martial law, many of the Party's erstwhile noncommunist allies struck deals with the dictator in order to retain their political and economic power, while others simply fled to the United States.

By 1989, even though a growing number of CPP officials expressed interest in broadening the appeal of the revolutionary popular front, there were no indications that the NDF would in the near future convince overwhelming numbers of middle-class, business, and professional elements to cast their lot with the revolution. What was emerging instead throughout the countryside was a bizarre patchwork of sometimes unlikely local alliances and accommodations, formal and informal, each providing sustenance to the revolution, but when taken collectively, still far short of the broad coalition that was capable of carrying the movement to victory in the years ahead.

While the urban mass movement struggled to regroup and a national popular front remained elusive, the CPP continued to pressure the Aquino government and its armed forces in the countryside. The movement began to devote more attention to improving the standard of living in rebel-controlled barrios, and provisional revolutionary governments were being organized in contiguous barrios to develop a communist municipal structure in the countryside. On the military front, by the late 1980s the NPA had added to its arsenal new weapons and tactics ranging from homemade land mines and hand grenades to hostage taking and prisoner exchanges. (Some veteran cadres only reluctantly accepted the policy of taking civilian hostages. "You might not be able to control it if any unit can do it, and it might get out of hand," one CPP cadre remarked to me.)

The revolutionary movement reaped military and propaganda benefits from innovations in weapons and tactics. The land mines enabled the

NPA to destroy military trucks and armored troop carriers in bloody ambushes dramatically reported on the front pages of national newspapers, giving the impression of a rebel army holding its own against the AFP, despite government suggestions to the contrary. A series of well-publicized negotiations for the release of civilian hostages and captured soldiers held by the guerrillas projected the image of NPA strength even further. Often the NPA delivered its demands over live public radio broadcasts. In some instances, in order to facilitate negotiations, the AFP even agreed to NPA demands to suspend operations against the rebels in the area.

Although a military triumph for the NPA appeared at best to be years in the future, there was one potential development that could dramatically change that timetable: the acquisition of heavy weapons. International representatives of the NDF, working from an office in Utrecht, Netherlands, were traveling throughout the world soliciting foreign political and material support for the revolution. Led by former Negros priest Luís Jalandoni, the NDF emissaries were in contact with established communist governments, fledgling revolutionary regimes such as Angola and Nicaragua, other rebel movements, and radical parties and organizations in noncommunist countries. By 1989, the NDF had also established solidarity committees in 15 European countries, the United States, Canada, Japan, Australia, New Zealand, and Latin America. The committees were assigned to conduct propaganda work, build political support, and solicit material aid, such as medical supplies. The long-term aim of the NDF's diplomatic efforts was to win recognition of the national provisional revolutionary government to be declared at some point in the future. The first step toward that goal was the establishment of municipal revolutionary governments under the auspices of the NDF, which was begun in 1988.

After years of building a remarkably independent, indigenous revolution, the CPP was actively searching for a source of heavy weapons and other aid. In the countryside, "foreign aid" and "heavy weapons" were words that were on the lips of every ranking Party official and NPA commander with whom I spoke in 1987 and 1988. "We have to have foreign aid now," one senior CPP official told me with a tone that had become characteristic of many leaders of the movement. "If we go without it, the revolution will take a very, very long time. To destroy the AFP's company camps and company headquarters, we should have better arms."[6]

Jalandoni acknowledged that the NDF was discussing with friendly governments and radical political movements and parties the procurement of heavy weapons, money, and even food, but he declined to discuss what offers the movement had received. A senior CPP official based in

Luzon said to me, "We are told many are offering help. There are many, many groups now—countries, parties and organizations—offering help. It is a question of how we can possibly receive the help."[7] Other Party officials said the problem was training rather than transporting the materiel to the Philippines. Another ranking CPP official told me in 1988 that NPA officers were already abroad receiving training in the use of heavy weapons, and Jalandoni seemed to confirm the revelation. Such training, Jalandoni said, was "within the framework of mutually beneficial relations," but it would be "unwise for any representative of the revolutionary movement to confirm."[8]

If the NPA were to acquire heavy weapons, communist forces might be able to force a military stalemate with government forces in a matter of months. With its armor and air dominance neutralized, the AFP would be hard pressed to conduct offensive operations against the guerrillas, and widespread new areas of the countryside would become virtually inaccessible to the government. The broader implications of such a development would be an almost certain reaction by the United States. A deeper U.S. role in the war would likely begin with the shipment of heavier weapons to the AFP to offset the communist hardware and possibly lead to even more direct U.S. involvement in the conflict. CPP strategists have factored the anticipated U.S. response into their plans for procuring heavy weapons, and the thinking of underground leaders is that a more overt role by the United States would result in a nationalist backlash that ultimately would benefit the revolution.

The most likely source of arms for the NPA by the late 1980s was North Korea. The CPP enjoyed warm relations with Pyongyang, a fact underscored by the visit of a delegation of Filipino communists to North Korea in September 1988 to attend ceremonies celebrating the fortieth anniversary of the communist regime. (The head of the CPP's International Department, who led the delegation to North Korea, had visited Nicaragua earlier in the year, although during a visit to Manila in 1988 senior Sandinista officials denied that the Nicaraguan government was supporting the Philippine guerrillas.[9])

In late October or early November 1987, a North Korean ship believed to be carrying arms was spotted sailing toward the Philippines. The vessel was tracked by Western intelligence operatives but subsequently disappeared. Afterward, President Aquino's national security adviser, Emanuel Soriano, told me the ship could have slipped into Philippine waters and unloaded its cargo. "We do not know where the vessel went," he admitted. "We've got a long shoreline, and it's very difficult to monitor all the beaches we have in this country."

Other Asian communist countries closer to the Philippines—notably China and Vietnam—seemed unlikely donors to the NPA. Following a visit to Vietnam in late 1988, Philippine foreign secretary Raul Manglapus said he had been told that the Vietnamese government had resisted suggestions from "other forces" to supply the NPA with surplus U.S. weapons captured from the former South Vietnamese regime.[10] China, the CPP's original patron, also appeared to have no interest in getting involved with the Maoist-oriented Filipino revolutionaries, which left the world arms market as the next most likely source of arms.

Although the Soviet Union had shown a greater interest in the Philippine revolutionary movement since the mid-1980s, and the Pentagon suggested in 1985 that the USSR was beginning to play a role in the insurgency, it seemed highly improbable that Moscow would get entangled with the NPA in the near future. With negotiations on the future of U.S. military bases in the Philippines beginning in 1989, the Soviet Union was obsequiously trying to curry favor with the Aquino government. Jalandoni virtually ruled out the possibility of aid from the Soviet Union, noting "there would be an understandable tendency on the part of the Soviet Union not to get involved in one national conflict which might complicate diplomatic efforts [with the United States]."[11] For the time being, the Soviet Union seemed to be content with forging greater contacts with Filipino communists through radical labor unions and with sponsoring legal NDF activists on visits to the USSR.

For the revolution, there were inherent dangers in the campaign to obtain foreign weapons. The movement had always stressed politics over military tactics, and some longtime NPA observers suggested that the communist army was in danger of lapsing into military adventurism. Furthermore, expectations for the delivery of heavy weapons were running high in the countryside among Party officials and NPA commanders with whom I spoke, and a failure by the leadership to deliver the promised materiel could ignite bitter recriminations that would plunge the movement into deeper crisis.

In contrast to the statements of NPA commanders in the Philippine countryside, Jalandoni seemed to be disturbed by the NPA leadership's growing talk about heavy weapons. "If you have 30,000 NPA fighters and 10,000 with automatic rifles, where is the stress in their thinking? I would prefer that they do not talk about expecting heavy weapons because your tendency will be [to think about] how to use these weapons."[12] Jalandoni maintained that the NPA was still capable of expanding without heavy weapons, adding that "advance of the revolutionary movement must not be made dependent on that."[13]

It seemed likely that at least some heavy weapons would find their way into the hands of the NPA. It was also possible that some heavy weapons had already been acquired by the rebel army and had been stockpiled in mountain or jungle caches in preparation for future escalation of the war. NPA commanders suggested to me that with or without heavy weapons, communist forces would have to begin attacking larger government camps by 1990 or risk a deterioration of support in the countryside.

In 1988, amid the euphoria of the arrests of several ranking communist leaders, the AFP and the defense establishment began talking of a "war of quick decision" that would defeat the insurgents by 1992. Such a victory was achieved against the Luzon-based Huk guerrillas in the 1950s, but the NPA in 1989 was too dispersed and had too many secure mountain and jungle bases—not to mention a committed civilian mass base—to be defeated overnight. Furthermore, there was adequate reason to question whether the AFP was capable of carrying out the effective military campaign that would be required to rout the guerrillas in the countryside.

The NPA's integration with peasant supporters stood in sharp contrast to the government armed forces. In many areas where the AFP had established outposts, government troops maintained a distrustful coexistence with local inhabitants. Despite some improvements in AFP discipline and performance by 1989, in general government soldiers remained prone to corruption and abuses against civilians, and many units were poorly disciplined, poorly motivated, and poorly led. A preponderance of the AFP's scarce combat forces, totaling about 70,000 troops, was still being deployed to protect town halls, communications facilities, government agencies, even private businesses, while vast areas of the Philippine countryside were being ceded virtually without contest to the NPA.

Despite a pay increase in 1987, following a nearly successful coup attempt, soldiers remained poorly paid. As 1989 began, AFP soldiers were being allotted 18 pesos (about 90 cents) a day for food, hardly enough for three decent meals. "Our soldiers are physically weak," Cagayan governor Rodolfo Aguinaldo, one of the AFP's most celebrated counterinsurgency experts until his retirement in late 1987, told me. "They are underfed and unable to support their families, and as a result, they resort to graft and corruption. It gets bigger as you go up the line. The soldier at the checkpoint may ask for 10 pesos, while the senior officers ask for 10,000 pesos."[14]

Morale in the ranks of the AFP remained low for other reasons as well. Field hospitals were nonexistent, and soldiers wounded in combat might wait hours for emergency medical care. Lieutenant Domito Mendoza and two other young officers recalled in late 1987 how a close friend, a second lieutenant only a few months out of the Philippine Military Academy, had been wounded in the stomach the previous week during an NPA attack on a police station on the northern coast of Cagayan. The provincial constabulary headquarters in Tuguegarao requested from the regional headquarters a helicopter to evacuate the wounded officer. The regional headquarters in turn had to course the request through the northern Luzon headquarters. Radio communications were poor, and it took several hours of haggling to get the helicopter dispatched. Twelve hours after the battle, the badly wounded officer finally arrived at a hospital in the provincial capital, only to die the following day.[15]

The optimistic pronouncements of AFP generals were more often than not contradicted by rank-and-file soldiers and lower-level officers. "I have been in the AFP for seven years, and I feel we are losing the war against the CPP-NPA," Mendoza told me in Cagayan province in late 1987, in a comment that seemed typical of the feeling of many government soldiers.

If the AFP was unable to crush the tiny NPA using the legal weapons of martial law, it seemed farfetched to assume that a much stronger, better-armed, and better-trained rebel army would be susceptible to quick defeat a decade later. Even if some guerrilla fronts collapsed quickly, others would almost certainly be in a position to carry on the fight for decades.

As the CPP celebrated the beginning of its third decade on December 26, 1988, the revolution was still being led by those onetime Vietnam War protesters and First Quarter Storm activists, the nationalist firebrands who, wearing their Mao caps and clutching the *Little Red Book*, had flocked to the countryside to "learn from the masses" and build a Philippine revolution from scratch. "I thought we would fight for 15 years and then we would win," one of those early CPP recruits recalled nearly 20 years later. The first generation of revolutionaries had traveled far and endured much since those heady days of the 1960s and early 1970s. They had learned to live with the peasants and share their hardships, and city-bred activists could now point with pride to their rough hands and splayed feet. Many had married comrades in the underground and had given birth to children who by now were teenagers. Thousands had died or gone to prison. Those who had survived in the rural underground had often done so with great physical suffering, and many were in poor health after years of trekking through remote mountains and inhospitable jungles. The ranks of the old guard were thinning by 1989, and the movement itself was undergoing revolutionary change as the torch was gradually passed to a new generation of Filipino revolutionaries.

No longer were the University of the Philippines and the Lyceum supplying the bulk of Party cadres, the future leaders of the revolution. At every level of the CPP hierarchy in the countryside, a growing number of recruits from the peasantry were filling leadership positions. The development should have been a proud moment for the university-educated CPP veterans who were finally seeing the fruits of their years of effort: a politically enlightened and militant peasantry rising up to lead what had been conceived as a peasant revolution. Yet, there was something ironic in the changing character of the movement. While veteran cadres obviously felt pride in watching the peasant radicals come of age, they quietly worried whether the rising generation of Party leaders were capable of leading the revolution into the future.

"Peasants are good fighters," Leny, a senior CPP cadre and a First Quarter Storm activist from UP, told me. "But training peasant recruits for cadre positions is a slow, tedious process." Expressing even greater concern, another senior CPP official said,"The peasants are determined. But if you don't provide them with the necessary skills, training and education, there comes a time when even their determination is affected."[16]

Some independent Filipino Marxists believe the emergence of poorly educated leaders from the ranks of the peasantry and workers is already resulting in a more dogmatic movement. According to these analysts, peasant and working-class cadres are more inclined to rigid acceptance of Marxist-Leninist principles and the Party line at the expense of creativity and debate. (Lending credence to that school of thought, CPP cadres from various areas of the countryside told me that peasant supporters had vehemently opposed the 60-day cease-fire with the Aquino government, a move that even the most hard-line revolutionary leaders deemed necessary to avoid political isolation.) A peasant-dominated leadership would likely be less willing to compromise with its opponents, both internal and external, and would add a sharper edge to the revolution's notion of class struggle. The current leadership still has extensive links with the middle and upper classes. These are the friends, relatives, and classmates of CPP leaders, and although in theory they might be class enemies, the importance Philippine culture places on interpersonal relations and loyalty to one's personal circle weighs heavily. CPP cadres from peasant backgrounds cannot be expected to identify with, or tolerate, the cautious nature of the middle and upper classes.

The rise of a less educated and less sophisticated leadership also raises the possibility of a movement less restrained in its application of military power. In the countryside, peasants grown accustomed to the violence of warlords, landowners, the military, and criminal gangs will likely have less qualms about using violence against class enemies. Many have grown up in the culture of the revolution and have grown hardened to the use of violence to achieve their political aims.

The same could be said of the tens of thousands of Filipino peasants who have fallen under the influence of the revolution. Having lived with oppression before and now having tasted what it was like to have the power to direct their own lives, peasants are less likely to simply abandon the struggle and return to the supplicant, feudal ways of the past. These revolutionary new attitudes are becoming institutionalized in many barrios as a generation of young peasant children who grew up under the sway of the revolution reach early adulthood. They have been reared in the movement and have been trained to carry on the ways of the revolution.

CPP leaders acknowledged that the revolutionary mood that had swept the country in the twilight of the Marcos regime was far from being recaptured three years into Corazón Aquino's presidency. Sotero Llamas said a prerequisite for an NPA military victory was for great masses of Filipinos "to feel there is no alternative. The people must be so angered that they will make the final push. At the moment," he conceded in 1988, "Cory is still a good alternative to [former defense secretary Juan Ponce] Enrile and the military." But Llamas and other CPP leaders argued that it was not necessary to have another repressive government, another Marcos, to create a revolutionary situation. "Now, the people are aware of the issues," Llamas assured me. "The presence of a strong Communist Party and New People's Army are enough to polarize the situation."[17]

In the meantime, the CPP and communist army were being sustained and strengthened by some unlikely allies. NPA and CPP officials were receiving varying degrees of cooperation from local government officials, businesspeople, and landowners in every area I visited. One of the demands the NPA had made on local officials seeking an accommodation with the rebels was not to organize anticommunist vigilantes in their towns, particularly in rural barrios. Gregorio Rosal, a veteran NPA commander in the Southern Tagalog provinces, said the NPA was not requiring local officials to actively support the guerrillas, but that "it will be enough if they do not support counterinsurgency activities against us."[18] In Bicol, Llamas talked openly about his many arrangements with the region's politicians—the "unholy alliance," as he jokingly described it. During the campaign for local and provincial elections in late 1987 and early 1988, hundreds of mayoral candidates had reached a modus vivendi with communist officials. In exchange for communist support in the election, the politicians agreed not push aggressive counterinsurgency measures against the guerrillas, Llamas said.

In the northern Luzon provinces of Nueva Vizcaya and Quirino, dramatic NPA growth was being nurtured by money, arms, radios, and free medical care provided by smaller landowners and minor politicians, the area Party secretary told me. Out-of-power politicians were courting the rebels in the hope of securing communist support in future elections. The process of cooptation in Nueva Vizcaya and Quirino was given greater impetus by the assassination of several prominent figures. Between mid-1987 and early 1988, the NPA had killed the Marcos-era governor of Nueva Vizcaya, a town mayor, and a town police chief. The NPA had forced local government officials to flee or collaborate in more than 150 barrios in 17 of the 21 municipalities in Nueva Vizcaya and Quirino provinces.

"Of the 21 town mayors, we have neutralized a good number of them—neutralized in the sense that they are not actively and openly involved in counterinsurgency," Bing, the area Party secretary, told me. "It doesn't matter to us if they keep their anticommunist sentiments to themselves. What matters is if they hold meetings to try to get people to fight us."[19]

The CPP, according to Llamas, had "revolutionized local politics" in Bicol. "Now, the politicians here don't have goons," he said, grinning broadly. "They ally with us so they are safe." The Party official's boasts were not idle. During a visit to Llamas' camp in Bicol in 1988, Party escorts suggested that we leave our van at the residence of the provincial governor, whom they cheerfully described as a friend. Back in Manila, I maintained contact with my Bicol CPP liaison by calling a phone pocket-beeper service paid for by a cooperative Bicol congressman, the cadre explained with a grin. Furthermore, the cadre said, if stopped at a military checkpoint en route to visit Llamas in his rural camp, I was to use the name of Congressman _____ as a reference. Happily, the Party cadre noted that the helpful congressman had "gotten all of his mayors elected" in local elections held a few days earlier, which would mean more favorable operating arrangements for the NPA in those towns.

During the local election campaign, the NPA forced candidates to pay fees in order to campaign in areas where the rebels were strong. One unfortunate candidate for Quezon governor, Eduardo Rodríguez, initially rejected NPA demands to pay a 100,000-peso ($5,000) campaign "tax." A few days later, Rodríguez was taken hostage by the NPA while campaigning in a rebel-controlled area. Later, Rosal (the NPA commander who was negotiating with the candidate) told me that Rodríguez was released after paying the full 100,000 pesos demanded by the NPA; his running mate for vice governor had paid 50,000 pesos. Rodríguez won the election.

The pliability of Philippine politicians seemed to know no bounds. A former deputy justice minister under Marcos who was running for Congress in 1987 recounted how the NPA had requested a meeting with him during the campaign. Afterward, the former government official took pride in noting that he had given the guerrillas only food and medical supplies, not weapons and ammunition, as other politicians did. The same process of cooptation was under way within the Philippines' economic elite. The CPP was also achieving some success in infiltrating the civilian bureaucracy.

Although the cooperation and support provided to the NPA by government officials, politicians, businesspeople, and landowners might never amount to enough to bring the movement to power, the arrangements had become a significant source of strength for communist forces by 1989. Perhaps more significantly, the unholy alliance was helping offset efforts by the armed forces and government to defeat the guerrillas.

In most areas of the countryside where I traveled with NPA units and CPP members in 1987 and 1988, the rebel successes still appeared to be coming mostly by default. The NPA was at least holding its own against the government by improving the lives of its supporters. The peasants of Barangay Rose for the first time in their lives were enjoying the fruits of a responsive government: health care, law enforcement, education, agrarian reform, and a higher standard of living, among other benefits. It was hard to imagine that the peasants of Barangay Rose and thousands of other barrios swept up in the revolution would ever be as passive as in the years before the NPA arrived.

Regardless of political developments, it appeared as 1989 began that the guerrilla war would simmer for years in the countryside—or at least as long as the roots of the revolution remain anchored in the poverty and injustice that weighed down the lives of Filipino peasants. Midway through Aquino's six-year term, the government had made little headway in addressing the economic, social, and political inequities that had historically oppressed the country's peasantry and growing urban underclass. The quality of government services to the majority of Filipinos living in poverty in the countryside had improved little, if any, since Marcos' time in the areas I visited. Unchecked lawlessness, a barely functioning criminal justice system, and official corruption all served to further erode Filipinos' faith in government, Aquino's popularity notwithstanding.

A 1988 World Bank report on poverty in the Philippines suggested an equally bleak future. In 1985, nearly 30 million people out of a population of 56 million were living below the poverty line, and that figure had risen by 1989. In rural areas, 58 percent of all families lived in poverty. The report noted grimly, "While rapid economic growth will help alleviate the poverty problem, alone it is not sufficient to solve the problem."[20]

Nevertheless, the government and its boosters clung to the hope that economic expansion would eventually undermine support for the rebels. Modest economic growth, aided considerably by falling world oil prices, had finally been recorded in 1987 and 1988 after years of deep recession. Higher world copra prices had marginally increased incomes for subsistence farmers and coconut industry employees and their families—roughly one-third of the country's population. But higher copra prices were at best a temporary boon, and a series of devastating typhoons in 1987 and 1988 had robbed millions of peasants of the benefits of the strong coconut market. Furthermore, declining productivity from the country's aging coconut trees was offsetting much of the effect of higher copra prices for many poor farmers.[21] Aquino's popularity and higher copra prices, to be sure, had made the NPA's organizing work more difficult in many areas of the countryside, but by 1989, these developments alone had not changed the course of the war.

Even if the government were able to sustain economic growth for several years, the peasant support upon which the revolution has flourished would not be cut substantially unless a radical restructuring of the rural economy were to occur. That seemed unlikely as Aquino began her final three years in office.[22] Rapid population growth had made the simple redistribution of land to peasants an impossibility, and intransigent landlords had sabotaged implementation of the modest government agrarian reform program enacted in 1988. The government faced other daunting problems that seemed certain to tear further at the country's social fabric. Topping the list was an annual birthrate of 2.8 percent, which was steadily adding to already staggering unemployment and underemployment. Watching from the sidelines, CPP strategists remained confident that the country's social and economic challenges would gradually overwhelm Aquino and those who succeed her.

One of the crowning achievements of the Philippine revolutionary movement was its success in turning the Left into a force in national politics, even if that influence had yet to translate into election victories. Although the National Democratic Front may never seize power, the movement has played a leading role in shaping the national agenda and framing debate on virtually every major issue affecting the Philippines during the past 20 years: agrarian reform, poverty, relations with the United States, the future of U.S. military bases, women's rights, education, the role of the Catholic Church in Philippine society, the plight of cultural minorities, and the rights of workers, among others. If not for the broad-based guerrilla war led by the NPA in the countryside, agrarian reform would not have been accorded such a prominent place in national debate during the rule of Marcos and Aquino. If not for the emergence of the NDF as a serious contender for political power in the twilight years of the Marcos regime, the United States would probably never have dumped its loyal ally, however corrupt and repressive he may have been.

At the very least, the revolution's legacy will be the changes that have transformed the lives of Filipino peasants. Poor farmers who had once slept with their livestock and produce for fear of thieves no longer did so in barrios ruled by the rebels. Peasants who before had paid two-thirds of their harvest to landlords now paid one-third. The elimination of usury had enabled some rural families to escape indebtedness for the first time in two generations. Illiterate peasants, young and old, had learned to read, write, and do arithmetic. They had also learned about political and civil rights and for the first time in their lives had exercised them. No Philippine president, governor or armed forces chief of staff could claim as much. The cost of these accomplishments had been fearful, paid in the blood of tens of thousands of Filipinos, many of them innocents caught in crossfires, others whose only transgression had been to cross the path of one side or the other in a relentless war. But however cruel and brutal the revolution might seem, it was a price many desperate Filipinos long accustomed to the institutionalized violence of the country's political and economic aristocracy were willing to pay.

The revolutionary ideas and methods that the communists have imparted to the rural peasants and urban workers may ultimately prove to be irreversible. Perhaps most significantly, the revolution has raised forever the expectations of hundreds of thousands, if not millions, of Filipinos who for decades had stoically suffered poverty, malnutrition, injustice, and illiteracy. Even if the CPP and its forces never triumph, and the New People's Army fades into oblivion, in these heightened expectations lie the seeds of future unrest and revolution.

Notes

CHAPTER 1

1. A *barangay* is the smallest administrative division in the Philippines, equivalent to a rural barrio or an urban neighborhood.

CHAPTER 2

1. The 12 people who were in attendance and formed the CPP Central Committee were (1) José María Sison, captured in 1977; (2) Monico Atienza, captured in 1974; (3) Ray Casipe, surrendered after a 1975 Central Committee plenum; (4) Leoncio Co, captured in 1970; (5) Manuel Collantes, captured in 1972, became a military intelligence officer, and was assassinated by the NPA at Manila's University of Santo Tomás in 1974; (6) Arthur García, killed by one of his men in a dispute in 1970; (7) Hermenigildo García, captured in 1974; (8) Reuben Guevarra, captured in 1981; (9) Art Pangilinan, surrendered around 1973 after a dispute with another ranking Party official; (10) Nilo Tayag, captured in 1970; (11) Fernando Tayag, captured in 1974; and (12) Ibarra Tubianosa, who broke with the movement while heading a secret CPP delegation to China in the 1970s. A thirteenth person, José Luneta, was in China at the time of the founding congress and was elected to the Central Committee in absentia. Of the 13, only Luneta was an active Central Committee member as of 1989. Sison was in self-exile in Holland. Although Philippine military officials suggested that Sison had reassumed leadership of the CPP, it seemed more likely that he did not hold a formal position within the Party.

The official CPP communique issued in January 1969 claimed that the founding congress lasted for two weeks.

2. This account of events surrounding the CPP founding was drawn from a series of interviews in 1988 with Sison and four other founding Central Committee members.

3. A founding CPP member related this to the author in a March 1, 1988, interview, which was subsequently corroborated by Salas.

4. Author's interview with Nemenzo, January 17, 1988.

5. Author's interview with a CPP associate of Sison, March 1, 1988.

6. Author's interview with Sison, April 19, 1988.

7. Author's interview with Nemenzo, January 17, 1988.

8. See Teodoro Agoncillo, *A Short History of the Philippines* (New York: Mentor, 1975), p. 291.

9. Author's interview with Co, March 1, 1988.

10. Author's interview with Fortuna, February 21, 1988.

11. Author's interviews with Sison, April 19, 1988, and with a founding Central Committee member, January 17, 1988.

12. Author's interview with Fortuna, January 31, 1988.

13. Author's interview with Co, March 1, 1988.

14. Author's interview with a founding CPP member, March 1, 1988.

15. Author's interview with José Feliciano, a prominent Tarlac province politician who sat in on many of these meetings with Sumulong in the 1960s, February 8, 1988.

16. Biographical material on Buscayno was compiled from Eduardo Lachica, *HUK: Philippine Agrarian Society in Revolt* (Manila: Solidaridad Publishing House, 1971), pp. 156–157; and a profile in *Philippines Daily Inquirer,* April 15, 1987, p. 5.

17. Author's interview with a Tarlac politician and landowner who has known Buscayno since his early days as a Huk, February 8, 1988.

18. Author's conversation with Aquino, October 1987.

19. Author's interview with a founding CPP member, March 1, 1988.

20. Author's interview with a founding CPP member, February 10, 1988.

21. Details of the meeting between Sison and Dante were gathered from separate interviews with four founding Central Committee members in 1988, including Sison.

CHAPTER 3

1. The account of the NPA founding was reconstructed from a series of interviews in 1988 with a CPP Central Committee member who was present and from an April 19, 1988, interview with Sison. The eight guerrilla lieutenants who were present, and who subsequently were included in the CPP Central Committee, were (1) Juanito Rivera, who would rise to head the Party's military commission and was a member of the CPP's powerful Executive Committee at the time of his capture in late 1987; (2) José Buscayno, Dante's younger brother; (3) Diosdado Layug, a former Huk rebel who eventually surrendered in 1973 and in 1988 was living on a small farm outside Capas, Tarlac; (4) Ben Tuason, killed in an encounter with the military in Nueva Ecija province in the 1970s; (5) Commander Goody, the nom de guerre of Ernesto Miranda, one of Dante's closest lieutenants, killed in Tarlac in 1973; (6) Commander Melody, who surrendered within the first year and later became a government informant; (7) Felman, the nom de guerre of a Huk commander later accused by his NPA comrades of several unauthorized executions (arrested by the military in 1974, he cooperated with his captors, then disappeared in 1979, believed murdered

by either military agents or former NPA colleagues); and (8) Elias, the name of a peasant representative, about whom little else is known.

2. NPA documents stated 35 rifles. Sison told me the NPA began with 35 weapons, only 9 of which were automatic rifles.

3. The description of Layug was drawn from the author's interviews with a founding CPP Central Committee member, March 1 and March 29, 1988; and author's interview with Ariel Almendral, an NPA field officer in Isabela in 1971–1972, January 28, 1988.

4. Author's interview with a founding CPP member, March 29, 1988; and interview with Rodolfo Salas, August 10, 1988.

5. In the beginning, the fledgling communist army was divided into nine squads of about seven guerrillas each.

6. CPP communique issued following the NPA founding, reprinted in a compilation of captured documents, *So the People May Know* (Quezon City: Armed Forces of the Philippines, 1970), pp. 59–80.

7. Benedict J. Kerkvliet, *The Huk Rebellion: A Study of Peasant Revolt in the Philippines* (Quezon City: New Day Publishers, 1979), p. 182.

8. From the constitution of the Communist Party of the Philippines, reprinted in *So the People May Know*, pp. 17–31.

9. Author's interview with a founding CPP member, March 29, 1988.

10. Ibid.

11. Author's interview with Co, one of those leading political discussions in the Tarlac countryside at the time, February 26, 1988.

12. Ibid.

13. Author's interview with a founding Central Committee member, March 1, 1988; and interview with Almendral, January 28, 1988.

14. Details of Arthur García's exploits and his death were gathered in interview with Sison, April 19, 1988; and interview with another founding Central Committee member, February 26, 1988.

15. Author's interview with a founding Central Committee member, March 29, 1988.

16. Sison's "Student Power?" was published in the January 8, 1970, issue of *The Philippine Collegian*.

17. The account of the events of late 1969 and early 1970 is drawn from reports in the *Manila Chronicle, Manila Times*, and *Philippines Herald;* and from Lachica, *HUK*, pp. 191–194.

18. Author's interview with Sison, April 19, 1988.

19. Cited in Daniel Boone Schirmer and Stephen Shalom (eds.), *The Philippine Reader: A History of Colonialism, Neocolonialism, Dictatorship, and Resistance* (Boston: South End Press, 1987), p. 125.

20. Cited in *Area Handbook for the Philippines* (Washington, D.C.: GPO, 1976), pp. 286–289.

21. See Lachica, *HUK*, pp. 258–259.

22. Cited in *Area Handbook for the Philippines*, p. 287.

23. See Lachica, *HUK*, p. 255.

24. Foreword to Renato Constantino (ed.), *M.A.N.'s Goal: The Democratic Filipino Society* (Quezon City: Malaya Books, 1969).

25. Cited in Lachica, *HUK*, pp. 193–194.

26. Author's interview with Nemenzo, January 17, 1988.

27. Amado Guerrero, *Philippine Society and Revolution* (Oakland, Calif.: International Association of Filipino Patriots, 1979), p. 144 (reprint).

28. Author's interview with Fortuna, December 10, 1987.

CHAPTER 4

1. Author's interview with Francisco, November 27, 1987.

2. One of Corpus' protégés was a cadet named Gregorio Honasan, who as an army colonel would later help lead the "people power" revolt against Ferdinand Marcos in 1986 and then a bloody, failed coup attempt against Corazón Aquino on August 28, 1987.

3. Author's interview with Corpus, October 28, 1987.

4. Ibid. Several NPA officers and CPP cadres whom I interviewed recalled being escorted in the early 1970s by Faustino Dy's police from Cauayan into the nearby Sierra Madre foothills, where they began the climb to the main NPA base camp. Dy, then a member of Benigno Aquino's Liberal party, forged an alliance with Marcos when martial law was declared and became a sworn enemy of the NPA. He remained governor until Marcos was forced from power in 1986 and Aquino's local governments secretary removed Dy and hundreds of other pro-Marcos officials from office. After Dy's handpicked candidates won easily in legislative elections in Isabela in 1987, the Aquino administration reversed itself and supported Dy's candidacy for governor in 1988 elections. He won in a landslide.

5. Cited in a CPP publication, "Why Lt. Victor Corpus Left the AFP to Join the New People's Army" (Manila: Gintong Silahis Publications, 1971), pp. 7–10.

6. Author's interview with Sison, April 19, 1988.

7. Author's interview with Corpus, January 21, 1988.

8. Author's interview with Almendral, January 28, 1988.

9. Ibid. Commander Dante's unpublished works on guerrilla warfare were later incorporated into Sison's 1974 essay entitled, "Specific Characteristics of Our People's War."

10. Author's interview with Sison, April 19, 1988.

11. Author's interview with Almendral, January 28, 1988.

12. Ibid.

13. Author's interviews with Corpus, October 28, 1987, and May 18, 1988; interview with Almendral, Feb. 3, 1988; and interview with a former CPP Central Committee member, March 29, 1988.

14. Author's interview with Corpus, October 28, 1987; and interview with Almendral, February 3, 1988.

15. Corpus' version of events during the *Karagatan* episode was corroborated by Manila press accounts. See "*Karagatan* Gunrunner, PC Insists," *Manila Chronicle*, July 14, 1972, p. 1.

16. Author's interviews with Corpus, October 28, 1987, and May 19, 1988; and interview with Almendral, who was with NPA forces that received the *Karagatan* arms shipment, February 3, 1988.

17. Author's interview with Almendral, February 3, 1988; Kintanar was NPA commander in chief as of the late 1980s.

18. Author's interview with Corpus, May 18, 1988. Additional details were obtained from "Captured NPA Man Says Corpus Wounded—Dead?" *Philippines Herald*, September 15, 1972, p. 1.

19. Author's interview with Corpus, October 28, 1987.

20. Ibid.

21. Author's interview with Almendral, January 28, 1988.

22. Ibid.

23. Author's interview with Almendral, February 3, 1988.

24. Author's interview with Tony, March 23, 1988.

25. Ruth Firmeza (pseudonym), "Long March of the NPA in the Cagayan Valley (1976–1978)" (August 8, 1986). Firmeza was a northern Luzon CPP official and veteran of the period.

26. Ibid.

27. Author's interview with Tony, March 23, 1988.

28. Firmeza, "Long March of the NPA in the Cagayan Valley (1976–1978)."

CHAPTER 5

1. The description of the Plaza Miranda bombing was compiled from newspaper photographs and articles. See "LP Miranda Rally Bombed—9 Die," *Philippines Herald*, August 22, 1971, p. 1.

2. Ibid.

3. Author's interview with a founding Central Committee member, May 21, 1988.

4. The story of Plaza Miranda was told by several former ranking CPP officials—including four former Central Committee members—at the time privy to various aspects of the plan. I have protected the identity of my sources, at their request. In instances in which the information was not corroborated by a second or third source, I have identified the source by Party position in the notes. Most of the interviews regarding Plaza Miranda took place in 1987 and 1988. In early 1989, I talked at length with a former senior Party official who figured prominently in the Plaza Miranda episode and its aftermath. Although no longer an active CPP member, the person continued to be sympathetic to the revolution. This source corroborated most of the basic facts of this chapter.

5. The early 1971 meeting was described to the author by a former ranking CPP official who was briefed about the plot by one of those in attendance at the session. Author's interview, April 1988. I intentionally have not named the CPP finance officer present at the meeting. As of 1989, this person was a legal political activist who had been the target of death threats by right-wing extremists.

6. Author's interviews with a CPP official who was briefed by one of the principals on the actual plans and the justification of Party leaders for carrying

out the bombing, April 1988; and interview with a former Central Committee member who personally heard Sison's explanation, October 28, 1987.

7. Author's interview with a founding Central Committee member, May 21, 1988.

8. Author's interview with Corpus, May 18, 1988.

9. Ibid.

10. This profile of Danny Cordero was provided to the author by a former KM activist from Cordero's district, May 3, 1988; Cordero was named as the leader of the team that carried out the Plaza Miranda attack by three former Party veterans interviewed separately by the author in late 1987 and early 1988.

11. Author's interview with one of those present at the meeting, May 21, 1988. Reuben Guevarra was captured by the military in 1981 and in a voluminous statement detailed this meeting. In addition to interviewing Guevarra, the author interviewed a senior military officer who read the statement, May 18, 1988. I purposely have not identified the Politburo member who was CPP organizational department chairman at the time. As of 1989, this person was trying to build a career outside the Party.

12. Ibid.

13. Author's interview with Guevarra, May 21, 1988.

14. Author's interview with a former CPP official who was a member of the tribunal that tried Cordero, May 21, 1988.

15. Ibid.

16. Author's interviews with a former NPA officer in Isabela, January 28 and February 3, 1988; interviews with Corpus, October 28, 1987, and January 21, 1988; and interview with a member of the tribunal, May 21, 1988. Cordero's accomplices in the bombing were reportedly killed in the 1970s in encounters with the military.

17. Author's interview with a former CPP Central Committee member, May 17, 1988.

18. Ibid.

19. The Party official alluded to the Plaza Miranda bombing in his resignation letter. The official's resignation was first described to the author during a May 17, 1988, interview with a former CPP Central Committee member who read the resignation letter. In January 1989, the former Manila Party secretary confirmed his resignation during a conversation with the author. As of 1989, he was a successful professional living in Manila. I have not named the former CPP official in order to spare him and his family from possible attack by right-wing extremists.

20. See "Marcos Links Aquino to 'Subversives' Plot," *Philippines Herald*, August 25, 1971, p. 1. As already noted, Aquino did have close links with the Huks and the NPA forces operating in Tarlac, but politicians from both the Nacionalista and Liberal parties had similar contacts.

21. The question of whether Aquino had prior knowledge of the Plaza Miranda bombing remains an intriguing mystery. Aquino was at home when the attack occurred. Later that evening, he told reporters he had received a phoned threat earlier in the day that "they would get me," so he had stopped at his house

to don a bulletproof vest before proceeding to the rally. See "Aquino: They Said They Would Get Me," *Philippines Herald*, August 22, 1971, p. 1. Almost immediately, Aquino's absence from the rally spawned rumors that he had knowledge of the bombing or even had arranged it to eliminate challengers from within his party. Marcos and his loyalists—and possibly the more cunning minds within the CPP—fanned the rumors of Aquino's possible hand in the bombing. On one hand, since Aquino was the Liberal party leader most often mentioned as the likely successor to Marcos, he would have had little to gain by decimating the ranks of his party. But Aquino's contacts with the CPP were extensive, and it is not beyond the realm of possibility that one of Aquino's Communist Party contacts had given him at least vague details about an attack that would occur during the Plaza Miranda rally.

In 1989, a former CPP official who was the Manila Party secretary at the time of the bombing suggested to me that Aquino did have prior knowledge of the attack. The source offered no details, but urged me to look further into this possibility. The only detailed testimony I gathered alleging Aquino's complicity came from a source who was hardly impartial: Rolando Abadilla, Marcos' former military intelligence chief. In 1972, Abadilla had been the arresting officer of CPP Central Committee member Manuel Collantes. Collantes had cooperated with his military captors, divulging considerable information on the innerworkings of the CPP. Abadilla told me in February 1989 that Collantes had also disclosed the Party's responsibility for the Plaza Miranda bombing and had implicated Aquino in the plot. Abadilla quoted Collantes as saying that Aquino's private helicopter had been used to transport Danny Cordero and his two accomplices to Isabela following the bombing. While the story sounded farfetched, Abadilla offered enough information gleaned from his conversations with Collantes— details that dovetailed with information I had gathered from Party sources—to merit some credibility. I asked Abadilla why the military had not attempted to use its knowledge of CPP complicity in the Plaza Miranda bombing, and Aquino's possible involvement, for propaganda purposes during the 1970s. "It was during martial law, you know, and nobody was interested in Plaza Miranda," he replied. "Nobody wanted to hear about it." Author's interview with Rolando Abadilla, February 8, 1989.

22. Raymond Bonner, *Waltzing with a Dictator: The Marcoses and the Making of American Policy* (New York: Times Books, 1987), p. 80. In the days preceding martial law, it was a simple task to buy guns and other weapons, including grenades, on the arms black market in Manila. Even now, a surprising number of NPA weapons and ammunition are bought from government soldiers.

23. During the course of several hours of conversation in late 1987 and 1988, I found Corpus to be coherent and articulate. During that same period, Corpus wrote a book on counterinsurgency theory and government policies toward the guerrilla movement.

24. Author's interview with a founding CPP member, May 17, 1988.

25. Ibid.

26. Author's interview with a former Party activist, March 30, 1988.

CHAPTER 6

1. When I broached the subject of Chinese aid with Sison during an April 19, 1988, interview, he refused to even acknowledge that an official relationship between the Philippine rebels and China had ever existed.

2. Author's interview with a former CPP official who was close to Sison, April 18, 1988.

3. Ibid.

4. Ibid.

5. Author's interview with a member of the China delegation, April 18, 1988; and conversation with two other delegation members, November 15, 1988.

6. The China delegation members were Ibarra and Calay Tubianosa; Ricardo and Charito Malay; Carlos and Frances del Rosario; Mario and Alma Miclat; and Roger Arcilla. Carlos del Rosario disappeared before the group left for China and was believed to have been abducted and murdered by pro-Lava PKP agents. Author's interview with a former senior CPP official, January 31, 1988.

7. Author's interviews with a member of the China delegation, April 1988.

8. Author's interview with Malay, April 18, 1988.

9. Author's interview with a former ranking CPP official who was briefed beforehand about the Plaza Miranda plan, April 1988.

10. Ibid.

11. Ibid.

12. Ibid.

13. Author's interview with a former Central Committee member, March 29, 1988; and interview with a China delegation member, April 1988.

14. Ibid.

15. Author's interview with a *Karagatan* crew member, December 7, 1988.

16. Marcos is quoted in "FM Sends More Men to Isabela," *Manila Chronicle*, July 8, 1972, p. 1.

17. See "Man Relates Capture by Isabela NPAs," *Manila Chronicle*, July 13, 1972, p. 1.

18. Author's interviews with a member of the China delegation, April 1988.

19. Author's interviews with a member of the China delegation, April 1988; and interviews with two members of the NPA forces receiving the arms, October 28, 1987, and February 3, 1988.

20. Author's interviews with a member of the China delegation, April 1988, corroborated in conversations with two delegation members, November 2 and November 15, 1988.

21. Ibid. Eventually, some of the criticism directed at the Central Committee was accepted, and the leaders responsible for the *Karagatan* project, Sison included, agreed to "self-criticism." Author's interview with a senior CPP official in Manila at the time, January 31, 1988.

22. Author's interviews with a member of the China delegation, April 1988. The former Party official said Alcid was suffering from seasickness at the moment the ship ran aground.

23. Ibid.

24. Ibid. When I talked to Tubianosa 14 years later, on May 22, 1988, he used almost the same words, although not naming Sison. "Whoever did that bombing was a madman," he glowered.

25. Author's interviews with a member of the China delegation, April 1988.

26. Ibid.

27. Ibid.

28. Ibid.

29. Ibid.

30. Author's interviews and conversations with three members of the China delegation in April and November 1988.

31. In December 1975, leadership of the CPP delegation shifted to a pair of young radical students, Ericson Baculinao and Santiago Santa Romana, who had been stranded in China when martial law was declared and were subsequently assigned to the official CPP delegation.

CHAPTER 7

1. Escandor later died in the war, and a clandestine communist medical brigade in the greater Manila area was named for him. In 1989, Ragos was a UP liberal arts professor.

2. Author's interview with Tibbs, November 26, 1987.

3. Ibid.

4. Author's interview with Sotero Llamas, Bicol CPP secretary, February 16, 1988; and interview with Tibbs, November 26, 1987.

5. Ibid.

6. Author's interview with Tibbs, March 4, 1988.

7. Ibid.

8. Quoted in Alfred McCoy, *Priests on Trial* (Ringwood: Penguin Books Australia, 1984), p. 127.

9. The opening of the Negros front was reconstructed from the author's interview with Sison, April 19, 1988; interview with one of the first Negros cadres, December 20, 1987; and from "Communist Exploitation of Student Radicalism in the Philippines," *So the People May Know*, p. 322. Other details were reported in "PC Lines Up Ex-Huk, Wife as Witnesses," *Philippines Herald*, August 27, 1971, p. 1.

10. Author's interview with Jalandoni, April 14, 1988.

11. Author's interview with one of the original Negros CPP cadres, December 20, 1987.

12. Author's interview with Leny, a veteran CPP cadre who served on Mindanao from 1975 to 1985, March 30, 1988.

13. Author's interview with Leny, November 11, 1987.

14. Ibid.

CHAPTER 8

1. José María Sison, "Rectify Errors and Rebuild the Party," reprinted in *So the People May Know*, pp. 99–152.

2. "Specific Characteristics" incorporates some of Commander Dante's writings on guerrilla warfare in the chapter entitled, "Fighting in a Small Mountainous Archipelago." Author's interview with a former Luzon NPA commander, January 28, 1988.

3. Author's interview with Sotero Llamas, February 16, 1988.

4. Author's interview with a CPP cadre who served in Sorsogon in the early 1970s, November 26, 1987.

5. Ibid.; also author's interview with Llamas, February 16, 1988.

6. Author's interview with Llamas, February 16, 1988.

7. Ibid.; also author's interview with Sison, April 19, 1988.

8. Author's interview with a CPP cadre who had served in Bicol, November 26, 1987.

9. Ibid.; also author's interview with Llamas, February 16, 1988.

10. Ibid.

11. Author's interview with a former ranking CPP cadre, December 10, 1987.

12. Author's interview with a Visayas CPP official who had served on Samar, September 1987.

13. Ibid.

14. *Ang Bayan* (June 1984), p. 11.

15. Author's interview with Leny, a veteran CPP cadre who served in various regions of Mindanao, November 11, 1987.

16. Ibid.

17. Amado Guerrero, "Our Urgent Tasks," July 1976, reprinted in *Philippine Society and Revolution*, pp. 219–263.

CHAPTER 9

1. Author's interview with Omy, February 26, 1988.

2. Ibid.

3. Author's interview with a national Party cadre, October 3, 1987.

4. Author's interview with Aguilar, August 1987.

5. Ibid.

6. Author's interview with a member of the National Liaison Commission, February 7, 1988.

7. Cited in Bonner, *Waltzing with a Dictator*, p. 118; corroborated by author's interview with Sison, April 19, 1988.

8. Author's interview with Sison, April 19, 1988.

9. Author's interview with Sancho, October 14, 1987.

10. Ibid.

11. Author's interview with Omy, February 26, 1988.

12. Author's interview with Fortuna, February 7, 1988.

13. Ibid.

14. "What's Happening in the Philippines?" *Far East Reporter* (November 1976), p. 44.

15. Author's interview with a former CPP student activist in the late 1970s, February 5, 1988.

16. Guerrero, "Our Urgent Tasks," pp. 232–233.

17. Author's interview with a member of the CPP's Manila Regional Committee in the late 1970s, February 26, 1988.

CHAPTER 10

1. Author's interview with a member of the Manila Party Committee at the time, February 26, 1988.

2. Ibid.

3. Ibid.

4. Author's interview with a former CPP activist, February 5, 1988.

5. Manila-Rizal Executive Committee, "Our Tactical Slogan for the Present Phase of the Revolution" (August 1975), quoted in Armando Malay, Jr., "The Dialectics of Kaluwagan: Echoes of a 1978 Debate," *Marxism in the Philippines, Second Series* (Quezon City: Third World Studies Center, University of the Philippines, 1988), p. 11.

6. Guerrero, "Our Urgent Tasks," p. 233.

7. Author's interview with a member of the CPP's Manila-Rizal Party Committee at the time, February 29, 1988.

8. Ibid.

9. Ibid.

10. Author's interview with a Manila Party activist who had access to communications between the Central Committee and the Manila-Rizal Committee, February 5, 1988.

11. Ibid.

12. Author's interview with a member of the Manila Party Committee at the time, February 29, 1988.

13. Ibid.

14. Author's interview with a Manila CPP activist, February 5, 1988.

15. Author's interview with a Manila Party Committee member, February 29, 1988.

16. Ibid.

17. Ibid.

18. Ibid.

19. Author's interview with one of the author's of the Manila–Rizal Party Committee's arguments, February 29, 1988.

20. Ibid.

21. Central Committee, "In Reply to 'Our Tactical Slogan for This Phase of the Revolution,'" quoted in Malay, "The Dialectics," p. 14.

22. Author's interview with a member of the Group of 11, February 29, 1988.

23. Ibid.

24. Author's interview with a Manila CPP activist, February 5, 1988.

25. Author's interview with a member of the Group of 11, February 29, 1988.

26. Ibid.

27. Ibid.

28. Author's interview with a Manila Party Committee member captured in the raid, February 29, 1988.

29. Author's interview with Sotero Llamas, February 16, 1988.

CHAPTER 11

1. Gareth Porter, "The Politics of Counterinsurgency in the Philippines: Military and Political Options," Philippine Studies Occasional Paper no. 9 (Honolulu: Center for Philippine Studies, University of Hawaii, 1987), p. 19.

2. See Carolina G. Hernandez, "The Role of the Military in Contemporary Philippine Society," *Diliman Review* 32, no. 1 (January-February 1984), p. 20.

3. See Larry Niksch, "Insurgency and Counterinsurgency in the Philippines" (Washington, D.C.: Congressional Research Service, July 1, 1985), pp. 22–23.

4. See Porter, "The Politics of Counterinsurgency," pp. 21–23; Niksch, ibid., pp. 22–24.

5. Author's interview with Happy, an NPA company commander in northern Luzon, April 2, 1988.

6. Author's interview with Rodolfo Aguinaldo, August 28, 1985.

7. Happy's account of the incident was corroborated by Aguinaldo in an interview on August 28, 1985. From 1982 to 1986, Aguinaldo commanded a Scout Ranger detachment near Naddungan.

8. Author's interview with residents of Barangay Calaoagan, August 28, 1985.

9. Author's interview with Aguinaldo, August 28, 1985.

10. Author's interview with Happy, April 2, 1988.

11. Ibid. As much of Happy's story was corroborated by earlier interviews with Aguinaldo, I found no reason to doubt this story.

12. Author's interviews with Calaoagan residents, August 28, 1985.

13. Author's interview with Aguinaldo, August 28, 1985.

14. *Ang Bayan* (December 1983), p. 5.

15. *Ang Bayan* (March 1984), p. 6.

16. *Liberation* (March 1984), p. 5.

17. Author's interview with a CPP official who was previously a member of the Eastern Visayan Command, September 12, 1987.

CHAPTER 12

1. Author's interview with Lucas Fernández, a veteran CPP cadre and former Mindanao NDF chairman, December 30, 1987.

2. Ibid.

3. Author's interview with Mila Aguilar, a Mindanao cadre from 1974 to 1980, July 20, 1988.

4. Ibid.

5. Author's interview with Fernández, December 30, 1987.

6. Ibid.

7. "NPA in Mindanao Grows Stronger, Intensifies Guerrilla Warfare," *Ang Bayan* (June 1984), pp. 11–13.

8. Author's interview with Fernández, December 30, 1987.

9. Author's interview with Ignacio, November 12, 1984.

10. Marty Villalobos, "For a Politico-Military Framework" (February 23, 1987, unpublished), p. 20.

11. Author's interview with Fernández, December 30, 1987.

12. Villalobos, "For a Politico-Military Framework," p. 20.

13. For example, in February 1985, a Philippine Constabulary lieutenant was arrested and charged with heading a Davao robbery gang. "Davao Death Toll Now 120," *Bulletin Today*, February 21, 1985, p. 3.

14. Author's interview with O'Brien, July 27, 1985.

15. Agence France Press report carried in "Violence: No. 1 Killer," *We Forum*, October 5, 1985, p. 1.

16. Author's interview with O'Brien, July 27, 1985.

17. "Red Slogans Fill Davao Slum Area," *Bulletin Today*, December 18, 1984, p. 1.

18. Author's interview with Fernández, December 30, 1987.

19. See "Davao Death Toll in June Lowest in Last 6 Months," *Bulletin Today*, July 7, 1985, p. 4.

20. "897 Persons Killed in Davao City in '85," *Bulletin Today*, January 10, 1986, p. 5.

21. Author's interview with Fernández, December 30, 1987.

CHAPTER 13

1. Sison, "Rectify Errors and Rebuild the Party," pp. 149–151.

2. Sison, "Programme for a People's Democratic Revolution in the Philippines," reprinted in *So the People May Know*, pp. 32–80.

3. Author's interview with Morales, October 6, 1987.

4. *Ang Bayan* (March 29, 1980).

5. Author's interview with Morales, October 6, 1987.

6. *Ang Bayan* (December 31, 1981), p. 5.

7. Author's interview with Mila Aguilar, July 20, 1988.

8. Ibid.

9. Central Committee, Communist Party of the Philippines, "Overthrow the U.S.-Marcos Fascist Dictatorship: An Urgent Message to the Filipino People," *Ang Bayan* (October 7, 1983).

10. *Ang Bayan* (August 1984).

11. "When a Zigzag Turn Is Shorter than a Straight Route," *Praktika* 1, no. 1 (May 14, 1986), pp. 21–22.

12. See *Marxism in the Philippines*, p. 122.

13. "National Democratic Front 10 Point Program" (1977 draft), p. 1.

14. Author's interview with Tripon, July 20, 1988.

15. Ibid.

16. Author's discussions with several non-NDF sources involved in the founding of Bayan, 1985–1988.

17. The split within Bayan affected the Manila chapter and national leadership more than the provincial chapters, which continued to attract an array of noncommunist elements.

18. Author's interview with Aquino, August 6, 1985.

CHAPTER 14

1. See "Snap Election: A Point of View," *We Forum*, November 19–25, 1985, p. 7.

2. *Ang Bayan* (December 1985).

3. The meetings were described to the author by a Bayan official, February 8, 1988, and corroborated by Salas, August 26, 1988.

4. Author's interview with a Bayan official involved in the discussions, February 8, 1988.

5. "Some Clarifications," *Praktika* 1, no. 2 (August 1986), pp. 111–112.

6. CPP Executive Committee memorandum to Party cadres, quoted in "What CPP/NPA Say About Elections," *Mr. & Ms. (Special Edition)*, February 7–13, 1986, p. 9.

7. "When a Zigzag Turn Is Shorter than a Straight Route," p. 16.

8. Candy Quimpo, "Boycotters Not Vital to Final Count," *Mr. & Ms. (Special Edition)*, February 7–13, 1986, pp. 8–11.

9. See CPP Politburo memorandum to members of the Central Committee, "Resolution on the Party's Tactics Regarding the Snap Election," (May 7, 1986); and "When a Zigzag Turn Is Shorter than a Straight Route," *Praktika* 1, no. 1, p. 15.

10. Interview with a CPP cadre, cited in Porter, "The Politics of Counter-insurgency in the Philippines," p. 36.

11. Author's interview with Froiland Maureal, Southeastern Mindanao CPP Committee member at the time, April 5, 1987.

12. "When a Zigzag Turn Is Shorter than a Straight Route," p. 16.

13. Author's interview with Maureal, April 5, 1987.

14. An excellent account of the CPP debates of 1986–1987 is Porter, "The Politics of Counterinsurgency in the Philippines," pp. 32–49; another valuable resource is Alex Magno, "CPP: Rethinking the Revolutionary Process?" *Diliman Review* 34, no. 4 (1986), pp. 17–22.

15. Villalobos, "Where the Party Faltered: An Analysis of the Snap Polls and the February Uprising" (unpublished, undated CPP paper), p. 4.

16. Ibid., pp. 6–8.

17. Villalobos, "On the Insurrectional Strategy" (unpublished paper, March 30, 1986), p. 5.

18. "When a Zigzag Turn Is Shorter than a Straight Route," pp. 19–22.

19. "Resolution on the Party's Tactics Regarding the Snap Election."

20. "Resolution on the Present Situation and the Immediate Revolutionary Tasks," CPP Executive Committee, May 31, 1986.

21. NDF press conference attended by the author, May 17, 1987.

22. "Our Program for Mass Struggle from August to December 1987," CPP Executive Committee, August 7, 1987.

23. Author's interview with a Negros CPP cadre, August 6, 1988; also "The Outlaws of Negros," *Midweek*, July 27, 1988, pp. 3–9.

CHAPTER 15

1. Author's interview with Mitra, February 12, 1988.

2. Author's interviews with several CPP officials, 1987–1988.

3. "Negotiations About a Cease-fire," CPP Executive Committee, July 1986.

4. Press conference given by Zumel, quoted in a subsequent NDF statement, March 31, 1986, p. 1.

5. See "Armitage Says Communist Insurgency in RP Worsens," an Associated Press dispatch published in *Manila Times*, July 12, 1986, p. 1.

6. Author's interview with a well-placed U.S. Embassy source, December 4, 1986.

7. See "Cory Yields to 2 Enrile Demands," *Manila Chronicle*, October 23, 1986, p. 1.

8. See Gregg Jones, "Communist Rebels Offer A Cease-fire to Manila," *International Herald Tribune*, November 3, 1986, p. 1.

9. See "The President on a Tightrope," *Newsweek*, November 24, 1986.

10. See "Cease-fire Brings Dancing in the Streets," *Manila Chronicle*, December 11, 1986, p. 1.

11. "Reds Propose Power-sharing," *Business Day*, December 15, 1986.

12. Ibid.

13. Author's interviews with several CPP officials, 1987–1988.

14. See "Peace Talks Suspended," *Business Day*, January 23, 1987.

15. Author's interview with the businessperson, February 8, 1987.

16. "A Case of Ceasefire," a Defense Department position paper dated January 31, 1987, quoted in "How the Military Views the Ceasefire Collapse," *Manila Chronicle*, March 15, 1987.

CHAPTER 16

1. The description of the lives of Nueva Vizcaya peasants is based on the author's conversations with peasants and former farmers who had become NPA members, March 31–April 5, 1988.

2. Author's interview with the Nueva Vizcaya–Quirino Party secretary, April 1, 1988.

3. Author's interview with an NPA platoon commander who led the raid, April 2, 1988.

4. Author's interview with Bing, April 1, 1988.

5. Ibid.

6. See "Programme for a People's Democratic Revolution in the Philippines," pp. 32–80.

7. A member of the CPP's Bicol Agrarian Reform Committee told me that five years of campaigning for rent reductions in the region's six provinces had by 1987 resulted in more than 4,000 farmers paying less rent. More than 4,500 farm workers had been given wage increases because of NPA intervention. The CPP had redistributed to nearly 2,000 peasant families 4,665 hectares of land that had been abandoned, confiscated, or donated. Author's interview, February 16, 1988.

8. Author's interview with the Nueva Vizcaya–Quirino CPP secretary, April 1, 1988.

9. The peasant association operates on the legal and the underground levels. The CPP's underground organization for peasants is the PKM, one of 14 member organizations of the NDF.

10. See "Reaping the Bounty of Their Fields," *Liberation* (December 1987), pp. 3–5.

11. Ibid.

12. Author's interview with a member of the CPP's Bicol Agrarian Reform Committee, February 16, 1988.

13. Author's interview with a national CPP cadre, March 24, 1988.

14. On the eve of Aquino's 1987 signing of an agrarian reform decree, the Securities and Exchange Commission was flooded by applications for the registration of agribusiness firms. Most were owned by only four families. One familiy on Negros had established 44 firms. The families were frantically cutting up their landholdings and transferring ownership to new agribusiness firms— owned and controlled by family members and friends—in an effort to circumvent the agrarian reform measures. See "Evading Land Reform," *Ibon Facts and Figures,* July 15, 1987, p. 8.

15. The excluded tracts were commercial farmlands, including vast sugar and coconut estates. See José Galang, "Landlocked in Manila," *Far Eastern Economic Review,* October 6, 1988, p. 64.

16. See "CL Listasaka Disappointing," *Manila Chronicle,* December 19, 1988, p. 3.

CHAPTER 17

1. An account of the proceedings was provided to the author by witnesses, including a CPP cadre and two peasants, October 31, 1987.

2. Author's interview with Francisco, November 27, 1987.

3. Author's interview with Llamas, February 16, 1988.

4. Details of the CPP's collective farm plot project were related to the author by Dante, Eladio, and other peasants during two visits to Barangay Rose in October and November 1987.

CHAPTER 18

1. See Agoncillo, *A Short History of the Philippines,* pp. 259–260.

2. Author's interview with Nick Ruíz, March 24, 1988.

3. Edicio de la Torre, *Touching Ground, Taking Root* (Quezon City: Socio-Pastoral Institute, 1986), p. 102.

4. Author's interview with Brendan Cruz, founding CNL member, March 24, 1988.

5. Author's interview with Luís Jalandoni, a key figure in the CNL's growth on Negros and elsewhere, April 14, 1988.

6. Author's interview with Ruíz, August 24, 1988.

7. Ibid.

8. Ibid.

9. Author's interview with Jalandoni, April 14, 1988.

10. McCoy, *Priests on Trial*, p. 125.

11. Author's interview with Jalandoni, April 14, 1988.

12. Ibid.

13. Ibid.

14. Author's interview with Ruíz, August 24, 1988.

15. Ibid.

16. Ibid.

17. Jalandoni was captured in September 1973 and upon his release went to Europe to establish an international NDF office.

18. Author's interview with Ruíz, August 24, 1988.

19. McCoy, *Priests on Trial*, p. 169.

20. Quoted in ibid., p. 202.

21. Ibid., pp. 203–204.

22. Author's interview with Brendan Cruz, who was a member of the committee, March 24, 1988.

23. Author's interview with Jalandoni, April 14, 1988.

24. Author's interview with Cruz, March 24, 1988.

25. Ibid. I have not named the organization to protect innocent members.

26. Author's interview with Cruz, March 22, 1988. Although it is impossible to accurately determine actual membership, the figures do not seem to be extravagantly inflated.

27. Author's interview with a regional CPP cadre, December 22, 1987.

28. Ibid.

29. Author's interview with Cruz, March 24, 1988.

30. Author's interview with Jalandoni, April 14, 1988.

CHAPTER 19

1. See "CPP Controls 341 Unions in Metro," *Daily Globe*, April 29, 1988, p. 1. These unions included an estimated 1,400 CPP members.

2. Author's interview with Bani, February 5, 1988. I have decided not to name the unions or factories discussed in this chapter to protect my source.

3. Ibid.

4. Ibid. I have not used the name of the factory and its precise location to avoid retribution against union members.

CHAPTER 20

1. Author's interview with the Southern Tagalog regional NPA commander, November 27, 1987.

2. Ibid.

3. The section on romance is taken from the author's interviews with several Party members in 1987 and 1988.

4. Author's interview with a CPP cadre, December 26, 1987.

5. Author's interview with Maya, August 6, 1988.

CHAPTER 21

1. Author's interview with Bing, April 1, 1988.

2. The AFP's helicopters posed difficulties for the NPA, but budget constraints significantly curtailed the use of its air superiority. Shortages of spare parts and fuel further restricted use of gunships against rebel forces. To give an idea of how limited the AFP's air capabilities were as of 1988, the entire Northern Luzon Command had only five helicopter gunships to cover a 13-province area with perhaps the highest incidence of guerrilla activity in the Philippines.

3. I saw no evidence to give credence to government claims that much of the NPA's support was the result of coercion. Nevertheless, in some areas peasants were motivated by fear to give food and shelter to the NPA. "We have no choice," explained a peasant on Mindanao. "The NPAs pass by our house . . . [and] they are courteous. Sometimes they ask for food. I give—why not? Besides, I'm afraid to refuse because they have arms." Quoted in "Zamboanga Caught Between the Red and the Right," *Mr. & Ms. (Special Edition)*, September 28–October 4, 1984, p. 35.

4. Author's interview with guerrillas who participated in the raid, March 11, 1988. The account was largely corroborated by official reports.

5. Author's interview with Gregorio Rosal, March 9, 1988.

6. Author's interview with the regional NPA commander, November 27, 1987.

7. Author's interview with a Negros CPP cadre, August 6, 1988.

8. Author's interview with the CPP's Southern Tagalog regional secretary, March 4, 1988.

9. NPA high-powered-rifle strength in early 1989 was estimated to be anywhere from 7,300 to 10,000. The lower figure was given in captured CPP documents in 1988; the higher figure was cited by the NPA in a twentieth anniversary statement.

10. The movement's policy on "revolutionary taxation" is spelled out in a 1987 position paper, "On NDF Tax Policy" (unpublished). According to this document, "small- and medium-scale businessmen and manufacturers . . . are not subject to the 'class enemy tax.'" Furthermore, "big businessmen and landowners" who support the revolution are exempted from the class enemy tax (pp. 1–3).

11. The AFP estimated in late 1987 that the NPA was collecting about $100,000 a month from the logging industry in Cagayan province alone. See John Peterman,

"Mixed Military Results," *Far Eastern Economic Review*, November 26, 1987, p. 39.

12. The author had access to transcripts and summarized notes from the captured disks.

13. Author's interview with Bing, the CPP regional secretary, April 4, 1988.

14. It was several days before the CPP took credit for the attacks, and subsequent conversations with several Party cadres and officials—as well as the captured computer disks—led me to conclude that the particular men killed had been targeted by local units and that the national CPP leadership was embarrassed by the apparent mixup. They were not the first U.S. citizens to die in the war. In April 1974, the NPA ambushed and killed three U.S. Navy Seabees outside Subic Bay Naval Base north of Manila. In an August 10, 1988, interview, Rodolfo Salas, who planned the ambush, told me the Seabees had been killed because their unit had bulldozed six barrios surrounding Subic to make way for base improvements. Salas said that before martial law the NPA had killed "two or three" GIs outside Clark Air Force Base.

15. Author's interview with a member of the NPA Manila Regional Command, December 17, 1987.

16. Ibid.

17. Author's interview with Gregorio Rosal, March 9, 1988.

18. Author's interview with a Negros cadre, August 6, 1988.

19. Author's interview with Rosal, March 9, 1988.

CHAPTER 22

1. The highest CPP policymaking body is the Central Committee, believed to number 29 members as of the late 1980s. Members are widely dispersed, as are members of the Politburo, which has between 11 and 15 members. As a result, day-to-day leadership falls to the 5-member Executive Committee, which comprises the Party's highest ranking officials.

2. Author's conversation with Aquino, October 1987.

3. Author's interviews with two former CPP officials who knew Tiamzon during the early 1970s, December 10, 1987, and February 29, 1988.

4. Author's interview with Rodolfo Salas, August 26, 1988; and interview with a CPP official who knew Tiamzon during the 1970s, February 29, 1988.

5. Author's interview with a former senior CPP official, December 10, 1987.

6. Ross H. Munro, "The New Khmer Rouge," *Commentary* 80 (December 1985), pp. 19–38.

7. Author's interview with a former CPP Central Committee member, July 20, 1988.

8. When Rivera was captured several months later, the letter from Salas was found in his possession. Sources close to Salas confirmed its authenticity.

9. As CPP United Front Commission chairman, Reyes had advocated "an expansive united front," which had brought him into bitter conflict with Salas. Author's interview with a former ranking CPP official, February 21, 1988. A former senior CPP official close to Salas told me that Reyes had been placed

under a cloud by his claim that he had been arrested by police in suburban Manila in November 1986, only to escape hours later. According to this source, Reyes was removed from the Executive Committee and transferred to the Visayas. Author's interview, March 29, 1988.

10. Quoted in Munro, "The New Khmer Rouge," p. 31.

11. Author's interview with a CPP official who was present, December 30, 1988.

12. Ibid.

13. Ibid.

14. Author's interview with Nemenzo, January 17, 1988.

15. Author's interview with Ocampo, November 12, 1986.

16. The account of Carolina Malay's political radicalization was drawn from the author's conversations during 1986–1989 with Malay, her mother, Paula, and Teodoro Benigno, a Filipino journalist who was studying with Malay in Paris during the late 1960s.

17. Author's conversation with Paula Malay, February 23, 1988.

18. Author's interview with Nemenzo, January 17, 1988.

CHAPTER 23

1. Author's interview with Fely, January 10, 1988.

2. Author's interview with a senior CPP official, December 30, 1987.

3. Ibid. This Party official was previously a member of the CPP's Mindanao Commission. Later, he participated in the Central Committee's investigation of the Mindanao infiltration and purge.

4. Ibid.

5. Ibid.

6. Ibid.

7. Author's conversation with Williams, August 18, 1988. Ms. Williams made available to the author taped interviews.

8. Author's interview with a veteran CPP cadre, November 11, 1987.

9. Author's interview with Aroma, January 10, 1988.

10. Author's interview with a senior CPP official, December 30, 1987.

11. For a more detailed description of the CPP organization in Punta Dumalag, see William Chapman, Inside the Philippine Revolution (New York: Norton, 1987), pp. 143–153.

12. Author's interviews with a national CPP cadre in 1988; and interview with two foreign missionaries sympathetic to the NDF, January 10, 1988.

13. Author's conversation with a journalist who accompanied Solarz, January 10, 1988.

14. See Munro, "The New Khmer Rouge," pp. 19–38.

CHAPTER 24

1. Author's interview with a senior CPP official, March 4, 1988.

2. See "Programme for a People's Democratic Revolution," pp. 32–80.

3. Author's interview with a senior CPP official, March 4, 1988. The Party official said "quite a number" of cadres were in Nicaragua studying problems the revolution had encountered after victory.

4. Author's interview with Salas, August 26, 1988.

5. See "Our Vision of a Just and Democratic Society" (NDF Publishing House, 1987), p. 7.

6. Ocampo was responding to written questions submitted by the *Far Eastern Economic Review* in November 1987. His responses were made available to the author.

7. Author's interview with Cruz, March 24, 1988.

8. Author's interview with Salas, August 26, 1988.

9. Author's interview with a CPP regional secretary, March 4, 1988.

10. See "Freedom of Religion Is an Inalienable Right," *Liberation* (September–October 1988), pp. 7–8.

11. Ibid.

12. See "Our Vision of a Just and Democratic Society," p. 22.

CHAPTER 25

1. Author's interview with Kulas, December 25, 1987.

CHAPTER 26

1. Author's interview with a national CPP cadre, September 2, 1988.

2. These comments are taken from captured CPP computer disks, the transcripts of which were viewed by the author.

3. Author's interview with a national CPP cadre, September 2, 1988.

4. Author's interview with Llamas, February 16, 1988.

5. Author's interview with Brendan Cruz, CNL spokesperson, March 24, 1988.

6. Author's interview with a senior CPP official, March 4, 1988.

7. Author's interview with Jalandoni, April 14, 1988.

8. Ibid.

9. Author's interview with a national CPP cadre, September 4, 1988.

10. See "Local Rebels Will Not Get Surplus Arms from Vietnam," *Manila Chronicle*, December 3, 1988, p. 3.

11. Author's interview with Jalandoni, April 14, 1988.

12. Ibid.

13. Ibid.

14. Author's interview with Rodolfo Aguinaldo, August 5, 1988.

15. Author's interview with three fellow officers, all friends of the victim, September 8, 1987.

16. Author's interview with a senior CPP official, March 4, 1988.

17. Author's interview with Llamas, February 16, 1988.

18. Author's interview with Rosal, March 9, 1988.

19. Author's interview with Bing, April 4, 1988.

20. World Bank, *The Philippine Poor: What Is to Be Done?* (Washington, D.C.: World Bank, 1988).

21. See José Galang, "The Coconut Crisis," *Far Eastern Economic Review*, November 24, 1988, pp. 72–73.

22. Aquino has repeatedly declared she will not run for reelection when her term expires in 1992. There is debate over whether the Philippine constitution approved in 1987 bars Aquino from seeking a second term.

Glossary

agaw armas: Literally "grab guns," the communist tactic of attacking individual or small groups of police or security personnel in order to capture their weapons; devised by the New People's Army command in the 1970s in an effort to increase the communist arsenal.

Alsa Masa: The anticommunist vigilante organization formed in Davao's Agdao slum in early 1986. The organization became the prototype for hundreds of anticommunist vigilante groups that were formed in the Philippines between 1986 and 1988.

Ang Bayan: The official publication of the Communist Party of the Philippines, produced clandestinely in Manila by the CPP Central Committee.

armed propaganda unit: The smallest unit of the New People's Army, made up of 7 to 10 lightly armed members, whose task is to propagandize and organize rural villagers.

banca: A small outrigger canoe.

barangay: The smallest administrative unit in the Philippines, roughly equivalent to a rural village or urban neighborhood.

barrio: A rural village.

bibingka: Sweetened rice cake.

cadre: A Communist Party member who has undergone specialized training and who is assigned to a position of political and administrative leadership.

carabao: Water buffalo.

fast-track insurrection theory: Strategy developed by the CPP's Mindanao Commission in 1983 that called for the quick seizure of power by fomenting urban uprisings in lieu of a lengthy NPA general offensive in the countryside.

First Quarter Storm: A series of violent student-led demonstrations in Manila that began in January 1970 and lasted until March 1970. The demonstrations were loosely directed and manipulated by the CPP.

fugasse: A crude anti-tank device developed by the NPA, constructed of a steel or bamboo tube packed with gunpowder and shrapnel. The tube is positioned alongside a road and is command-detonated when an army tank or troop carrier passes by.

hacendero: The wealthy owner of a large plantation, usually referring to the owner of a sugar hacienda in the Philippines.

hacienda: A large plantation or ranch.

hopia: A small pastry, usually filled with sweetened bean paste.

kaingero: An upland slash-and-burn farmer, among the poorest of the Philippine peasantry.

kamote: A starchy tuber, easily cultivated, that is a major food source for Philippine peasants and urban poor.

kasama: Roughly translated as comrade, a respectful term to address elders; adopted by Filipino communists to refer to all members of the revolutionary movement.

Liberation: The official publication of the National Democratic Front, produced clandestinely in Manila.

masa: The mass base or pool of lower-class supporters of the revolutionary movement.

pancit: Thin rice noodles.

pera-frente-bahay: Literally "money-front-house," a derogatory term used by some CPP cadres in the early 1980s to describe the Party's unwillingness to develop working alliances with middle- and upper-class supporters in Manila.

sacada: A seasonal field-worker on a sugar plantation.

salvaging: A term used to describe extrajudicial killings, usually connoting those murders carried out by Philippine security forces.

sparrow unit: NPA assassination squad, usually composed of three members.

welgang bayan: Literally "people's strike," the CPP's answer to the general strike of more developed nations. It is a combination of work stoppages and coordinated demonstrations and rallies. The first *welgang bayan* was carried out in Davao in August 1984.

Bibliography

BOOKS AND MONOGRAPHS

Agoncillo, Teodoro A. *Filipino Nationalism: 1872–1970.* Quezon City: R. P. Garcia Publishing, 1974.

———. *A Short History of the Philippines.* New York: Mentor, 1975.

Agoncillo, Teodoro A., and Milagros C. Guerrero. *History of the Filipino People.* Quezon City: R. P. Garcia Publishing, 1977.

Aguirre, Alexander P., with Ismael Z. Villareal. *Readings on Counterinsurgency.* Quezon City: Pan Service Masters Consultants, 1987.

Area Handbook for the Philippines, 2nd ed. Washington, D.C.: GPO, 1976.

Bain, David Haward. *Sitting in Darkness: Americans in the Philippines.* Boston: Houghton Mifflin, 1984.

Bonner, Raymond. *Waltzing with a Dictator: The Marcoses and the Making of American Policy.* New York: Times Books, 1987.

Bresnan, John, ed. *Crisis in the Philippines: The Marcos Era and Beyond.* Princeton, N.J.: Princeton University Press, 1986.

Buss, Claude A. *The Arc of Crisis.* Garden City, N.Y.: Doubleday, 1961.

Chapman, William. *Inside the Philippine Revolution.* New York: Norton, 1987.

Constantino, Renato. *The Filipinos in the Philippines and Other Essays.* Filipinia Reprint Series. Mandaluyong: Cacho Hermanos, 1985.

———. *The Nationalist Alternative,* 2nd ed. Quezon City: Foundation for Nationalist Studies, 1984.

———. *The Philippines: A Past Revisited.* Manila: Renato Constantino, 1975.

———, ed. *M.A.N.'s Goal: The Democratic Filipino Society.* Quezon City: Malaya Books, 1969.

———. *Recto Reader.* Manila: Recto Memorial Foundation, 1983.

Constantino, Renato, and Letizia Constantino. *The Philippines: The Continuing Past.* Manila: Foundation for Nationalist Studies, 1978.

The Filipino People Will Triumph! Conversations with Filipino Revolutionary Leaders. Communist Party of the Philippines, Central Publishing House (location unknown), 1988.

Friend, Theodore. *Between Two Empires.* New Haven, Conn.: Yale University Press, 1965.

Guerrero, Amado (José María Sison). *Philippine Society and Revolution*. Oakland: International Association of Filipino Patriots, 1979.

Jenkins, Shirley. *American Economic Policy Toward the Philippines*. Stanford, Calif.: Stanford University Press, 1954.

Kasama. Makati: International Concerns for Philippine Struggles, 1987.

Kerkvliet, Benedict J. *The Huk Rebellion: A Study of Peasant Revolt in the Philippines*. Quezon City: New Day Publishers, 1979.

Lachica, Eduardo. *HUK: Philippine Agrarian Society in Revolt*. Manila: Solidaridad Publishing, 1971.

Lenin, V. I. *State and Revolution*. New York: International Publishers, 1981.

_____. *What Is to Be Done?* New York: International Publishers, 1978.

McCoy, Alfred W. *Priests on Trial*. Ringwood, Australia: Penguin Books, 1984.

McLellan, David. *Marxism After Marx*. Boston: Houghton Mifflin, 1981.

Malay, Armando, Jr. "The Dialectics of Kaluwagan." *Marxism in the Philippines, Second Series*. Quezon City: University of the Philippines, Third World Studies Center, 1988.

Mao Zedong. *Quotations from Chairman Mao Zedong (Little Red Book)*. New York: Universal-Award House, 1971.

Mijares, Primitivo. *The Conjugal Dictatorship of Ferdinand and Imelda Marcos*. San Francisco: Union Square, 1976.

Nemenzo, Franciso, "Rectification Process in the Philippine Communist Movement," *Armed Communist Movements in Southeast Asia*, edited by Lim Joo-Jock and S. Vani. Hampshire, England: Gower, 1984.

Pomeroy, William J., ed. *Guerrilla Warfare and Marxism*. New York: International Publishers, 1968.

Porter, Gareth. "The Politics of Counterinsurgency in the Philippines: Military and Political Options." Philippine Studies Occasional Paper no. 9. Honolulu: Center for Philippine Studies, University of Hawaii, 1987.

Rosario, Simeon G. del. *Surfacing the Underground*. Quezon City: Republic of the Philippines, nd., Part II, vol. 1.

Saulo, Alfred B. *Communism in the Philippines: An Introduction*. Manila: Ateneo de Manila Publications, 1969.

Scaff, Alvin H. *The Philippine Answer to Communism*. Stanford, Calif.: Stanford University Press, 1955.

Schirmer, Daniel Boone, and Stephen Shalom, eds. *The Philippine Reader: A History of Colonialism, Neocolonialism, Dictatorship, and Resistance*. Boston: South End Press, 1987.

Schott, Joseph L. *The Ordeal of Samar*. Manila: Solar, 1986.

Simbulan, Roland G. *The Bases of Our Insecurity: A Study of the U.S. Military Bases in the Philippines*. Manila: Balai Fellowship, 1983.

Simons, Lewis M. *Worth Dying For*. New York: Morrow, 1987.

Smith, Joseph B. *Portrait of a Cold Warrior*. Quezon City: Plaridel Books, 1987.

So the People May Know. Quezon City: Armed Forces of the Philippines, 1970.

Sturtevant, David R. *Popular Uprisings in the Philippines, 1840–1940*. Ithaca, N.Y.: Cornell University Press, 1976.

Taber, Robert. *The War of the Flea: A Study of Guerrilla Warfare Theory and Practice.* St. Albans: Granada, 1977.

The Theology of Liberation. Quezon City: Claretian Publications, 1986.

Torre, Edicio de la. *Touching Ground, Taking Root: Theological and Political Reflections on the Philippine Struggle.* Quezon City: Socio-Pastoral Institute, 1986.

Wilson, Dick. *Mao: The People's Emperor.* London: Futura, 1980.

REPORTS, PAMPHLETS, ARTICLES, AND MILITARY DOCUMENTS

Bayani, Samuel P. (pseudonym). "What's Happening in the Philippines? Background and Perspectives on the Liberation Struggle," *Far East Reporter* (November 1976), pp. 1–57.

Clad, James. "Anatomy of a Red Revolution." *Far Eastern Economic Review,* July 28, 1988, pp. 12–14.

"COIN (Counterinsurgency) Appraisal Report for 1st Qtr CY 88." Quezon City: Armed Forces of the Philippines intelligence report, classified secret. May 10, 1988.

The Communist Insurgency in the Philippines. Manila: Republic of the Philippines, 1985.

Conger, E. E., A. H. Peterson, and G. C. Reinhardt, eds. "Symposium on the Role of Airpower in Counterinsurgency and Unconventional Warfare: The Philippine Huk Campaign." Santa Monica, Calif.: Rand Corporation, July 1963.

"CPP/NDF Disinformation, Propaganda and Fund-raising Activities Abroad." Quezon City: Confidential Armed Forces of the Philippines Intelligence report, November 1987.

"CPP/NPA Strength and Armaments" and "Summary of Combat Statistics— 1st Quarter 1988." Quezon City: Intelligence Service of the Armed Forces of the Philippines, documents classified as secret, first quarter, 1988.

"Evading Land Reform." *Ibon Facts and Figures,* July 15, 1987, p. 8.

Galang, José. "Landlocked in Manila." *Far Eastern Economic Review,* October 6, 1988.

———. "The Coconut Crisis." *Far Eastern Economic Review,* November 24, 1988. pp. 72–73.

Hernandez, Carolina G. "The Role of the Military in Contemporary Philippine Society." *Diliman Review* 32, no. 1 (January-February 1984).

"The Insurgency Situation in the Philippines." Quezon City: A confidential intelligence report of the Philippine Constabulary/Integrated National Police, February 12, 1988.

Leighton, Richard M., Ralph Sanders, and José N. Tinio. "The Huk Rebellion: A Case Study in the Social Dynamics of Insurrection," Publication no. R-231. Washington, D.C.: Industrial College of the Armed Forces, March 1964.

Lorimer, Norman, "Philippine Communism—An Historical Overview." *Journal of Contemporary Asia* 7, no. 4, (1977), pp. 462–485.

Magno, Alex. "CPP: Rethinking the Revolutionary Process?" *Diliman Review* 34, no. 4 (1986), pp. 17–22.

MAKIBAKA: Join Us in Struggle! London: Friends of the Philippines, 1978.

"Memorandum of Agreement on a Preliminary Ceasefire." Manila: Document drafted and signed by the Republic of the Philippines and the National Democratic Front, 1986.

Munro, Ross H. "The New Khmer Rouge." *Commentary* 80 (December 1985), pp. 19–38.

Niksch, Larry. "Insurgency and Counterinsurgency in the Philippines." Washington, D.C.: Congressional Research Service, Library of Congress, July 1, 1985.

Peterman, John. "Mixed Military Results." *Far Eastern Economic Review*, November 26, 1987, p. 39.

Pimentel, Benjamin. "The Outlaws of Negros." *Midweek*, July 27, 1988, pp. 3–9.

Porter, Gareth. "Philippine Communism After Marcos." *Problems of Communism* 36 (September-October 1987), pp. 14–35.

Quimpo, Candy. "Boycotters Not Vital to Final Count." *Mr. & Ms. (Special Edition)*, February 7–13, 1986, pp. 8–11.

_____. "What CPP/NPA Say About Elections." *Mr. & Ms. (Special Edition)*, February 7–13, 1986, pp. 8–9.

Salas, Rodolfo. Letter to Juanito Rivera, May 1, 1987.

Shalom, Stephen R. "Counter-Insurgency in the Philippines." *Journal of Contemporary Asia* 7, no. 2 (1977), pp. 153–177.

Sison, José María, "Lectures on Philippine Crisis and Revolution." Delivered at the Asian Center, University of the Philippines, 1986.

"Special Report on the NDF's International Strategy and Tactics." Classified document of the Philippine National Intelligence Coordinating Agency, December 1987.

"Vigilantes in the Philippines: A Threat to Democratic Rule." New York: Lawyers Committee for Human Rights, 1988.

World Bank. *The Philippine Poor: What Is to Be Done?* Washington, D.C.: World Bank, 1988.

CPP, NPA, AND NDF DOCUMENTS, POSITION PAPERS, AND PUBLICATIONS

Alex Boncayao Brigade, New People's Army-National Capital Region. Press statement, April 11, 1987.

Ang Bayan 13, no. 23 (December 31, 1981).

_____ 15, no. 5 (July 1983).

_____ 15, no. 10 (December 1983).

_____ 16, no. 1 (March 1984).

_____ 16, no. 4 (June 1984).

_____ 16, no, 6 (August 1984).

_____ 16, no. 9 (November 1984).

———— 17, no. 2 (April 1985).
———— 18, no. 9 (November 1986).
————. Special Release (November 14, 1986).
————. Special Release (November 16, 1986).
———— 19, no. 2 (April 1987).
———— 19, no 4 (June 1987).
————. Special Release (July 7, 1987).
————. Special Release (August 29, 1987).
———— 19, no. 7 (September 1987).
———— 19, no. 8 (October 1987).
———— 19, no. 9 (November 1987).
———— 19, no. 10 (December 1987).
———— 19, no. 11 (January 1988).
————. Special Release (January 12, 1988).
———— 19, no. 12 (February 1988).
———— 20, no. 1 (March 1988).
———— 20, no. 2 (April 1988).
———— 20, no. 3 (May 1988).
———— 20, no. 4 (June 1988).
———— 20, no. 5 (July 1988).
————. Special Release (August 1, 1988).
"Economic Upliftment of the Masses Is the Road to Peace." CPP/NPA/NDF position paper, Negros Island, June 8, 1986.
Fernández, Frank, and Celso Magsilang. "The Burning of the DYHM and DYEZ Transmitters: A Response to a Challenge (An Open Letter)." NDF Negros Island, NPA Negros Island Regional Operation Command, July 31, 1988.
Firmeza, Ruth (pseudonym). "Long March of the NPA in the Cagayan Valley (1976–1978)." CPP document, August 8, 1986.
"General Program of the Cordillera Peoples' Democratic Front." Revised draft, December 1986.
"General Program of the National Democratic Front." Undated.
Guerrero, Amado (José María Sison). "Our Urgent Tasks." July 1, 1976. Reprinted in *Philippine Society and Revolution*.
————. "Specific Characteristics of Our People's War." December 1, 1974. Reprinted in *Philippine Society and Revolution*.
Kalatas. Official organ of the National Democratic Front, Southern Tagalog, November-December 1987.
Liberation 13, no. 2 (March-April 1985).
———— 13, no. 3 (May-June 1985).
————. Special Issue no. 1 (August 21, 1985).
———— 13, no. 5 (September-October 1985).
————. Special Issue no. 2 (September 11, 1985).
————. Special Issue no. 3 (September 21, 1985).
————. Special Issue no. 4 (October 21, 1985).
———— 14, no. 2 (February-March 1986).
———— 14, no. 3 (April-May 1986).

———— 14, no. 4 (June 1986).
———— 14, no. 5 (July-August 1986).
———— 14, no. 6 (August 21, 1986).
———— 14, no. 7 (September 1986).
————. Special Issue no. 1 (September 1986).
———— 14, no. 8 (December 15, 1986).
———— 15, no. 1 (January 1, 1987).
———— 15, no. 3 (June-July 1987).
———— 15, no. 5 (September 1987).
———— 15, no. 6 (October-November 1987).
———— 15, no. 7 (December 1987).
———— 16, no. 1 (January-February 1988).
———— 16, no. 2 (March-April 1988).
———— 16, no. 4 (July-August 1988).
———— 16, no. 5 (September-October 1988).
———— 16, no. 6 (November-December 1988).
"Living Out the Passion, Death, and Resurrection of the Filipino People." A primer on the Christians for National Liberation, undated.
Luchar, Carlos (pseudonym). "Wishing to Go South by Driving the Chariot North Is Forfeiting Victory: A Position Paper on the Draft 1986 Constitution," December 1986.
Manalo, Pepe (pseudonym). "Political Strategy and the Political Negotiations." Draft position paper, January 17, 1987.
National Democratic Front. "A Statement Condemning Fraud and Terrorism," February 13, 1986.
————. "NDF Business Collective Condemns Fraud," February 13, 1986.
————. "NDF Hails People's Ouster of Marcos," February 28, 1986.
————. "NDF Calls for Vigilance Against U.S. Meddling," March 8, 1986.
————. "NDF Declares Openness to Ceasefire," March 21, 1986.
————. "NDF Declares Openness to a Ceasefire," March 31, 1986.
————. "NDF Calls on Filipino People to Condemn Barbaric U.S. Attacks on the Libyan People," April 19, 1986.
————. "Why the Fighting Goes On," April 28, 1986.
————. "Beware U.S. Officials Bearing Gifts," May 9, 1986.
————. "NDF Names Emissary," May 28, 1986.
————. "Ocampo Accepts Emissary Task," June 10, 1986.
————. "An Open Letter," from Satur C. Ocampo, June 10, 1986.
————. "The Government Must Create the Climate for Peace," August 31, 1986.
————. "NDF Restates Position on Ceasefire," September 8, 1986.
————. "Two Years After: Carry on the Struggle to Victory (Statement on the Occasion of the Second Anniversary of the February 1986 Events)," February 24, 1988.
————. "On the State of the Nation," July 24, 1988.
————. "Get Rid of the U.S. Bases Now!" July 26, 1988.
————. "National Democratic Front 10 Point Program." 1977 draft.
————. "The NDF Philippines: A Profile." Undated.

————. "On NDF Tax Policy." Unpublished position paper, 1987.

"Negotiations About a Cease-fire." CPP Executive Committee, July 1986.

"On the Electoral Campaign." Central Committee guidelines on legislative elections, March 1987.

"An Open Letter: To Our Beloved Filipino People." Christians for National Liberation, National Council, February 17, 1988.

"Our Program for Mass Struggle from August to December 1987." CPP Executive Committee, August 7, 1987.

"Our Vision of a Just and Democratic Society: A Primer on the General Program of the National Democratic Front of the Philippines." NDF Publishing House (location unknown), March 1987.

Praktika 1, no. 1 (May 14, 1986).

Praktika 1, no. 2 (August 1986).

"Resolution on the Party's Tactics Regarding the Snap Election." CPP Political Bureau, May 7, 1986.

"Resolution on the Present Situation and the Immediate Revolutionary Tasks." CPP Executive Committee, May 31, 1986.

"Revolutionary Guide on Land Reform." Central Committee, Communist Party of the Philippines, revised, 1977.

Sison, José María. "Rectify Errors and Rebuild the Party." Reprinted in *So the People May Know*.

"Statement on President Aquino's Call for a Ceasefire." Military Commission, Communist Party of the Philippines and General Staff, New People's Army, March 18, 1986.

Victoria, Carol (pseudonym). "A Reply to the Resolution." Draft position paper, September 1986.

Villalobos, Marty (pseudonym). "For a Politico-Military Framework." Draft position paper, February 23, 1987.

————. "Notes on the Coming Elections." Unpublished paper, March 10, 1987.

————. "On the Insurrectional Strategy." Unpublished paper, March 30, 1986.

————. "Parallelisms: The Philippines Now and El Salvador in 1979–80." Draft position paper, undated.

————. "Where the Party Faltered: An Analysis of the Snap Polls and the February Uprising." Undated.

"Why Lt. Victor Corpus Left the AFP to Join the New People's Army." Manila: Gintong Silahis Publications, 1971.

NEWSPAPERS

Atlanta Constitution
Bulletin Today
Business Day
International Herald Tribune
Manila Chronicle

New York Times
Philippine Daily Globe
Philippine Daily Inquirer
Philippines Herald
Washington Post

Index

Abaya, Hernando, 20
Adam (communist peasant), 293
Afable, Jaíme, 272
AFP. *See* Armed Forces of the Philippines
Aga (guerrilla), 248–249
Agaw armas campaign, 8
Agcaoili, Fidel, 75
Agdao (Davao slum), 140–141, 268–269, 274
Agoncillo, Teodoro, 26, 43
Agrarian reform, 12, 21, 22, 31, 32, 41, 99, 177, 182–183, 280
   NPA, 176–181, 182, 314
Aguilar, Mila, 105–106, 147
Aguinaldo, Emilio, 20
Aguinaldo, Rodolfo, 307
Agusan del Norte province, 266–267, 302
Agusan de Sur province, 302
Aidit, D. N., 72
Albania, 277
Albay province, 90, 99, 100
Alcid, Edwin, 75, 76, 78
Alejandro, Leandro, 152, 300
Aleng (CPP cadre), 56
Alex Boncayao Brigade, 248
Alliance of Urban Poor, 135
Almendral, Ariel, 49, 64
Alsa Masa, 268, 269, 270, 271–273, 274
Amy (peasant), 186, 188, 189, 190, 191, 192, 194
Andrea (ship), 78–79, 82

Ang Bayan (CPP newspaper), 105, 150, 156, 161, 250
Angola, 304
Anticommunist vigilantes, 7, 124–125, 240, 268, 269, 273–274, 292, 296, 299, 300. *See also* Alsa Masa
Apo Hiking Society, 169
Apostal, Cecil, 63
Aquino, Agapito, 115, 148–149, 152, 153
Aquino, Benigno, Jr., 27, 28, 29, 61, 66, 67, 76, 86, 104, 110, 115, 320–321(n21)
   assassination (1983), 66, 110, 147–148
   exile in U.S. (1980–1983), 147
Aquino, Corazón, 1, 7, 27, 46, 67, 173, 252, 253, 290, 292, 293, 296, 312
   candidacy, 156, 157–158, 210
   on CPP, 156, 162, 211. *See also* Communist Party of the Philippines, and Aquino government
   on Dante, Commander, 28–29
   and labor unions, 301
   and land reform, 182–183, 188, 211, 313
   on Marcos, Ferdinand, 147, 153
   and military, 7, 66, 166, 167, 168, 169
   popularity, 7, 156, 174, 178, 210, 211, 220, 302, 312
   and reelection, 336(n22)

and the Right, 7, 256
and vigilante groups, 273
Aquino, Rodolfo, 139
Aquino, Wilfredo "Baby," 139, 140
Arcilla, Roger, 322(n6)
Araneta, Concha, 170, 171
Arevalo, Arceli, 268–269
Arevalo, George, 269
Arguillas, Carolyn, 273
Armed Forces of the Philippines
    (AFP), 8, 89, 99, 147, 225–226
  and cease-fire, 166–167, 168, 169
  combat-effective troops, 9, 307
  corruption, 123–124, 125, 139, 307
  coup attempts (1986, 1987), 159,
    163
  and CPP, 109, 121–122, 124, 135–
    136, 138, 165, 166, 174
  and criminal syndicates, 138
  Forty-eighth Infantry Battalion, 245
  loyalty check, 48
  marines, 142
  morale, 307
  and NPA, 6–7, 14–16, 36, 38, 50,
    51–52, 53, 54–56, 57, 88–89, 99,
    100, 101, 105, 110, 124, 125,
    126, 127, 131, 136, 139, 141,
    234, 237, 240, 241, 245–246,
    248, 258–259, 268, 274, 290,
    298, 304, 307–308
  and peasants, 6, 16, 102, 124, 126,
    127, 128, 182, 226
  and private businesses, 245
  size, 124
  in South Vietnam, 22, 260
  Thirty-first Infantry Battalion, 1, 2
  Thirty-seventh Infantry Battalion,
    128
  See also Aquino, Corazón, and
    military
Armitage, Richard, 167
Aroma, Eddie, 268
Arquilino (Alsa Masa member), 271
Atienza, Monico, 24, 315(n1)
August Twenty-first Movement, 152
Aurora province, 55
Australia, 304

Bacolod, 170, 207, 250
Baguio, 36, 47
Bais, 206, 207

Baldo (guerrilla), 228, 229, 288; Plate
  1
Bamboo cannons, 287
Bananas, 94, 189, 195
Bancas (outrigger canoes), 51, 76
Bani (CPP cadre), 216–217, 218, 219,
  220
Barangay Ibaba, 180
Barangay Naddungan, 125, 126, 127,
  128
Barangay Rose, 13, 14, 15, 16, 187,
  198, 199, 234, 248, 312; Plates 5,
  8, 11
  artesian well, 188
  CPP anniversary festivities, 285–
    294
  cultural group, 193–194
  farming, 188–189, 190–191
  people's court, 185–186
  typhoon (1987), 194–196
Barangays, 8, 13, 315(n1)
Barcelona (Sorsogon province), 88, 89
Barican, Gerry, 115
Barrio revolutionary council, 13, 15,
  270, 288
Barrio Self-Defense Units. *See*
  Civilian Home Defense Force
BARs. *See* Browning automatic rifles
Basic Christian Communities (BCCs),
  208
Bataan province, 34, 179, 180, 181
Batangas province, 26, 37, 46
Bayan (Bagong Alyansang
  Makabayan), 152, 153, 156, 157,
  158
Baylosis, Rafael, 38, 119, 130, 157,
  161, 254, 255, 259–260, 263
BCCs. *See* Basic Christian
  Communities
Bel (guerrilla), 1, 2, 3
Benguet Corp., 152
Benny, Commander, 36
Bertrand Russell Peace Foundation,
  25
Betta (peasant), 293
Biazon, Rodolfo, 142
Bibingka, 286, 288
Bicol, 12, 85, 89, 98, 100, 123, 150,
  310
  Agrarian Reform Committee (CPP),
    180, 181

CPP organization, 122, 180, 187, 242, 244, 311
Bilog. *See* Salas, Rodolfo
Bing (CPP secretary), 177, 179, 239, 240–241, 311
Black market, 29
Bohol, 93, 204, 208
Boncayao, Alex, 115
Bondoc peninsula, 1, 3, 13, 194, 237
Bonifacio, Andrés, 20
Bonner, Raymond, 66
"Bourgeois reformism," 110, 111, 117
Boy Gat. *See* Gatmaitan, Apolinario
Browning automatic rifles (BARs), 50
Bukidnon province, 266
Bureaucrat capitalism, 13
Buscayno, Bernabe. *See* Dante, Commander
Buscayno, José, 38, 316–317(n1)
Butak, Nene, 124

Cabardo, Jorge, 100
Cacao, 190
CAFGUs. *See* Civilian Armed Forces Geographical Units
Cagayan province, 56, 57, 126, 240
Cagayan de Oro, 258, 266
Cagayan River, 54
Calixijan, Hermando, 141
Camarines Norte province, 229
Camarines Sur province, 85, 88, 89
Cambaya, Victor, 128–129
Cambodia, 278, 279, 280, 281, 283
Camp Crame stockade (Manila), 255
Canada, 304
Canello, Mario, 139
Canlas, Melchor, 52
Capegsan, Ignacio, 119, 130
Capitalism, 280, 281
Capitalists, 43
Carabaos. *See* Water buffalos
Casipe, Ray, 315(n1)
Catholic Church, 8, 92, 94, 170–171, 201, 282
  BCCs, 208–209
  and CNL, 213
  and CPP, 202–203, 207–208, 209, 210–212, 297
  groups, 134, 135
  landholdings, 201
  and Marcos regime, 208, 209–210

social action centers, 201–202, 203, 204, 205, 210
Cattle ranches, 176
Cauayan, 47
Cease-fire negotiations (1987), 7, 161, 162, 165, 166, 168–171, 174
Cebu, 93, 267, 300
Center-Right student party, 300
Central Intelligence Agency (CIA), 166, 167
Central Luzon, 6, 12, 18, 21, 25, 27, 29, 34, 37, 45, 49, 107, 174, 183
  flooding, 109
  population density, 42
  rebel bands, 32
  Regional Party Committee, 120, 181, 254, 298
Charcoal, 182
CHDF. *See* Civilian Home Defense Force
Chess, 231
Chiang Ching, 74, 77, 80
Christians for National Liberation (CNL), 146, 203, 209, 211, 212, 213
Christian Socialist movement, 85
CIA. *See* Central Intelligence Agency
Civilian Armed Forces Geographical Units (CAFGUs), 273
Civilian Home Defense Force (CHDF), 124–125, 126, 129, 299
Civilian "self-defense units," 102
Civil liberties, 282
Clark Air Force Base, 21, 22, 28, 29, 247
Claudia (CPP official), 186, 288, 292
Clavell, James, 255
Club Filipino (Manila), 170
CNL. *See* Christians for National Liberation
Co, Leoncio, 22, 27, 35, 36–37, 38, 315(n1)
Coalition of Organizations for the Realization of Democracy, 138
Cockfights, 35, 93
Coconuts, 189, 195, 313
Coffee, 175, 190
Cogon grass, 224
Cojuangco family, 27
Collantes, Manuel, 63, 91, 315(n1)
Collectivized farming, 190

Commentary magazine, 254, 256, 257, 274
Committee on Anti-Filipino Activities, 20
Communist barrio peasants' association, 14. *See also* Peasants, associations
Communist Party of the Philippines (CPP), 1, 9, 11–12, 36, 42, 308, 314
anniversary festivities, 285–294
and Aquino government, 7, 8, 10, 14, 151, 161, 162, 163, 165–166, 171–173, 295, 297, 298–299, 300, 303, 310
businesses, 245
cadres, 13, 34, 37, 93, 95, 96, 102, 106, 109, 130, 134, 149, 159, 278, 309
Central Committee, 27, 31, 34, 37, 38, 48, 61, 63, 91, 94, 96, 97, 100, 101, 110, 111, 112, 114, 115, 116, 117, 118, 119, 122, 129, 130, 131, 146, 148, 149, 156, 256, 257, 260, 263, 298, 316–317(n1)
Central Committee Executive Committee, 119–120, 121, 130, 147, 157, 158, 160–161, 162, 254, 298
centralized leadership, decentralized operations, 96, 298
changes in, 309
Church sector, 211. *See also* Catholic Church, and CPP
demonstrations, 40
discipline, 6, 33, 64, 118, 186, 235, 236
Education Bureau, 157, 254
election boycott (1980), 155
election boycott (1981), 135, 146
election boycott (1984), 149, 155
election boycott (1986), 157, 158–159, 160
election boycott order (1978), 116, 122, 155
flag, 138
and foreign aid, 8, 9, 50, 62, 64, 72, 79, 83, 304–306
founders, 17–19, 26, 27, 315(n1)

front organizations, 104, 107, 135, 138, 143, 145, 146–153, 161, 300–301
ideology, 7, 119, 150, 155, 160, 177, 296, 297. *See also* Maoism; Marxism-Leninism
International Department, 305
and labor unions, 8, 19, 37, 40, 45, 111, 138, 151, 159, 215–221, 296, 301
Manila underground organization, 103–106, 107, 108, 109, 111, 112, 203, 301
–Marxist-Leninist (Mao Zedong Thought), 17, 296, 297, 309
membership, 6, 37, 48, 62, 107, 129, 309
Military Commission, 63, 157
National Liaison Commission, 106
National Urban Commission, 157, 160
and Netherlands, 83
organization, 8, 92, 298
and People's Republic of China, 8, 50, 62, 64, 71, 72–75, 77, 78, 79–82, 83, 306; Plate 26
and Plaza Miranda bombing (1971), 60–64, 65, 66–67, 68–69, 73, 79
Political Bureau (Politburo), 48, 63, 65, 157, 160–161
political network, 9–12, 15, 48, 135, 302, 303
publications. *See Ang Bayan; Praktika*
regional commands, 129, 130, 298
Southern Luzon Commission, 297
Southern Tagalog Region, 46
strategy, 215, 298, 299, 301–302
strategy debates, 7, 110, 111, 112, 113, 114, 116–117, 120–121, 122, 137, 146, 147, 159–162, 163
sympathizers, 10–11, 92, 94, 134, 138, 310
and terrorism, 69
United Front Commission, 147, 157, 300
urban insurrection strategy, 137, 142, 147, 215, 270, 300
See also Manila, -Rizal (CPP) Committee; National Democratic

Front; New People's Army;
Student political radicalism
Congress dissolved, 110
Congress of the Filipino People
(KOMPIL), 148–149
Constantino, Renato, 42, 43, 44
Constitution
1935, suspended, 110
1987, 336(n22)
proposed, 172
Cooperatives, 179, 182, 190, 205,
270, 280
Copra, 313
Cordero, Danny, 62, 63–64, 65, 69
Cordillera Mountains, 18, 123, 125,
175, 302
Corn, 175, 190
Corpus, Victor, 46–48, 49, 50, 51,
52, 53, 62, 63, 66–67, 68, 130
Corruption, 6, 42, 47, 123, 312. *See
also under* Armed Forces of the
Philippines
CPP. *See* Communist Party of the
Philippines
Crime, 42
Cruz, Brendan, 202, 210, 213, 280
Cua, Junie, 239
Cuba, 9, 91
Cultural Revolution (People's
Republic of China), 5, 23, 24,
74, 80, 81, 108

Damit (guerrilla), 10
Danny (CPP activist), 63
Dante (peasant), 12–13, 14, 15–16,
188, 193, 194, 199, 292, 293,
294; Plates 5, 11
Dante, Commander (Bernabe
Buscayno), 27–30, 31, 32, 34–35,
38, 47, 48, 49, 50, 62, 91, 129,
255; Plate 23
arrested (1976), 129
released (1986), 253
Davao, 93, 101, 133, 268–270
Chamber of Commerce, 140
and CPP, 134, 135, 137–138, 142,
143, 300
economy, 139–140
and NPA, 133–134, 136, 138–139,
140, 142, 143
population, 133

Davao, Gulf of, 270
Davao del Norte province, 94, 101,
267
Davao del Sur province, 94
Davao Oriental province, 101
David, Randolph, 149–150
Day care program, 191
Death squads. *See* Monkees
Deep penetration agents (DPAs), 265,
266–267, 268, 269
De La Salle University (Manila), 46
De la Torre, Edicio, 209
Democratic coalition government, 150
"Democratic space," 161
Democratic Union of Peasants. *See*
Malayang Samahan ng
Magsasaka
Democratic Youth Association. *See*
Samahang Demokratiko ng
Kabataan
Deng Xiaoping, 80, 82, 281
Development Academy of the
Philippines, 146
de Vera, Benjamin, 135, 136, 255,
258, 259
Diarrhea, 231
Digoyo Point, 50, 76, 77
Diliman Commune, 108
Dimafiles, Nemesio, 250
Diokno, José, 148, 152, 166, 172
Diokno, María, 172
Disease, 216, 231, 232–233
Divorce, 235
Doña Cassandra (ferry) sinking (1983),
259
DPAs. *See* Deep penetration agents
Dumagat tribespeople, 50
Dumaguete Times, 37
Dumlao, Patricio, 176, 177
Dy, Faustino, 47
Dysentery, 232

Eddie, Commander. *See* Layug,
Diosdado
"Eight Points of Attention" (Mao),
33–34
Eladio (peasant), 188–189, 191, 192,
194, 195
Election
1969, 39, 104
1978, 115–117, 155

1980, 155
1981, 135, 146, 155
1984, 149, 155
1986, 7, 143, 157–159, 210
Electricity, 187
Elias (guerrilla), 316–317(n1)
Elvie (guerrilla), 194
English (language), 6, 35
Enrile, Juan Ponce, 66, 67, 104, 142,
    166, 167, 168, 169, 310
Erosion, 175
Estella, Mercedes, 141

Family planning, 236
Family ties, 283
Far Eastern University (Manila), 40
Farmers' league. See Malayang
    Samahan ng Magsasaka
Fascism, 104, 109
Favali, Tullio, 125
Federation of Free Farmers (FFF), 93,
    201, 203, 204, 205, 206, 207,
    208
Federation of Free Workers, 201
Feliciano, José, 156, 157
Felman (Huk commander), 316–
    317(n1)
Fely (guerrilla), 265
Fernández, Lucas, 134, 136, 137, 269
Feudalism, 6, 13, 20, 32, 175
FFF. See Federation of Free Farmers
First Quarter Storm (1970), 39, 40,
    42, 45, 87, 104, 113
Fish farms, 176, 191
"Five Golden Rays" (Mao), 35
Flores, Henry, 141
Flores, Lucila, 141
Foreign investment, 281
Fort Bonifacio, 253
Fortich, Antonio, 206
Fortuna, Julius, 23, 24, 26, 40, 44,
    110
Francisco (guerrilla), 45–46, 186, 241,
    244
Freddie (guerrilla), 225
Free Philippines News Service, 263
Fugasse, 243

Gambalay rehabilitation center, Plate
    2
Gambling lords, 35

Gang of Four (People's Republic of
    China), 80
García, Arthur, 18, 19, 37, 62,
    315(n1)
García, Hermenigildo, 37, 65, 91, 92,
    315(n1)
Garduce, Lourdes, 121
Gatmaitan, Apolinario (Boy Gat), 91–
    92
General Textile Company strike
    (1970), 253
General trade unionism course
    (GTU), 216
Goiter, 232
Goody, Commander (Ernesto
    Miranda), 316–317(n1)
Gorbachev, Mikhail, 281
Greg (peasant), 198
Group of 11, 119, 120–121
GTU. See General trade unionism
    course
Guavas, 176, 177
Guerrero, Amado (Sison's
    pseudonym), 43, 96, 252
Guerrillas. See New People's Army;
    Urban guerrillas
Guevarra, Reuben, 63, 64–65,
    315(n1)
Guingona, Teofisto, 166, 172
"Guns, goons and gold," 207
Guring (peasant), 288, 291
Gutierrez, Gustavo, 208

Habeas corpus, writ of
    reinstated, 104
    suspended (1971), 60, 65, 66, 68,
    85, 103
Hacenderos, 90, 91
Hacienda Luisita, 27, 28, 37
Hainan Island, 78
Happy, Commander, 125–126, 128
Health care, 12, 42, 45, 46, 205, 233,
    270
Heidi (guerrilla), 227–228, 229
Hernia, 233
Herrera, Trinidad, 115
Hilton Hotel (Manila), 39
Holland. See Netherlands
Hotel del Rio (Iloilo), 171

Hukbalahap (Huk) guerrillas, 18, 22, 25, 26, 27, 29, 31, 32, 34, 36, 303, 307
  peasant rebellion (1950s), 41, 85
Human rights, 125, 135, 257, 290
  organizations, 134–135, 171, 247
Hunan province (People's Republic of China), 80; Plate 26

Ignacio, Avelino, 135, 136
Ignacio, Robertson, 135–136
Ilocos Sur province, 20
Iloilo, 170, 171
Imperialism, 6, 13, 14, 22, 24, 32, 35, 43, 104, 108, 109, 151, 230
Income, per capita (1969), 41
Indonesia, 23, 72
International Monetary Fund, 151
"Investigation of the Peasant Movement in Hunan Province" (Mao), 40
Irrigation, 179, 190
Isabela province, 6, 34, 36, 38, 45, 47, 48, 49, 50, 55, 56, 62, 95, 96, 107
  "free-fire zones," 54
  Plains Platoon, 54
Isidro (Alsa Masa member), 271–272
Ivan (guerrilla), 247

JAJA. *See* Justice for Aquino, Justice for All
Jalandoni, Luís, 92, 93, 205–207, 212, 213, 304, 305, 306
Japan, 11, 32, 75, 281, 304
Jesena, Arsenio, 91
Johnson, Lyndon, 22, 23
Jones, Aleli, 285, 288, 292, 293, 294
Jopson, Edgar, 117, 119, 121, 135, 259
Jopson, Gloria, 259
Joy (CPP cadre), 14, 186, 187, 196–197, 198, 237, 285, 286; Plate 11
Joyce (CPP cadre), 281
JPE logging company and sawmill, 239
Justice, 12, 186–187, 312
Justice for Aquino, Justice for All (JAJA), 148, 151

Kabataang Makabayan (KM), 21, 22, 23, 24, 25–26, 29, 36, 37, 40, 45, 46, 62, 85, 87, 88, 93, 103, 104, 145, 202
Kabataan para sa Demokrasya at Nasyonalismo (KADENA), 300
KADENA. *See* Kabataan para sa Demokrasya at Nasyonalismo
Kaingeros. See Slash-and-burn farming
Kaisahan Settlement Project (Negros), 205
Kamote, 89, 90, 175, 177
Kang Sheng, 72
Karagatan (boat), 51, 52, 64, 75–76, 77–78, 82, 104, 105; Plates 24, 25
Karagatan Fishing Corp., 76–77
Karingal, Tomás, 248
Kasamas, 226, 227
Katipunan (secret society), 20
Khi Rho (radical Christian youth organization), 93
Khmer Rouge, 274
Kilusang Magbubukid ng Pilipinas, 301
Kilusang Mayo Uno (KMU), 152, 156, 169, 215, 218, 219, 220, 301
Kintanar, Galileo, 209
Kintanar, Romulo, 52, 53, 101, 135, 136, 255, 257–259
  prison escape (1988), 258
Kishi Maru. See Karagatan
KM. *See* Kabataang Makabayan
KMU. *See* Kilusang Mayo Uno
KOMPIL. *See* Congress of the Filipino People
Koniev, Ivan, 247
Kulas (communist peasant), 288, 289–291, 293–294; Plates 8, 10

Labor Department, 217, 220
Labor unions
  yellow, 217, 218
  See also under Communist Party of the Philippines
Lagman, Filemon, 113, 117, 118, 119, 121
Laguna province, 37
Lakas ng Bayan party, 115, 279
La Morena, Victorino, 269
Lanao del Norte province, 266

Landownership, 41, 43, 123, 175,
176, 203–205
Land Reform Act
1955, 41
1988, 183
Latin America, 208, 304
Laudiangco, Juanito, 2, 237
La Union province, 78
Lava brothers, 17, 18, 19, 25, 26, 30,
32, 79, 95, 253
Law enforcement, 12
Laya (NPA cadre), 291
Layug, Diosdado (Commander
Eddie), 32, 34, 36, 316–317(n1)
League of Filipino Students, 152,
156, 300
Lenin, V. I., 5, 22, 118, 130, 192
Leny (CPP cadre), 309
Lerma (peasant), 288
Liberal democrats, 152
Liberal party, 41, 62, 77, 104, 110
and communists, 60, 65, 66, 68
rally killings (1971), 59–64
Liberation (NDF publication), 180
Liberation theology, 208
Libya, 9
Lin Piao, 260
Lisa (CPP cadre), 233–234, 285
Little Red Book (Mao), 24, 25, 29, 85,
88, 90
Liu Shaoqi, 26
Llamas, Sotero, 85, 90, 187, 302,
310, 311; Plate 6
Logging, 175
Luneta, José, 38, 61, 72, 263, 315(n1)
Luzon, 6, 12, 20, 33, 48, 57, 96, 123,
128, 233, 240, 245, 266, 302,
311; Plate 20
Lyceum University, 19, 21, 260, 309

Macapagal, Diosdado, 41
MacArthur, Douglas, 21
Macau, 71, 73
Magpantay, Caridad, 117, 119, 121
Magsaysay, Ramón, 41
Mahjong, 271
Majul, Cesar Adib, 20
Malabon (Manila slum), 248
Malaria, 232, 233
Malay, Carolina, 156, 166, 169, 170,
260, 261–263

Malay, Charito, 73, 322(n6)
Malay, Ricardo, 73, 78, 322(n6); Plate
26
Malayang Samahan ng Magsasaka
(MASAKA), 22
Malnutrition, 216
MAN. *See* Movement for the
Advancement of Nationalism
Mangatarem, 18
Manglapus, Raul, 306
Manila, 1, 8, 35, 39, 45, 48, 59, 94,
300
Aquino assassination demonstration
(1983), 148
bombings (1972), 104
NPA attacks in, 247–248
-Rizal (CPP) Committee, 62, 110–
111, 112, 113–122, 146
student and worker protest
movement (1970s), 103, 110, 111,
113
summit (1966), 23
U.S. embassy in, 39
Manila Times, 260, 262
Maoism, 8, 18, 25, 26, 30, 33, 35,
38, 43, 95, 103, 111, 113, 118,
137, 202, 230, 277
Mao Zedong, 5, 6, 24, 32, 33, 35,
38, 40, 43, 79, 80, 81, 88, 92,
95, 98, 99, 103, 108, 111, 118,
119, 192, 227
Marcos, Ferdinand, 6, 7, 22, 29, 39,
42, 47, 48, 54, 60, 61, 62, 65–
66, 68, 76, 77, 133, 143, 150,
155, 159, 167–168, 187, 210, 290,
314
anti-, 105, 110, 111, 115, 135, 148,
152–153. *See also* Liberal party
and Aquino assassination, 147
counterinsurgency strategy, 124
exile (1986), 66, 83, 159, 210
and land reform, 41, 177
and oil prices, 104
See also Martial law
Marcos, Imelda, 39
Marcos Resign movement, 148
Marikina (Manila suburb), 103
Marriage, 235–236
Martial law (1972), 6, 39, 54, 61, 66,
68, 77, 89, 97, 102, 104–105,

106–109, 123, 124, 145, 207, 208, 303

Marx, Karl, 5, 20, 22, 35, 38, 61, 62, 103, 192

Marxism, 20, 21, 22, 24, 110, 296
and Christianity, 202, 208

Marxism-Leninism, 121, 173, 218–219, 230, 278, 279, 297

Marybelle (peasant), 288

Masa, 237

MASAKA. *See* Malayang Samahan ng Magsasaka

Maureal, Froiland, 236

May (guerrilla), 286–287

Maya (CPP cadre), 236

May Day Statement (Sison), 26

May First Movement. *See* Kilusang Mayo Uno

MDP. *See* Movement for a Democratic Philippines

Meding (peasant), 286, 287

Melody, Commander, 32, 316–317(n1)

Mendoza, Domito, 307, 308

Menorah, 124

Miclat, Alma, 322(n6)

Miclat, Mario, 82, 83, 322(n6)

Middle class, 8, 10, 24, 134, 145, 147, 148, 150, 173, 279, 280, 302, 309

Mike (CPP secretary), 1, 2, 3, 198, 228

Militarism, 104

Mindanao, 12, 48, 93, 94, 101, 102, 123, 128, 133, 245, 265, 267–268, 274, 299
CPP Commission, 134, 136, 137, 141, 158, 258, 266, 267, 269
and NPA, 135

Mines, 243–244

Minguez, Celso, 100

Miranda, Ernesto. *See* Goody, Commander

Mitra, Ramón, 76, 165, 166, 168, 172

Mon, Comrade, 82

Monkees (death squads), 36

Morales, Horacio, 146, 147

Movement for a Democratic Philippines (MDP), 40, 107, 145

Movement for the Advancement of Nationalism (MAN), 25, 145

Movement of Concerned Citizens for Civil Liberties, 107

Multinational companies, 219

Mundo, Faustino del. *See* Sumulong, Commander

Munro, Ross, 274

Mushrooms, 48

Muslims, 9, 101, 124, 199

Nacionalista party, 41, 61, 62, 77

Nap (guerrilla), 223, 224, 225

National Assembly election (1978), 115–117

National Association of Trade Unions (NATU), 21

National bourgeoisie, 145, 279

National Democratic Front (NDF), 7, 8, 145, 146, 147, 149, 150, 152, 153, 155, 163, 168, 169, 171, 172, 174, 179, 180, 183, 210, 211, 212, 213, 290, 300, 302, 313–314
Committee for the Participation of Christians, Chinese, and Moros, 209
coordinating committee, 146
economic scenario, 280–281
election boycott, 146–147
government scenario, 278–279, 282
livelihood projects, 271, 272
policy issues, 278, 280–283
popular fronts, 302–303
publication. *See Liberation*
social agenda, 281–282
solidarity committees, 304

National Farmers Movement. *See* Pambansang Katipunan ng Magsasaka

National Federation of Sugarcane Workers, 206

National Highway, 14, 224, 237, 250

Nationalism, 5, 20–21, 22–23, 24, 25, 46, 108, 202

Nationalist Alliance for Justice, Freedom, and Democracy, 148, 151

Nationalist Corps, 24

Nationalization, 280

National Liberation Front, 23

National police force, 139

National Reconciliation and
  Development Program, 172
Nato. See Ruíz, Nick
NATU. See National Association of
  Trade Unions
NDF. See National Democratic Front
Negros, 37, 56, 90–91, 92, 93, 123,
  163, 170, 205–207, 208, 244,
  245, 250; Plate 19
Nemenzo, Francisco, 20, 21, 42, 260,
  263
Nestlé plants strike (1987), 219–220
Netherlands, 83, 212, 252, 304
New Nationalist Alliance. See Bayan
New People's Army (NPA), 1, 2, 6,
  8, 12, 28–29, 30, 48, 61, 62, 87,
  163, 175, 185, 223, 250, 295,
  314; Plates 3–5, 7–9, 13–14, 16
ages of members, 229
ammunition, 243
assassinations, 247–248, 249, 257,
  269, 298
and BCCs, 208–209
camp, typical, 231–233
and cease-fire, 170–171, 172–173,
  174, 309
and CNL, 212
communications, 242, 244, 298,
  304
and CPP, 34, 96–97, 98, 101, 129,
  163, 230, 266, 279
discipline, 7, 32, 33–34, 39, 94,
  225, 235, 236, 243, 289
Eastern Mindanao Front, 101, 102
egalitarianism, 226
financing, 244–245, 246, 304
founded (1969), 31
growth, 130–131, 135, 239–240,
  241, 242, 254, 265, 297, 311
Manila Command, 220
medics, 233
mobile bases, 96, 101
Northern Luzon Command, 54, 57,
  63
operating costs, 242
organization, 7, 49, 87, 95, 105,
  135, 229–230, 242
platoons, 230, 242
political education, 34, 35, 37, 49,
  88, 92, 97, 98, 225, 229, 230–
  231, 298

propaganda teams, 46, 85, 87, 89,
  97, 99, 129, 134, 229, 246
purges, 265–268, 274–275, 277
rural influence, 10–11, 12–14, 15,
  53, 87, 90, 93, 94, 98–99, 101,
  102, 126, 127, 128, 150, 186,
  225, 226, 239, 246–247, 249–
  250, 291, 296, 310–312
size, 8, 45, 49, 55, 57, 107, 129,
  131
Sorsogon Command, 88
Southern Quezon Front, 15, 228,
  233, 237, 248
Southern Tagalog Regional
  Command, 220, 233, 243, 249,
  310
squads, 6, 33, 93, 94, 129, 242
strategy, 33, 49, 50, 93, 96, 98,
  102, 166, 296
sympathizers and support, 88, 107,
  123, 127–128, 133, 174, 203,
  225, 226–227, 230, 236–237,
  249, 297, 310–312
tactics, 241, 250, 303
Third Red Company, 55
weapons, 8, 9, 14, 15, 32, 49, 50,
  51–52, 62, 64, 72, 74, 75–76, 78,
  87, 88, 89, 101, 107, 129, 131,
  171, 242, 243–244, 303–304,
  305–307
Western Mindanao Front, 101
See also Revolution; Urban
  guerrillas; under Agrarian reform;
  Armed Forces of the Philippines;
  Davao; Peasants
"New Society," 123
New Zealand, 304
Nicaragua, 9, 136, 160, 278, 279,
  302, 304, 305
North Cotabato province, 265
North Korea, 9, 277, 278, 305
NPA. See New People's Army
"NPA Yenan," 38 56, 95
Nueva Ecija province, 55, 121
Nueva Vizcaya province, 53, 125,
  175, 176, 177, 223, 233, 239,
  240, 241, 245, 311

O'Brien, Allan, 139

Ocampo, Saturnino, 23, 156, 162,
    166, 169, 170, 171, 173, 260–261,
    263, 279
  prison escape (1985), 261
Olalia, Rolando, 152, 169
Omy (student activist), 103–104, 105,
    109–110
"On Contradiction" (Mao), 118
Ongpin, Jaíme, 152
"On Tactics" (Mao), 118
Oriental Falcon (Hong Kong salvage
    ship), 79
Oriental province, 93
"Our Urgent Tasks" (Sison), 102,
    111, 114

Padilla, Carlos, 176
Palanan, 50
Palestine Liberation Organization, 9
Pambansang Katipunan ng
    Magsasaka (PKM), 176, 177, 181
Pampanga, 36, 37, 174
Pampango (dialect), 34
Panay, 93, 123, 170
Pancit, 288
Pangasinan, 18, 26, 182
Pangilinan, Art, 315(n1)
Paris Commune, 108
Partai Kommunist Indonesia, 23, 72
Partido Komunista ng Pilipinas
    (PKP), 17, 18, 19, 21, 22, 24–25,
    26, 29, 32, 43, 95, 97, 118, 130,
    145, 297, 303
Partido ng Bayan (PnB), 162, 169,
    302
Patriotic Youth. See Kabataang
    Makabayan
Payawal, Edgardo, 36
Peanuts, 190
Peasants, 5, 12–13, 14, 21, 42, 91,
    94, 123, 134, 175, 204–205, 206;
    Plates 4–7, 16, 19–20
  associations, 21, 22, 50, 176, 179,
    180–181, 182, 189, 190, 301
  and Catholic Church, 204–206,
    207, 208
  and KM, 24
  loan payments, 175–176
  medical training, 188, 191
  middle, 286

and NPA, 13, 15–16, 34, 38, 49,
    87–88, 89, 90, 98–101, 126, 127–
    128, 129, 176–181, 182, 188,
    189–191, 194, 196–199, 225,
    226–227, 234, 241, 243, 286,
    287, 301, 307, 312, 313, 314,
    332(n3)
  and PKP, 25, 29
  politicization of, 13, 14, 109, 191–
    194, 298, 309–310
  rich, 181, 182
  unrest, 5, 6, 9, 19, 22, 41, 206
  See also under Armed Forces of the
    Philippines
Peking Review, 24
Pelayo, José, 156
Pena, Rolando, Plate 26
People's Liberation Army (People's
    Republic of China), 32, 33
People's Party. See Partido ng Bayan
People's Republic of China, 5, 8, 9,
    23, 26, 50, 62, 64, 108, 261,
    277, 278, 281, 305
  labor mutual-aid societies, 190
  opera, 74, 77
  See also under Communist Party of
    the Philippines
Pepper, 190
Perestroika, 281
Philippine Army. See Armed Forces
    of the Philippines
Philippine Collegian, 24, 25, 103
Philippine Military Academy (PMA)
    (Baguio), 46, 47
  armory raid (1970), 47, 50
Philippines
  economy, 133, 140, 313
  education, 283
  of the 1960s, 5, 6, 19, 21, 23, 39–
    42
  and People's Republic of China, 8
  revolution (1896), 303
  Right, 7, 60
  and U.S., 5, 6, 9, 11, 20–21, 22,
    38, 40–41, 90, 91, 106, 147, 150,
    166–168, 303, 305, 314
  and U.S. military bases, 156, 158,
    282, 300
Philippines Herald, 59
Philippine Society and Revolution
    (PSR) (Sison), 43–44, 206, 230

Piggeries, 176, 190–191
Pilipino (language), 28
Pimentel, Aquilino, 115
PKM. See Pambansang Katipunan ng
    Magsasaka
PKP. See Partido Komunista ng
    Philipinas
Planas, Charito, 115
Plaza Miranda (Manila) bombing
    (1971), 59–64, 65, 66–67, 68–69,
    71, 73, 79, 82, 104; Plates 17, 18
PMA. See Philippine Military
    Academy
PnB. See Partido ng Bayan
Political parties, 40, 41, 115, 162,
    279
Political pluralism, 150, 278
Pol Pot, 278
Pop group. See Apo Hiking Society
Population growth, 41–42
Poverty, 6, 12, 13, 42, 91, 123, 125,
    155, 274, 312–313
    line, 175
Praktika (CPP journal), 160
Principe, Elizabeth, 53, 65
Programme for a People's Democratic
    Revolution (CPP), 277
Prostitution, 216
Protestant Church, 211
PSR. See Philippine Society and
    Revolution
Pumpboat, 246
Punding (peasant), 286, 287, 288
Punta Dumalag, 270–273, 274

Quezon City, 18, 104
Quezon province, 1, 12, 13, 15, 16,
    37, 46, 229, 231, 234, 237, 243,
    246
Quiapo flea market, 1–2
Quirino province, 125, 175, 176, 177,
    239, 240, 245, 311
Quotations from Mao Zedong, 260

Radio Beijing, 72
Radio Moscow, 81
Ragay Gulf, 3, 197
Ramos, Fidel, 169
Rattan, 176
"Rectify Errors and Rebuild the
    Party" (Sison), 19, 95, 145

Recto, Claro, 20, 22, 44
"Red Detachment of Women, The"
    (opera), 74
Red Guards (People's Republic of
    China), 6, 23, 108
Reggie (guerrilla), 223, 224, 225
Repression (Philippine government),
    60–61, 65, 68, 104, 150
Revolution (1968–), 4, 5, 6, 7, 17,
    26–27, 43, 85, 91, 150, 308
    deaths, 8
    future climax, 295, 296
    as indigenous, 8–9
    leadership, 251–263
Revolutionary songs and skits, 192–
    194, 231, 292–293
Reyes, Ricardo, 256
Rice, 175, 176, 189, 190
    bowl. See Central Luzon
"Right opportunism," 111, 114
Risen Masses. See Alsa Masa
Rivera, Juanito, 29, 36, 157, 255,
    256, 316–317(n1)
Rodríguez, Eddie, 56
Rodríguez, Eduardo, 311–312
Roland (guerrilla), 230, 231
Roque, Magtanggol, 102, 105
Rosal, Gregorio, 310, 311
Rosario, Carlos del, 18, 72, 322(n6)
Rowe, James N., 247
Roxas, Gerry, 146
Roy (CPP cadre), 236
Rudy (guerrilla), 197, 229
Ruíz, Nick (Nato), 203, 204, 205,
    207, 208
Rustlers, 13, 86, 88, 186, 289

Sacadas, 91
Salas, Josefina, 255
Salas, Rodolfo (Bilog), 18, 22, 26, 27,
    35, 37, 115, 118, 119, 120, 121,
    129, 130, 147, 148–149, 156, 157,
    161, 254–257, 278, 279, 281, 296
    arrested (1986), 161, 168, 255;
    Plate 22
Salvagings, 138
Samahang Demokratiko ng Kabataan
    (SDK), 26, 45, 103, 104, 202,
    253
Samal, 179–180

Samar, 93, 100–101, 130, 245, 254, 302
Sanchez, Ramón, 98, 100
Sancho, Nelia, 108–109
Sandinistas (Nicaragua), 136, 302, 305
Sandra (guerrilla), 246
Santa Ana, 174
Santa Rita, 29, 31, 34, 36
SCAUP. *See* Student Cultural Association of the University of the Philippines
SDK. *See* Samahang Demokratiko ng Kabataan
Seasonal workers. *See* Sacadas
Second Vatican Council (1965), 201, 202, 203, 208
Secret society. *See* Katipunan
Serve the People Brigades, 24
Shakey's pizza parlors (Manila), 197
Share-Tenancy Law (1954), 204
Shirley (guerrilla), 287
Shogun (Clavell), 255
Sierra Madre, 6, 34, 36, 53, 56
Sin, Jaíme, 171, 210, 213
Sison, Janos, Plate 26
Sison, José María (Joema), 5, 46, 47, 48, 66, 80, 105, 107, 108, 114, 206, 252–253, 259
    arrested (1977), 115, 120; Plate 21
    and CPP, 6, 17–19, 27, 29, 32, 34, 35, 36, 38, 40, 43, 49, 60, 61–62, 79, 82, 83, 95, 97, 102, 107, 110, 111, 114, 129, 130, 145, 202, 252, 254
    and KM, 22, 23, 24, 26
    and KOMPIL, 148
    and NPA, 30, 31, 32, 33, 36, 49, 56, 72, 73, 78, 87, 95, 96, 100, 101, 102, 131, 227
    and peasants, 178
    pen name. *See* Guerrero, Amado
    and People's Republic of China, 72–73, 74–75, 77, 78, 79
    and PKP, 21, 25, 78, 95, 118
    and Plaza Miranda bombing, 60, 61, 62, 63, 65, 66, 67, 68–69, 79
    and PnB, 162
    released from prison (1986), 162
    and SCAUP, 20, 24
    self-exile, 252, 297

successor, 115
Sison, Julieta, 148, 252
Slash-and-burn farming, 14, 175
Smuggling, 29
Social services, 12
Social Democrats, 145, 151, 152
Socialist state, 280, 296
Solarz, Stephen, 274
Solo Brothers, 292
Soriano, Emanuel, 152, 305
Sorsogon province, 85, 87, 88, 89, 98, 99–100
    CPP organization, 182
SOTs. *See* Special operations teams
Soul-hunting, 194
South Vietnam, 22, 98, 136, 260
Soviet Union, 9, 26, 278, 281, 306
Spain, 11, 20, 201
Sparrows, 249, 269
Special operations teams (SOTs), 298
"Specific Characteristics of Our People's War" (Guerrero), 96, 114
Squatter slums, 42, 111, 270
Stalin, Joseph, 29
Stalinists, 24
"Stalin University," 29
State, U.S. Department of, 6, 167
Stockman, David, 255
Strategic hamletting, 127
Strikes, 219, 220
    1970s, 111, 206, 253
    1980s, 137, 142, 219–220, 301
Stringbeans, 175
Student Christian Movement, 202
Student Cultural Association of the University of the Philippines (SCAUP), 20, 21, 24, 26
Student political radicalism, 5, 6, 20, 21, 22, 23, 24, 26, 38–39, 40, 45, 85, 107, 108, 109–110, 202
    decline, 300
"Student Power?" (Sison), 38
Suarez, José, 156
Subic Bay Naval Base, 21, 22
Sugar, 27, 28, 90–91, 205, 206
Sumulong, Commander (Faustino del Mundo), 18, 27, 28, 29, 30, 32, 33, 35, 37, 130
Surigao del Sur province, 267
Sweet potato. *See* Kamote

Tactical offensives (TOs), 230
Tadeo, Jaíme, 152
Tagalog (language), 24, 34, 35, 72, 231
Tañada, Lorenzo, 148, 152, 157
Tarlac province, 27, 28, 29, 34, 35, 36, 37, 49, 157
Tayag, Fernando, 22, 315(n1)
Tayag, Nilo, 19, 37, 315(n1)
Teach-ins, 38, 39, 108
Tenant farmers, 41, 123, 175, 176
Theologies of liberation, 202
Theology of Liberation (Gutierrez), 208
"Three Main Rules of Discipline" (Mao), 33
Tiamzon, Benito, 119, 120, 121, 130, 157, 253–254
Tibbs (guerrilla), 86–87, 88, 89, 196, 199
Tobacco, 190
Tony (guerrilla), 55, 56
Torre, José, 170, 171
TOs. *See* Tactical offensives
Tripon, Firmo, 150–151, 157
Triumph of Politics, The (Stockman), 255
Tuason, Ben, 316–317(n1)
Tuberculosis, 233
Tubianosa, Ibarra, 19, 36, 61, 72, 73, 74, 75, 77, 78, 79, 80, 82, 83, 315(n1), 322(n6)
Tuition protests, 111, 113
Typhoid fever, 232, 234
Typhoon
1972, 108
1987, 194–196

Ulcers, 232
Underemployment, 41
Unemployment, 41, 42
United States, 279, 281
image of, 198, 230–231, 293
and NDF, 304
See also Imperialism; Vietnam War; *under* Philippines
University of Santo Tomás (Manila), 45
University of the Philippines (UP), 20, 21, 24, 25, 38, 104, 108, 300, 309
High School, 103

UP. *See* University of the Philippines
Upper class, 8, 10, 11, 147, 148, 150, 309
Urban guerrillas, 8, 133, 247–248, 257
"Urgent Message to the Filipino People" (CPP) (1983), 148
U.S. Tobacco Company, 19, 36
Utrecht (Netherlands), 304

Vatican II. *See* Second Vatican Council
Vietnam, 278, 279, 281, 305, 306
Vietnam War, 5, 22–23, 38, 72, 107
Village militia, 13, 14, 185, 186, 188
Villalobos, Marty, 160
Villano, José, 139
Virgie (guerrilla), 236
Visayan islands, 93, 131
Visayas, 48, 94, 100, 298
Voice of America, 81
relay station, 31, 35

Wages, 41, 301
Waltzing with a Dictator: The Marcoses and the Making of American Policy (Bonner), 66
Water buffalos, 3, 13, 179, 186, 188; Plate 16
Welgang bayan, 137–138, 142
Western Europe, 281
West Germany, 252
Whirlwind (Clavell), 255
"White-haired Girl" (opera), 74
Williams, Louise, 267
World Bank, 151, 313

Xinhua news agency (People's Republic of China), 261

Yap, José, 27, 29
Yoly (domestic helper), 288–289
Youth for Democracy and Nationalism. *See* Kabataan para sa Demokrasya at Nasyonalismo

Zambales Mountains, 29, 34
Zamboanga peninsula, 93
Zone One Tondo Organization, 115
Zumel, Antonio, 120, 130, 156, 157, 166, 169, 170, 256, 260